Resources and the Environment

Resources and the Environment: Policy Perspectives for Canada

edited by O.P. Dwivedi

McCLELLAND AND STEWART

Copyright © 1980 McClelland and Stewart Limited

McClelland and Stewart Limited
The Canadian Publishers
25 Hollinger Road
Toronto Ontario
M4B 3G2

CANADIAN CATALOGUING IN PUBLICATION DATA

Main entry under title:
Resources and the environment

ISBN 0-7710-2962-4

1. Environmental policy – Canada.   2. Natural
resources – Canada.   3. Environmental protection –
Canada – Case studies.   I. Dwivedi, O.P., 1937-
II. Title.

HC120.E5R47   333.7 '15 '0971   C80-094227-2

Printed and bound in Canada

Contents

TO MY FATHER AND MOTHER

who have spent their lives protecting
the forestry resources of India

CONTRIBUTORS

FIKRET BERKES is an Assistant Professor of Environmental Studies, Institute of Urban and Environmental Studies, Brock University, and has published on the management of living resources and on human ecology.

JOHN E. CARROLL is Associate Professor of Environmental Conservation, Institute of Natural and Environmental Resources, University of New Hampshire, and currently is writing a book on Canada-U.S. environmental relations.

EDGAR J. DOSMAN, Associate Professor of Political Science, York University, edited *The Arctic in Question* (1976) and is the author of *The National Interest: The Politics of Northern Development, 1968-75* (1975).

O.P. DWIVEDI, Professor and Chairman, Department of Political Studies, University of Guelph, has published numerous scholarly articles on Canadian environmental questions and edited *Protecting the Environment* (1974).

DAVID G. LEMARQUAND, Research Associate, Westwater Research Centre, University of British Columbia, is author of *International Rivers: The Politics of Cooperation* (1977).

BRUCE MITCHELL, Professor of Geography, University of Waterloo, is author of *Geography and Resource Analysis* (1979) and co-edited *Managing Canada's Renewable Resources* (1977).

DON MUNTON, Associate Professor of Political Science and a member of the Centre for Foreign Policy Studies at Dalhousie University, is the author of several articles on Canadian foreign policy and of a forthcoming book on the 1972 Great Lakes Water Quality Agreement.

ROBERT PAEHLKE, Associate Professor of Political Studies at Trent University, is the founding editor of *Alternatives: Perspectives on Society and Environment* and was a contributor to the book, *James Bay Forum* (1973).

A. PAUL PROSS is Professor in the School of Public Administration and Research Associate in the Institute of Public Affairs at Dalhousie University.

JOHN B. ROBINSON teaches geography at Erindale College, University of Toronto, and has published several recent articles on Canadian energy planning.

TED SCHRECKER is a graduate student in Political Science at York University and an editor of *Alternatives* magazine.

ANTHONY SCOTT is Professor of Economics, University of British Columbia, and a former commissioner in the Canadian Section of the International Joint Commission.

W.R. DERRICK SEWELL is Professor and Chairman in the Department of Geography, University of Victoria, Victoria, British Columbia.

NEIL A. SWAINSON is Professor of Political Science, University of Victoria, the editor of *Managing the Water Environment* (1976), and author of *Conflict on the Columbia* (1979).

GEOFFREY R. WELLER is Associate Professor in the Department of Political Studies, Lakehead University.

R. BRIAN WOODROW is Assistant Professor, Department of Political Studies, University of Guelph.

PREFACE

In the early 1970's, there was a widespread belief that the governments at every level in Canada would be able to control the excessive depletion of the country's natural resources and to avert ecological disasters. Public pressure forced government to closely scrutinize major resource development schemes while pollution problems continued to demand attention and appropriate governmental response. However, the decade of the seventies has now gone by without any major persuasive evidence of substantial improvement. It appears that our historical reliance on exploitation and export of our "abundant" natural resources has continued to be the primary source of our national economic well-being, without much regard to any consequent effects on the environment. And the main reason seems to be the absence of any policy framework which clarifies the intimate relationship between the exploitation and use of natural resources and its consequence for the environment. Part of the reason would seem to lie in the conflict between development of natural resources in a responsible manner and the trade-off between economic growth and environmental quality. At the same time, it would also seem to be due to the lack of our ability to understand the role and importance of political and economic forces. For, it is certain that these forces do ultimately govern whether and how much of the environment will be further degraded and the extent of natural resource exploitation. It is with this view in mind that these essays, mostly written by political scientists, have been assembled in this volume.

The decade of the 1970's was indeed a period of intermittent concern for environmental quality coupled with increasing apprehension about resource scarcities. These problems continue to be with us. But the time has come for reflections and stock-taking, particularly by those who are concerned about the complex relationship between economic interests, governmental machinery, and political forces. The essays in this book stress the interplay between these three sets of actors, by highlighting and providing comparative perspectives on natural resources development and the environmental problems. The major purpose of this publication is to analyze the dynamics and implications of public policy process in Canada as it relates to natural resources management (including energy development) and related environmental problems. Policy overviews and selected case studies seek to provide a better understanding of the specifics involved so that the reader is able to appreciate this important area of public policy.

I acknowledge with gratitude the contributions made by colleagues who generously spent time and energy to prepare essays for the book. The scope of their knowledge and expertise has ensured that the book has a breadth and depth it might not have had. I owe a special debt to Professor Brian Woodrow whose help at the various stages of the book planning was extremely valuable. I am also grateful to Dr. Richard S. Tallman for doing an excellent job at copy editing. Finally, I am thankful to Jean Edmiston and Diane Perozzo of the Department of Political Studies at the University of Guelph for their secretarial assistance.

O.P. Dwivedi
Guelph, Ontario
March, 1980

Resources and the Environment: An Introduction
by O.P. Dwivedi

An Overview

The history of Canadian economic development has been dominated by trade in natural resources. Unlike other highly industrialized nations, industrialization of Canada has been based on the fortuitous discovery of minerals, natural gas, and petroleum, and on the exploitation of waterways for hydroelectricity, inland and coastal waters for the fisheries, and forests for the lumber industry. Over the years, a succession of staple exports – fish, furs, wheat, minerals, timber products – has made us one of the richest nations. The prosperity of Canada, then and now, is based on the exploitation of natural resources, and their export to foreign lands. At the same time, the seeming abundance of land, forests, bodies of water, and conflicting estimates about our mineral resources have ill-prepared us to devise a framework of intimate relationship between the exploitation and use of natural resources and consequences on the environment.

Until a few years ago, the major question before government policy-makers was how to facilitate the extraction of these resources so that the use yielded the greatest benefit. The general rule was, and to some extent still prevails, that each segment of every natural resource – water, land, minerals, forests, etc. – should be exploited for its highest and best use. If two or more simultaneous uses of a resource could yield a greater benefit than one use alone, then that policy was pursued. For this, technology was developed to reach previously inaccessible resources. Furthermore, because Canada is not endowed with an abundance of human resources, it became essential, to minimize the labour and capital cost, that the intensity of natural resources extraction be increased; and sometimes this extraction has been indiscriminate. Private industry has successfully appealed to governments that, for economic survival of the nation, no serious restraints be imposed; that instead, subsidies and rebates be given in order to open up the frontier and otherwise unlock the doors to nature's bounty.[1] Economic arguments have greatly impressed the politicians; consequently, the natural resource entrepreneurs have been able to expand our primary industrial base to the extent that the resource development activity has become the most important element in our economy. To expand that base, both foreign and domestic capital was invested. While the extraction was done in Canada, the resource was taken out of the country for final processing. Thus, the interest of private industry has been limited mainly to exploitation rather than to conservation and protection of the environment.

A framework for understanding the unity and interdependence of natural resources to the environment is yet to be properly advanced. It should be realized that any change in the character of one influences the character of the other. Exploitation of a natural resource without understanding the concept of composite environment results in a narrowed vision and piecemeal solutions, while abuse and waste continue to rise. This piecemeal approach to natural resources exploitation has led to contamination of some of our precious water resources – for example, decaying Lake Erie. While efforts have been made to conserve one resource or another, apparently we have not been able to devise an integrated plan. Conservation and environmental protection cannot be accomplished in detached segments. Historically, the conservation movement in Canada was limited to only one source, forestry, with little or no emphasis on fostering a comprehensive national strategy. A unified policy, incorporating all aspects and consequences of natural resource development must replace divergent, piecemeal approaches and isolated efforts. Our environment is a mosaic of many parts, each of which influences the other. Unity in nature, as demonstrated by the interdependence and balance, should be the guiding force to good natural resource management and environmental protection.

Natural resource policies in Canada have been designed within the framework of existing constitutional and federal-provincial conflicts over jurisdiction. The division of powers between the two levels of government was based on the needs of the mid-nineteenth century. While the control of natural resources and management and the sale of public lands (including timber and wood on these lands) belong to the provinces, the federal government has power to regulate trade and commerce, navigation and shipping (including interprovincial transportation), and inland and coastal fisheries. And to confuse the matter further, environmental concerns are not specifically mentioned in any constitutional document. At present, there is no agreement as to who has the constitutional jurisdiction to control pollution arising out of the exploitation and use of natural resources in the country as a whole. In reality, there is an interdependence of federal and provincial functions which can be used to formulate, co-operatively, a national policy; the same interdependence of functions can be used by one level of government to avoid taking responsibility. At the same time, this conflict can be used by private industries to try to prevent either level of government from acting or to promote action at one level or another. We have evidence for all three of these situations.[2]

Management of environment and resources policy, in both political and economic senses, involved action through organizations (both in public and private sectors) and piloting through an intricate web of policy directions and administrative constraints. This book stresses the management of environmental policy as it has emerged through the exploration, extraction, transportation, and use of natural resources. This is based on a process which is increasingly becoming complex and which is influenced by competing economic goals, monitored by public interest groups, and controlled by the political institutions. The emphasis on policy management arises mainly because of the growing complexity of these three forces: market economy, defenders of public interest acting as guardians of perceived societal needs and values, and governmental machinery.[3] A word of caution is essential here: in the domain of environment and resources, policy management does not imply that these three elements co-ordinate their goals by participating in a national and sub-national policy planning process. First, there is no nationally conceived and negotiated environmental and resource management policy in Canada. Secondly, market forces have exerted greater influence on the enforcement of environmental standards. One example of such influence occurred in 1978 when the Ontario Ministry of the Environment extended its earlier order of erecting pollution control devices in the INCO plant in Sudbury. The fear of loss of jobs was sufficient to slacken environmental standards. That complexity – the interplay of three sets of actors – has meant that while economics will greatly influence the policy outcome, politics eventually will decide the allocation of current values and goals and will determine the mode of compliance. The essays in this book stress the interplay among industry, public interest, and governments, and while the focus of the book is on specific case studies, these cases provide comparative perspectives on the issues of environmental quality as seen from the issue of natural resources management.

The Essays

The collection of essays is based on the view that the exploitation, use, and transportation of natural resources create, and have created, environmental problems. Our understanding of these problems can benefit from the examination of political, legal, and institutional forces which shape the policy process. We should recognize that while economic factors greatly influence the nature of resources use and exploitation, ultimately the domain of political and bureaucratic devices is responsible for policy realization and its consequences. Thus, the basic intent of this book is to examine the political and institutional roles, structures, and processes, and to evaluate and explain the nature and importance of the complex linkages between natural resources management and inherent environmental problems. We should appreciate that the protection of the environment will depend largely on how much weight we, as users, would like to place on the judicious use and adequate conservation of our precious natural resources. These essays attempt to highlight this basic challenge all of us face in Canada.

The book is organized into two parts. Part I analyzes the policy process of Canadian environmental and resources management, and carries this analysis into the three specific levels of the policy-making: the national, provincial, and international domains. Through a comprehensive overview of policy perspectives, these authors examine the interplay of various factors that the federal and provincial governments employ to achieve their objectives. The essay by R. Brian Woodrow, on policy-making at the national level, examines the resources-environment complex as it has evolved in Canada, describes its main structural features and operating characteristics, and assesses its capability for making those difficult national choices. In particular, this essay explores the desirability and feasibility of comprehensive, explicit national environmental and the natural resources policy. Woodrow acknowledges that such a policy must take shape within the context of divided jurisdiction between the federal and provincial governments and of fragmented responsibilities among various government departments and agencies. The essay sketches the roles of some federal government agencies with direct operational responsibilities on the subject, and then analyzes the basic positions of the three major political parties and some of the more significant interest groups. Woodrow concludes by suggesting that the 1980's will require a new national policy designed to consolidate the gains made through the existing resources and environmental policy, which was geared primarily toward nation-building and the creation of an advanced industrial economy based on a clear strategy of industrial and resources use.

The provincial domain is surveyed by Bruce Mitchell, who provides an overview of provincial policies and administration pertaining to resources development and the environment. He considers jurisdictional responsibility, surveys pollution control policies of the provinces, and examines three specific issues: land-use planning and the threat of foreign ownership, a case study of the potash industry in Saskatchewan, and a comparative overview of provincial approaches to environmental impact assessment; and concludes by identifying and discussing the significant trends and patterns. The final essay in Part I, by David LeMarquand and Anthony Scott, surveys Canadian international environmental concerns, and demonstrates in detail the transboundary environmental and resource development issues between Canada and the United States. Specific cases such as water quality, air quality, the Great Lakes water levels, and coastal, marine, and fisheries issues are examined. The essay also discusses institutional mechanisms used in environmental diplomacy and the role of the International Joint Commission. The purpose of these three essays, then, is to examine the central processes of policy-making and management in regard to the environment and natural resources of Canada.

Part II presents detailed case studies of the major environmental and resource development projects in Canada. These studies demonstrate the earlier assertion that policy-makers in Canada either have not fully comprehended or have ignored the consequences to the environment of their policies for the development of natural resources. Economic arguments, as usual, have gained the upper hand whenever a clear-cut choice between economic pay-off and environmental quality has been presented.

The first chapter in Part II, by A. Paul Pross, is on the issue of coastal zone management. Pross examines briefly the concept of coastal zone management and the various approaches taken by federal and provincial governments in Canada. The paper outlines policy interactions of major interests involved in the seaward side of the zone (fishing, oil, and transportation interests) and those primarily concerned with the use of the shore itself (environmental and industrial development interests). Finally, Pross considers policy options open to governments by drawing on the process used thus far in attempts to develop coastal zone policy. The next essay, by Robert Paehlke, focuses on the James Bay Project, on how the realities of federal and Quebec politics in the 1970's foreshortened environmental considerations in this mammoth hydroelectric project. Paehlke also indicates that the James Bay Project is a benchmark in Canadian recognition of the need for thorough environmental impact assessment. This need was especially great in the case of James Bay, where a public project became bigger than the political institutions meant to oversee its development.

The water and land resources of the Great Lakes have attracted a great concentration of industries and urban population. Over the years the population and industrialization pressures on the limited resources of the Great Lakes Basin increased at an accelerating rate, with the result that such proliferation brought considerable stress on the physical limits of the water system of the basin. The situation was further complicated because the Lakes are shared (except for Lake Michigan) between Canada and the United States. The essay on the politics of Great Lakes water quality, by Don Munton, illustrates how this fact – the involvement of two countries and several jurisdictions – tends to inhibit joint, comprehensive efforts on resource planning and on the clean-up of polluted air and water. Munton examines both the adequacy of institutional mechanisms and the constraints on governments in resolving transboundary environmental problems.

In the next case study, on the National Energy Board's northern pipeline hearings, John Robinson thoroughly delineates the shortcomings in the NEB hearing process by comparing its deliberations with those of the Berger Inquiry on the social and environmental impact of the proposed Mackenzie Valley pipeline. Robinson's conclusions point to a need for a more "open" decision-making process that involves more publicity and greater participation by public interest groups. Elsewise, hasty approval of projects may result in the long run in greater economic and environmental costs. To date, it should be added, Foothills Pipelines of Calgary, the successful applicant, has yet to lay a foot of pipeline while incurring many millions of dollars in expenses.

Another case study of public involvement in the planning and decision-making process, by W. R. D. Sewell and N. A. Swainson, examines the evolution of the west coast oil pollution issue. Sewell and Swainson trace the manner in which the issue became increasingly complex and changed in the course of a decade, and assess how the public as well as the various levels of government responded to the question. This case illustrates how an issue rises to the public agenda, and then, in time, disappears from it. The study concludes by suggesting that governments should try to facilitate the emergence of a social consensus. This might be done by generating the broadest possible analysis of environmental questions. The next essay, by G. R. Weller, also discusses the nature of public inquiry and the involvement of public interest groups. Weller focuses on northern Ontario by examining the influence of private industries – their size, power, and wealth based on the exploitation of natural resources; the competing views of those for development and those against development; and policy responses by the various levels of government.

The next two essays deal with cases where not enough has been known for intelligent decisions to be made or for dissemination of information to be anything but confusing. Ted Schrecker considers Canada's nuclear commitment, and concludes that the historically esoteric, industry-controlled assessment of its own technology has short-circuited the decision-making process. In effect, Schrecker suggests, unless more neutral and informed non-industry input soon becomes part of Canadian decisions on nuclear energy, we may be irrevocably committed to an essentially untenable nuclear path in our energy future. Nuclear waste, and its potential hazards, will be with us for a *long* time. Fikret Berkes then examines mercury pollution, which perhaps has proven more difficult to control than other kinds of pollution. This essay discusses controversies surrounding the evolution of public policy on mercury pollution. Intra-jurisdictional confusion, the lack of co-ordinated action by various levels of government, appears to be the major cause of inadequate treatment of the mercury hazard in Canada. The second part of this essay deals with the effects of industrial mercury on the native populations of Ojibway, Cree, and Algonquin. Nutritional problems among the native people are linked to the environmental consequences of industrial policy and programs, and incomplete information and poorly explained test-ing are seen to have caused undue reaction and confusion in the native population.

The final essay, by O. P. Dwivedi and John E. Carroll, deals with issues in Canadian-American environmental relations. Dwivedi and Carroll examine the relationship by analyzing the in-stitutional mechanisms for consultation and decision-making, and by selecting three cases (the Eastport tanker route, the Garrison Diversion, and the Skagit River-Ross Dam) that illustrate the problem both countries face in the search for mutually beneficial solutions to environmental problems that arise from resources-use projects.

Concluding Observations

The essays in this book stress the need to integrate environmental questions at the planning and development stage of a natural resource project, before other scientific and technical studies have been completed, rather than later when policy options have been narrowed. A needed reform would entail the recognition of public interest groups as a necessary instrument of policy-making by awarding them costs of participation in the process, by including direct representation of the public on regulatory and licensing boards and agencies, and by providing access to corporate infor-mation. Also, such reform must include the provision that en-vironmental costs of resource development should be extracted from the economic benefits accruing from such use.

The Science Council of Canada, in a 1968 report, summed up the close relationship between our environment and our natural resources by emphasizing the extent to which we, as a nation, had taken these for granted:

Without water, air and a place to stand men cannot live, but nature has provided these elements so abundantly in Canada that we take them for granted. To our great benefit we have har-nessed our waters as sources of energy, used them as channels for transportation, developed them for industrial and municipal use and spent our leisure hours in recreation upon them, but in the process we have often reduced our streams, lakes and rivers to sewers for refuse. When we examine our vital surroundings we often see that careless advance has left us with the smell of polluted air, the taste of dirty water and the sight of devastated landscapes. We have not learned to conserve and care for natural riches.[4]

The 1970's found Canada solving some environmental problems, creating new ones, still struggling with others, and too often continuing to take this vast land and its resources for granted. My hope, in bringing together the essays in this book, is that the 1980's will see a renewed concern for the delicate balance between resource exploitation and environmental protection. The present volume, with its perspective on public issues and government policies, points both to our successes and failures in the recent past and to the directions we should consider for the future.

NOTES

1. P. H. Pearse, "Natural Resources Policies: An Economist's Critique," in Ralph R. Krueger and Bruce Mitchell (eds.), *Managing Canada's Renewable Resources* (Toronto, 1977), 18.
2. See, for example, Mary A. Carswell and John Swaigen, *Environment on Trial* (revised edition, Toronto, 1978), 3-79.
3. For further elaboration, see R. W. Phidd and G. Bruce Doern, *The Politics and Management of Canadian Economic Policy* (Toronto, 1978), especially the introduction.
4. Science Council of Canada, *A Major Program of Water Resources Research in Canada*, Report No. 3 (Ottawa, 1968), 3.

Part I
Policy Process

Resources and Environmental Policy-making at the National Level: The Search for Focus

by R. Brian Woodrow

Over the decade of the 1970's, issues relating to natural resources and the environment received unprecedented attention at the national level in Canada. Grandiose resource development schemes like the James Bay Hydroelectric Project in Quebec, the Syncrude Tar Sands development in Alberta, and the Mackenzie Valley Pipeline through the Canadian North have each been subjected to prolonged public scrutiny and investigation. Persistent pollution problems, whether the long-term effects of mercury or other toxic chemicals on man and his environment, the threat of oil spills off Canada's coastlines, the multiple ills affecting the Great Lakes or whatever, likewise have been studied and treated but not yet resolved. Major national and international conferences like the Stockholm Conference on the Human Environment in 1972, the Man and Resources Conference in Montreal in 1973, and the Habitat Conference in Vancouver in 1976, not to mention the sporadic Law of the Sea conferences held since 1974, have all served to focus attention and bring expertise to bear on one aspect or another relating to natural resources and the environment. Northern development, urban decay, population growth, agricultural land-use, and occupational health have all in some sense emerged as derivative national concerns as have new ideas and concepts like "eco-system planning," "energy self-sufficiency," and the "conserver society." To be sure, natural resources and the environment have commanded unprecedented attention during the past decade!

How can this unprecedented attention to matters of natural resources and the environment be explained? What impact has this unprecedented attention at the national level had on public policy over the past decade? Answers to these questions must be sought in the way these issues have emerged on the public agenda and the basic challenges they pose. For most of its history, Canada has been committed to the forthright exploitation of its abundant natural resources as a primary element of national economic policy and with only slight regard for any consequent effects on the surrounding environment or on overall social well-being. During the late 1960's and early 1970's, however, the dramatic emergence of pollution as a salient public issue forced government and citizens alike to begin to reassess that wholesale commitment to the growth ethic and established environmental quality as a national goal of at least intermediate importance. Somewhat later, the onset of the energy crisis in 1973 highlighted the fundamental reality of resource scarcities as both a national and global concern and gave heightened importance to the practical problems of finding and developing new sources while at the same time making better use of available reserves. Whether treated individually and separately or as different sides of the same coin, the goal of enhanced environmental quality and the reality of important resource scarcities portend increasingly difficult national choices in the 1980's.

A Tale of Two Crises

On its most elemental level, the increasing prominence of natural resources and environmental issues at the national level can be explained as "a tale of two crises." Governments in the modern liberal democratic state do not readily take on new areas of public policy on their own initiative but rather are usually forced to do so as the result of mounting public awareness and concern. As one perceptive author has noted, there would seem to be a fairly systematic "issue-attention cycle" whereby new issues are constantly being raised and gradually institutionalized though not necessarily resolved.[1] The dynamics of this issue-attention cycle fit into several stages. During the "pre-problem stage," an undesirable social problem exists but receives little serious attention except from a few specialists and other individuals particularly interested in the problem. Then, often as a result of some dramatic event or series of events, the public at large suddenly becomes much more aware of and concerned about the problem and blithely looks to governments at any level for quick and painless solutions. A variety of political forces–political parties, interest groups, and the like–mobilize around the issue but intense public interest soon begins to decline as the initial novelty of the issue wears off and the real costs of dealing with the problem become apparent. In the final stage, the issue typically has spawned some committed supporters and brought about some limited institutional and policy changes, but eventually it loses its high ranking on the public agenda and is relegated to a position of lesser importance or spasmodic recurrences of interest. In many but not all respects, such would seem to have been the case with the pollution issue and the energy crisis during the 1970's.

The rapid rise and subsequent decline of the pollution issue in Canada can be treated here only briefly.[2] Prior to the late 1960's, pollution was not generally considered to be a major national concern in this country but rather was regarded primarily as a private or local matter. As a result of serious pollution incidents like a major fish kill in Placentia Bay, Newfoundland, the grounding of the oil tanker *Arrow* off the Nova Scotia coast, and the discovery of high mercury levels in fish caught in the Great Lakes, public awareness and concern about pollution problems in Canada rose dramatically, just as was happening at the same time in the United States and elsewhere. Mass media coverage, public opinion polls, and parliamentary interest in the subject all registered sharp jumps during 1969 and 1970 and the major political parties and important interest groups began to stake out their positions on the issue. As well, the federal and several provincial governments came into conflict over who should deal with pollution problems and how these problems should be handled at the same time that various federal departments and agencies were likewise jockeying for power and influence on the issue. During the early 1970's, public awareness and concern reached its peak and has since dropped off, although by no means back to its earlier low level. What is perhaps more important, however, is that the initial, rather narrow focus on immediate pollution problems gradually became diffused over a whole range of environmental concerns from land-use planning to northern development.

In somewhat similar fashion, the so-called "energy crisis" of 1973 also served to focus attention on natural resources and environmental issues at the national level in Canada.[3] The Arab oil boycott initiated after the Middle East War brought about apparent scarcities in the supply of oil to North America and Western Europe and occasioned a rapid escalation in world energy prices. In Canada, public awareness and concern about energy supply and pricing had been relatively low prior to 1973 but rose dramatically as a result of this bold action. Once again, mass media coverage, public opinion polls, and parliamentary interest in the issue increased dramatically and the major political parties and important interest groups began to articulate their views on the various aspects of the energy crisis. In particular, the battle lines were soon drawn on three not always separate fronts: conflict between the federal government and Alberta as producer provinces sought to assert their supply and pricing interests vis-a-vis consumer provinces; contention between both the federal and Alberta governments and the oil and gas industry over how windfall revenues should be shared and incentives created for new exploration and development; and skirmishing between Canada and the United States over energy exports and continental energy planning. During 1974, however, the energy crisis, at least in its public manifestations, began to disappear almost as quickly as it had originally appeared, although the issue did flare up again on more than one occasion as the decade progressed.

Several key features of this "tale of two crises" are noteworthy in attempting to explain the heightened importance of natural resources and environmental issues during the 1970's. (1) It is difficult to escape the conclusion that the mass media and other modes of communication played a crucial, catalytic role in fostering and promoting public awareness and concern about the pollution issue and the energy crisis. In this regard, they were very much instrumental in initially placing these issues on the public agenda but, largely owing to their own internal characteristics, ill-suited to the task of sustaining public interest over the long term. (2) In characteristically Canadian fashion, the pollution issue and energy crisis came to be expressed predominantly in jurisdictional and administrative terms. Conflict between levels of government, jockeying among different departments and agencies, and skirmishing between government and private interests became central to public policy-making. (3) Governmental responses to the pollution issue and the energy crisis have taken the form primarily of piecemeal initiatives in which short-term considerations have outweighed long-term concerns. This pattern became particularly evident in the case of response to the pollution issue; the response to the energy crisis was perhaps somewhat more calculated. (4) A new and potentially powerful configuration of political forces has emerged in the wake of the pollution issue and the energy crisis. During the 1970's these political forces have demonstrated considerable ability in keeping natural resources and environmental problems before government and the public at large. (5) One very important consequence of this "tale of two crises" has been to highlight the national dimensions of natural resources and environmental problems in Canada. While differences of opinion remain over how such problems should be handled by the federal and/or provincial governments, there would seem to be no substantial disagreement over the legitimacy and importance of pursuing national solutions.

Canada's Historic Pattern of Growth and Development

While contemporary happenings are undoubtedly important, Canada's historic pattern of growth and development also has affected not only the scope and distribution of her natural resources and environmental problems but her ability as a nation to deal with them. The earliest European visitors to North America found a culture and lifestyle among the indigenous inhabitants which was modest and simple and made few demands upon natural resources and the environment. However, as more Europeans came to the continent to trade and to settle, that idyllic situation was bound to be challenged. The exploitation of a succession of abundant natural resources and primary products for an external metropolitan centre set the pace and pattern for Canadian growth and development and the future economy began to evolve according to what economic historians were later to identify as the "staples model."[4] First with regard to fish and furs and later with other resources, the pace of exploitation became synchronized to changing fashion and demand in the export market and the tendency was soon established to creaming off only the most desirable resources in an area and then moving on with little regard for the impact on the natural environment. Moreover, the very character of the resources themselves necessitated something approaching monopoly control and placed a high premium on the role of government in promoting and sustaining growth. And finally, widespread settlement was not at first a primary goal until agriculture beyond the subsistence level became established during the early nineteenth century and the frontier of settlement began to expand. In these circumstances, matters of proper husbandry and the conservation of resources received little attention but the gross impact on the natural environment was still largely benign.

By the middle of the nineteenth century, however, changes began to take place in the character of growth and development in British North America even though many of the features of the "staples model" continued to persist. British North Americans themselves sought to replicate essentially the same mode of metropolitan dominance on a continental scale and, with the growing diversification of the economy and the fresh challenges posed by nation-building, the state began to take on an expanded and more active role in facilitating and promoting growth and development.[5] Under the aegis of the National Policy of 1879, the settlement of the West proceeded slowly at first but eventually proved successful with the establishment of the "wheat economy."[6] As well, a "new industrialism" – capital-intensive and requiring more sophisticated technology than in the past and centred on the production of pulp and paper, minerals, hydroelectricity, oil and gas, and other primary products – was in large part superimposed upon the earlier "staples model," but this time at much higher cost in terms of the resource endowment and the natural environment.[7] And lastly, in spite of the clear advantage to be gained by retaining and exercising public control over much of the land and resources of the country, governments in Canada – and especially those at the provincial level – consistently showed themselves more anxious to reap the "spoils of progress" and promote "the manufacturing condition" and largely unwilling to deal in any serious fashion with the broader environmental and social problems attendant upon private development of natural resources.[8]

The conservation movement, which emerged upon the North American scene at the turn of the century, represented the first major reaction against this well-established pattern of growth and development. In Canada, however, it never elicited the same degree of enthusiastic support and commitment as it did in the United States. To be sure, the Commission on Conservation was established in 1911 and carried out extensive investigations over the next decade into Canada's natural resources as well as a number of other topics like public health, town planning, and even pollution control.[9] It resulted in the adoption of a few notable reforms and gave a spur to other developments, but for the most part the conservation movement never become firmly rooted in Canada. "Wise use" conservationists, who were primarily interested in promoting the efficient utilization of natural resources and the environment, tended to emphasize new resource management principles like sustained-yield forestry or extensive resource development activities, which were not fundamentally incompatible with good business practices and soon came to be accepted by government and industry alike.[10] The smaller group of "preservationists," who were more concerned about protecting natural resources and the environment from exploitation and retaining them in a relatively untouched state, could not be so easily accommodated and consequently continued over the years to be little more than voices crying in the wilderness.[11] More to point, however, conservation came to prominence in Canada at a time when the country's frontier was still open and a steady stream of settlers was making its way westward and when industrialization was really beginning to flourish in areas like Ontario, Quebec, and British Columbia. Under these circumstances, it should not be surprising that the early conservation movement in Canada achieved only modest success and placed only minimal pressure on government and industry to deal with resources and environmental problems.[12] Nevertheless, the ideal of conservation has remained alive over the years, experiencing somewhat of a resurgence after World War II and during the late 1950's and eventually becoming one important component of the "environmental movement" as it emerged during the late 1960's and early 1970's.

Specifically with regard to environmental problems, it was not so much the conservation movement as rapid urban growth that stimulated the greatest interest in pollution control. The earliest concern in this regard stemmed primarily from the threat of epidemics and came to be associated with the provision of adequate sanitation facilities for Canada's growing cities.[13] Between 1910 and 1930, the purification of urban drinking water and the extension of solid waste disposal services brought about a dramatic reduction in the incidence of death from water-borne diseases. However, faced with escalating demands for urban services and with revenues squeezed as a consequence of depression and war, Canadian municipalities often had to give low priority to other capital-intensive projects like the installation of municipal sewage treatment facilities.[14] After 1945, Canada experienced extremely high rates of urbanization and the country was transformed rapidly but somewhat unevenly from the essentially rural society implicit in the "staples model" into a predominantly urban one where problems of pollution and congestion became increasingly salient. In these circumstances, not only the provincial governments but also the federal government became concerned about these problems and mounted programs that attempted to deal with such matters as the financing of municipal sewage treatment, the regulation of motor vehicle emissions, and national standards for industrial pollution.[15] In large part because of this growing concern for urban problems the conception of environment that has emerged in Canada is one that focuses more broadly on the *human* environment and not solely on the *natural* environment.[16]

One final theme, which increasingly shapes present-day conceptions of natural resources and the environment, is a growing unease about Canada's historic pattern of growth and development and especially about industrialization. In the past Canadians had been willing by and large to accept their appropriate role as "hewers of wood and drawers of water," but that attitude began to change somewhat during the 1950's. Dating at least from the Royal Commission on Canada's Economic Prospects, there has been increasing concern about overdependence on Canada's resource sector and the weakness of domestic manufacturing and technology.[17] Some have argued that foreign ownership of Canadian industry, which had become particularly extensive in the resource sector, raised the specter of increasing continentalism and had serious implications for national sovereignty and continued economic prosperity.[18] Others have stressed the crucial importance of advanced science and technology in an increasingly competitive world economy and suggested that Canada's bounteous nature may have actually done the country a disservice in that its easy availability detracted from the need for continuing innovation and adaptation.[19] Still others have expressed concern about the excesses of the consumer society spawned by industrialization and the way that it tended to abuse natural resources for trivial ends and to disregard the integrity of the natural environment.[20] While it is somewhat ironic that the effect of the energy crisis in Canada has been to throw the country back even more onto reliance on her resource endowment, the foundations of a more critical approach toward industrialization have been laid and the need for comprehensive and explicit national policy is becoming more and more evident.

Constitutional, Administrative, and Policy Framework

National policy with regard to natural resources and the environment must take shape within the context of divided jurisdiction between the federal and provincial governments and fragmented responsibilities among different government departments and agencies. There are two main parameters of jurisdiction over natural resources and the environment in Canada: proprietary rights and legislative authority.[21] Under Section 109 of the British North America Act, ownership of all Crown lands and natural resources not given over into private hands was granted to each of the provinces, although in the cases of Manitoba, Saskatchewan, and Alberta these proprietary rights were retained by the federal government until 1930. For its part, the federal government continues to hold proprietary rights to land and resources in the Canadian North, at least until such time as these territories become provinces, as well as to sea-bed resources off Canada's coastlines, although some provinces have challenged these claims. In fact, however, public ownership by the two levels of government is not nearly as extensive or as significant as it might seem.[22] Over the years, proprietary rights to much of Canada's land and many of her natural resources have passed through sale or lease into private hands. Virtually all farmland in Canada is now owned privately; oil and gas and mineral rights have either been transferred with surface grants of land or leased by government to private individuals or corporations; and forest lands, while still largely under public ownership, have also been allocated under conditional tenure to large forest products companies. As well, water, fish, and wildlife resources, traditionally viewed as incapable of normal ownership because of their fugitive and common property character, have nevertheless been subjected to some degree of control through common law doctrines like riparian rights and limitations on the right to hunt and fish.[23] Thus, proprietary rights confer a form of jurisdiction over publicly-owned unalienated resources that is scarcely less far-reaching than legislative authority.

In addition to any proprietary rights, there also are several provisions of the British North America Act which confer explicit legislative authority over natural resources and the environment upon either the provincial or federal governments. Under various heads of power, the provincial governments hold a particularly wide-ranging legislative jurisdiction within their boundaries. Their power over "the management and sale of public lands" has been utilized extensively to allocate rights to forests, minerals, and oil and gas among public and private users and to regulate the production and conservation of those resources within the province. Their power over "municipal institutions" has allowed them to establish compulsory frameworks for municipal and regional planning as well as to delegate the delivery of municipal services like sewage treatment and solid waste disposal. Their power over many "local works and undertakings" has been used to construct and operate large hydroelectric and other resource projects and to provide the necessary infrastructure of road, rail, and transmission lines for their development. As well, their powers over "property and civil rights" and "matters of a merely local and private nature within the province" have been particularly instrumental in allowing them to regulate intraprovincial transportation and marketing of resources and to set province-wide standards for environmental protection and occupational health and safety. And finally, concurrent jurisdiction with the federal government over agriculture has meant that the provincial governments hold a wide-ranging authority over livestock and crop production and agricultural land use within their boundaries. On the face of it, then, the provincial governments would seem to hold virtually an inclusive jurisdiction insofar as natural resources and the environment within the province are concerned.

Federal jurisdiction over matters of natural resources and the environment is considerably narrower and more restrictive than that of the provincial governments, but it is by no means insignificant. Among its exclusive heads of power, the federal government holds legislative authority over "seacoast and inland fisheries" and has acted extensively to manage the fisheries as both a resource and an environment even though in seven of the ten provinces much of the administration has been delegated to the provincial governments. It can legislate with regard to "navigation and shipping" and has relied upon this power to regulate the use of navigable waters across the country and the conduct of shipping in both domestic and international waters. It can legislate with regard to "Indians and lands reserved for Indians" and consequently can exercise some control over the resources and environment of these lands wherever they may be located in Canada. More importantly, the federal government is responsible for "trade and commerce" and can exercise substantial control over interprovincial and export marketing of resources. As well, it is primarily responsible for the conduct of Canada's external relations and, with some limitations on implementation within areas of provincial jurisdiction, can enter into a wide range of resource and environmental conventions, treaties, or agreements with other countries. The federal government also possesses certain broader conceptual powers which might bear upon matters of natural resources and the environment: through its virtually unrestricted "spending power," it can attempt to induce provincial governments or private interests to undertake actions it regards as desirable in the resources/environmental field; with its "declatory power," it can take control over physical facilities associated with a particular resource such as has occurred with wheat marketing; and in the "peace, order, and good government" clause, it can find solid grounds for federal control over matters of "national dimensions" like aeronautics or atomic energy and one possible justification for "emergency" intervention in case of serious pollution incidents or resource scarcities. Thus, while the federal government cannot claim the same comprehensive jurisdiction with regard to natural resources and the environment as can the provincial governments, its legislative authority remains significant.

Given the historical and constitutional situation, it should not be surprising that policy and administration with regard to natural resources and the environment have tended to be fragmented among different government departments and agencies at the national level. Environment Canada was established in 1970 at the very height of public interest in the pollution issue and has since become the main standard-bearer for environmental concern at the national level. Bringing together diverse federal activities relating to fisheries, forestry, water resources, wildlife, meteorology, and pollution control under a single roof, it is essentially a renewable resources department with an environmental perspective superimposed upon it.[24] During the 1970's Environmental Services and Fisheries and Marine Services quickly emerged as the two main components within Environment Canada, joined together in a somewhat uneasy partnership and subject to continuing argumentation that they should be split into separate departments under different ministers.[25]

In dealing with environmental matters, Environment Canada has pursued a mix of regulatory and managerial strategies with primary emphasis on the former. In 1971, it began slowly and tentatively to promulgate national effluent and emission standards for major industries like pulp and paper and petroleum under the Fisheries Act and the Clean Air Act.[26] In 1973, it introduced environmental impact analysis procedures for new programs and projects under federal jurisdiction, but there have been continuing criticisms about the adequacy and ultimate influence of these procedures on decision-making.[27] In 1975, it secured the enactment of the Environmental Contaminants Act, which mandates the testing and evaluation of pctentially harmful substances being introduced into the natural environment, but again concern has been expressed that the legislation is not as inclusive and foolproof as it could be.[28] In addition, Environment Canada has also taken the lead in negotiating important federal-provincial and international agreements for the management of specific environmental problems. On the federal-provincial front, Environment Canada has been able to negotiate planning agreements with provincial governments affected by specific environmental problems like the Peace-Athabaska Delta or the St. Lawrence River; as well, since 1974, it has negotiated accords with individual provincial governments which delineate the roles and responsibilities of the respective levels of government and provide for specific environmental quality objectives, financial arrangements, timetables, and the like, but leave the actual implementation largely to the provinces.[29] Likewise, as first negotiated in 1972 and subsequently renegotiated in 1978, Canada and the United States have entered into a Great Lakes Water Quality Agreement which prescribes common objectives for these boundary waters and sets out program commitments and institutional arrangements designed to allow the federal and provincial or state governments on both sides of the border to meet those objectives.[30] However, lacking any clear determination of a proper federal role and often in conflict with other government departments and agencies, under severe budget constraints, and with little evidence of marked public concern, Environment Canada has found it increasingly difficult to make environmental quality a government priority and to exert a continuing and vital influence on national decision-making.

The Department of Energy, Mines and Resources originally was established in 1966 as a new "glamour" portfolio designed to promote the future scientific and economic development of the nation. Since 1973, the main focus of attention within the Department has been on the Energy Policy Sector and its attempts to forge a national energy policy in response to the crisis spawned by the OPEC oil increase and exacerbated by Canada's own unpreparedness and indecision.[31] On this latter point, Alberta and the federal government were soon locked in conflict over increases in the domestic price of oil and gas, the imposition of export taxes on Canadian oil going to the United States, and the appropriate distribution of the windfall revenues gained among the producing and consuming provinces and the oil and gas industry.[32] As well, the National Energy Board, which was supposed to operate as a quasi-independent watchdog over energy policy, had been persuaded after 1970 to authorize long-term exports of oil and natural gas to the United States but by 1975 was being asked to approve the massive Mackenzie Valley pipeline project with its serious social and environmental consequences in order to replace supplies of gas already exported.[33] Likewise, Atomic Energy of Canada Limited – the Crown corporation responsible for the manufacture and sale of CANDU nuclear reactors – was also busily engaged in extensive promotional and marketing activities at the same time that serious questions were being raised about the adequacy of international safeguards to ensure their peaceful use and the safety and waste disposal characteristics of the system itself.[34] By 1976, the Department of Energy, Mines and Resources was able to produce a national energy strategy directed to the goal of "energy self-reliance" and based upon ten policy elements ranging from "appropriate energy pricing," "energy conservation," and "increased exploration and development," down to "greater Canadian content and participation."[35] However, given the complexity and the increasing pressure for exploration and development, no mere statement of government policy is likely to overcome the continuing disarray affecting decision-making nor can it assure the effective application of such a strategy to the numerous and difficult decisions about Canada's energy future.

The Department of Indian and Northern Affairs also was originally established in 1966 and given a particular mandate to oversee the economic, social, and political development of Canada's North. The discovery of substantial quantities of oil and gas off Alaska's north shore in 1968 brought about increasing pressures for exploration and development in Canada's North.[36] The test voyages of the tanker *Manhattan* through the Northwest Passage in 1969 and 1970 raised questions about Canada's sovereignty in the Arctic, and Canada's equivocal position between 1971 and 1973 on the possibility of a Mackenzie Valley route as an alternative to the eventually successful trans-Alaska pipeline plus shipment by oil tanker down the west coast revealed the difficult technical and political problems associated with northern development.[37] Meanwhile, during the late 1960's and early 1970's, the Department secured the enactment of legislation and regulations including the Arctic Waters Act and the Arctic Land Use Regulations and also enunciated a set of policy guidelines designed to ensure orderly development compatible with environmental protection and preservation of the indigenous way of life.[38] After 1973, the idea of northern pipelines received new life, first with the Arctic Gas proposal to bring gas down the Mackenzie Valley and later with the Alcan proposal for a route following the Alaska Highway. Extensive technical and environmental studies supervised by the Advisory Committee on Northern Development revealed numerous shortcomings in the Arctic Gas proposal and the Commission of Inquiry under Mr. Justice Thomas Berger focused particular attention on the need for a settlement of native land claims as well as measures to protect the northern environment and way of life before any Mackenzie Valley pipeline should be considered.[39] In the meantime, the Alcan proposal had emerged as a promising alternative and, after less extensive studies and another less-elaborate Commission of Inquiry under Mr. Kenneth Lysyk, the government agreed to proceed with the Alaska Highway pipeline after being persuaded to accept a number of important conditions relating to native claims, environmental protection, and project financing and management.[40] On this issue as on many others, the Department of Indian and Northern Affairs found itself in a particularly awkward kind of double jeopardy – not only charged with promoting development and protecting the environment but also responsible for settling native land claims and supervising the overall well-being of a region of the country that is becoming increasingly important to the national interest.

In addition to those federal governments and agencies with direct operational responsibilities relating to natural resources and the environment, other bodies play an important role in matters of co-ordination and conceptualization at the national level. On transboundary problems between Canada and the United States, the International Joint Commission, first established in 1909 and consisting of three appointed members from each country, has played a crucial role in investigating and arbitrating potential conflicts as well as stimulating government action to deal with these problems. Its continuing investigations of pollution problems affecting the Great Lakes were instrumental in leading to the 1972 and 1978 agreements and the Joint Commission has been called upon to examine a number of other current problems, including the Skagit River flooding proposal, the Garrison Diversion Project, and the regulation of water levels in the Great Lakes and the St. Lawrence River.[41] Likewise on problems of mutual concern and interest to both the federal and provincial governments, the Canadian Council of Resource and Environmental Ministers has served as a forum for continuing discussion and consultation and a useful vehicle for raising consciousness and mobilizing participation by specialists and the public. In 1966, the Council sponsored the Pollution and Our Environment Conference in Montreal, which contributed greatly to the emergence and progressive definition of environmental concern in Canada. This was followed up in 1973 with the Man and Resources Conference, which helped to focus attention on the wide-ranging implications of renewable and non-renewable resource development.[42] Finally, the Science Council, which has operated as an independent advisory body to the federal government since 1966, has shown a special interest in issues relating to natural resources and the environment and has taken the lead in developing new and integrative concepts such as the "conserver society," which attempts to outline a constructive, responsible approach for Canadians and their governments to follow in responding to the challenges posed by resource scarcity and environmental quality.[43]

Building upon their extensive jurisdiction and long-standing involvement in the natural resources and environmental field, provincial governments have been able to play an increasingly important role in national policy-making during the 1970's. Several prominent examples come quickly to mind. In Quebec, the James Bay Project shows clearly that a provincial government determined to undertake large-scale resource development for employment, energy, and other reasons can do so quite effectively and independently and with little regard for the wishes of the affected population or for broader national concerns;[44] in Alberta, the Tar Sands Development demonstrates how a provincial government can use its proprietary and legislative jurisdiction to control the production and conservation of a resource so as to obtain a favourable outcome in its dealings with the federal government and the consuming provinces as well as with the multinational oil companies;[45] and, in northern Ontario, the compelling problem of mercury pollution of the English-Wabigoon river system reveals the tangled web of jurisdiction and administration that has only served to complicate the task of dealing with a major threat to human health and environmental safety.[46] In short, the provincial governments in Canada have both the capability and the incentive to exert a major influence on national policy-making with regard to natural resources and the environment.

The Changing Configuration of Political Forces

While the jurisdictional and administrative framework has remained relatively stable during the 1970's, the configuration of political forces on natural resources and environmental issues has been undergoing important changes. To be sure, there has been a long-standing interest in these matters as a theme in Canadian development, but the dramatic emergence of the pollution issue and the onset of the energy crisis added new dimensions and heightened importance. The major political parties at the federal level have all staked out basic positions on many of the issues involved; organized groups representing diverse sectors of Canadian society have more or less clarified the views and interests; and, after the unprecedented attention of the past decade and with the uncertain prospects for the 1980's, a more realistic public opinion on natural resources and environmental issues may be emerging.

All three of the major political parties at the federal level basically accept the continuing importance of a staples model of growth and development but do so with varying degrees of enthusiasm and with different views as to its implications for Canada. This substantial consensus as well as important points of difference became evident in the recent debate over the issue of northern pipelines. The Liberal government took a rather cautious approach to the issue, actively promoting the idea of such a pipeline in both Canada and the United States but waiting for the results of technical and environmental studies as well as the Berger and Lysyk inquiries before finally committing itself to the Alaska Highway route and negotiating the necessary treaty with the United States.[47] On the one hand, the Progressive Conservatives were placed eventually in the position of supporting the government decision, forced to dismiss any Mackenzie Valley route for environmental and other reasons, and able only to argue for the best possible deal with the United States and as much private enterprise participation in the project as possible.[48] On the other hand, the New Democrats came out in forthright opposition to any northern pipeline, rejecting not only the Mackenzie Valley route but also the Alaska Highway route, attacking any deal with the U.S. as unwarranted continentalism and a sell-out to American multinationals, and promoting a policy of greater public ownership and control and effective energy conservation to husband Canada's depleting non-renewable resources.[49] With appropriate modifications and additions, the same basic themes of continentalism, public versus private ownership, conservation, and environmental quality have been prominent in partisan debate on natural resources policy.

With regard to environmental protection, both the Progressive Conservatives and New Democrats generally supported the mix of regulatory and managerial strategies adopted by the governing Liberals during the 1970's. Both opposition parties were strongly in favour of national standards for water and air quality and supported the government's environmental impact analysis procedures and its environmental contaminants legislation. As well, both opposition parties endorsed the Great Lakes and West Coast pollution agreements with the United States and have been satisfied by and large with most of the joint federal-provincial planning agreements. The Progressive Conservatives and the New Democrats differed with the governing Liberals primarily on matters of style and organization rather than substance. As might be expected, both opposition parties argued for a stronger federal role on environmental matters, preferring a more direct assertion of Arctic sovereignty to go along with the pollution control measures adopted and pressing for enhanced federal powers vis-a-vis the provincial governments on certain issues like mercury pollution.[50] Likewise, on matters of government organization, the New Democrats emphasized the need for greater public participation in environmental policy-making through such mechanisms as an independent Environmental Council while the Progressive Conservatives urged repeatedly that Environment Canada's fisheries and environmental responsibilities be separated.[51] In the final analysis, however, each of the political parties at federal level has come to adopt one variation or another of the notion that economic growth and environmental quality must be balanced and that pollution control should be prosecuted in the most efficient technical manner but with due regard for the various societal interests involved.

In addition to the positions taken by political parties, a wider range of organized groups in Canadian society also have contributed to the elaboration of a basic pattern of demand on resources and environmental issues at the national level. For purposes of analysis, these various groups can be divided into three characteristic types: (1) the "promoters," whose views and interests derive from their commitment to exploitation as the key to economic growth and development and who press for free rein and appropriate incentives within which to pursue their entrepreneurial activity; (2) the "conservationists and environmentalists," who advocate restraint and regulation because they are concerned about the unthinking and wasteful exploitation of resources and the consequent impact on the natural and urban environment; (3) the "technologists," who primarily are interested in natural resources and environment for their own sake and whose orientation is to design the best technical and administrative solutions without much reference to broad economic and social considerations.[52] Needless to say, no specific organized group will fit exactly into any category nor are the lines of demarcation between categories always clearly drawn, but these three basic types do capture the essence of conflict on resources and environmental issues.

Among the various organized groups in Canada, the major "promoters" at the national level come from the ranks of business and industry, but support for their views is by no means limited to this narrow circle. Canadian business and industry have a well-established tradition of relying upon both the federal and provincial governments for encouragement, assistance, and protection in carrying out their entrepreneurial function. The actual pattern of business and industry representation on natural resources and environmental issues will vary from one instance to another, but certain patterns become readily apparent. "Peak associations" like the Canadian Manufacturers' Association, the Canadian Chamber of Commerce, and the Conference Board are concerned primarily that the proper "climate" for investment and development is created and that undue restrictions on exports or on industrial pollution are not imposed.[53] Industry or trade associations are left to promote the shared views and common interests of their various members. For example, the oil and gas industry represented by the Canadian Petroleum Association and the Independent Petroleum Association of Canada have been particularly adept at using their links with the Alberta government to exert influence at the national level.[54] The Canadian Pulp and Paper Association has long had close relations with the forest managers within Environment Canada and can use this access to good advantage in getting across its views on pollution controls affecting the industry.[55] And the interests of the Canadian Nuclear Association and Atomic Energy of Canada Limited are so close as to be virtually synonymous.[56] Finally, individual companies or their officers may and often do choose to bring their views and interests on natural resources issues directly to the attention of governments and the public, as has been clearly evident in the competition between the Arctic Gas consortium and Alcan interests over the northern pipeline.[57] It is misleading, however, to identify business and industry as the main "promoters" at the national level; it should be recognized that many societal interests – labour and consumers as well as government itself – have at least a tacit stake in sustaining the present pattern of growth and development.

For its part, the "environmental movement" is not nearly as disorganized and powerless at the national level in Canada as it was even a decade ago. Originating in part from the various conservation groups that for many years fostered understanding and respect for the natural world, it built upon the many citizen action groups that emerged spontaneously in response to the pollution issue and the energy crisis during the 1970's.[58] The "environmental movement" is now comprised of several hundred different organizations across the country, some of which are becoming well-organized and increasingly visible at the national level and able to gain the support of other organized groups affected by natural resources and environmental issues.[59] For example, the Canadian Wildlife Federation maintains a modest Ottawa office with a few full-time researchers and support staff and has been particularly active in keeping its members and the public informed of current issues through publications and public hearings.[60] Similarly, the Canadian Arctic Resources Committee, a group of academics and others concerned about the future development of Canada's North, has played an important role in providing independent information and analysis on the various northern pipeline proposals before regulatory and advisory bodies.[61] As well, the Canadian Coalition for Nuclear Responsibility has just begun to raise public consciousness of the dilemmas and dangers facing Canada with regard to nuclear energy.[62] Of further importance, these various groups have been forging links with other organized groups, ranging from trade unions and consumer associations to native rights groups, on an increasing number of natural resources and environmental issues of common interest and shared concern. Thus, the "environmental movement," composed of highly motivated individuals with a good flair for public relations and a solid scientific grounding, has begun to exercise greater influence at the national level while remaining primarily a grassroots phenomenon.

"Technologists" are those individuals with expertise in the natural, physical, and social sciences whose concern is primarily with the resource or environment itself and how it can best be utilized and managed. Over the past decade, a notable expansion in resources and environmental studies has occurred within and among many diverse disciplines ranging from economics, law, and geography to biology and engineering.[63] This has produced a growing number of academics, consultants, and public and private sector officials with interest and expertise on many of the emerging problems in the field. Proposed schemes for forest management in northern Ontario, fisheries development and conservation within Canada's 200-mile offshore limit, and oil and gas exploration in the High Arctic all raise difficult technical questions that require at least tentative answers before agreement to proceed with such schemes can reasonably be undertaken.[64] Procedures for environmental planning – whether applied in urban or rural settings, to coastal zone regions, or in the Canadian North – have received increasing attention and are steadily becoming accepted as standard practice.[65] Energy conservation as both a goal and a strategy has led to heightened interest and burgeoning opportunities in the development and application of new technologies, ranging from solar energy to wind power and new fuels.[66] In their preoccupation with resources and/or environment, "technologists" court several very real dangers. On the one hand, they run the risk of becoming little more than hired guns for "promoters" or the "environmental movement" in their efforts to place pressure on public and private decision-making. On the other hand, they are liable to be too narrow in their perspective and orientation and badly in need of the corrective provided by broad-based concepts and integrative ideas. Nevertheless, the "technologist" has become a prominent figure on resources and environmental issues at the national level during the 1970's and will likely become even more so in the future.

In a very important sense, the public remains the ultimate arbiter (although admittedly a rather unwieldy and sometimes capricious one) of what happens with regard to resources and environmental issues. Through popular attitudes and opinions, consumer preferences and buying habits, and participation in group action, public meetings, and the election of governments, the public plays a crucial role in setting the agenda and establishing the limits within which governments and other actors must operate. Judged by the simple measure of public opinion, the 1970's have been both a cause for optimism and a source of pessimism as far as natural resources and environmental issues in Canada are concerned. The decade began with a generous outpouring of public concern about pollution problems but this gradually dropped off. In 1970, one nation-wide survey revealed that 91 per cent of respondents were aware of pollution problems and 69 per cent felt them to be "very serious" in Canada; another survey found that pollution was ranked highest by the general public as an issue deserving more attention from government.[67] By 1975, however, a further nation-wide survey revealed virtually the same high degree of awareness of pollution problems, yet there was a modest decrease in the number of respondents who felt that these problems were "very serious" and almost no disposition to view pollution as a major political issue at the time.[68] Similarly, the energy crisis mobilized much immediate concern about the issue but revealed a continuing disbelief in its reality. In 1973, nation-wide surveys showed that Canadians were becoming increasingly concerned about oil and gas shortages but another poll in 1974 found that only one-fourth of all Canadians felt that energy problems constituted a real crisis. Subsequent surveys in 1976 and 1978 indicated that a large majority of Canadians expected no energy crisis in the upcoming five years.[69]

A similar mix of concern and resignation is seen in Canadian attitudes on a number of more specific resources and environmental issues. In 1974, a majority of Canadians were against expropriation of Indian lands for the James Bay Project, yet support for this view was considerably lower in Quebec itself.[70] In 1975, there was strong nation-wide support for a government role in the Athabaska Tar-Sands, although again support was somewhat lower in Alberta.[71] In 1976, one survey suggested that more Canadians favoured than opposed increased reliance on nuclear power, but the following year another survey found that a majority of Canadians would halt rather than increase its use.[72] Public opinion in 1977 was split on the Berger Report, with about equal percentages of Canadians who were aware of its recommendations supporting and opposing them.[73] And in 1978, a nation-wide survey revealed the hardly surprising fact that 55 per cent of Canadians felt that development of natural resources for foreign markets was "bad" for the country.[74] What all of this data actually means is not always obvious, but it does suggest a basic ambivalence and continuing volatility to Canadian attitudes toward natural resources and the environment.

Concluding Comments

This essay has explored the complex and disjointed character of natural resources and environmental policy-making at the national level in Canada. It has shown how the emergence of the pollution issue and the onset of the "energy crisis" mobilized public awareness and concern during the 1970's and how Canada's historic pattern of growth and development has consistently underlined the need for national policy. In the past, governmental response to natural resources and environmental issues and the development of a national policy have been much constrained by divided jurisdiction between the federal and provincial governments and the fragmentation of administrative responsibility among different departments and agencies. As well, a configuration of political forces sensitive to natural resources and environmental issues has gradually emerged and undoubtedly will continue to influence policy-making at the national level in the coming decade. In these circumstances, it is useful to consider the desirability and feasibility of overall national policy relating to natural resources and the environment.

Such a national policy clearly must not be segmented in character, as are so many of the present policies and programs undertaken by government, but must provide a focus and framework for integrating diverse and wide-ranging concerns. It must include a comprehensive, explicit statement of national goals and interests with regard to natural resources and the environment; it must be developed within the context of a clear industrial strategy, a rational energy strategy, and a wise northern development strategy; and it must deal with such knotty questions as native rights, technological dependence, and foreign control. Nevertheless, the preconditions for such a national policy are becoming clearer. First, there is a growing recognition of the need for a more precise determination of the trade-offs required among economic growth, resource scarcities, and environmental quality so that intelligent choices can be made. Second, there is also recognition of the need for revision in the relationship between the federal and provincial governments so that natural resources and environmental issues can be confronted more comprehensively. And third, new and integrative concepts that order our perception of natural resources and environmental issues are being developed. On each of these accounts, some progress has been made during the 1970's. More will be required during the 1980's if a proper national policy for natural resources and the environment is to be forthcoming.

NOTES

1. See Anthony Downs, "Up and Down with Ecology – The 'Issue-Attention Cycle,' " *The Public Interest*, 28 (Summer, 1972), 37-50.
2. For a more complete treatment of the rise and decline of the pollution issue in Canada, see R. Brian Woodrow, *Pollution, Politics and Public Policy* (forthcoming).
3. On the "energy crisis" as an issue in Canada, see G. R. Berry, "The Oil Industry and the Energy Crisis," *Canadian Public Administration*, 17 (Winter, 1974), 600-35.
4. For a review of the historiography of the "staples model," see Irene M. Spry, "Historical Perspective," in Philippe Crabbe and Irene M. Spry (eds.), *Natural Resource Development in Canada* (Ottawa, 1973), 23-47. Of course, the basic references include H. A. Innis, *The Fur Trade in Canada* (Toronto, 1930); Innis, *The Cod Fisheries* (Toronto, 1940); and A. R. M. Lower, *The North American Assault on the Canadian Forest* (Toronto, 1938).
5. On these points, see D. G. Creighton, *The Empire of the St. Lawrence* (Toronto, 1956); and H. G. Aitken, *American Capital and Canadian Resources* (Cambridge, Mass., 1961).
6. On the pattern of development in the West, see A. S. Martin and Chester Martin, *History of Prairie Settlement and Dominion Lands* (Toronto, 1948);

and V. S. Fowke, *The National Policy and the Wheat Economy* (Toronto, 1957).

7. The "new industrialism" is described briefly in W. T. Easterbrook and H. G. J. Aitken, *Canadian Economic History* (Toronto, 1956), chapter 21.

8. For excellent treatments of how this commitment to growth and development affected the ability of government to regulate industry in the public interest, see J. H. Dales, *Hydroelectricity and Industrial Development: Quebec, 1898-1940* (Cambridge, Mass., 1957); H. V. Nelles, *The Politics of Development* (Toronto, 1974); and Martin Robin, *The Spoils of Progress* (Toronto, 1973).

9. For a brief account of the conservation movement in Canada, see T. J. Burton, *Natural Resource Policy in Canada* (Toronto, 1972), chapter 2.

10. For a case study of how conservation came to be assimilated by one industry, see Peter Gillies, "The Ottawa Lumber Barons and the Conservation Movement," *Journal of Canadian Studies*, 9 (February, 1974), 14-30; on its acceptance within a single profession, see A. Paul Pross, "Development of Professions in the Public Service: The Foresters of Ontario," *Canadian Public Administration*, 10 (September, 1967), 367-404.

11. On the origins of the "preservationist" strain in Canada, see Janet Foster, *Working For Wildlife* (Toronto, 1978).

12. "Conservation . . . has scarcely become a 'movement' in Canada. Canadian intellectuals have been less sentimental and Canadian legislators have taken a more commercial attitude to the conservation movement than their opposites in the United States." Anthony Scott, *Natural Resources: The Economics of Conservation* (Toronto, 1955), 253.

13. On the history of urban development in Canada, see John C. Weaver, *Shaping the Canadian City* (Toronto, 1977); and Paul Rutherford (ed.), *Saving the Canadian City* (Toronto, 1972).

14. On the growth of sanitation problems in Canada, see Albert Berry, "Environmental Pollution and Its Control in Canada," in Canadian Council of Resource Ministers, *Background Papers for the Pollution and Our Environment Conference*, vol. I (Montreal, 1966), A-1.

15. For a case study of governmental response to the municipal sewage treatment problem, see R. Brian Woodrow, "Municipal Sewage Treatment: The 'Political Miseconomy' of Pollution Control in Canada," in O. P. Dwivedi (ed.), *Protecting the Environment* (Toronto, 1974), 211-29.

16. For evidence of this emerging conception of environment in Canada, see N. H. Lithwick, *Urban Canada: Problems and Prospects* (Ottawa: Central Mortgage and Housing Corporation, 1970); Environment Canada, *Canada and the Human Environment* (Ottawa, 1972); and Department of National Health and Welfare, *New Perspectives on the Health of Canadians* (Ottawa, 1974).

17. On the growth of nationalist sentiment, see David Godfrey, *From Gordon to Watkins to You* (Toronto, 1970).

18. For a classic statement of this view, see Kari Levitt, *Silent Surrender* (Toronto, 1970).

19. Evidence of this view can be found in Economic Council of Canada, *Looking Outward* (Ottawa, 1975); and Science Council of Canada, *Population Resources and Technology* (Ottawa, 1976).

20. On the reaction against the consumer society, see Kimon Valaskakis, P. S. Sindell, and J. G. Smith, *The Selective Conserver Society* (Montreal, 1977), especially chapter 5.

21. The following discussion of jurisdictional matters is based primarily upon A. R. Thompson and H. R. Eddy, "Jurisdictional Problems of Natural Resource Management in Canada," in W. D. Bennett *et al.*, *Essays on Aspects of Resource Policy* (Ottawa: Science Council, 1973), 67-96; and Dale Gibson, "The Environment and the Constitution: New Wine in Old Bottles," in Dwivedi (ed.), *Protecting the Environment*, 105-22.

22. For treatments of public land use at both the federal and provincial levels, see J. G. Nelson, R. C. Scace, and R. Kouri (eds.), *Canadian Land Use in Perspective* (Ottawa: Social Science Research Council, 1974).

23. For a series of essays which implicitly demonstrate the extent to which proprietary rights to natural resources have been alienated, see R. R. Krueger and Bruce Mitchell, *Managing Canada's Renewable Resources* (Toronto, 1977).

24. On the original goals and organization of the Department, see Environment Canada, *Its Organization and Objectives* (Ottawa, 1971).

25. See *Organization of the Government of Canada* (Ottawa, 1976), 180 ff. In October, 1978, the government finally introduced legislation to separate these two components and create both Environment Canada and Fisheries and Oceans Canada.

26. As of 1978, national standards or guidelines had been promulgated for industries across the country. For a review of this approach, see Environment Canada, *Annual Report, 1976-77* (Ottawa, 1977), 71-80.

27. The basic procedures for environmental impact analysis can be found in P. J. B. Duffy, *The Development and Practice of Environmental Impact Assessment Concepts in Canada* (Otawa: Environment Canada, 1975).

28. On the adequacy of environmental contaminants legislation, see Science Council of Canada, *Policies and Poisons* (Ottawa, 1977), especially chapter VII.

29. For a review of the various agreements and accords, see Environment Canada, *Canada Water Year Book*, (Ottawa, 1976), 1-62.

30. On the 1972 and 1978 agreements, see the essay by Don Munton in this book.

31. There are now several treatments of Canadian energy policy during the 1970's. In particular, see Philip Sykes, *Sellout: The Giveaway of Canada's Energy Resources* (Edmonton, 1973); Wade Rowland, *Fueling Canada's Future* (Toronto, 1974); and James Laxer, *Canada's Energy Crisis* (Toronto, 1974).

32. On the federal-provincial aspects, see D. V. Smiley, "The Political Context of Resource Development in Canada," in Anthony Scott (ed.), *Natural Resource Revenues: A Test of Federalism* (Vancouver, 1976).

33. On the regulatory process involved, see A. R. Lucas, "The National Energy Board," in G. Bruce Doern (ed.), *The Regulatory Process in Canada* (Toronto, 1978), 259-313.

34. On AECL and the nuclear option, see Charles Law and Ron Glen, *Critical Choice: Nuclear Power in Canada* (Toronto, 1978).

35. The basic statements of federal energy policy are Energy, Mines and Resources, *An Energy Strategy of Canada: Policies for Self-Reliance* (Ottawa, 1976); and Energy, Mines and Resources, *Energy Conservation in Canada: Programs and Perspectives* (Ottawa, 1977).

36. For an overview of the northern development issue during the early 1970's, see Edgar Dosman, *The National Interest: The Politics of Northern Development, 1968-1975* (Toronto, 1976).

37. On the specific issues of Arctic sovereignty and the trans-Alaska pipeline, see Edgar Dosman (ed.), *The Arctic in Question* (Toronto, 1976); and P. H. Pearse, *The Mackenzie Pipeline: Arctic Gas and Canadian Energy Policy* (Toronto, 1974).

38. The basic statement of federal policy is Department of Indian Affairs and Northern Development, *Canada's North 1970-80* (Ottawa, 1972).

39. See Mr. Justice Thomas Berger, *Northern Frontier, Northern Homeland: The Report of the Mackenzie Valley Pipeline Inquiry* (Ottawa, 1977).

40. See Kenneth Lysyk, *Alaska Highway Pipeline Inquiry* (Ottawa, 1977).

41. For treatments of this body, see O. P. Dwivedi, "The International Joint Commission: Its Role in United States-Canada Boundary Pollution Control," *International Review of Administrative Sciences*, 40 (Fall, 1974), 369-76; and F. J. E. Jordan, "The International Joint Commission and Canada-United States Boundary Relations," in R. St. J. Macdonald *et al.*, *Canadian Perspectives on International Law and Organization* (Toronto, 1974), 525-41.

42. On the role of the Canadian Council of Resource and Environmental Ministers, see Michael Whittington, "Environmental Policy," in G. B. Doern and V. S. Wilson (eds.), *Issues in Canadian Public Policy* (Toronto, 1974), 203-27.

43. For a review of its various activities in this regard, see Science Council of Canada, *Canada as a Conserver Society* (Ottawa, 1977), especially chapter I.

44. See Boyce Richardson, *Strangers Devour the Land* (Toronto, 1976).

45. See Larry Pratt, *The Tar Sands* (Edmonton, 1976).

46. See Warner Troyer, *No Safe Place* (Toronto, 1977).

47. For the Liberal government position, see House of Commons, *Debates*, May 13, 1977, pp. 5638-40, and February 13, 1978, pp. 2787-94.

48. For the Progressive Conservative position, see House of Commons, *Debates*, August 4, 1977, pp. 8036-40, and February 13, 1978, pp. 2794-2800.

49. For the NDP position, see House of Commons, *Debates*, May 13, 1977, pp. 5628-32, and February 13, 1978, pp. 2811-15.

50. For the positions of the opposition parties on Arctic sovereignty, see House of Commons, *Debates*, May 15, 1969, pp. 8720-21, and April 16, 1970, pp. 5922-25; on a stronger federal role vis-a-vis the provinces, see House of Commons, *Debates*, December 12, 1974, pp. 2213-22, and June 28, 1977, pp. 7163-69.

51. On the need for an independent Environmental Council, see House of Commons, *Debates*, June 27, 1972, pp. 3567-73, and May 8, 1973, pp. 3543-44 and 3588-89; on the creation of separate documents, see House of Commons, *Debates*, December 20, 1976, pp. 2159-66.

52. This typology has been adopted from P. H. Pearse, "Natural Resource Policies: An Economist's Critique," in Krueger and Mitchell (eds.), *Managing Canada's Renewable Resources*, especially pp. 17-19.

53. For a typical example of this activity, see Conference Board, *Pollution Control in Canada: Government and Industry Viewpoints* (Montreal, 1971).

54. On the oil and gas industry, see Glyn R. Berry, "The Oil Lobby and the Energy Crisis," *Canadian Public Administration*, 17 (Winter, 1974), 600-35.

55. On the pulp and paper industry and its relations with government, see Canadian Pulp and Paper Association, *From Watershed to Watermark* (Montreal, 1974).

56. On the nuclear industry, see Doug Torgenson, "From Dream to Nightmare:

The Historical Origins of Canada's Nuclear Energy Future," *Alternatives*, 7 (Fall, 1977), 8-17.

57. For a series of essays on how a large company can influence energy policies, see J. Laxer and A. Martin (eds.), *The Big Tough Expensive Job: Imperial Oil and the Canadian Economy* (Toronto, 1976).

58. On some of the key differences between conservation and the "environmental movement," see Burton, *Natural Resource Policy in Canada*, chapter 6.

59. For a comprehensive listing of conservation and environmental groups in Canada, see Canadian Nature Federation, *Canadian Conservation Directory*, published biennially.

60. Among its various activities, the Canadian Wildlife Federation published a very informative *Pipeline Update* during 1976 and 1977 so as to keep interested individuals informed on the rapid development of this issue.

61. The Canadian Arctic Resources Committee has sponsored a number of special publications relating to the North, including D. H. Pimlott *et al.*, *Arctic Alternatives* (Ottawa, 1973); and D. H. Pimlott, *Oil Under the Ice* (Ottawa, 1976).

62. For a major statement by this group, see Canadian Coalition for Nuclear Responsibility, "Nuclear Power: Time to Stop and Think," *Alternatives*, 7 (Fall, 1977), 26-33.

63. On the growth of resources and environmental studies in Canada, see Science Council of Canada, *It's Not Too Late – Yet* (Ottawa, 1972), 29-33; and *Natural Resource Policy Issues in Canada* (Ottawa, 1973), 35-40.

64. For recent articles on these technical issues, see, for example, Kari Lie, "The Plight of Ontario's Northern Forests," *Alternatives*, 7 (Fall, 1978), 17-26; C. L. Mitchell, "The 200-Mile Limit: New Issues, Old Problems for Canada's East Coast Fisheries," *Canadian Public Policy*, 4 (Spring, 1978), 172-83.

65. For a series of essays on various planning problems in Canada, see G. R. McBoyle and E. Sommerville (eds.), *Canada's Natural Environment* (Toronto, 1977).

66. On this issue, see F. H. Knelman, *Energy Conservation* (Ottawa: Science Council, 1975).

67. *The Gallup Report*, March 25, 1970; and December 2, 1970.

68. *Ibid.*, February 26, 1975; and August 13, 1975.

69. *Ibid.*, December 5, 1973; April 6, 1974; October 27, 1976; and October 21, 1978.

70. *Ibid.*, March 27, 1974.

71. *Ibid.*, April 19, 1975.

72. *Ibid.*, October 30, 1976; and November 3, 1977.

73. *Ibid.*, July 16, 1977.

74. *Ibid.*, August 7, 1978.

CHAPTER TWO

The Provincial Domain in Environmental Management and Resource Development

by Bruce Mitchell

Attempts to develop a comprehensive national policy for environmental management and resource development must recognize varying regional needs and aspirations in Canada. These regional differences raise many difficult issues in developing national policies and strategies. For example, in tackling control of water pollution, the question has arisen whether Canada should adopt uniform national quality standards or devise standards specific to given areas. In this context, a decision must be made as to whether water quality should be the same in Lake Louise and Hamilton Harbour. In other words, are the same approaches appropriate for all regions, or is it necessary to accommodate different regional characteristics?

Varying regional concerns are complicated by the divided jurisdiction between the federal and provincial governments concerning the environment and resources. In the preceding paper, Woodrow clearly described the ambiguity in the BNA Act regarding responsibility over natural resources.[1] Furthermore, the provinces are seeking increased power over resources. This situation makes understanding of provincial attitudes and approaches a prerequisite for development of any national policy.

Against this background of varying regional requirements and divided jurisdiction, the present study considers selected provincial approaches to environmental management and resource development. The objectives are to illustrate the way in which existing jurisdictional arrangements facilitate or constrain provincial strategies and to explore the implications for establishing a comprehensive national approach toward environmental management and resource development. Particular attention will be given to identifying areas in which current arrangements encourage or impede federal-provincial co-operation and to considering pressures which are likely to result in altered arrangements in the future.

Whether classified by resource sector (water, minerals, forests) or resource problem (pollution, offshore fisheries, energy, foreign investment), many policy areas could be covered in such an analysis. As length constraints preclude consideration of them all, four examples are presented. The first two (pollution and environmental impact assessment) represent policy areas in which jurisdictional arrangements have facilitated management by provincial governments, although conflict with the federal government has not been totally absent. The other two examples (foreign investment and mineral and petroleum development) involve situations in which national and regional interests have conflicted directly. Efforts to design national policies will have to overcome the types of difficulty encountered in these latter two policy areas.

Pollution Management

Pollution management focuses upon water, air, and soil. Water was the first to receive attention because of the clear link between water pollution and the spread of disease. Air quality did not receive the same early attention, but with urbanization and industrialization it, too, became an issue for concern. Soil pollution is the most recent policy issue, reflecting growth of the chemical industry and the use of herbicides and pesticides.[2] In this section, the general approaches of the provincial governments to pollution control will be outlined, general trends noted, and implications discussed.

Although pollution attracted widespread attention during the mid-1960's, it was a concern long before then. The implications for public health drew early attention to water quality relative to drinking water and sewage disposal. Since public health responsibilities were allocated mainly to the provinces under the BNA Act, the first response to pollution usually came from provincial health agencies. Furthermore, since many of the health problems were associated most with urban and industrial areas, the provinces had to work closely with municipalities. As a result, pollution management in Canada initially was characterized by health concerns and joint efforts by provincial and municipal governments.

These public health efforts were effective. For example, in Ontario the Provincial Board of Health initiated sanitary engineering in 1912. The subsequent sanitation projects reduced typhoid fever rates substantially. For Toronto, the typhoid death rate was 40.8 per 100,000 population in 1910. By 1931 this rate had dropped close to the "vanishing" point of 0.5.[3] While sanitation received recognition for controlling disease, there was less success in resolving pollution problems that did not have a direct and obvious relationship with disease. Consequently, while progress was realized with water pollution control programs, air and soil pollution control attracted little support.

A second approach toward provincial pollution control emerged during the 1950's and 1960's. It became apparent that pollution control involved more than ensuring safe domestic water supplies and effective waste disposal systems. Since water also served industry, agriculture, recreation, and wildlife, it was recognized that a public health focus, while important, was too narrow. The outcome was establishment of specialized provincial agencies responsible for controlling pollution. The creation of the Ontario Water Resources Commission in 1956 set a precedent which was followed by other provinces.

These specialized agencies often dealt with water, air, and soil pollution, although initial concern was with water. In addition to implementing their own policies and programs, these agencies had to co-ordinate other agency interests. The number of laws and regulations in each province reflects appreciation that pollution problems are not confined to urban places and that activities in rural areas (run-off of fertilizers, pesticides, and herbicides from farmers' fields, leaching from mine wastes) also may have adverse impacts on the environment.

Other considerations arose. In situations where pollution problems transcended provincial boundaries, the specialized provincial agencies became involved with the federal government.[4] Examples are air pollution in the Detroit-Windsor area and pollution in the Great Lakes. Indeed, a necessary prerequisite to the Great Lakes Water Quality Agreement signed in April, 1972, by Canada and the United States was a federal-provincial agreement between Canada and Ontario in 1971 on Great Lakes water quality.[5]

The specialized agencies often found themselves being reorganized and their roles recast during the 1970's. From 1956 to early 1972, the primary responsibility for water pollution control in Ontario was with the Ontario Water Resources Commission. In the spring of 1972, this commission was dissolved. Its functions became part of a new Ministry of the Environment and pollution control fell under the Environmental Protection Act of 1971. In Newfoundland, a Department of Provincial Affairs and Environment Act in 1973 replaced the Clean Air, Water and Soil Authority Act of 1970. And, in Quebec, where responsibility for water pollution had been governed by the Quebec Water Board, an Environment Quality Act in 1972 shifted authority for pollution control to the Minister of the Environment.

This reorganization of responsibilities stresses an important aspect – the provincial approach to pollution control has steadily been broadened. From initial concern with public health, pollution management became a concern of specialized pollution agencies in the 1950's and 1960's. During the 1970's, a third phase emerged when pollution control was approached not as a specialized issue but as one of many issues associated with environmental management and quality. As a result, responsibility shifted from specialized pollution agencies to more broadly based environment departments. At the same time, while environment departments became the lead agencies, the interests of other government departments had to be incorporated into the policy approach. Of the other agencies, health and municipal affairs continue to be significant, reflecting their long-standing concern with pollution.

Set in the context of these organizational structures, the provinces have had to address important policy issues. First, what is pollution? This question is a difficult one, particularly given the problems created from two or more polluting substances interacting in the environment. But until pollution is defined, provincial agencies have difficulty in establishing environmental quality objectives. Second, how should pollution control be approached? Most provinces have adopted a combination of two strategies.

One alternative is called *regulatory*, and involves the establishment of quality objectives or standards. These usually are stated in fairly general terms, and are used as the basis for negotiation with different industries or individual firms. For example, British Columbia established environmental quality objectives for the forest products industry (sawmills, veneer and plywood plants, pulp and paper mills) and Quebec developed quality directives for petroleum refineries, pulp and paper plants, mines, wood processing, and meat products, as well as for the milk and textile industries. Such objectives provide potential or actual pollutors with an indication of what is expected, and "these requirements may then be modified through bilateral negotiations between the applicant and the Ministry in the light of the circumstances of the particular water course."[6]

This regulatory approach seeks both to minimize environmental pollution and to ensure that economic development is not checked unduly. Obviously, a delicate trade-off is involved, which usually satisfies neither the advocate of economic growth nor the supporter of environmental quality. In reality, this procedure may result in varying treatment of different pollutors in the same industry. Most new facilities are designed to satisfy the government objectives or standards. In contrast, many older facilities do not meet the standards, and the government and firms try to negotiate a mutually acceptable schedule to bring treatment up to requirements. The government agencies frequently are hesitant to push too vigorously because they do not want to force major sources of employment (e.g., a pulp mill in an isolated rural community) to close down.

The other approach involves *economic incentives*. That is, the governments provide financial incentives for municipalities or industry to upgrade their pollution treatment. Thus, firms may be allowed generous tax write-offs for expenses associated with pollution control equipment. Or, provincial governments may offer to share the costs of a municipal sewage treatment plant. To illustrate, Nova Scotia supplemented federal Central Mortgage and Housing Corporation loans for municipal sewage treatment plants by paying 20 per cent of capital costs. Saskatchewan provided 10 per cent grants to cities for secondary treatment and 15 per cent grants for advanced treatment.[7] Thus, through the use of carrots (economic incentives) and sticks (regulations) the provinces have attempted to control environmental pollution. Throughout, a difficult task has been to balance the importance of environmental quality against the provision of jobs and other benefits for economic growth. That decision often becomes a political rather than a technical one.

In addition to defining pollution and determining appropriate strategies, other issues need to be faced. One involves enforcement. In other words, definitions and strategies have little merit if the willingness to implement and enforce them is absent. And, as noted earlier, enforcement may be a difficult matter when a province attempts to enhance environmental quality and to avoid unemployment.

Another issue involves the roles of different levels of government. Through their responsibility for health under the BNA Act, the provinces took initial responsibility for pollution management. They continue to have a leading role, but increasingly find themselves in joint approaches with the federal and municipal governments. The relationship with municipalities often is a difficult one, since the province frequently has veto power over urban expansion if pollution regulations are not satisfied.[8] This aspect reiterates that any attempt to develop a national policy for pollution control will have to recognize the interests and roles of three levels of government. To date, this situation has led to an uneven quality to pollution control, reflecting such factors as differing levels of economic development and differing priorities being given to environmental problems relative to other societal concerns in various regions of the country.

Environmental Impact Assessment

Both the federal and provincial governments have developed procedures for conducting environmental impact assessments.[9] In this policy area, procedures have facilitated provincial government assessments of environmental consequences of development projects, or joint studies between federal and provincial governments. Thus, unlike the issues of mineral and petroleum development or foreign ownership of resources, environmental impact assessment has not generated as much conflict between national and regional interests.

As this paper focuses upon provincial attitudes and approaches, the federal procedure is described only briefly. Attention is devoted to experiences in New Brunswick, Ontario, Alberta, and British Columbia. Given the disputes that have arisen over legislation dealing with resources, it is appropriate to note that only Ontario and Alberta have legislation specifically requiring environmental impact assessments. However, during 1979, Newfoundland was in the process of drafting a bill to establish an Environmental Assessment Act to replace a procedure whereby environmental impact assessments of major resource development projects were requested as a matter of policy by the Department of Consumer Affairs and Environment with approval of the provincial Cabinet.[10] The other governments' approach is based upon administrative and executive decisions by the federal and provincial Cabinets.

The Federal Approach

The approach of the Canadian government is based upon a Cabinet decision of December 20, 1973, which was modified on February 8, 1977.[11] The decision emphasized that environmental effects of federal projects should be considered as early as possible in the planning process. All new projects initiated by federal departments or agencies or involving federal property or funds could require such assessments. This latter aspect ensured that the federal approach would come into contact with the provinces through the many jointly funded projects and has led to joint federal-provincial studies in addition to those conducted by the federal government itself.

The Provincial Approaches

1. New Brunswick

New Brunswick officially established its environmental impact assessment policy by a Cabinet decision on October 8, 1975.[12] All major developments being considered by a provincial department or agency were to have an environmental assessment prior to implementation. However, environmental impact assessments were made prior to 1975. The first one was completed in January, 1973, as a joint federal-provincial analysis of the impact of a proposed supertanker port and thermal generating station for the Lorneville area. In another case, New Brunswick and the federal government agreed to prepare a detailed assessment after tentatively identifying Point Lepreau as a nuclear power plant site in the spring of 1974. The Point Lepreau study was the first one to be completed under the federal environmental assessment process. The first project to come fully under the provincial policy was a highway between the village of Welsford and the city of Saint John. This study was completed late in 1977.

The New Brunswick procedure involves two phases. The first is an environmental feasibility study conducted at the same time as engineering and economic feasibility studies. The second phase involves a detailed environmental assessment intended to ameliorate undesirable environmental effects and to strengthen potential benefits. The Department of the Environment establishes guidelines, reviews the environmental impact statement, arranges public meetings, and prepares a recommendation. The final decision for a project is the responsibility of the Government.

New Brunswick has had experience with assessments for a range of projects in the province, and has become involved with assessments involving more than one jurisdiction. The latter include Fundy tidal power, the Dickey-Lincoln dam on the Saint John River in Maine, an oil terminal and refinery at Eastport, Maine, a natural gas pipeline from Saint John to the U.S. border, and a liquid natural gas terminal at Saint John. Based on these and other experiences, the Department of the Environment has considered making several changes to its procedure, including establishment of an independent review board to judge the adequacy of assessments, extension of the process to include policies and programs as well as projects, and development of legislation to bring the private sector into the process.[13]

2. Ontario

Environmental impact assessments are authorized by the Environmental Assessment Act of 1975, which was proclaimed in October, 1976. The act requires that all proposals, plans, or projects of provincial departments have environmental impact assessments subject to the development of guidelines to identify environmentally significant proposals. At a later date, the Cabinet will include municipal and private sector projects.

After a proponent has prepared an environmental impact assessment, the Department of the Environment co-ordinates a review. The impact statement normally is made available to the public for study. If any individual requests one, the Minister will arrange for a hearing unless he believes that the request is frivolous. The hearings are organized by an Environmental Assessment Board, which consists of five or more persons who are not public servants. The Environmental Assessment Board may accept or reject the study, and also makes a recommendation about the project. This recommendation is final unless altered by the Minister with Cabinet approval within twenty-eight days.

The process has been slow in being implemented due to difficulties in developing regulations that identify projects requiring assessments. The government indicated that the regulations would identify such developments as highways, sewage and water treatment plants, master plans for parks, hydro projects, and major construction. However, Orders-in-Council have exempted hundreds of such projects. The exemptions were justified because the government "will be interfered with and damaged by the undue delay and expense required to prepare environmental assessments. The public will be interfered with and damaged by the undue delay in the carrying out of the programs."[14]

By the spring of 1979, the procedure had gained little momentum. At that time, environmental impact assessments had been prepared for only a few projects, including: (1) two road widenings and alignment improvements; (2) minor transmission lines, transformer stations, and communications for Ontario Hydro; (3) an expansion of the Welland water treatment plant; and (4) expansion of residence facilities at a college. The government explained that the delay occurred because of the time needed to prepare regulations. A further concern was a need to give the Environmental Assessment Board opportunity to gain experience.

3. *Alberta*

Alberta is the second province to have legislation specifically requiring environmental impact assessments.[15] Section 8 of the Land Surface Conservation and Reclamation Act of 1973 authorizes the preparation of reports containing an assessment of the environmental impact of proposed developments. By January, 1976, seventeen impact assessments had been completed. During 1976, twenty-six assessments were reviewed and seven were in preparation; of these, there were eleven proposals for coal developments, three for oil sands proposals, sixteen for industrial plants, one for a highway, and two for pipelines. Of this number, eleven of the assessments led to project approval, one was rejected, and five were withdrawn.[16]

The Department of the Environment has prepared guidelines for proponents of projects. The Minister may ask for an environmental assessment, or the public, elected representatives, or government agencies may request the Minister to call for one. The Department of the Environment co-ordinates the review of impact statements and makes a recommendation to the Minister. A Cabinet committee then reaches a decision. Approval by the Cabinet committee does not ensure that the project will go ahead. It only means that the requirements of the environmental impact assessment process have been met. The proponent must still satisfy all of the stipulations of other permitting and licensing agencies.

4. *British Columbia*

Although no one piece of legislation requires impact assessments, four different acts provide the statutory basis for them. The major legislation is the Environment and Land Use Act of 1971, which established an Environment and Land Use Committee comprised of the ministers of nine departments. A secretariat to this committee has the co-ordinating role in ensuring that environmental, social, and economic impact studies are included in the feasibility and planning stages of all major developments in the province. This secretariat has published a number of guidelines to assist in the preparation of impact statements. For example, specific guidelines have been prepared for coal development proposals and for such linear developments as power corridors or pipelines. All of the guidelines follow a three-phase reporting process which evolves from a general overview to a more detailed assessment of specific alternatives.

Overview

Within Canada, environmental impact assessment procedures did not develop until the early- to mid-1970's. From experience to date, several aspects have created substantial problems. Development of *regulations* has proven to be difficult. That is, which actions should be required to have assessments? Several related matters have arisen. Most procedures have focused upon assessments for *projects* whereas many feel that *policies* and *programs* also should be reviewed for their environmental consequences. *Scale* is another factor. In other words, several small projects in isolation may create minimum environmental disturbance. When their cumulative effect is considered, their impact may be significant.

The *discretionary nature* of most procedures is also important. Most jurisdictions give elected representatives considerable leeway to decide which proposals will be included or exempted, what information will be made available, and what role the public will have. Such discretion permits flexibility but must be watched to ensure that it is not abused. *Monitoring* and *enforcement* are important. Most procedures have yet to determine adequately how to monitor the long-term impacts of projects, and thereby how to enforce regulations whose significance may not be apparent for years or decades.

How environmental assessment should be *co-ordinated* with other policies is a concern. Many jurisdictions had environmental quality or pollution control legislation prior to environmental impact regulations. A worry is that the environmental regulations should not add unnecessary overlapping controls relative to other legislation or requirements. The concern for co-ordination also is important at the intergovernmental level. Projects, programs, and policies often touch upon different government jurisdictions. Distinct intergovernmental relationships include: (1) provincial-municipal, (2) interprovincial, (3) federal-provincial, and (4) international.

Foreign Land-Ownership

Foreign ownership of recreational and agricultural land emerged as a policy issue during the early 1970's and created conflict between national and provincial interests.[17] As governments became aware of this issue, they recognized that information about the nature and extent of foreign land-ownership was poor. A select committee in Ontario observed during 1973 that "no systematic and comprehensive study of the extent and pattern of foreign ownership of real property in the province has been undertaken"[18] whereas a federal-provincial committee reported in 1975 that "generally comprehensive data on the nature and extent of foreign land ownership in Canada are not available."[19] The two levels of government were placed in the unenviable position of having to address a policy question without thorough understanding of the nature of the problem.

During the early- and mid-1970's, many of the provincial governments initiated studies regarding foreign land-ownership. Furthermore, in May, 1973, a conference of First Ministers established a joint committee to examine this matter on a nation-wide basis. The committee was requested to identify legal, constitutional, and land-use problems related to alien and non-resident ownership in Canada as well as to consider approaches through which the federal and provincial governments might work together to handle this matter and to avoid legal or constitutional problems.

Despite the inadequate data base, the committee was able to identify a range of problems which arose through foreign ownership of land. The report stressed that these problems, with varying significance among and within provinces, included the following:

(1) restriction on public access for resident citizens to prime recreational areas such as beach and shoreline areas;

(2) limit on the amount of land that is available for public recreational use by resident citizens;

(3) acceleration of the subdivision of agricultural land and the removal of productive farmland from production;

(4) rising property values, which in turn may lead to higher tax assessments for local residents;

(5) changes in the character of communities, in that areas become depopulated or primarily populated by summer or occasional residents;

(6) an increased demand for land resulting in higher prices, thus making it more difficult for resident citizens to purchase land;

(7) the possibility that a majority of the total land mass of a province or an area within a province might shift to non-resident and/or alien ownership;

(8) creation of a potential for conflict between the priorities of foreign investors and Canadian economic goals.[20]

At the same time, it was recognized by this committee and other studies that foreign ownership can generate benefits. Non-residents often have shown a greater regard for protecting the environment than Canadians, and have permitted access to beaches and shorelines. In many instances, the non-residents purchased land in isolated areas long before Canadians showed any interest in such purchase. Outsiders willing to pay higher prices often provide a retiring farmer or landowner with an income that serves as a base for a retirement pension. A related concern is that Canadians enjoy the opportunity to purchase land in other countries. Controls on non-resident ownership in Canada could spark retaliatory action by other governments. And finally, it was recognized that *land use* might be more significant than *land ownership*.[21] It is against this background that any policies regarding foreign land-ownership must be assessed. To elaborate on the way in which policies have developed, the experiences of several provinces are discussed.

Prince Edward Island

Prince Edward Island was the first jurisdiction in Canada to establish legislation to regulate non-resident ownership of land.[22] In brief, the province amended existing legislation in 1972 to stipulate that all non-resident purchases exceeding 10 acres (4 hectares) in size or 330 feet (100.6 metres) of shore frontage required approval by the Cabinet. This amendment was challenged in the courts, and upheld by a Supreme Court of Canada decision in June, 1975.

Prince Edward Island is relatively small and nearly all of the land is privately held. During the late 1960's, the attractive Prince Edward Island landscape came to the attention of recreational property buyers in central and eastern Canada and the northeastern United States. Some of the property being purchased by non-residents was among the best quality recreation land and productive farmland in the province. The government frequently was outbid for property it wished to acquire and a tradition of public access to shorelines was threatened by appearance of "no trespassing" signs on newly acquired properties.[23] Most large purchases were of farmlands by non-farmers who did not rent the land to adjacent farmers. Instead, the land was withdrawn from agricultural production and often reverted to shrubs and weeds that spread to neighbouring farms.

Legislation restricting non-resident ownership of land had existed for many years, dating back to 1859. In 1964, the Real Property Act was amended to reduce the amount of property which non-Canadians could acquire without Cabinet approval to 10 acres (4 hectares) and also stipulated that ownership of shore frontage was limited to not more than five chains or 330 feet (100.6 metres). However, for a variety of reasons, the legislation was not administered or enforced. In the early 1970's the provincial government made further amendments to the Real Property Act. Non-residents, meaning other Canadians as well as aliens, in 1972 were limited without Cabinet consent to purchases of up to 10 acres (4 hectares) or 330 feet (100.6 metres) of shore frontage. The amended legislation did not prohibit non-residents from acquiring land in the province. Instead, the amended act placed restrictions on the amount that could be purchased without Cabinet approval. Amounts less than the limits did not need approval. While larger amounts required permission, the Cabinet generally allowed such sales.

Two Americans from New York State challenged the legality of the regulations relative to their attempt to purchase about 12 hectares of land. The Supreme Court of Prince Edward Island upheld the legislation in 1973 on the basis that the statute fell under the provincial power over property and civil rights specified under Section 92(13) of the BNA Act (Table 1). This decision was appealed to the Supreme Court of Canada. At issue was a difference of legal opinion concerning the jurisdictional responsibility of the federal and provincial governments concerning foreign (alien) and non-resident land-ownership. Relative provincial powers were derived from Sections 92(5), 92(13), and 92(16) of the BNA Act (Table 1). Federal power was identified in Sections 91 (Preamble) and 91(2) and in several other subsections. A further complication arose over Section 24 of the federal Canadian Citizenship Act which stated that aliens had the right to own land or interests in land throughout Canada. The provinces argued that Section 24 of the Canadian Citizenship Act conflicted with their rights under Sections 92(13) and 92(16) of the BNA Act.

In simplified fashion, the dispute took the following form. Prince Edward Island, supported by all the other provinces, argued that provinces had the right to restrict land ownership within their boundaries to both foreigners and residents from other Canadian provinces. Not all provinces were enthusiastic about restricting ownership by Canadians from other provinces, but they were concerned about federal intrusion into an area viewed to be within provincial jurisdiction. The federal govern-

**Table 1: Jurisdictional Responsibility
for Resource Development**

Federal Government

BNA Act, Section 91 (Preamble) . . . for the peace, order and good government of Canada, in relation to all matters not coming directly within the classes of subjects by this Act assigned exclusively to the Legislatures of the Provinces . . . .

91(2)	The regulation of Trade and Commerce
91(3)	The raising of money by any mode or system of taxation
91(12)	Sea Coast and Inland Fisheries
91(24)	Indians and lands reserved for Indians
91(29)	Such classes of subjects as are expressly excepted in the enumeration of the classes of subjects by this Act assigned exclusively to the Legislatures of the Provinces

Provincial Governments

BNA Act, Section 92(2)	Direct Taxation within the Province in order to the raising of a Revenue for Provincial purposes
92(5)	The management and sale of the Public Lands belonging to the Province, and of the timber and wood thereon
92(10a)	Local works and undertakings other than such as are of the following classes: Lines of steam or other ships, railways, canals, telegraphs and other works and undertakings connecting the Province with any other or others of the Provinces, or extending beyond the limits of the Province. . . .
92(13)	Property and civil rights in the Province
92(16)	Generally all matters of merely local or private nature in the Province
109	All lands, mines, minerals and royalties belonging to the several provinces of Canada. . . .

ment was sympathetic to controlling land ownership by aliens, but disagreed that non-resident Canadians should be restricted from acquiring land in any province. The federal government thus supported the two Americans. If the provincial action could be shown to be invalid under the Canadian Citizenship Act, then the amendment would have to be revoked and Canadians would not be restricted from owning property in any province.

The Supreme Court of Canada upheld the provincial legislation in June, 1975. The Court dismissed the argument that the law was invalid because it dealt with aliens, a matter for federal jurisdiction. In the view of Chief Justice Bora Laskin, the law did not regulate alien residents per se, but rather landholdings by nonresidents. The Chief Justice also rejected the argument that the legislation discriminated against other Canadians since anyone could enter the province and take up residence there. The decision affirmed that it was entirely within provincial jurisdiction to pass laws dealing with land and that absentee ownership of land in a province was a legitimate provincial concern. The outcome was that the right of provinces to legislate control over non-resident ownership of land was upheld. This decision was important since Prince Edward Island was the first province to pass such legislation and its confirmation established an important precedent.

Saskatchewan

The major concern in Saskatchewan has been non-resident ownership of agricultural land. A study of land-ownership patterns in the nine townships along the southern border of the province showed that as of December 31, 1970, Americans owned about 2.3 per cent of land in that area.[24] Some municipalities had very little such ownership while others had over 9 per cent. It also noted that land acquisition by Americans provided benefits to retiring Canadian farmers through higher prices for properties but made it more difficult for beginning farmers to get started. A survey completed during 1972 by a select committee confirmed the figures from the first study, showing that American ownership was 2.2 per cent for the southern part of the province and just under one per cent for the province as a whole.[25] A third study, by the Saskatchewan Farm Ownership Board, suggested that by September 30, 1978, non-residents owned 3.1 per cent of agricultural land in the province.[26]

During 1974, Saskatchewan became the second province to enact legislation to limit and reduce non-resident ownership of agricultural land. The Saskatchewan Farm Ownership Act applied to both aliens and Canadians living in other provinces. Under the legislation, a non-resident is any individual who does not reside in Saskatchewan for more than half of each year or who is not a farmer living within twenty miles (thirty-two kilometres) of the Saskatchewan border for more than half of each year. The act stipulated that a non-resident could acquire agricultural land with an assessed value of up to $15,000. This regulation applied to all land purchased after March 31, 1974. For land acquired before that date, non-residents had five years to reduce their aggregate holdings to this limit.

The intent of the legislation was to prevent non-agricultural corporations and non-residents from gaining control over large tracts of agricultural land. The act did serve as a deterrent. However, experience showed that non-residents were continuing to acquire land. The outcome was an amendment in 1978 that reduced the maximum limit on non-residents from $15,000 assessed value to 160 acres (65 hectares). This amendment took effect retroactive to September 15, 1977. Non-residents who purchased land in excess of the limit after September 15, 1977, had five years to bring their total holdings into accordance with the new limits.

Saskatchewan thus became the second province to introduce legislation to control non-resident ownership of land resources. Its action did not trigger a confrontation with the federal government over jurisdictional responsibilities because of the precedent set in the Supreme Court of Canada decision concerning Prince Edward Island.

Manitoba

As in Saskatchewan, the main concern in Manitoba has been with agricultural land. Between 1973 and 1977 there had been active buying of large tracts of prime agricultural land by non-resident individuals or corporations.[27] The outcome was the passing of the Farm Lands Protection Act during June, 1977, retroactive to April 1 of that year. The act was intended to control purchases of agricultural and recreational land by non-residents of Canada to a maximum of 160 acres (65 hectares). Unlike Prince Edward Island and Saskatchewan, the Manitoba legislation did not place restrictions on Canadians living in other provinces.

The legislation stopped corporate purchases. However, a loophole allowed groups of individuals to get together to purchase adjoining properties of 65 hectares each. This situation led to amendment to the Farm Lands Protection Act. Effective July 20, 1978, the legislation became known as the Agricultural Lands Protection Act and applied only to agricultural land. Two key provisions were established. First, purchase of agricultural lands by non-residents was restricted to a new limit of not more than 20 acres (8 hectares). Second, as a result of an associated amendment to the Real Property Act, a statutory declaration became required before any change of land title would be made by a district registrar. The name and address of the purchaser had to be filed along with information indicating whether the purchaser was a resident of Canada. If the purchaser were not a Canadian, he had to indicate the aggregate amount of any other holdings in the province. The Manitoba Lands Protection Branch maintains a computerized record of all such transactions, and thereby monitors land sales to non-residents.

Ontario

Like other provinces, Ontario has had a poor information base from which to tackle the issue of non-resident ownership. Available studies and public concern suggest, however, that recreational land-ownership has been a main issue. For example, Wolfe had shown in 1964 that 12 per cent of cottage owners in Ontario were from the United States with the percentage of non-resident owners extending as high as 68 per cent in the Windsor area and also being high in the Kenora, Rainy River, Algoma, Manitoulin, St. Clair River, and Lake Erie areas.[28]

A Select Committee on Economic and Cultural Nationalism made a range of recommendations in 1975 that touched upon restrictions on non-residents and taxation adjustments.[29] The Ontario government did not adopt these recommendations but did introduce regulations to discourage non-resident ownership of land. During 1974, the government introduced a 20 per cent land transfer tax on real estate sales to non-residents. Prior to that date, non-residents could purchase land at the same tax rate as residents – less than one per cent. In addition to discouraging non-resident ownership of recreational land, the intent was to curb land speculation and high profits. However, during October, 1978, the government introduced a bill to rescind the land transfer tax. The Provincial Treasurer stated that while the tax had dampened land speculation, it also was discouraging needed investment in the province and had never earned more than $9 million in any one year.

A second strategy focused upon the sale of Crown land for cottages. In 1971, the government stopped all sales of Crown land and allowed only leases for up to thirty years, renewable for two further ten-year periods. Foreign ownership of cottage land had been one of the factors that led to this decision. During the Speech from the Throne in February, 1978, the government stated that Crown land in northern Ontario would be sold for private recreational use to increase construction jobs and to promote development. During the subsequent debate, a question emerged as to whether foreigners would have the same opportunity as Canadians to purchase Crown land.

In May, 1978, the actual details of the program were announced. When lots went up for sale, any Ontario residents would be able to buy for the first year. During the second year, unsold lots could be bought by other Canadian citizens and landed immigrants outside the province. After two years had elapsed, non-Canadians would be allowed to lease lots. However, a loophole was left. Once Canadians had purchased the land, they could sell it without restrictions to non-Canadians. The government recognized this loophole but declined to close it on the grounds that all land was once Crown land and it was not right to restrict what a Canadian could do with land once a title for it had been obtained.

Overview

The experiences of these four provinces show that a variety of approaches may be used to control non-resident ownership of land. Since the jurisdictional dispute between the federal government and Prince Edward Island was addressed by the Supreme Court, the alternative strategies have become clearer. As identified by the federal-provincial committee on foreign land-ownership, the alternatives include:

(1) assuring public access to prime recreational areas such as beaches by, for example, public easements;
(2) purchasing or expropriating land for public recreational use;
(3) limiting directly the purchase of land by non-residents;
(4) implementing differential tax structures, so that local landowners using their land for specified purposes, such as agriculture, do not bear the burden of increased property assessments that result from non-resident purchases;
(5) establishing minimum maintenance standards for landowners and levying compensatory payments on those who do not meet the required standards;
(6) generally restricting corporate holdings;
(7) establishing land use and zoning controls;
(8) requiring disclosure of place of residence, citizenship, and other pertinent information concerning all persons owning or purchasing land in the province.[30]

Mineral and Petroleum Development

Development of minerals and petroleum has led to a different type of conflict between national and provincial interests. The focus has been upon the roles of the federal and provincial governments concerning the nature of pricing and taxation of resources. The conflict has occurred because of ambiguity in the BNA Act (Table 1). While the provinces have control over property rights (92-13), the federal government regulates trade and commerce (91-2). Thus, once resources cross provincial or international boundaries, they are no longer a matter of local concern (92-16) but fall under the jurisdiction of the federal government. This situation has generated disputes over the appropriate selling price for resources, with the provinces usually advocating a higher price than the federal government will sanction. Taxation powers also have caused disagreement. The provinces are restricted to direct taxation (92-2) whereas the federal government may use direct or indirect taxation (91-3). This division has raised the question as to what is an indirect tax, and whether some provincial resource taxes are constitutional. The experience of Saskatchewan with potash and petroleum indicates the disagreements that have occurred due to varying national and provincial aspirations.

Potash

Potash refers to a number of salts containing potassium. Potassium chloride is produced during mining, and is a basic element in fertilizer. Saskatchewan and the Soviet Union are the major world potash producers, and it has been estimated that Saskatchewan potash reserves could supply the entire world for about 3,000 years, assuming the rate of consumption that existed in the mid-1970's.[31] Saskatchewan potash production is based on ten mines, most of which are in the Saskatoon and Esterhazy regions. By 1978, five of these were owned by the provincial government.

Potash was first discovered during exploratory drilling for oil in 1943. Several attempts were made to extract the ore commercially, but technological problems resulted in the first continuous operation not starting until 1962. In that year, a schedule of relatively low royalties was approved. During 1964, a newly-elected Liberal government extended the existing royalty rates until 1981. However, it indicated that potential producers would have to commit themselves to begin operations by October, 1967, or face higher royalties. This arrangement, combined with the rich potash deposits in the province, generated rapid expansion. By the late 1960's, overproduction existed and mines were laying off employees as operations were cut back.

With the support of the companies, the Liberal government established a prorationing formula in 1969 under which a minimum production price was set and a production quota was allocated to each mine. This practice ensured that each mine had a guaranteed output, and the minimum price provided an ensured income. The prorationing regulations allowed all of the mines to continue operating. Furthermore, because the quota system reduced production, the price jumped substantially. As a result, even though production was constrained, profits increased because of the rising revenues obtained for the potash, nearly all of which was exported from Saskatchewan.[32]

During 1972, one potash producer challenged the prorationing system. Central Canada Potash had a long-term agreement with a farmers' co-operative based in Chicago. With the prorationing controls, it was unable to provide the amounts of potash for which it had an ensured market. This situation led the company to question the legality of the prorationing system. It argued that prorationing affected international trade and commerce, a matter which the BNA Act had placed under the jurisdiction of the federal government (Table 1).

Central Canada Potash went to court and won a declaration that the potash prorationing system was unconstitutional. The provincial government appealed, however, and the Saskatchewan Court of Queen's Bench overturned the earlier decision. In his decision, the Saskatchewan Chief Justice observed that prorationing was not a simple marketing scheme but rather one directed to the conservation and orderly development of a provincial resource. As a result, he saw no intent to interfere with the flow of interprovincial or international trade. If the American farmers' co-operative could not obtain its full supply from Central Canada Potash, other Saskatchewan sources were available.

The issue was subsequently referred to the Supreme Court of Canada.[33] During early October, 1978, in the midst of a Saskatchewan election campaign, the Supreme Court ruled the prorationing legislation to be unconstitutional. The federal government had supported Central Canada Potash during the Supreme Court proceedings in order to protect its constitutional powers. Since almost all Saskatchewan potash was exported, it and the company maintained that prorationing affected interprovincial and international trade over which Ottawa had exclusive authority. On the other hand, Saskatchewan was supported by Alberta, Manitoba, Ontario, New Brunswick, and Newfoundland in arguing that prorationing dealt with a matter which fell under provincial control.

Chief Justice Bora Laskin accepted the company and federal government argument and stated that because almost all of Saskatchewan potash was exported the province had been regulating exports and fixing prices in an area over which it had no authority. He indicated that production controls and conservation measures with respect to natural resources normally fell under

Figure 1: Western Perspective on Control of Resources
(from *Saskatoon Star-Phoenix,* October 14, 1978, p. 11.)

Saskatchewan resources. Ottawa wants control. Blakeney says NO.

The Trudeau Government is making a determined effort to take control of resources away from Saskatchewan.

At every turn, they have supported large international resource companies against the people of this province. In spite of the fact that resource ownership is clearly given to the provinces under the terms of the British North America Act.

The Trudeau Resource Policy.

The Trudeau "national" resource policy consists of battling with every resource producing province except Quebec and Ontario.

The Trudeau resource policy says Alberta oil prices must be set by Ottawa; that B.C cannot control its natural gas; and that Saskatchewan oil and potash are Ottawa's business.

But the Trudeau Government has a "hands off" policy towards Quebec asbestos, iron ore and hydro electric power. And a "hands off" policy towards Ontario nickel and pulp production.

There is definitely a double-standard resource policy that favors Eastern interests at the expense of the West.

The Supreme Court Decision.

The two recent Supreme Court decisions on resource control have no immediate effects on Saskatchewan people. But they have long-range implications.

The main implication is that whenever a mineral resource is destined for sale outside Saskatchewan's borders, the provincial government cannot control the price at which it is sold or the amount produced.

If we cannot control the price, we cannot recover the resource dollars that rightfully belong to the people of Saskatchewan — money that will amount to billions of dollars in the next few years — more jobs, lower taxes and even better health care. If we cannot control the amounts, we cannot conserve oil and gas to meet our own future needs. We cannot guarantee fuel for our farmers to run their tractors in the 1990's.

Allan Blakeney's answer to Ottawa.

Allan Blakeney is fighting to make sure Saskatchewan people benefit from Saskatchewan resources.

To forge a truly national resource policy that does not exploit the West.

Allan Blakeney has the support of most other Canadian provinces. Together they will make the federal government redefine its resource policy and keep resource control where it belongs — in the hands of the provinces.

It's Your Choice.

On October 18, you have to decide who can best handle Ottawa to make sure control of our resource heritage remains in Saskatchewan.

To make a strong case in Ottawa — and win — Allan Blakeney needs your support. On October 18, vote for Premier Blakeney. Let Ottawa know — resource control belongs to Saskatchewan.

Blakeney NDP

provincial jurisdiction. Nevertheless, he maintained that the situation "may be different" when price fixing was the central feature of a marketing scheme because provincial authority did not extend to control over marketing of provincial products, minerals, or natural resources in interprovincial or export trade.

Petroleum

Saskatchewan and Ottawa also have encountered conflict over taxation policies. At the same time that it overturned the potash prorationing legislation, the Supreme Court ruled that Saskatchewan had to pay interest on millions of dollars collected under a mineral income tax and crude oil surcharge found to be unconstitutional by the Supreme Court in a decision rendered in 1977. Following the world oil crisis in 1973, the Saskatchewan New Democratic Party government introduced an Oil and Gas Conservation, Stabilization and Development Act. This legislation initially claimed for the government the difference between the 1973 price for oil and the world price for oil. An amendment later claimed the difference between the 1973 price and the domestic price. The objective was to ensure that the province rather than the oil companies gained the windfall profits created by sharply rising oil prices after 1973.

Canadian Industrial Gas and Oil Ltd. challenged the royalty. Two issues arose. The first was whether the Saskatchewan income tax-royalty system represented a direct tax (Saskatchewan's view) or an indirect tax (the company's contention). Under the BNA Act, while both governments may levy direct taxes, only the federal government may apply indirect taxes (Table 1). The second was whether the Saskatchewan legislation intruded on federal control over interprovincial and international trade. The Supreme Court decided in 1977 that the royalty system was an indirect tax and an infringement on commerce and trade. On this basis, the legislation was found to be unconstitutional even though the Court did not challenge provincial jurisdiction over natural resources or its right to tax resources. The decision centred on the way in which the tax had been established. This approach by the Supreme Court led one observer to remark:

The Supreme Court of Canada rendered judgement in a major constitutional case this week. But it did it in such a way as to confuse, more than clarify, questions of provincial jurisdiction over natural resources, federal and provincial taxing powers, and inter-provincial trade.[34]

However, the long legal battle with Canadian Industrial Gas and Oil was effectively ended in February, 1979, when the company received $3.7 million from Saskatchewan. The payment included $3,152,000 in back taxes, $75,000 in court costs, and interest on back taxes.[35]

Overview

The Supreme Court decision concerning oil and potash may serve as a landmark for any renegotiation of federal and provincial control over natural resources. The two Supreme Court decisions occurred during a Saskatchewan election campaign. The New Democratic Party, which was re-elected, used the decisions as an election issue. The NDP leader declared that the federal Liberal government's support of challenges to provincial legislation demonstrated that Ottawa had been attacking Saskatchewan resource policy "at every turn." Premier Blakeney called for a mandate to obtain changes to the BNA Act which would clarify the constitution regarding resources. To this end, he sent a letter to Ottawa in which he indicated that the following points needed attention: (1) provinces should be allowed to levy indirect as well as direct taxes on resource production, and (2) federal trade and commerce power should be clarified so that "it can no longer be used to frustrate a province's legitimate efforts to influence the production and marketing of natural resources."[36] This position of greater provincial control for resources was endorsed by the Alberta Conservative Party of Premier Lougheed.

The concern for increased provincial control over resources re-emerged at a First Ministers' conference at the beginning of November, 1978. Premier Blakeney of Saskatchewan promoted a package deal between Ottawa and the provinces that included guarantees for provincial control over natural resources. Premier Lougheed of Alberta also was determined to make gains in this direction, and stated that "I can't see Alberta agreeing to anything that doesn't strengthen provincial control of natural resources."[37]

For its part, the federal government indicated that it was willing to negotiate. Prior to the First Ministers' conference, Prime Minister Trudeau stated that his government would consider permitting provinces to levy indirect taxes on resources as long as it did not interfere with interprovincial or international trade. At the conclusion of the First Ministers' conference, the Prime Minister agreed to study seven provincial demands for limits on federal constitutional powers. One of these points was clarification of federal and provincial jurisdiction over control, management, and taxation of natural resources as well as control and regulation of interprovincial and international trade. Inclusion of this point represented a breakthrough as it was the first time the federal government offered to consider this area. This action also responded to the arguments of Alberta and Saskatchewan, both of which had stated that provincial control over resources was a minimum condition for their agreeing to constitutional changes.

Although agreeing that resource control was open for negotiation, the federal position suggested that it may be sometime before any agreement is reached. Trudeau insisted that any changes could not weaken Ottawa's ability to equalize opportunity across the country. Furthermore, he indicated that all Canadians and not just one region should benefit from resource development.[38] The difficult road in renegotiating jurisdictional control was illustrated in late November, 1978, when the First Ministers met to discuss the economy. A central issue was pricing of oil, and the federal decision to postpone an earlier agreed upon price increase but to have two delayed, higher price increases within a year. The federal government later indicated that the postponement held, but that the delayed increases would not be automatic. This stance prompted an angry retort from Premier Lougheed, who claimed that Alberta would "not tolerate unilateral action" and that such a breach of the original agreement could lead to "the most serious crisis in Confederation."[39]

Further evidence appeared during 1979 to emphasize the problems in clarifying responsibility over natural resources. During a Constitutional Conference in February, 1979, the provincial and federal leaders agreed that any constitutional change should allow provinces to impose indirect taxes on natural resources, a right not permitted under the BNA Act. However, the First Ministers did not reach agreement over the appropriate federal role in regulating interprovincial trade in natural resources. Indeed, Premier Lougheed objected to a federal suggestion that Ottawa should have the right to intervene in natural resource policy for reasons of "compelling national interest." The Alberta leader believed that this proposal was too general and would allow the federal government to obstruct the provincial right to exploit and sell natural resources. Following the federal elections in May, 1979, and in February, 1980, the debate over the appropriate roles of federal and provincial governments continued, stressing that the different viewpoints are deeper than political party affiliations. The types of statements made by provincial and federal leaders indicate that the national and provincial interests often are incompatible. As a result, any national policy for environmental management and resource development will have to go beyond identifying national goals and interests and clarifying jurisdictional responsibility. While necessary, such steps are too simplistic and insufficient. It must be recognized that regional aspirations may conflict with national concerns.

Implications

Analysis of provincial approaches to pollution management, environmental impact assessment, foreign land-ownership, and mineral and oil development identifies several critical aspects that must be considered in the planning of national policies for environmental management and resource development. Four implications can be discerned. (1) Fragmentation and ambiguity of jurisdictional responsibility obviously hinders a comprehensive approach to environmental and resource issues in Canada. Sections of the BNA Act, and other federal and provincial statutes, contradict one another concerning appropriate roles of different governments for natural resources. If the BNA Act is to be revised, jurisdiction over natural resources is of fundamental importance. Yet, while alterations in the legal basis for jurisdiction are a necessary condition for improved natural resource management, such changes will not be sufficient in themselves. (2) It will be necessary to recognize varying regional needs and aspirations. It is a fact of life that provincial or regional goals can conflict sharply with national goals. Consequently, any national policies will have to incorporate the idea of regional diversity. Acceptance of this idea should eliminate attempts to devise standardized approaches to be applied in a blanket-like fashion across the nation. (3) The disagreements between the provincial and federal governments over some aspects of environmental management and resource development emphasize that a national perspective is not synonymous with a federal viewpoint. A national perspective and associated policies will have to transcend the federal vantage point. This point is easy to make, but it is much more difficult to determine *how* this would be realized. Indeed, this aspect may well become a fundamental issue for the 1980's. (4) Although problems exist, we should not focus exclusively on the weaknesses in the system. Policy fields exist for which progress is being realized, and co-operation among three levels of government (municipal, provincial, federal) is occurring. We should seek to build upon these existing strengths while recognizing the limitations. Being at the interface between the municipal and federal levels, the provinces have a crucial role in environmental management and resource development. Nevertheless, the problems often are larger than any one provincial jurisdiction, and their resolution increasingly will require combined governmental efforts.

NOTES

1. See also Gerard V. La Forest, *Natural Resources and Public Property under the Canadian Constitution* (Toronto, 1969).
2. Albert E. Berry, "Environmental Pollution and Its Control in Canada: A Historical Perspective," *Background Papers for the National Conference on Pollution and Our Environment*, vol. 1 (Ottawa, 1966), A1: 1-9.
3. *Ibid.*, A1: 3.
4. Denis Bellinger, "Canadian Water Management Policy Instruments – A National Overview," in B. Mitchell (ed.), *Institutional Arrangements for Water Management: Canadian Experiences*, University of Waterloo, Department of Geography Publication Series No. 5 (Waterloo, Ont., 1975), 1-42.
5. Ronald Shimizu, "Evolving Institutional Arrangements for Water Quality Management in the Great Lakes," in Mitchell (ed.), *Institutional Arrangements for Water Management*, 55-7.
6. Richard S. Campbell *et al.*, "Water Management in Ontario – An Economic Evaluation of Public Policy," *Osgoode Hall Law Journal*, 12 (December, 1974), 508.
7. Bellinger, "Canadian Water Management," 17.
8. R. Brian Woodrow, "Municipal Sewage Treatment: The 'Political Miseconomy' of Pollution Control in Canada," in O. P. Dwivedi (ed.), *Protecting the Environment* (Toronto, 1974), 211-29.
9. Bruce Mitchell and Richard Turkheim, "Environmental Impact Assessment: Principles, Practices and Canadian Experiences," in R. R. Krueger and B. Mitchell (eds.), *Managing Canada's Renewable Resources* (Toronto, 1977), 47-66; British Columbia, Ministry of the Environment, *Environmental Impact Assessments in Canada: A Review of Current Legislation and Practice* (Victoria, 1977); Canadian Council of Resource and Environment Ministers, EIA Task Force, *Canadian Environmental Impact Assessment Processes* (Toronto, 1978).
10. Correspondence from the Research and Assessment Branch, Newfoundland Department of Consumer Affairs and Environment, April 2, 1979.
11. Office of the Chairman, Environmental Assessment Panel, *A Guide to the Federal Environmental Assessment and Review Process* (Ottawa: Fisheries and Environment Canada, 1977); Environmental Assessment Review Office, *Guide for Environmental Screening* (Ottawa: Environmental Protection Service and Federal Environmental Assessment Review Office, 1978).
12. New Brunswick, Department of the Environment, *Environmental Impact Assessment in New Brunswick* (Fredericton, 1975), 1-2.
13. Correspondence with the New Brunswick Department of the Environment, March 31, 1978.

14. "Province Skirts Law to Push Projects," *Kitchener-Waterloo Record,* November 4, 1976, p. 2.
15. Alberta Environment, *Environmental Impact Assessment Guidelines* (Edmonton: Alberta Environment, Land Conservation and Reclamation Division, 1977).
16. Alberta Environment, *Annual Report for the Year ended March 31, 1977* (Edmonton, 1977), 57.
17. Maurice Cutler, "Foreign Demand for Our Land and Resources," *Canadian Geographical Journal,* 90 (April, 1975), 5.
18. Ontario Select Committee on Economic and Cultural Nationalism, *Foreign Ownership of Ontario Real Estate: Interim Report* (Toronto, 1973), 12.
19. Canadian Intergovernmental Conference Secretariat, *Federal-Provincial Committee on Foreign Ownership of Land: Report to the First Ministers* (Ottawa: Information Canada, 1975), 3.
20. *Ibid.,* 35-36.
21. Maurice Cutler, "Shall Canada's Land Go to the Richest Bidders?" *Canadian Geographical Journal,* 90 (July/August, 1975), 27.
22. P.E.I. Land Use Service Centre and the Maritime Resource Management Service Council of Maritime Premiers, *Non-Resident Land Ownership Legislation and Administration in Prince Edward Island,* Environment Canada Land Use in Canada Series No. 12 (Ottawa, 1978).
23. C. W. Raymond, J. Wells, and C. Jones, *Report of the Prince Edward Island Royal Commission on Land Ownership and Land Use* (Charlottetown, 1973), 40.
24. J. A. Brown, *A Study of Purchases and Ownership of Saskatchewan Farm Lands by Citizens and Companies of the United States of America to December 31, 1970* (Saskatoon: University of Saskatchewan, Department of Agricultural Economics, 1972).
25. Legislative Assembly of Saskatchewan, *Final Report of the Special Committee on the Ownership of Agricultural Lands* (Regina, 1973), 31-2.
26. Correspondence from the Saskatchewan Farm Ownership Board, November 30, 1978.
27. Correspondence from the Manitoba Agricultural Lands Protection Board, November 17, 1978.
28. R. I. Wolfe, *Parameters of Recreational Travel in Ontario: A Progress Report* (Toronto: Ontario Department of Highways, 1966).
29. Ontario Select Committee on Economic and Cultural Nationalism, *Final Report on Economic Nationalism* (Toronto, 1975), 137.
30. *Federal-Provincial Committee on Foreign Ownership of Land: Report,* 38-9.
31. Saskatchewan, Department of Mineral Resources, *Potash: Challenge for Development* (Regina, 1976), 15.
32. J. Richards, "New Saskatchewan Prairie 'Free Enterprise' Politicians Say Howdy to the Potash Cartel," *Canadian Dimension,* 7 (January-February, 1971), 28-33.
33. R. Shaffner, *New Risks in Resource Development: The Potash Case* (Montreal: C. D. Howe Research Institute, 1976); J. Richards, "Potash, Populists and Fabians," *Canadian Forum,* 57 (November, 1977), 14-21.
34. Geoffrey Stevens, "A Muddied Theory," Toronto *Globe and Mail,* November 17, 1977, p. 6.
35. "CIGOL Gets Repayment from Saskatchewan," Toronto *Globe and Mail,* February 15, 1979, p. B1.

36. "BNA Act Change Urged," *Saskatoon Star-Phoenix,* October 10, 1978, p. 31.
37. "Accord on Constitutional Reform Unlikely, Lougheed, Blakeney Say," Toronto *Globe and Mail,* October 30, 1978, p. 1.
38. See "Division of Power Now Negotiable, PM Tells Premiers," Toronto *Globe and Mail,* November 1, 1978, pp. 1-2.
39. "Ottawa Firm on Delaying Oil Increase," Toronto *Globe and Mail,* December 1, 1978, p. 1.

CHAPTER THREE

Canada's International Environmental Relations

by David G. LeMarquand and Anthony Scott

A glance at a globe reveals two immediate geo-political facts about Canada. First, it takes up a good portion of the world's land mass; yet it shares international boundaries with only one country, the United States. Second, it has a very long coastline. Its oceanic interests and its close proximity to the United States are the two key concerns of the Canadian federal government's international resource policies. The government does have interests in the broader question of protecting and managing the global environment, but the government's more pressing policy commitments are regional.

Law of the Sea policy and Canada-U.S. environmental relations sometimes have been conducted from the same department, and overlap both legally and geographically in some cases, but for the most part the Canadian federal government treats them quite separately. Canada-U.S. environmental relations engender a steady flow of irritants. These demand continuing, and often it seems, interminable attention from the governments, if not finally to resolve the issues, at least to keep them from harming other aspects of Canada-U.S. relations. The experience and the precedents in this essentially fire-fighting operation build up a body of policy and institutional arrangements for the ongoing management of the common environment. Nevertheless, the attention of civil servants and political leaders is devoted less to seeing Canadian policy accepted by the United States than to solving common problems or easing an irritation.

On land, the International Joint Commission (IJC) has a widely recognized and important role in this international problem of management. Few, if any, procedures are borrowed from wider international practice. On the other hand, the IJC and similar Canadian-American institutions are serving as models or object lessons for other pairs of countries whose resources and environments overlap. Particularly in the field of transfrontier pollution, the IJC is held up to European countries as an example of common management of rivers, lakes, and airsheds.

On the seas, the governments of the world recognize some immediate and swiftly worsening international problems arising from competitive uses of the oceans and the resources therein and underneath. For the most part, international action is directed to forming multinational principles of law that avoid future disputes over resource exploitation and, occasionally, may recommend arrangements for the sharing of benefits. Canada has been an active participant, but only one of many, in framing these arrangements. In the management of fisheries, however, Canadian-American precedents have, as with the IJC, been somewhat influential elsewhere, although the Canadian-American fisheries' management commission idea has not, in the end, found favour over competing principles of sovereignty over and division of the catch.

The boundary between Canada and the United States is the source of many bilateral problems. Environmental systems do not respect political boundaries and the Canada-U.S. boundary was drawn without much respect for environmental systems and the physical features of the continent. The boundary line (over 8,900 kilometers) cuts across common mountain ranges, forest areas, wildlife and fishery migration routes, airsheds, and watersheds. Canada and the United States are thus joined through innumerable environmental and physical interconnections. Many of these interconnections link resource-rich regions and industrial, urban, and agricultural areas. When groups in one country exploit a nearby boundary resource or engage in some other activity that alters the environment the effects of those actions are felt across the boundary. A development project that seems on balance a good idea to people on one side of the border, who can weigh the project's environmental damages against its benefits, will be seen far differently by people on the other side who experience only environmental damages.

This paper presents an overview of Canadian international environmental concerns. Canada's Law of the Sea policy is also touched on, but the main emphasis is on Canada's environmental relations with the United States. First some features of Canadian environmental diplomacy are examined, particularly the use made of the IJC. This is followed by a review of the types of issues affecting boundary and coastal international relations and a discussion of some of the characteristics of Canadian international environmental policies.

Environmental Diplomacy

Much attention is directed toward the IJC as an instrument for frontier management.[1] Nevertheless, the great load of work needed to maintain stable relations is handled by normal diplomatic exchange among government officials and political leaders in both countries. Within the confines of the Department of State, the Environmental Protection Agency, the Department of the Interior, the Departments of External Affairs, Environment, and Transport, and the Canadian and American embassies, ideas are batted about, information exchanged, policies and positions proposed, notes passed, ministerial meetings arranged, and agreements signed. Many issues never reach the IJC or do so only at certain stages in the history of a particular issue. An issue like diversion of water from Lake Michigan has been present on the diplomatic agenda since early in this century. But only in 1977 was the IJC given any part of it to investigate. The IJC does not often touch coastal environmental problems, yet these can not be easily divorced from other boundary issues. This point, that most management responsibility remains within traditional government and diplomatic confines, is perhaps obvious. But the point is worth emphasizing. Governments determine what approaches are to be used to settle boundary disputes or promote joint management schemes, and just when and for what purpose the IJC will be used.

To the outsider the internal working of the governments is obscure and difficult to examine. The style of exchange between Canada and the United States does not help the observer. Apart from the IJC and the fisheries' commissions there are remarkably few formal mechanisms of exchange between the countries.[2] The emphasis is on informal contact. There is a commitment to hold periodic ministerial meetings to discuss environmental issues. And when the Prime Minister and President meet, one or more boundary or fishery issues are usually on the agenda. At the legislative level contact is maintained by Canadian embassy personnel in Washington with key congressmen and congressional staff. Also, there is the bilateral legislative group, the Canada-United States Inter-Parliamentary Group, which when it meets spends time informing the others of each country's perspective on particular bilateral environmental issues. Close personal contact, however, among officials in both governments and their embassies through letters, telex, meetings, and prevalent toll-free telephone calls is the preferred style of diplomatic exchange. Of course, normal diplomatic procedures are used by each country in presenting their formal positions.

This easy-going personal style is increasingly followed by provincial and state officials. For certain issues along the border the lower levels of government take the initiative or at least share responsibility for their settlement with federal authorities. Formal procedure usually requires that exchanges between provinces and states go through the respective foreign affairs departments. But for some problems a direct exchange is more appropriate, and it is difficult to judge the extent of this common-sense network of local arrangements. In the last decade regional meetings have also been held between provincial premiers and state governors. Common environmental and boundary issues are often discussed to clear away misconceptions, establish respective positions, or form a consensus on particular transfrontier issues and policies.

The IJC, nevertheless, has an important and vital role in boundary relations. Under the Boundary Waters Treaty of 1909 and other agreements, such as the Great Lakes Water Quality Agreement of 1972, the IJC has a number of duties. The 1909 treaty gives the commission administrative and quasi-judicial functions to approve and regulate works that alter the natural water levels at the boundary (Articles III and IV) and a so-far-unused arbitration function, while the Great Lakes agreement has expanded the commission's work in that basin and added new surveillance, monitoring, and investigatory duties. But the most important function and the one discussed here is the "reference" function, authorized under Article IX of the Boundary Waters Treaty. This function is of interest not just because of the substantive contribution the commission makes in providing information for the governments and proposing alternative courses of action to settle the boundary issues assigned to it, but also because the way the governments use the IJC to handle references suggests some of their concerns and constraints in their conduct of boundary relations. At the request of the two governments, the commission carries out investigations of a wide range of transfrontier problems. The investigation need not even have anything to do with water or the environment. For example, in 1971 the commission was asked to look into the problem of transfrontier urbanization of Point Roberts, Washington, a small peninsula jutting below the 49th parallel boundary. IJC references, however, are not usually so far-removed from traditional boundary environmental and resource issues.

The commission's reference work has in recent years given it much credit. Its reports and recommendations on a number of major issues have led to agreement. The 1964 and earlier references on pollution of the lower Great Lakes led to the signing of the 1972 Great Lakes Water Quality Agreement.[3] Other IJC reports formed the basis for the Columbia River Treaty of 1961.[4] The IJC's reports on the Garrison[5] and the Poplar references will no doubt be central to finding a satisfactory solution to those problems. All the same, for reference questions the role of the IJC is circumscribed. Because governments reserve to themselves the right to make decisions that affect their constituents, and the responsibility to face the reaction to those decisions, they control international issues as flexibly as possible by narrowing the role the IJC plays. By tradition, the two governments only submit to the IJC questions on which they have come to complete prior agreement on the terms of reference. As a result, the commission may be asked to look at only one aspect of an issue. For example, for the Skagit reference the IJC was asked to look only at the "environmental consequences in Canada" of raising Ross Dam.[6] It was not to look at either such consequences downstream in the United States where the dam is located, or the energy benefits from the project itself.

If the governments thus limit the freedom of the commission, why do they employ the commission to carry out boundary investigations? It must first be said that the IJC is very good at fact-finding. When an issue is contentious the IJC provides a means of obtaining agreed upon and trusted technical and social data. Rarely, by the time it reports, are there any facts in dispute. Without use of the IJC's unique technical-board procedures neither side would have the same confidence in each other's proposals, and the resolution of problems might be needlessly hindered by endless debate about facts, effects, and opportunities.

Second, the commission is used by the governments to make detailed proposals to implement negotiations already carried out. Particularly for issues with a potentially negative effect on one country there is often little common ground on which the commission could be expected to devise proposals acceptable to both sides. Thus, the principles and objectives that form the common basis for settlement are largely arranged by prior bilateral negotiation. The commission is then asked to provide the substance. Both countries can be reasonably assured through the past performance of the IJC that, with restricted terms of reference, its proposals will be within a range of alternatives considered acceptable. By relying on IJC investigations, the governments side-step political search for, and negotiation of, verifiable elements. Once the commission has reported, the recognized impartiality of its findings can then be used by the governments to elicit political support or calm domestic opposition to proposals that both seek.

Third, the IJC is used to conduct studies in which its findings are to be the basis for further negotiation of a joint policy, program, or regulation scheme. For the most part these references are complex, bewildering situations in which the two countries share a common interest and incentive to co-operate, such as regulation of lake levels, pollution abatement in a common pool resource, or integrated development. The commission is used to map issues, identify alternatives, and sketch joint recommendations as the basis for bilateral negotiations or further work by the commission.

Fourth, the governments also use the commission to administer knotty problems, or use its investigations to delay final decisions. A contentious issue, like high lake levels, may require the governments to be doing something. There the IJC can be given authority to manage levels on a seasonal basis, while its studies can provide the opportunity to put off project decisions. Through its boards of control and directly, the IJC has administered some aspects of the flows in "connecting channels" of the Great Lakes for decades.

Fifth, and most simply, the governments may be genuinely puzzled by a problem. In the Point Roberts and Niagara Falls environmental references the commission was given a free hand to recommend proposals suitable for joint action. The IJC's reference recommendations are subsequently most successful, however, when the governments already implicitly agree and will support anticipated solutions to specific problems; in other words, when only technical issues need to be resolved.

Range of Issues

The government faces a number of different kinds of international resource and environmental problems along its border with the United States and its coastal seas. For the purpose of review of existing and emerging issues these boundary and coastal problems can be grouped into different categories. Many of the specific transboundary problems are examined elsewhere in this volume. Here we consider some of the broad policy features of the issues.

Water Quality

The Canadian-American boundary includes 3,800 kilometers of fresh-water rivers and lakes. The St. Croix River, the Saint John River, the St. Lawrence River, the Great Lakes, the Pigeon-Rainy Rivers, and the Lake of the Woods make up this discontinuous water boundary. Some of these, of course, are very important rivers for many purposes, and are the focus of active, densely populated industrial regions. Thus, pollution of these waterways is not merely an appendix to the widespread pollution problems of both countries; it is, particularly for central Canada and the northern tier of states, the essence of their pollution problem.

The pollution of the Great Lakes is the most important water quality problem faced by the two countries. For several of the pollutants affecting the lakes, the international issue is not only the equitable division of the responsibility for cleaning up, although much time is spent keeping an eye on each other's performance. A more interesting problem is the freedom of the respective countries to adopt a different type of policy instrument for the particular pollutants. An outstanding example has been the phosphate problem. To the domestic problem of eutrophication caused by nutrient enrichment from the phosphates in detergents, Canada's answer, befitting a compact nation almost forty per cent of whose population live near the Great Lakes, was to control or weaken household detergents. The United States, following the general principle that its restrictive chemical inputs policies should be uniform over the entire nation (as also with gasoline and coal composition), could not agree to a detergent policy that would be useful and effective only in the Great Lakes area. Hence, the American answer was to undertake extremely heavy investment in domestic-waste purifying plants – possibly a scientifically more effective response, but more costly and more time-consuming from the point of view of reversing the continuing deterioration of Great Lakes water quality.

Today, major attention has been switched from such organic pollution to the difficulty and costly program of controlling diffuse sources of discharge of heavy metals and toxic chemicals. In the five-year review of the Great Lakes Water Quality Agreement, for 1977-78 the U.S. government took the offensive by demanding more comprehensive pollution abatement efforts, arguing that for control of toxic and hazardous substances the Great Lakes should be regulated as an entire system. This is because, even if water quality meets the objectives for toxic substances at the outlets of tributaries into the lakes, those substances will be accumulated in the larger lakes' food chain. The U.S. government has wanted Canada to follow its lead and control toxic substances at the industrial or domestic source, control to be imposed by the introduction of effluent standards based on the American approach of best available technology (BAT), which American industry is supposed to have fully adopted by 1985. Canada and Ontario, on the other hand, have not accepted the BAT/effluent standard approach. Perhaps fearful of depending solely on national (U.S.) policing of its own effluents, they have held out for joint surveillance of common water quality as a criterion for monitoring national abatement performance, however administered.

It appears, however, that the U.S. "source" approach for toxic materials has been accepted in part. Publicity claims that the new agreement calls for a so-called cradle-to-grave strategy, monitoring the introduction of toxic materials and their use and disposal, presumably in addition to monitoring their final effect on water quality. The co-ordination and administration of this broad strategy may pose a serious problem for the IJC if Ottawa and Ontario are not willing to legislate source procedures similar to those already called for by orders under the U.S. Clean Water Act of 1977 and similar state legislation. However, some such policy had been recommended to the IJC by its Water Quality Board and by the IJC to the two governments; so it is to be presumed that Ottawa and Ontario will be led to increasing acceptance of the U.S. approach. Indeed, it is likely that Ontario policy-makers welcomed the U.S. pressure to help justify stronger legislation for dealing with its purely internal toxic-materials problems in northern Ontario.

The Saint John River, like the Great Lakes, requires a joint effort to restore the river, which receives industrial and municipal waste discharges from both sides of the border. In the Great Lakes, the Saint John, and other boundary fresh waters, the water quality problems that exist result from waste management practices in both countries. Both sides contribute to the problem and both sides suffer. Thus, there is a strong incentive to take joint action to ease the problem, though as we have seen the approach each side favours can differ and lead to problems. The potential water quality problems in the Souris and Red Rivers from the Garrison Diversion Project, on the Poplar River from Saskatchewan

Power Corporation's thermal power plants, and in the Flathead River from possible coal mining in the Cabin Creek region of British Columbia produce a different kind of political response. One side suffers at the expense of the other and thus the emphasis is less on joint efforts than on reminding the other side of its responsibility not to pollute.

Air Quality

Various types of air quality problems exist. First is the problem within the Detroit-Windsor airshed that arises from coal-fired thermal power plants and other industrial coal-fired boilers. The air quality problem is being tackled by federal, state, and provincial efforts, the results of which are being monitored by the IJC. The IJC reports that these efforts are not strenuous enough to permit the abatement program to attain the air quality standards set by the commission.[7]

For this type of air quality issue the United States would like Canada to accept the reciprocity provision offered in the United States Clean Air Act. The act instructs its administrator to demand that a plan of revision be drawn up for sources of pollution if a duly authorized international agency has reason to believe transfrontier pollution originates in the United States (Section 115(a)). The act gives foreign countries affected by the emission of pollutants the right to appear at any public hearing associated with revision of the implementation plan (Section 115(b)). In return, the act states this right applies only to those countries that offer the United States the same right (Section 115(c)).[8] In a sense this opportunity raises anew the very issues that the Boundary Waters Treaty was designed to settle. As we shall see below, it is a form of exposing complainants or respondents to the decision of a tribunal set up under the laws and customs of only one of the two countries, instead of an international tribunal.

A new problem for Canada-U.S. boundary relations is long-range air pollution. Already familiar in industrialized western Europe, this phenomenon is becoming increasingly evident along the eastern edge of the continent and around the Great Lakes. The pollutants were thought to have come from as far away as St. Louis, but it is now believed that they may be the waste products of large-scale coal combustion in the mountain or even the west coast states. In any case, they are carried northeast by prevailing winds which pick up further pollutants in industrial centres from Chicago to Buffalo. Part of the polluted air mass ends up over eastern Canada where the pollutants are washed from the air by rain and snow. In the winter, when the winds come from the north, sulphur dioxide is carried south from the huge smelter at Sudbury, Ontario. The damage from this smelter used to be local but very high stacks were built and now the detrimental effects of the sulphur dioxide emissions can be detected hundreds of miles away in the United States.

The Canadian government fears the pollution, especially from sulphur dioxide, may become much worse. The number of coal-fired thermal power plants in the northeast United States is increasing greatly as a result of the conversion to domestic sources of fuel supply. Although the United States has higher standards for desulphurization than Canada, the tremendous increase in the size and number of U.S. plants means that the concentration of sulphur dioxide in the air is going to keep increasing. Both governments have extensive research programs directed to the problem. Canadian diplomatic activity, at present, focuses on increasing Canadian participation in American studies to ensure that consideration of the effects on Canada are taken into account and to direct the studies to include Canadian interests.

Boundary Water Levels

Boundary water-level applications are generally handled by the IJC and their boards of control. The commission works out regulation schemes for the control of boundary and transboundary waters over which it has authority. It tries to balance riparian interests. As the waters are shared it often happens that the different interest groups are more or less equally distributed between the countries so that the commission has little trouble finding a "golden mean." Bilateral controversies do occur, however, such as over-regulation of the levels of Lake Champlain where Canadian interests, which seek protection from flooding downstream along the Richelieu River, are opposed to American conservation groups, who want to regulate the lake to protect wetland areas in New York State.

The most baffling, complex, and important issue is the regulation of Great Lakes levels. It is generally agreed, following the submission of the IJC's ten-year study of the problem, that a co-ordinated basin-wide scheme is needed to replace the controls independently regulated by the IJC on the St. Mary's and St. Lawrence Rivers. Nevertheless, co-ordinated operation of these works, even with the addition of control over the inflows and outflows from the Chicago, Long-Lac, Welland Canal, and New

York State Barge Canal diversions, cannot prevent extreme natural fluctuation of the lake levels. Damage must occur somewhere during extreme fluctuations. With regulation, the lakes to which the water is shifted will receive greater damage than they would naturally (or under the previous regulation schemes.) For the United States, the net benefits from regulation are anticipated to be substantial[9] and the government is willing to endure the political reaction from lake-side interests that suffer damage and the consequent legal liability. It has encouraged the IJC in its desire for more basin-wide control. Canada, on the other hand, has less to gain and its government is much more cautious in face of the liability and compensation problems of shifting damages.[10]

System-wide regulation without regard to the boundary may yield significant benefits. All the same, when those benefits are shared disproportionately, the country receiving less benefits will want to be assured that it will not be at a permanent disadvantage before committing itself to a costly or irrevocable management scheme. It will want to ensure either a flexible or a larger net share of benefits and costs. Nevertheless, the commission is no doubt right in thinking basin-wide regulation is appropriate. The weight of its studies and the fact that the lakes are boundary waters in which both sides have a stake in reducing extreme fluctuations should lead to a more systematic regulation arrangement, with some redistributive or reallocative mechanism built in.

Bilateral Coastal Issues

The safe handling and transport of oil are the source of a number of bilateral coastal controversies between Canada and the United States. Two port-refinery projects, Cherry Point in Washington and Eastport in Maine, have the Canadian government worried because of the potential damage from spills to nearby Canadian marine resources. The American government, on the other hand, is concerned about Canadian oil drilling and exploration in the Beaufort Sea and the potential damage to the fragile arctic environment, though that concern is being expressed less as the American government itself takes increasing interest in the prospect of oil discoveries in the Beaufort Sea off the Alaska coast.

Like most projects that are a consequence of the international energy crisis, the Cherry Point terminal is continually reconsidered in drastically changing contexts. It should not be assumed that the government of Washington or residents of different parts of the Puget Sound shore have reached any consensus about the need for a refinery or about its location. Neither is British Columbia able to speak with one voice: the Kitimat proposal produced a surprising local uproar proclaiming the possible environmental damages to be expected from the use of a narrow fjord by tankers from Alaska. In the meantime, such projects rise and fall in favour in the headquarters of oil companies and energy ministries with each new perception of oversupply or undersupply in long-range "energy independence" policies. At the time of writing, neither country is even sure which, if any, of these self-sufficiency policies are worth struggling for. The debate frequently degenerates from consideration of high principle to that of the short-term plight of energy consumers in particular regions and of energy producers to whom such new ports would be a competitive threat. Furthermore, the disappearance of a west coast American oil shortage in 1978-79 led to alternative destinations for Alaska oil, ranging from Atlantic ports to Japan and southeast Asia.

Similar on-again, off-again perceptions of necessity influence the demand for the Eastport, Maine, project. In addition to the environmental considerations affecting the two governments, the drama is being played out against a shifting background of import and export policies, and against the possibility that alternative refineries in Newfoundland, New Brunswick, and the Caribbean might be developed to fulfil the Eastport project's role. Eastport is one of the few remaining undeveloped U.S. sites, but it is by no means indispensable from a technical point of view.

Marine and Fisheries Issues

The relations of the two countries concerning their common use of inshore waters and the high seas are by no means as institutionalized as in the inland situations we have so far described. This is apparent in the contrast between those conflicts where the IJC or similar bodies are calmly proceeding to approvals and recommendations and those in the adjoining waters of Passamaquoddy, Head Harbour Passage, and the Gulf of Georgia, where no decisive rules (or too many) are available. Most of these irritating issues have involved the Law of the Sea, or coastal fisheries.[11]

Until very recently, bilateral fisheries problems had been assigned for the most part to commissions set up under international agreements or treaties. Among these were the oldest truly Canadian treaty, that dealing with Pacific halibut, and a series of later arrangements on the west coast for protecting and enhancing salmon and herring stocks. In most cases the international commissions were given some implicit or explicit independent authority to make day-to-day decisions about closing the fishery for certain species or sizes on given dates or in particular fishing grounds. The two countries were also the chief members of two high-seas agreements: the unusual Pacific seal treaty, wherein the U.S. protects and harvests seals on behalf of several signatories, including Canada, and the International North Pacific Treaty, which has gradually become a means for setting the extent to which Japan (and to a lesser extent Russia) can take fish not under protection of or extensive exploitation by Canada or the United States.

In more recent years, the good will inherent in these treaties and in the liberal style of management employed by their commissions has become depleted by what are essentially territorial disputes. The question "for whom?", which once divided the two nations and was eventually influential in establishing the treaties just mentioned, has once again come to the fore in regulation of the fisheries. The essentially distributional questions have had domestic as well as international ramifications. In Canada, the implementation of an entry-restriction scheme in the salmon fisheries has aggravated frictions between those included and those excluded; between sports and commercial salmon fishermen; and between fishermen employing different techniques of catching for the same species. Similar frictions have arisen in Alaska and Washington, and added to these frictions has been a revolutionary judicial decision that in effect exempts native fishermen in Puget Sound from the edicts of the state government and the international commissions regarding fish-catch sharing and protection of spawning grounds.

If these frictions were not enough, the fisheries have been rent by geographical disputes regarding the division of fish that cross boundaries, especially around Prince Rupert and in the Straits of Juan de Fuca. It may be possible to settle the former by a local arbitration or negotiation. But the latter involves very complicated cross-claims. On the one hand, British Columbia fishermen, using a variety of gear, have been catching coho and other salmon feeding in Canadian or international waters but undoubtedly reared in Washington's state hatcheries. On the other hand, American fishermen have been pressing their claim to half of the sockeye-salmon run on the Fraser River, a run which has been protected and augmented by river-improvement expenditures over many years by an international salmon commission. Now Canada has declared its willingness to take on the entire financial burden of enhancing the salmon fishery in inland British Columbia, but it is no longer willing to split evenly the resulting increased catch. This policy is of course difficult to enforce unilaterally because the salmon cut through U.S. waters on their way to the Fraser River.

These B.C. salmon questions are frequently paired with a parallel dispute in Atlantic waters over rights to harvest the rich fisheries of George's Bank, rights which are asserted, by both New England and Maritime fisherman, on historical grounds and with further basis in the International Commission for Northwest Atlantic Fisheries. Although little similarity exists between the eastern and western disputes, they are seen by heads of state and top-level diplomats as "fisheries questions," and are more than likely, after some further months of intensive staff work and local fact-finding, to be settled jointly by diplomatic compromise. Fishing-grounds disputes have been endemic in Atlantic waters for hundreds of years, and the George's Bank quarrel is nothing new. But it is a pity that on the west coast, where joint maximization and equitable sharing on the basis of equal sacrifice have been the rule, disputes about how to read maps or how to apply *ad hoc* historic principles should have been allowed to flair up and to sour well-working understandings in the fisheries.

These disputes have simmered while the global Law of the Sea conferences have proceeded since the first of the current cycle in 1973. In general, Canada and the United States have not worked closely on this grandiose international maritime constitution-forming exercise. The United States has been profoundly concerned about offshore military and mineral rights not only in waters adjoining its own shores but over the world as a whole. It has had to act, on different issues, as the leading spokesman for what might be called the NATO position on naval claims and for the great-powers position on minerals and navigation, while assuming a modified coastal-state position on fisheries. Canada, hardly visualizing itself as a global military, mining, energy, or shipping power, has found it easier to align itself with coalitions of developing nations in Africa, Latin America, and Asia and with an overlapping "coastal-state" bloc. In most ways, therefore, because the two nations have not made common cause in the Law of the Sea, a greater burden has been thrown onto their *ad hoc* agreements or *modus vivendi* whenever navigational, maritime, or fishing questions have arisen.

Three specific implications are worth mentioning. One is that the United States ultimately has joined the larger bloc, of which Canada is a member, that favours a wide economic zone under coastal control, taken from what was previously the *res nullius* of the high-seas regime. For fisheries, this coastal belt will be at least two hundred miles wide, and will reduce the scope of or need for the fishing treaties already mentioned and create a much larger area in which artificial straight boundary lines are drawn at sea across migratory paths and stationary fishing grounds. The resulting need for common understanding about respective rights in constricted waters also may occur, from an environmental point of view, in connection with jurisdiction over navigation and over the control of shipping.

Another result was that fear of possible internationalization of the straits and sounds of the Arctic led Canada in 1970 to pass and proclaim many portions of the Arctic Waters Protection bill. This unilateral action was aimed chiefly at multinational oil companies and associated transportional systems then initiating exploration for oil and minerals in northern waters. American firms were most affected. In effect, Canada has claimed for most of the northern seas the status of "inland waters," in which the environmental, navigational, and mineral jurisdiction are, with many qualifications to govern a modified form of innocent passage, no longer to be regarded as anything but domestic.

Finally, perhaps more than the United States or other Law of the Sea participants, Canadian concern has focused on the vulnerability of coastlines to oil pollution by tankers and freighters. The broadening of the coastal economic zone and creation of the Arctic Waters legislation may be seen as just two elements in the Canadian campaign to protect the coastal environment. Concern about migratory salmon and seals in the Pacific and Atlantic, and the dependence of the Inuit people on fishing in the Arctic, are other explanations. Consequently, Canada at times has taken a leading role in the Intergovernmental Maritime Consultative Organization and other forums where tanker design, liability, insurance, spills, dumping, and remedial measures are discussed and evolved for global adoption.

These events have occurred quickly, and have passed into international law, treaty, or negotiation at a very rapid rate compared with progress thirty years ago. In the past the uses of the sea were primarily navigation and fishing, and there was still much room for both while giving the world's navies unrestricted access on each other's doorsteps. Today there are many more nations, many more consumers of fish and minerals, many more navies, and a much more vulnerable ocean. The *res nullius* status of the high seas is rapidly disappearing, and Canada and the United States are just two of scores of states rapidly adjusting to the task of protecting and managing their parts of it.

The Pattern of Response

The preceding section describes the types of Canadian international environmental issues. What then are the features that affect the government's response to them? The most basic observation about Canada-U.S. environmental relations is that issues may be classified into those in which there is some mutual incentive to co-operate and those in which there is no real incentive on the part of one country to work with the other. Accepting this distinction, a number of economic, political, diplomatic, and institutional points can be made about the two types of issues that indicate the pressures and constraints on governments in their efforts to resolve outstanding environmental resource issues.

Most often the controversies arise because the flows of air and water across the boundary are one-directional. No reciprocal interest in controlling transfrontier damages means no incentive to co-operate. For example, in the Garrison project, the United States can use whatever economic (or, more likely, political) calculus it likes to determine whether to go ahead with it. Canadians have no direct access to the project's evaluation. Nor does Canada reap benefits from it to compensate for the expected environmental damages. But there are other issues, like those of the East Poplar River and Atikokan, where the Americans are on the receiving end of anticipated environmental damages. In the country where the project is located the beneficial goods and services outweigh the damages, whereas the neighbouring country receives mostly negative effects. The country on the receiving end of the damages quite naturally becomes upset at the actual or threatened transboundary damage and will initiate high-level diplomatic action to remedy the problem. The country of origin has little local incentive to respond, much less to improve its performance, when the cost of doing so would reduce the net benefit from the project. Furthermore, the region suffering damage from its neighbour has no offsetting employment or other benefits, so that local politicians, unconstrained by interest groups benefiting from the project causing the damage, are free to exploit the irritation.

Take, for example, the Skagit issue.[12] In the early 1970's, with no compensating employment or regional investment and few benefits to offset the expected losses from raising further the High

Ross Dam, environmental groups and other political interests in Canada protested loudly. National sentiment at the time heightened the sense of violation and sharpened the protest. Since no domestic trade-offs had to be made with other sectoral or regional interests, regional politicians won an uncritical and sympathetic hearing at the national level. The climax came when an opposition MP introduced a resolution to Parliament which expressed opposition to the project. It passed unanimously.[13] What surely would have remained a local controversy within an entirely domestic jurisdiction developed into a significant national cause and an international irritant between Canada and the United States. As the project benefits were not shared in Canada, there was no Canadian group to defend the project and restrain criticism of the American plan.

A variant of the unidirectional-flow example and one that has been important in recent years is the controversy over accidental spills. The transportation of oil by sea to United States refineries on both coasts, the exploration for oil in the Beaufort Sea, and the location of nuclear facilities near the border raise fears in the neighbouring country. Nothing may ever happen. But the fear that there will be an accident across the border causing transfrontier damage motivates activity at the diplomatic level to lessen the risks. The economic and political characteristics of living-with-risk issues are much like the one-sided damage issues, except the damage is statistical and potential. Since no one locally has much stake in the activity creating the danger the same volatile emotions are raised, unrestrained by any countervailing domestic interests. In fact, the first unanimous resolution by Parliament against the United States for activities that might threaten the environment was protest against nuclear testing at Amchitka in the Aleutian Islands.

As such protests are against potential damage rather than actual damage, the country in which the project will originate is even less likely to be responsive to the protests of its neighbour than in the case of one-sided damage issues. It will not admit that the safety of its project is questionable, especially if it meets domestic standards. Also, on principle it may object to a neighbouring country having a say in an entirely domestic project that satisfies domestic requirements, is not expected to have any transfrontier impact, and may be in the national interest. The spirit of international law, as in the Stockholm and Helsinki declarations, at least imposes some censure on the upstream polluter, but for this type of issue the endangered country has no recognized claim to take action where no damage has yet been experienced.[14] As a fall-back, to prepare for the probability that an accident will happen, the endangered country can make do with arranging and negotiating contingency plans and compensation arrangements with its neighbour. For oil pollution there has been much progress, though problems remain in making each country's program reciprocal and equitable.[15]

Perhaps because of the nationalist sensitivity in Canada to American transgressions, unrestrained criticism has been more a Canadian practice than an American one. However, the righteous Canadian protests of the early 1970's are more subdued today. Many of the dangers remain but the nationalist sentiment that fueled protest has subsided somewhat. Equally important, Canada is less obviously the victim. As American pollution programs are implemented and Canadian standards for some projects clearly are less stringent than American ones, the United States is increasingly the victim of Canadian pollution. The long frontier between the two countries works to mute criticism. Canada (or the United States) may be at a geographic advantage in one region but at a disadvantage in another. Thus, for any particular regional conflict or type of damage a position has to be taken with thought to how it conforms to a broader policy for other contrary conflicts along the frontier.

Aside from the long border, a number of other factors soothe irritants and work to offset the incentive of one country to use its geographic advantage to the detriment of its neighbour. Article IV of the Boundary Waters Treaty of 1909 creates an obligation on each side not to pollute. It states: "boundary waters and water flowing across the boundary shall not be polluted on either side to the injury of health or property on the other." In the past Article IV has not been much noticed or observed in stopping transfrontier pollution, but in recent years, for pending projects, its invocation by either side has been more effectively used as a point of departure for the governments in negotiation and in submitting references to the IJC. The commission is asked whether or not the project will cause transfrontier pollution. The Garrison and Poplar references are, in part, the result of new recognition by governments that Article IV should not be disregarded and that an impartial study is needed to determine the environmental effects of the proposed projects and the standard that should be set to indicate what constitutes transfrontier pollution for the particular river.

This attention to the antipollution section of Article IV is part of a wider community of values. Environmental perceptions and values in both countries are fundamentally similar. Neither government can easily justify activities that blatantly do environmental damage, even abroad. Similar values and perceptions greatly facilitate diplomatic exchange, for seldom do the negotiators argue over their responsibilities. The arguments are over different standards of environmental damage, different approaches to maintain or improve environmental quality, and different senses of urgency or desirable timing. Common attitudes and perceptions also form the basis for transnational exchange and lobbying. A government sometimes can rely on allied sentiment across the boundary and transnational groups to further its own objectives. For many issues–Eastport, Garrison, the Chicago diversion, for example–the Canadian government's position is in sympathy with some U.S. interest groups. Reciprocally, especially on the Great Lakes, U.S. government attitudes have been echoed by Canadian interest groups. There is, then, opportunity for a government to stand aside and let disagreeable projects be shot down domestically, without ever having to dissipate international goodwill by diplomatic action that can raise the ire of the State Department and congressional critics.

This suggests common action at levels below national diplomacy. The United States is remarkably open in its government processes. Unlike Canadian practice, foreign groups affected by U.S. projects are permitted to intervene in the administrative and judicial processes that approve projects. This privilege led Canadian groups allied with American environmental interests (and with tacit support from the Canadian government) to challenge the Alaska pipeline in American courts. But such use by Canadians of the American equal-access rights, however thoughtfully invoked by Canadian groups, is not a desirable substitute for bilateral political and diplomatic initiatives. It does supplement them when these measures are having little apparent effect. As already remarked, Canadians are better served in the long run by having their government represent their interests than by submitting to foreign government authority, no matter how benign. Usually, they do so only as a final recourse, and the use of transnational groups and mechanisms by the governments is only of minor importance. But the close links between the countries that make such transnational action possible illustrate the shared perceptions along the boundary which have a moderating effect on many issues.

Reciprocal incentives to co-operate reinforce common perceptions and transnational policies. Both governments need the physical co-operation of the other to achieve their management goals. For example, Canada and the United States both wish to improve Great Lakes water quality and to devise, if possible, some flows-regulation scheme to reduce damage from extremes of high and low levels. In such situations, where the governments cannot succeed unless they work together to regulate, manage, or develop a shared resource, there is common ground for negotiation, even if goals are at variance and strategies at odds; each side needs the other. The reciprocal dependence arises because the action is a "public good" intended to improve an indivisible resource. Neither country has sufficient control over the Great Lakes or the Detroit-Windsor airshed, for example, for its waste discharges not to cause almost equal damage in the neighbouring country. More important, neither country can exclude its neighbour when it cleans up pollution on its side of the border, nor will it wish to do so unless its neighbour makes an equal effort. Thus, the reciprocal flow of damages and benefits and the common experience of pollution and abatement efforts engenders co-operation. Additionally, each can achieve a given standard of water quality at much less cost than by unco-ordinated, independent abatement. For water levels, too, the physical interconnections of the watershed require co-ordinated and sometimes joint efforts to regulate tributaries and strategic points within the basin.

But joint action requires simultaneous political agreement. This means that politicians on each side must gather domestic support and neutralize opposition at the same time. This is not easy. Agreement requiring regulation of the major industrial and municipal waste discharges, and so imposing significant costs on them, creates political opposition. A discharger's lobby, if organized and powerful, may win its demands for exceptions and modifications at the expense of damage to the neighbouring country. The neighbour can muster few electoral allies, compared to such interest groups. Co-operative regulation is likely to be more successful if the proposed agreement is in line with national regulatory proposals; here the interest groups against regulation may be balanced by other strong domestic groups elsewhere. Often what matters is whether the domestic legislation in the two countries has proceeded at the same rate. In Canada-U.S. relations, if regulation of dischargers north of the border is in advance of American control over its sector, the Canadian government cannot hope the United States government will respond with complementary controls. Canada cannot generate U.S. policy, and therefore must wait until court decisions, executive action, and congressional allies combine to force a domestic change.

When the positions are reversed and U.S. policy is more

vigorous, Canadian standards or policies likely will be re-shaped to complement American. While provincial autonomy may slow a uniform Canadian response, one or more Canadian provinces may be able to emulate U.S. policy with surprising speed. If uniformity is essential, the federal government has sufficient power in situations where the province is not absolutely immovable because of Ottawa's superior financial power and its *de facto* supremacy when federal and provincial regulations conflict. Within the federal government itself, the centralization of power in the Cabinet provides an obvious single target for U.S. diplomacy and persuasion. Politicians find unexpected allies in going along with U.S. proposals. Multinational companies in Canada, for example, may not object too vehemently to proposed regulations already in effect in the U.S. and accepted by their own parent companies. Environmental pressure groups, too, are less bothersome, for they often take U.S. practice or U.S. standards as a norm for Canadian attainment. In sum, even though the resource or the pollution is enjoyed or experienced in common, the tail does not wag the dog; the dog wags the tail.[16] For example, the 1972 Great Lakes Water Quality Agreement was not in advance of United States water quality policy. It simply adapted recently legislated national policy to the needs of the international agreement and the problem of the Great Lakes. Even then, Canadian complaints about slowness in the American municipal treatment program could not induce the United States to speed up implementation.

The United States is taking the initiative not just in common pool resources but in all transboundary issues. It is getting into full stride in its pollution abatement programs based on best practical technology (BPT) and, as already noted, best available technology (BAT). The Canadian authorities have accepted this regulatory approach for air pollution control and for certain toxic water pollutants. But they are reluctant to abandon their water quality, or environmental quality, standards approach. The Canadian argument, in brief, is that emphasis on water quality standards is more efficient and practical domestically because of Canada's sparse population and industrial settlement in relation to her water resources. Internationally, the Canadian position is based as much on a conception of equity as of efficiency. The prevailing economic teaching, for example, is directed at abating pollution at the lowest social cost by distributing the task of reducing discharges, and so pollution, to those sources that can abate least expensively. This makes sense within one community, and has led both Canada and the U.S. to consider a whole-hearted adoption of a general emission-control approach, with all its administrative headaches, instead of uniform standards or objectives for water or air quality. But BPT (or BAT) is not really the economists' ideal of emission control; it simply is an edict that every party using the same toxic materials must adopt the same abatement equipment and practices, regardless of their costs relative to one another. Thus, both the Canadian emphasis on water quality and the U.S. toxic-materials emphasis on BAT miss the economic efficiency boat. The U.S. claims that only the draconian BAT approach is adequate to stop the urgent toxic-materials threat. This view is not uniquely American but an adaptation of the earlier universalistic approach of automobile-emissions requirements, the emphasis on unleaded gas, detergent control, PCB and insecticide-spray control, and so on.

A more fundamental debate is becoming clearer, although neither country's position is articulated or consistent. In many matters concerning shared or transboundary pollution problems, the United States is tending toward a policy that was inherent in some of the earlier IJC reports on water resource projects: ignoring the boundary and adopting internationally efficient management policies, with the burdens and costs falling indiscriminately on citizens in both countries. This was also the approach embodied forty years ago in the U.S. benefit-cost procedure, which tended to ignore gains wherever they occurred. After some hesitation, Canada's authorities argue that Canada must be dealt with organically, not as a group of citizens or a group of regions subject to the same burdens and benefits as the United States, but in an undifferentiated approach to joint maximization.

For example, consider the Canadian argument on BAT for toxic materials. In detail, it is stressed that, as with other pollutants, the Canadian discharge into the jointly-owned lakes is very small. Furthermore, many Canadian dischargers are marginal firms in their respective industries. Canada claims it is not appropriate to adopt a uniform approach when either the minimization of the total international cost of abatement or the application of sweeping American uniform requirements to Canadian dischargers would be particularly costly for Canada. This claim is derived from an earlier Canadian position that the availability of the Great Lakes as a waste receptor must be shared in proportion to the two country's respective *ownership* of the lakes, not in proportion to their respective needs for or *costs* of waste disposal.

Seen from the Canadian point of view, the U.S. leadership in abatement regulations and its demands that Canada follow this leadership are reminiscent of the earlier American demand in the 1960's for a "continental resources policy." Of course, this raises problems in Canada about how the provinces and Ottawa are to co-ordinate their responses, just as it did with the original Great Lakes Water Quality Agreement and as is now the case with gas exports. But, more seriously, it raises the fundamental question of whether joint management of common resources calls for uniform regulatory policies by the two nations. The Canadian school of thought could be represented as arguing that, as long as each country makes its negotiated and agreed contribution to management, or to pollution abatement, each should be free to choose the domestic policies most suitable to mobilizing that contribution. This school is unenthusiastic or even hostile to the American demand for uniformity, which stems from other American notions about joint management of resources based on individualistic equality of requirements and responsibilities on citizens on both sides of the border. Not only do the Canadians dislike a uniform BAT requirement, but they also reject the American demand for reciprocity in marine insurance that now allows Canadians affected by U.S. projects the same protection as Americans and, further, allows them to argue environmental-review cases with the same freedom as Americans, under American hearings procedures. This, they point out, has already led to the anomoly that projects supported by U.S. funds anywhere in the world *must* be analyzed by an American environmental impact statement: for example, the Alaska pipeline in Canada must meet American environmental-impact requirements.

The American counter-argument is easy for Canadians to understand, however, especially in political terms. As we have already noticed, it is difficult to get congressional approval for measures designed mostly to protect Canadians from environmental damage. This task would be made easier if the American executive could assure Congress of consistent, equal burdens and policies being imposed in both countries. Thus, a fear that American industry might be put at a competitive disadvantage (by having to bear higher abatement costs than their Canadian rivals) would be allayed. More generally, congressmen do not want to hear that in common endeavours, say in the Detroit-Windsor area, American citizens are being forced to go to greater expense or inconvenience than Canadians.

Concluding Comments

Trends in Canada-U.S. environmental relations suggest that the IJC can have a greater role in boundary relations. As noted, one of the principal uses of the IJC's reference function, particularly in unidirectional-flow issues, is to fill in the details of agreement implicitly reached by the governments. Although these issues will continue to trouble relations, the stark incentives for and against co-operation are softening. Now Canada is often the origin of transfrontier pollution and the government must face up to its responsibilities along the frontier. It can no longer claim environmental purity and decry American transgressions. Unidirectional-flow issues are being treated more like common-pool issues—less disputes to resolve and more problems to solve. Particular issues are not looked at in isolation but as members of classes of issues (e.g., sulphur dioxide, toxic substances, marine traffic safety, etc.). Since the issues are regarded less in terms of conflict resolution, the IJC can have a greater role. The governments are using the commission in unidirectional issues not just to dot the i's and cross the t's of particular issues like the Poplar and Garrison, but also to set quality objectives for particular streams that give the standards for future conduct at the boundary, standards that the commission is given the task of monitoring.

As we have said, Canada and the United States share similar objectives for high environmental quality; the two countries thus have agreed to a co-ordinated approach to maintain environmental quality along the frontier. The American government seeks a modified continental approach through reciprocal equal access arrangements and the adoption of the effluent standard/BAT approach to pollution regulation. Canada in theory can have little argument against reciprocal provisions, but in principle it still favours absolute environmental standards as the strategy to guarantee each side protection from the other; alternatively it might support *equal* division of the lakes as receptors.

Should either approach be accepted there will be a common framework for looking at most transboundary problems. Within this framework the governments can afford, without a significant loss of sovereignty, to permit the IJC an expanded and more independent role. If the American approach is accepted, the relative freedom the IJC has long had, under both its earlier connecting-channels responsibilities and its present Great Lakes Water Quality Agreement, can be applied boundary-wide. If the Canadian approach is accepted, the IJC will have an expanded role to set air and water quality standards at the boundary and to monitor whether or not they are being met by each country.

Whichever approach prevails, the IJC is well-placed to interpret the new transfrontier pollution principles Canada and the United States accept within the Organization for Economic Co-operation and Development, aimed at providing guidelines for governments to avoid disputes over transfrontier pollution. These include means to harmonize laws, to ensure non-discrimination in the application of legislation, to provide equal rights of access in administrative and legal procedures, to implement warning systems, and to ensure full exchange of relevant information. The OECD principles, then, are designed to put boundary relations on a solid basis. It is not always recognized that Canada's acquiescence in these principles (such as that providing equal rights of access to foreign procedures and tribunals) may contradict our professed faith in direct regulation and in the IJC. Perhaps Canada kept its fingers crossed in approving some of the principles, as it must have years ago in agreeing to the OECD's "Polluter Pays Principle." Nevertheless, without a recognized impartial authority to adjudicate whether certain agreed principles are being met when one side complains that they are not, all principles may be ineffective: the IJC can provide the indicated monitoring and review implementation of principles. What it already does is indispensable: to make official that there is some real international injury, something the offending country may have been denying in its replies to its neighbour's complaints. In the same manner, future notice given by the IJC on one government's failure to implement any OECD transfrontier principle may be all that is required to remedy the deficiency.

The IJC has many possible additional and intermediate roles.[17] As with the fishery commissions, the IJC can deal almost directly with individuals, both in hearings and in administration, or it may merely stand between the responsible government bureaus. It has been suggested at the OECD that if a national view like Canada's is accepted, international financial payments eventually may be necessary to assure that the two countries gain equal benefit from their boundary waters. This idea raises two questions: should the international payments be passed on to those who have experienced the excess damage (a principle that is not in general followed when some citizens suffer from undue damage from an internal source of pollution); and should the countries enter the business of selling their pollution-absorption capacities to one another? The latter idea is anathema today in environmental matters, but it is not so far away in fisheries management systems. Indeed, it has long been embodied in the U.S. participation in the upkeep of the Fraser River salmon-passage works. The IJC or a similar agency or offshoot could handle these financial aspects instead of eternally attempting to find formulae by which both countries can be assured that absolute equality has been achieved in dividing the physical services of the environment, the rivers and lakes, or the fisheries.[18]

NOTES

1. "Summary of the International Joint Commission Seminar on the IJC, its Achievements, Needs and Potential, Montreal, 1974," available from IJC Canadian Section, 151 Slater Street, Ottawa, Ontario.
2. Maxwell Cohen, "Canada and the United States: Dispute Settlement and the International Joint Commission – Can this Experience be Applied to Law of the Sea Issues?" *Journal of International Law of Case-Western Reserve University,* 8 (1976), 68-83.
3. For an official history of the agreement see: Canada, Department of the Environment, "A History and Analysis of the Agreement between Canada and the United States on Great Lakes Water Quality," prepared for the NATO/CCMS Workshop Symposium on Approaches to Water Quality Objectives and Standards in an International River Basin, Presque Isle, Maine, September 18-22, 1972 (mimeo, 1972).
4. For summaries of the IJC and its engineering board reports see Canada, Department of External Affairs, *The Columbia River Treaty, Protocol and Related Documents* (Ottawa, 1964).
5. International Joint Commission, *Transboundary Implications of the Garrison Diversion Unit* (Ottawa, 1977).
6. International Joint Commission, *Environmental and Ecological Consequences in Canada of Raising Ross in the Skagit Valley to Elevation 1725* (Ottawa, 1971).
7. International Joint Commission, *Annual Report 1976* (Ottawa, 1977), 23. See also *Annual Report 1977* (Ottawa, 1978), 30.
8. United States Clean Air Act as amended August, 1977, Section 115.
9. International Joint Commission, International Great Lakes Board, *Regulation of Great Lakes Water Levels: A Summary Report/1974* (Ottawa, 1974), 30.
10. David LeMarquand and Anthony D. Scott, "Canada-United States Environmental Relations," *Proceedings of the Academy of Political Science,* 32, 2 (1976), 152-3.
11. For surveys, see the following, many of which contain recent bibliographies: Barbara Johnson and M. W. Zacher (eds.), *Canadian Foreign Policy and the Law of the Sea* (Vancouver, 1977); Paul G. Bradley and Anthony Scott, "Coastal Oil Spills: Alternative Courses for Canadian Policy," to be published in *Marine Policy*; and Gordon R. Munro, "Extended Fisheries Jurisdiction and International Cooperation," *International Perspectives* (March/April, 1978), 12-18. See also, in general, the items by Bourne, Langdon, Heaver, Waters, McRae, Zacher and others listed in "Publications by Participants in the Research Project on Canada and the International Management of the Oceans, 1975-78," Institute of International Relations, University of British Columbia, Vancouver, December, 1978.
12. For a discussion of the Skagit controversy, see David G. LeMarquand, *International Rivers: The Politics of Cooperation* (Vancouver: Westwater Research Centre, 1977), chapter 5.

13. House of Commons, *Debates,* November 2, 1973, p. 7473.
14. For further information, see Douglas M. Johnston, "International Environmental Law: Recent Developments and Canadian Contributions," in R. St. J. MacDonald *et al., Canadian Perspectives on International Law and Organization* (Toronto, 1974), 560-611.
15. Liability and compensation funds for oil spills are in place in both countries. The United States has a $200 million overall fund and Canada a $40 million fund. Problems occur over reciprocal access. The United States is limited to a fixed amount under the Canadian fund while Canada is unrestricted in the amount it can claim for damages. Canada has urged the United States government to consider construction of off-loading facilities closer to the open sea.
16. See Anthony Scott, "Fisheries, Pollution and Canadian-American Transnational Relations," in Annette Baker Fox *et al.* (eds.), *Canada and the United States – Transnational and Transgovernmental Relations* (New York, 1976), 234-57.
17. Remarks by Anthony Scott in "Summary of the International Joint Commission Seminar. . ."
18. The authors wish to acknowledge the influence and assistance, in different ways, of Irving Fox, Westwater Research Centre, University of British Columbia, and Murray Thompson, International Joint Commission, Ottawa.

Part II
Selected Case Studies

CHAPTER FOUR

The Coastal Zone Management Debate: Putting an Issue on the Public Agenda

by A. Paul Pross

The Emergent Significance of the Coastal Zone

Sea coasts and lakeshores have been an essential part of Canadian life and consciousness for centuries. Only in recent decades have their use and preservation become a public policy issue, however, and only in recent years have governments considered the possibility that they must be managed as an integrated and exceedingly complex biological and social system. In fact, the concept of "shore zone" or "coastal zone" management is still far from being widely accepted and is currently the subject of some debate in government circles. The course of that debate is the concern of the following discussion.

While the debate itself is a significant development in the evolution of Canadian environmental policy, and therefore worth studying in its own right, its twists and turns through the policy process make it an interesting case study in the evolution of a certain type of government policy. Consequently, the following discussion will go beyond the description of the development of a particular policy issue to help in answering a question that is frequently asked by students of public policy: How is an issue placed on the public agenda? For, unlike many environmental issues, the question of coastal zone management has not been pressed on governments by a concerned public. Rather, it has emerged from within specific government agencies in a fashion which suggests that, in Canada at least, the environmental movement may be well into a new and highly institutionalized phase.

First, however, it is necessary to explain some of the various meanings of "coastal zone" management and to indicate how the term has been used in Canada. There is no really satisfactory way of describing the "coastal zone," or "shore zone" as some prefer to call it. Like the term "environment" itself, it is generally used in a very broad fashion to emphasize the holistic qualities of the phenomenon. This is clearly an asset when the speaker is attempting to assert the need for developing a rather inclusive management regime for the zone; it is less helpful when scientists want to establish a precisely defined area for ecological analysis. Consequently, some biologists may define the zone as being between high and low water marks. Oceanographers, on the other hand, may trace the influence of a river system far out to sea and call the distance between that point and the river's headwaters the coastal zone. Similarly, the policy-maker and administrator will select definitions that reflect specific functional and legal understandings of the zone. Indeed, the term "shore zone" is a recent and particularly Canadian addition to the lexicon of coastal management, and is used to refer not only to ocean coastal zones but to the zones found around lakes and along rivers. Its use, in fact, perhaps has helped to convince Canada's central provinces that they, too, have coastal zones that require thoughtful management. This will be discussed later, but the use of the term here will be very limited since the general understanding of "coastal zone" embraces lacustrine and riverine as well as ocean phenomena.

As a result of this variety of opinion and approach most discussions of coastal zone management are content to cite the very broad definition of the term elaborated at one of the first major U.S. conferences on coastal zone issues:

The coastal zone is the band of dry land and adjacent ocean space (water and submerged land) in which ecology and use directly affect ocean space ecology, and vice versa. The coastal zone is a band of variable width which borders the continents, the inland seas, and the great lakes. Functionally, it is the broad interface between land and water where production, consumption, and exchange processes occur at high rates of intensity. Ecologically, it is an area of dynamic biogeochemical activity, but with limited capacity for supporting various forms of human use. Geographically, the landward boundary of the coastal zone is necessarily vague. The oceans may affect climate far inland from the sea. Ocean salt penetrates estuaries to various extents, depending largely upon geometry of the estuary and river flow, and the ocean tides may extend even farther upstream than the salt penetration. Pollutants added even to the fresh water part of the river ultimately reach the sea after passing through the estuary.

The seaward boundary is easier to define scientifically, but it has been the cause of extensive political argument and disagreement. Coastal waters differ chemically from those of the open sea, even in areas where man's impact is minimal. Generally, the coastal water can be identified at least to the edge of the continental shelf (depth of about two hundred meters), but the influence of major rivers may extend many miles beyond this boundary. For the purposes of Coastal Zone Workshop, the seaward boundary has been defined as the extent to which man's land based activities have a measureable influence on the chemistry of the water or on the ecology of marine life.[1]

For Canadian purposes, this writer and a group of colleagues have suggested that it is "too early . . . to fret over alternative statutory definitions," but that a working definition might perceive the zone as the area which includes:

(i) the ocean coastline and adjacent areas directly affected by the interaction of the land and ocean environments, but

(ii) extending as far seaward as the maximum limits of national jurisdiction and control within which Canada has managerial rights and responsibilities in international law, and

(iii) extending as far landward as may be deemed practicable and desirable for the purpose of coastal zone management studies and consultations.[2]

These definitions should adequately serve our needs in the following discussion. Coastal zone management, then, is the application to coastal areas of the "process of decision making whereby resources are allocated over space and time according to the needs, aspirations, and desires of man within the framework of his technological inventiveness, his political and social institutions, and his legal and administrative arrangements."[3]

Even this brief exercise in definition gives us some idea of the reasons why coastal zone management is emerging as a public policy issue not only in Canada but in many other countries. By stressing the holistic features of the zone, our definitions draw attention to the fact that scientists, policy-makers, and to some extent the general public have realized that the bio-physical interactions which occur at the water's edge are extremely complex, and that any attempt to regulate man's intrusion into these processes must appreciate the interconnectedness of social and natural systems. In fact, this perception of the systemic nature of the coastal zone, the interrelatedness of coastal use and coastal problems, presents the only really new aspect of the concern for coastal zone management. In one way or another we have experienced these problems many times, but only recently have we realized that resource management and environmental problems along the shorelines must be dealt with in an integrated way. Beanlands has typified these problems and the growing consensus of expert opinion concerning them as follows:

(1) Incompatible uses of coastal resources may continue for a long period of time with serious environmental and social effects before the general public will become sufficiently frustrated or concerned to demand that action be taken to resolve the issues. On the other hand, a well informed public can usually be relied upon to support policies or programs which are designed for the long term benefit of the coastal zone and rational use of the resources therein.

(2) There are situations where only government intervention can resolve user conflicts in the coastal zone, particularly where the resolution of such conflicts cannot be based on a compromise position between the parties involved.

(3) Procuring long term solutions to problems in the coastal zone is highly dependent upon an adequate understanding of the physical and biological systems involved. A lack of knowledge of the dynamic forces acting between land and water can lead to wasteful actions resulting in only short term solutions.

(4) As in most problem solving exercises, the resolution of coastal zone problems often hinges on the formulation of acceptable alternatives. A "cease and desist" order designed to stop some damaging historical use of coastal resources is likely to fail in the long run if realistic alternatives are not identified for the parties affected.

(5) Finally and most important, in Canada the long term solution to most of our problems in the coastal zone depends upon a co-operative effort between all levels of government. This not only applies to the interplay of jurisdictions, but also to the development of national, regional or provincial policies in general, which can have an indirect, but significant, effect on the policies, plans and programs of other agencies with coastal zone responsibilities.[4]

Few parts of Canada's extensive fresh- and salt-water coastlines fail to illustrate in some way or another the problems creating a growing consensus that Canada has a diverse but interrelated set of coastal problems which require a management solution. Many of these seem quite insignificant when we consider the extent of Canada's coastlines. Aggregate removed from a beach here; a sewage outfall there; siltation of a harbour following the building of a causeway; the draining of a salt-marsh; and the gradual closing off of access to a public beach: each in itself seems relatively insignificant yet each such use of the zone closes off other uses, and cumulatively they spell its deterioration. The fact that Canada's population is concentrated along a few key coastlines compounds their effect. In all, our coastlines may be incredibly long but they are subject to intensive use where our populations have clustered.

Major development projects have drawn most attention to the need for coastal zone management. Industrial conglomerations along the Great Lakes and the St. Lawrence have hastened the eutrophication of Lake Erie and created toxicity problems which are gradually finding their way to the fishing grounds of the Gulf of St. Lawrence. The Gulf, too, is affected by the building of hydroelectric dams on its tributary streams. Scientists are still not certain how the climate, the water temperature, and the ecology of the Gulf are affected, but there is no doubt that significant man-induced changes are underway. Similar changes have been noted on the west coast where the Fraser estuary has suffered immensely as a consequence of upstream developments. In the north the protracted debate over offshore drilling continually reminds us of the problems of coastal zone management in that region, problems not dissimilar to those off the east coast. Indeed, twice in the past decade the east coast has suffered dramatically the consequences of poor coastal zone management as first the *Arrow* and then the *Kurdistan* disasters destroyed bird populations, damaged the fishery, and fouled the beaches upon which the tourist industry depends. When we consider both the cumulative effects of small-scale modifications of the zone and the major impact of massive developments, it is impossible to over-emphasize the need for overall planning and co-ordination of coastal zone use: the need for coastal zone management.

Barriers to Effective Management

Our failure in the past to take account of the systemic aspect of our use of the coasts has had much to do with creating the problems which have at last forced us to consider the necessity of "managing" the coastal zone. The existence of a growing appreciation of coastal zone issues at the expert and administrative levels, however, does not mean public policy will necessarily reflect that appreciation. There are several reasons for this, not the least of them being the fact that coastal zone management issues are almost invariably complex, not only in ecological terms but in human terms as well. Run-off following clear cutting along a salmon stream, for example, may affect the migratory patterns of an important fish resource and disrupt a downstream economy. Yet efforts to change logging practices can encounter considerable resistance because they involve the introduction of new logging techniques and perhaps the replacement of costly equipment with labour-intensive selective cutting. Many forest industries accept such changes reluctantly and their resistance is often mirrored in public forestry agencies. The difficulties attending small-scale problems of this sort are magnified any number of times when major developments are at issue. The many disputes over the climatological effects of the James Bay development or the effect on tide levels and wildlife of Fundy tidal power, for example, suggest some of the difficulties to be encountered when the idea of managing the coastal zone is broached.

It is helpful to specify the public policy aspect of these difficulties. Broadly speaking, there are three major factors at play. First, much of the zone has been treated for centuries as a common property resource by a variety of human systems whose complexity rivals that of the ecology of the zone itself. Buttressed by long-standing freedom of access to the resource and by an ideology which rejects government interference, and aware that ameliorative environmental policies will involve short-run costs for most of them, traditional users have resisted a management approach. Thus, for example, the ideology of land – which holds that the ownership of property brings with it the right to use it and dispose of it as one wishes – has stopped short attempts to curtail nonresident ownership and to introduce more effective planning in the coastal zone. Similarly, municipalities and industrial users such as the pulp and paper industry and even fish processors have been extremely slow to install pollution control equipment.

Private sector reluctance is reinforced by the second factor impeding the introduction of a management approach to public policy in the coastal zone. Not only are the interests of users fragmented and often in conflict, but public agencies concerned with the zone are equally fragmented and at loggerheads with one another because each to some extent reflects the concerns of particular clientele. Clamour and discord are more likely than co-ordination and consensus to characterize discussions of coastal zone policy. The problem is compounded by the multiplicity and variety of public agencies which in one way or another administer policies relating to the coastal zone. A Dalhousie University study carried out in 1973-74 identified eight federal and thirty-four provincial agencies in the Atlantic region that have a significant impact on the zone and whose commitment must be secured if genuine coastal zone management is to be achieved.[5] It takes little imagination to appreciate how very difficult it is to secure agreement on coastal management policies when such a varied and extensive group of policy actors must be consulted and persuaded.

The third factor that makes the problem of achieving a coastal zone management policy so intractable is that, even if it were possible to secure a co-ordinative approach within any one government, the difficulties of divided jurisdiction create a formidable barrier to joint federal-provincial action, as current disputes over the management of the fishery testify. As I have suggested elsewhere:

Political divisions do not recognize the ecological unity of the zone, nor that the zone is for the most part a common property. Nor do they neatly divide the multiplicity of human uses to which the zone is put. We observed the practical difficulties of reconciling ecological and political systems in the tortuous international negotiations Canada . . . engaged in to establish a 200-mile management zone. . . . We recognize them as well in the reluctance with which Ottawa and the provinces subordinate their individual claims and aspirations to the needs of a biological system that is differently organized. Since administrative mandates are defined within political jurisdictions, it follows that organizational structures for management must be equally oblivious to the fundamental reality of the zone. Indeed, the functional specialization which is a necessary part of large-scale administration erects still more barriers to ecologically oriented management. In short, the ecological system of the coastal zone is inherently incompatible with the political and administrative structures we have developed to serve social systems. To manage the zone, then, we must find ways of reconciling human systems, particularly administrative structures, with the unyielding realities of nature.[6]

Despite such barriers a debate over the need for a management approach to the coastal zone has developed in Canada, chiefly within those few government agencies whose responsibilities permit an overview of what is happening in the zone. Indeed, the story of the coastal zone management issue in Canada is the story of how an initially small group of individuals located primarily in government have drawn the attention of an ever-expanding group to their concerns about the deterioration of our coastal zones. In the jargon of political science, it is an excellent illustration of how "withinput" sets about creating and mobilizing input demands for specific types of government action. Just how withinput has attempted to achieve this "agenda-setting activity" is the concern of the rest of this discussion.

Withinput: Early Stirrings of Government Concern

In a sense it is misleading to suggest that the broadening interest in coastal zone management has resulted from the missionary work of a small group of officials and scientists. After all, as we have noted, very few coastal problems are new and the trend toward a holistic approach can be seen as a logical outgrowth of the environmentalism now dominant in most federal and provincial departments of the environment. In Canada, at least, the coastal zone seems seldom to have been explicitly referred to during the heyday of the environmental movement. But concern for water pollution ranked very high, and it is hardly surprising that, as government agencies fleshed-out the mandates they were given in the early seventies, they attempted to overcome the barriers to holistic management of "the land/water interface" created by the fact that governments divide responsibilities internally and between one another to accomplish their objectives. Consequently, we can relate the evolution of a concern for coastal zone management to the most basic tenets of environmentalism in general, and to the development of policies for water management in particular. A concern for coastal zone management as a specific aspect of environmental management nevertheless seems to emerge in Canada primarily within the environmental agencies themselves, rather than as a concern expressed by the general public. At most, this governmental concern can be seen as a response to a rather vaguely felt and expressed public concern for coastal pollution and use.

In this, Canada has differed remarkably from the United States. There, a concern for coastal zone management was explicitly articulated as a part of the environmental movement of the late 1960's and early 1970's. As early as 1972 California created, through referendum, a coastal zone conservation commission with very extensive powers, especially in the regulation of land use in coastal areas.[7] In that same year Wood's Hole, Massachusetts, was the site of a major gathering of scientists and public officials who discussed virtually every aspect of the coastal zone management problem as it affected the United States. The published report of the conference, entitled *The Water's Edge*, has been extremely influential in the United States, Canada, and probably elsewhere. At the national level 1972 also saw Congress pass and the President approve a Coastal Zone Management Act which has been described as being rooted in a long-standing concern for the deterioration of the U.S. coastal areas.[8] Though weak, the act subsequently has been an important influence in encouraging broad-based public discussion of coastal zone management issues.[9] In Canada, on the other hand, the only broad-based public forum to address itself to questions of coastal zone management prior to 1978 was a conference held at Mount Allison University in May, 1973. However, even the Mount Allison conference was strongly linked to the four or five governmental units on the east coast which had developed a clear perception of the coastal zone management issue and which then and subsequently have been in the forefront of the debate in Canada.

The earliest explicit reference to Canadian coastal zone management issues seems to have occurred at a meeting of government experts held at Banff in early 1971. They are reported to have discussed problems of recreational land use in coastal areas.[10] This is not to suggest that there are not numerous examples of government activity in the field prior to 1971. In 1970, for example, the director of the Resource Development Branch of the Department of Fisheries and Forestry, K. C. Lucas, emphasized his agency's interest in coastal waters to the House of Commons Special Committee on Environmental Pollution.[11] Two years later the Department of the Environment prepared a forty-eight page partial summary of its activities in the coastal zone.[12] Most of these had been inherited from Fisheries and Forestry and the other agencies that contributed units to the environment department. Similar interest had developed at provincial levels. Nevertheless, the 1971 Banff session does seem to be the first discussion explicitly linked with the concept of the coastal zone in Canada. By late 1971, however, two meetings on the east coast had addressed themselves to two issues closely identified with the coastal zone management issue. At Amherst a group of scientists and administrators from the three Maritime provinces, the federal government, and the universities explored the problem of non-resident land-ownership, a problem that generally has affected coastal areas rather than inland regions.[13] At the same time a group of scientists and officials in the Department of Environment attended a workshop on the Bay of Fundy held by the Marine Sciences Branch of Water Management Services. Its main objective "was to provide some rationale and some guidelines for branch activities in the Bay of Fundy. Out of our discussions we further recognized the need for coastal zone management there as well as consideration of socio-economic issues."[14]

This appears to have been the first truly explicit discussion of coastal zone management, *per se,* in Canadian governmental circles. The fact that the vocabulary of coastal management creeps into discussions at this particular time suggests that the increasing publicity given coastal zone issues in the United States in 1971 and 1972 may have had some effect on the direction of Canadian approaches to coastal problems. At any rate, shortly before the highly regarded Wood's Hole meeting the Atlantic Unit of Environment Canada's Water Management Service held its own seminar on the coastal zone at the Bedford Institute of Oceanography. Though strictly an in-house conference, the seminar reviewed some two dozen papers dealing with a wide variety of concerns related to water management, land-use planning, and fisheries and wildlife administration. About ninety members of the department attended, as well as several observers from the Ministry of Transport and from Energy, Mines and Resources. The meeting was not the sort of session that could be expected to develop major new policies, or even policy guidelines. Rather, its significance lay in the educational function it performed for members of the department and in the fact that a considerable group of officials reached a consensus of sorts concerning the nature of the coastal zone management problem. That consensus has echoed and re-echoed through the subsequent years and still expresses our understanding of the major problem we find in trying to manage the coastal zone.

Basically, the Bedford seminar participants came to the meetings convinced that the coastal environment was suffering from an increasing rate of deterioration and that governments needed to take remedial action through a broad range of policies and programs. Though most were scientists, their discussion of the coastal problems invariably emphasized the social aspects of the zone's management. By the end of the seminar, discussion had focused on three types of problems to be resolved before coastal zone management could be achieved. These were: inadequate scientific information; cumbersome and unsuitable procedural devices creating and implementing coastal zone policy; and the complexity of the jurisdictional issue. The call for better information was inevitable, given the unevenly developed knowledge that was, and still is, available. Information is also seen as a part of the process problem: too often, environment agencies lacked sufficient advance information concerning development plans and so were unable to properly advise policy-makers concerning their feasibility. Again, government and the general public all too often did not understand one another or communicate effectively with each other. But there were other issues as well. The capabilities of the new Department of the Environment were discussed with concern by several workshops. As one workshop reported, of the four "critical functions" related to coastal zone management – information gathering and analysis, enforcement, planning, and management – "it is only in the first that we have clear-cut responsibilities, facilities and resources."[15] Another suggested that a "lead agency," perhaps the Marine Sciences Branch, should be assigned to set the pace in the field.[16]

In considering the last of these three categories of problems the seminar identified a series of difficulties that have dogged the attempt to promote coastal zone management then and now. Several of the background papers referred to jurisdictional problems, but perhaps it was most clearly articulated in a paper by W. N. English which examined competing uses in the Strait of Georgia. As English put it:

Perhaps the most difficult aspect of marine conservation is the co-ordination of the efforts of all the different levels of government, in a situation where their respective jurisdictions are not yet entirely agreed. In the federal-provincial sphere in British Columbia, the relevant existing legislation is contained in not less than seventeen federal and nine provincial acts, of which the most important are those concerning shipping (federal) and fisheries, parks and water (federal and provincial).[17]

The point was re-enforced by one of the workshop reports:

If many of the concerns being expressed about the use and misuse of coastal zone resources are to be resolved, and if the recommendations of environmental impact studies are to be reviewed seriously by jurisdictions empowered to act on them, some modus operandus enabling the involved jurisdictions to work together effectively on resolving coastal zone resource problems is required.[18]

Not all of the activity in this phase of the coastal zone management debate took place at the federal level, nor was it confined to the holding of conferences. In Prince Edward Island, for example, the Canada Water Act provided the federal and provincial governments with an opportunity to develop a joint approach toward coastal zone management in that province. For obvious reasons, Prince Edward Island has a clearly articulated interest in coastal issues and the provincial government seems to have approached this exercise with vigour. In January, 1972, a joint task force, chaired by Stanley Vass of the Prince Edward Island Environmental Control Commission, was assigned to review the Island's coastal zone situation and to recommend short- and long-range projects that would facilitate the management of the coastal areas.[19] By the end of the year, the task force had recommended a two million dollar program of inventory and research. Like so many initiatives of this sort, the proposal was never properly funded.[20] In British Columbia, the Westwater Research Centre was established in 1971 under the auspices of the University of British Columbia with federal financial encouragement. Intended to "make a major contribution to Canadian policy and institutional development within a defined part of the water resources field," the Centre's early interest in the problems of the lower Fraser soon led it to take a prominent part in public discussions of coastal zone issues on the west coast.[21]

Public discussion of environmental issues, including coastal issues, was a major feature of British Columbia's approach to the coastal zone debate.[22] As we have noted, it was much less a feature of development on the east coast. Consequently, the Maritimes Coastal Zone Seminar held at Mount Allison University from May 16-18, 1973, stands out as a virtually unique experience for the east coast. Sponsored by the Nova Scotia Resources Council, the Conservation Council of New Brunswick, and interested persons in New Brunswick, the conference was clearly influenced by the U.S. Wood's Hole conference. In fact, Bostwick Ketchum, editor of the Wood's Hole proceedings, gave the keynote speech. The one hundred or so delegates, drawn from a variety of occupations and interest groups, enunciated a series of recommendations that have characterized east coast discussion of zone problems. Asserting that "the coastal zone is an important national resource and *the* most important asset of the Maritime provinces," the conference suggested to governments that though they had a "considerable amount of human and financial resources already at work on aspects of the problem in the region . . . there is a need for much greater co-ordination, communication and team work, to use these resources more effectively in meeting the problem." In particular they urged that the Maritime Council of Premiers and the federal government appoint a joint Maritime coastal zone planning committee to assist, advise, and to some extent co-ordinate the various governments in carrying out coastal zone measures and to engage in a public information program.[23]

Encouraged by the momentum built up by the Bedford and Mount Allison meetings, Environment Canada officials in Halifax secured authority to commission the Dalhousie Institute of Public Affairs to carry out a study of "the legal and institutional frameworks for coastal zone management in the Atlantic region." The Institute put together a research team consisting of two specialists in resource and ocean law, Douglas M. Johnston and Ian McDougall, biologist Norman C. Dale, and the author, a political scientist. The team set to work in early 1974 to "analyze the legislation, institutions and management practices applicable to the coastal zone of Atlantic Canada; to compare the local situation with coastal zone trends in other countries, and to propose policy recommendations for ways and means of improving the management of the environment and resources of the coastal zone of Atlantic Canada."[24]

The resulting study, published in 1975, recorded a distressing degree of legal and administrative fragmentation in the field, but resisted the temptation to prescribe the creation of a super-agency with co-ordinative powers. This was seen as politically and administratively impractical. Instead, the study proposed creating institutions capable of drawing public and official attention to coastal zone management in the region. It also suggested steps that could be taken to ameliorate the effects of administrative fragmentation in the field. The major source of improvement and change, however, was seen as an attitudinal one. There was an urgent need to achieve a climate of opinion that favours co-operation rather than competition among the agencies involved in coastal zone management.

Because the institutional remedies proposed by the Dalhousie group have generated some debate recently it is worth describing them here. The study proposed the appointment of two coastal zone commissions, one for the Maritimes, the other for Newfoundland and Labrador, because the shore zone concerns of these two regions are very different. They were conceived as intergovernmental co-ordinating and advisory bodies possessing a research capacity and a responsibility for "speaking for, or acting as a kind of Ombudsman for, the coastal zone."[25] Their public information responsibilities would be quite prominent. We proposed that the commissions be composed of appointees representing the federal and provincial governments, plus representatives from local governments, the private sector, and the universities. The commission for the Maritime region would be under the general aegis of the Council of Maritime Premiers. Our terms of reference did not extend to the Quebec portion of the Gulf of St. Lawrence, consequently no reference was made to the inclusion of Quebec officials, in either coastal zone commission, even though Quebec would have to participate in any structure aimed at a comprehensive management of the east coast zone. As for the mandate, we recommended that it be the task of the commission to

... identify, appraise, and articulate the needs of the coastal zone in each region with a view to influencing policy discussions at all three levels of government that have an impact on the coastal zone to gradually create a climate of opinion and practice in which coastal zone management is a reality. Furthermore, it would be the responsibility of the Coastal Zone Commissions to seek to obtain throughout the regions under their jurisdiction a heightened degree of intergovernmental and interagency co-operation in the development and implementation of coastal zone administrative operations.[26]

We hoped that the commissions' work would be facilitated by their involvement in research, advisory, and liaison capacities in the management of special ecological reserves and in the "establishment of a system of designation, whereby a body consisting of representatives of the appropriate federal, provincial, and municipal pollution control agencies would be authorized to bring under a special protective regime any area . . . deemed to be especially vulnerable to a particular type of pollution which [could not] be combatted effectively under the jurisdiction of any one existing agency."[27] Especially important would be their connection to various internal government committees reporting ultimately to a committee of each Cabinet. These would use the coastal zone commissions as an information resource and contact point with other governments and perhaps periodically would exchange staff with the commissions. Several of these committees, and particularly the Cabinet committees, would review coastal zone commission recommendations and annual reports with a view to developing government policy. Helpful though these connections would be, the success of the coastal zone commissions would depend upon their establishing "a pattern of co-operative activity that would convince affected agencies of the soundness of their judgement and the integrity of their intentions."

In the final analysis, the Commissions' authority depends on public opinion, since effective Commissions having the respect of the public can do a great deal to influence public debate on policy issues. In this respect, the Commissions would have something of the authority of the Economic Council of Canada within the coastal zone field. Consequently, it is extremely important, first, that the Commissions receive the support needed to secure for them research capability, both in-house and on contract, in private agencies or government agencies. Secondly, it is important that the Commissions' pronouncements iest on adequate research and careful considerations embracing the opinion, not only of the Commissions' staff and their advisors, but of all agencies potentially affected by Commissions' opinions. Finally, it is important that the range of areas open to Commission inquiry within the field of coastal zone policy not be restricted. Restriction would not only blunt the thrust of Commission opinion, but would reduce both their credibility with the public and their utility to resource management agencies, concerned as they are with an extremely broad range of administrative questions.

. . . The proposed Coastal Zone Commissions can meet the need for a body with an appropriate geographical focus, a mandate to ensure the consideration of the coastal zone's requirements in policy discussions, and the interest in encouraging a heightened co-operation amongst coastal agencies while avoiding the danger of creating yet another agency impelled, through force of circumstances, to compete for scarce financial resources and limited jurisdictional assignments in the field of coastal zone administration.[28]

The structure described here sounds more complex and ambitious than it actually is. In reality, it would provide for zone management the kind of formal structures and policy apparatus common in other sectors. Figure 1 illustrates this point. Commit-

Figure 1: Organization Chart Showing the Possible Relationship Between
the Maritimes Coastal Zone Commission and One of the Provincial Governments

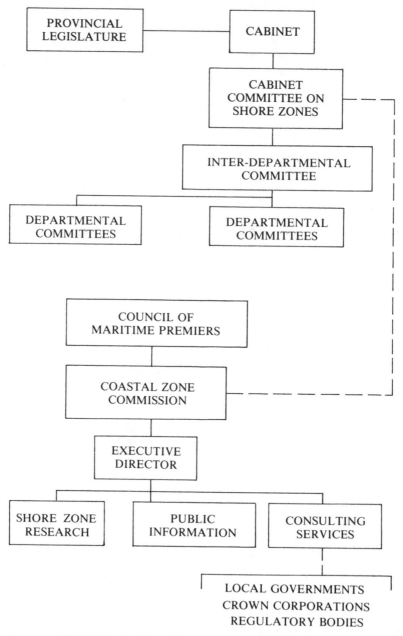

———— = Lines of authority and responsibility

--- = Lines of communication

tee systems within and between departments are commonplace in most policy fields, and a few already exist in the shore zone management field. Thus far, Cabinet committees rarely address themselves to shore zone issues and almost never in a continuing fashion such as would be required of a standing committee. Even with the current heightened interest in shore zone problems, it is unlikely that more than one or two Cabinets would want to establish standing committees of this sort. However, it is not unreasonable to expect more governments to establish standing committees of senior officials, and occasionally special Cabinet committees. As we have noted, the establishment of senior committees would be essential to the success of the coastal zone commissions. Without them, coastal zone commission policy recommendations could not easily be processed by either provincial or federal governments. They are consequently the mundane but essential links in the proposed system. The coastal zone commissions would be composed of appointed representatives participating on a part-time basis. Their staff could be organized along the lines suggested in Figure 1. Not shown, but an important element in the commission-government relationship, would be the many informal links between commission and departmental staff formed in the course of carrying out research and consulting functions.

Some critics of the Dalhousie study[29] have suggested that too much is made of the administrative impediments to a unified structure and that the study runs "headlong into the jurisdictional morass that seems to engulf all management-related activities in the shore zone." Perhaps this is true, but it is interesting to note how many studies of coastal zone management problems have dwelt on this point.[30] Administrative fragmentation was and remains a universal stumbling block to effective shore zone management. Furthermore, any institutional framework for bringing about coastal zone management in the Atlantic region can not succeed unless it is adapted to the reality of political, economic, and administrative fragmentation. The coastal zone commissions we envisaged would not, as critics have suggested, impose a new superstructure on an already complex situation; rather, they would provide a formal and much needed link between existing administrative structures. We should also bear in mind that, in the context of the Atlantic region, a properly run commission system could give the provincial governments the opportunity to pool their resources for hiring staff and obtaining information in this field. Such an opportunity would lessen the strain placed on provincial treasuries if individual agencies were left to develop their own expertise in various research and informal aspects of shoreline management. Similarly, such a pooling of resources would enable the provincial governments to meet the federal government on more equal terms.

Very few of these meetings, studies, and initiatives have led to concrete policy action. They have, however, served to identify a group of individuals – most of them located initially inside government – who either possess or have acquired an interest in the coastal zone management question. An information network has been created which, over time, has aspired to become an integral part of the various policy communities concerned with what are conceived to be coastal zone issues.[31] Just as the Bedford seminar identified interested officials within the Department of the Environment, other meetings like those at Banff, Amherst, and Mount Allison introduced individuals from other levels of government and from the private sector. A few of these, like C. W. Raymond, have played a key role in linking rather diverse elements of the network. Raymond, for example, as director of the Maritimes Resource Management Service, an agency of the Maritime Council of Premiers, was able to move easily across the jurisdictional barriers that often inhibit easy communication between federal and provincial officials. His interest in a variety of resource issues and his stature in the Maritimes government community (he later chaired the Prince Edward Island Royal Commission on non-resident land-ownership, for example) enabled him to link sectors in the network that normally would have had little contact with one another. Thus, he appears to have done a great deal to facilitate communication between officials in Environment Canada concerned with land-use policy in the zone and those in Parks Canada and the provincial agencies who were anxious to resolve the issue of foreign ownership and to work out a parks policy for the shore zone before private developments could forestall public use of key sections of the shore zone.

Administrative Change and the Decline of Momentum

Despite the emergence of the coastal zone network, those who were most intimately involved in forwarding the concept seem to have felt a great deal of discouragement in the period between 1973 and 1977. It was not that there were no advances during this time. In Prince Edward Island, for example, nine provincial and two federal agencies together with a representative committee of

local citizens engaged in an important concept development plan
for the north shore central region.[32] In Nova Scotia the provincial
Cabinet established a land-use committee which explored a
number of issues, including some coastal zone issues,[33] and in 1976
the Nova Scotia government appointed an executive director for
coastal zone management – recognition, at least, that the issue had
some importance. At the federal level the Department of the Environment was putting in place the Federal Environment Assessment and Review Process which, though confined to federally
assisted projects, has "provided the means for monitoring and to
some extent checking unwise coastal zone uses."[34] On the west
coast the various studies of the coastal resource were beginning to
come up with some usable results. The Dalhousie study, too, had
identified major institutional problems and proposed solutions.
The publication of these and other studies was broadening the base
of public discussion of coastal zone issues.

However, these advances seemed to be not enough to offset an
accumulation of setbacks elsewhere. As we have noted, the joint
Canada-P.E.I. Inventory and Research proposal petered out. A
similar proposal for a "coastal resource and inventory mapping
program for the Maritime provinces and Newfoundland" failed to
receive funding from the Department of Regional and Economic
Expansion. The Dalhousie study elicited no response from Environment Canada or provincial agencies for more than a year
after its publication in 1975. Overshadowing all of these successes
and failures, however, was a decision taken in January, 1973, to
dismantle the Water Management Service of the Department of
the Environment. Created only two years earlier, with the foundation of the department, the Service had amalgamated elements of
the Marine Service of the former Department of Fisheries and
Forestry and the Inland Waters Branch of Energy, Mines and
Resources. It had taken the lead in "developing a departmental
view of coastal zone management and [had] established a departmental committee on coastal waters [which] built upon a series of
activities carried out by the Water Management Service and
directed towards establishing policies for the effective management of the coastal zone. These included in particular the Bedford
Seminar on the Coastal Zone . . . which focused departmental
concern and assisted considerably in giving some direction to the
pattern of policy development in the field."[35]

Dissolution of the Service halted the building of a consensus on
the coastal zone issue; it dispersed a major part of the network
which had been formed and discouraged many of those who had

thought that the build-up of research activities and small programs was gradually leading to the creation of a Canadian coastal zone policy. A number of individuals who had been active in the field left it at this point.

The internal problems of the federal Department of the Environment, though important, were by no means the most significant barrier to the evolution of a coastal zone policy. Far more important was the jurisdictional issue at the intergovernmental level. As we have seen, its significance had been noted at the Bedford seminar. The Mount Allison conference had been very critical of the fact that the sum of discrete federal and provincial policies affecting the coastal zone "is a coastal zone policy which is neither consistent nor comprehensive." That conference demanded "an integrated coastal zone policy for the Maritimes" and the evolution of "a workable set of mechanisms for coastal zone management."[36] As the abortive proposal for an Atlantic region resource mapping program put it:

Too often the interface between land and sea has been used to divide jurisdictional and administrative responsibilities, producing anachronous coastal planning and development. Rather than producing a symbiosis of provincial and federal management, the coastal boundary line between land and water has produced a 'no-man's' land.[37]

The research group at Dalhousie discovered the extent of the jurisdictional division: since their research had been sponsored by the federal department some provincial officials refused to co-operate. Inevitably, the subsequent report stressed the importance of the jurisdictional issue and proposed institutional frameworks for achieving co-ordinated, if not unified, coastal zone policies.[38] Even so, the intractability of the jurisdictional problem has frequently been cited as the reason for a lack of government action on the report's proposals.

As well as being discouraged by the internal organizational problems of the Department of the Environment and by the extent of the jurisdictional problem, proponents of coastal zone management felt that their urgings and suggestions were falling into a vast pit of indifference at the national level. One of the bitter realities of Canadian politics is that if an issue cannot be made to seem significant as far as central Canada is concerned, then it makes very little headway achieving a place on the national public agenda. The coastal zone management issue is a case in point. Even though initiatives had developed on the east and west coasts and major, though different, questions had emerged in the north, the issues seemed to arouse very little interest at senior levels in Ottawa and Toronto, or even in Quebec City. Unfortunately, given the nature of the issue, significant policy action would have to come at the national level. For these and other reasons, by 1976 the prospects for a coastal zone management policy seemed exceedingly dim.

Revival: Putting the Debate on a Broader Base

Nevertheless, a new initiative did materialize, this time from the west coast and from the recreation and conservation sector rather than from the water management sector that had been so influential in the east. Lloyd Brooks, Deputy Minister of the British Columbia Department of Recreation and Conservation, had conducted a cross-Canada survey of coastal zone conditions in 1975 and by 1976 was ready to urge the Canadian Council of Resource and Environment Ministers (CCREM) to sponsor a national seminar on coastal zone issues. In addition to tackling the CCREM itself, Brooks also brought his case to the 1976 Federal-Provincial Parks Conference because, while parks agencies are not in the forefront of coastal zone users, their particular interest in the coastal zone, its use and preservation, has made them fairly prominent in the coastal zone debate. Brooks argued that "we are now faced with the shocking situation in this young country of ours where in many regions recreational shorelines of the right type in the right place are in very short supply and public access is severely limited. Also, much of that richest of all land and water areas, our estuaries, have been abused beyond recovery."[39] The conference agreed to look more closely at the problems and prospects of coastal zone parks at its 1977 meeting. Similarly, the CCREM proved responsive. As Brooks told the 1976 parks conference, "I think I was able to convince them that there really was not very much being done except on a rather localized basis and that nowhere in Canada is there any effective shore zone management legislation."[40] The council agreed to permit Brooks and his colleagues to present a one-day technical session at its June, 1977, meeting, with a view to convincing the Ministers of the need for a special CRREM-sponsored conference on the subject at a later date.[41]

The technical session also proved successful, perhaps because the federal government had recognized the need for an official who could speak for the interests of the coastal zone and had appointed a national coastal zone co-ordinator, J. G. Michael Parkes. Perhaps, too, because Brooks succeeded in giving coastal zone issues a "national" salience by adopting the term "shore zone" in order, as a long-time participant in the debate suggested, "to gain better support for the desired new approach to coastal resource management."[42] Whether or not the influential central provinces were convinced by the argument that they, too, possessed coastal problems, the council agreed to sponsor a major shore management symposium at Victoria in October, 1978.

The symposium perhaps marks a new stage in the coastal zone management debate. In particular, public involvement was encouraged for the first time. In the past, individual participants in the discussion had urged the importance of public involvement. Raymond, for example, in 1976 had pointed out that

Of overriding importance to the solution of these problems is an increased awareness both within government and amongst the general public with respect to the coastal zone and its problems. Ignorance of the coast and its importance continues to be the root cause of most of its problems. Unless professionals involved in coastal studies are successful in publicizing their work and their concerns, and making their information available in forms that are useful and understandable to decision makers, solutions are likely to be ill-conceived or unattainable.[43]

Others, too, had argued that little could be done to put coastal zone management in place unless there was broad public understanding and support, but thus far, particularly on the east coast, the public's role had been very limited. With its agreement that one of the objectives of the symposium should be to "focus national attention on Canada's shore areas as sensitive and complex human and natural resources,"[44] CCREM gave proponents of coastal zone management the strongest support they had yet received for placing the issue on the public agenda. In analytical terms, this objective suggested that the process of policy development had gone about as far as it could within government circles. To go further, the issue would require external, public endorsement. Withinput would have to be buttressed by input.

It is too early to tell whether or not the Victoria symposium achieved this objective. Certainly a considerable effort was made. In several provinces elaborate briefings and preliminary discussions took place; equally elaborate post mortems were also held. For many of those attending–nineteen from each province, twenty-five from the Government of Canada and the Territories–it was their first exposure to the debate. Since most non-governmental delegates were chosen because they were representative of both special interest groups and geographic areas, there is some reason to believe that the conference may have achieved part of its goal of diffusing coastal zone concepts more broadly through the population.

Whether the symposium will have a more immediate policy impact is much less certain. For the moment, perhaps, we can expect proposals such as the Dalhousie group's proposal for coastal zone commissions to receive a sympathetic hearing, but given the financial constraints of the present period and widespread suspicion of any sort of administrative expansion it is unlikely that such schemes will be implemented in the near future. We probably can expect to see some further co-ordination at the federal interdepartmental level, but intergovernmental co-ordination will depend on the reaction of individual governments to the report of the Victoria meeting, which at the time of writing had not yet been released. In October, 1979, Ottawa and British Columbia signed a two-year agreement covering the preparation of a management plan for the Fraser estuary. In general, we probably will see the continued piecemeal elaboration of the coastal policies and programs of individual governments on a sectoral basis, despite the need for government-wide policies concerning coastal land and water use. Even these steps, however, can produce in aggregate an impressive body of policy, as a recent review suggests.[45] To go further governments will need the kind of public understanding and participation that the Victoria symposium aimed for.

In the meanwhile, the coastal zone management debate teeters on the lowest rungs of the public agenda. At the Victoria symposium the Honourable Len Marchand declared that "the federal government recognizes the critical importance of the shore zone for economic, environmental and social reasons. We have, as a result, a strong interest in promoting its orderly, long-range development."[46] It will take an effort on the part of individuals within and outside government surpassing that which has gone before to translate that recognition into a generally acceptable system of coastal zone management for Canada.

NOTES

1. Bostwick H. Ketchum (ed.), *The Water's Edge: Critical Problems of the Coastal Zone* (Cambridge, Mass., 1972), 254. The discussion in question took place at Wood's Hole, Mass., May-June, 1972.
2. Adapted from Douglas M. Johnston, A. Paul Pross, and Ian McDougall, with Norman G. Dale, *Coastal Zone: Framework for Management in Atlantic Canada* (Halifax: Dalhousie Institute of Public Affairs for Environment Canada, 1975), 151.
3. Timothy O'Riordan, *Perspectives on Resource Management* (London, 1971), 19.
4. G. E. Beanlands, "Coastal Problems in Canada: A Case Study Approach," paper presented to Canadian Council of Resource and Environment Ministers, Shore Management Symposium, Victoria, B.C., October 4-5, 1978, pp. 31-2. Ketchum (ed.), *The Water's Edge*, presents an extensive survey of the problems that occur in the coastal zone. Most of them are to be found in Canada as well as in the United States.
5. For a detailed chart listing these agencies and their functional areas, see Johnston *et al.*, *Coastal Zone: Framework for Management*, 58.
6. "Atlantic Canada: Conditions and Prospects for Coastal Zone Management," in Bruce Mitchell (ed.), *Institutional Arrangements for Water Management: Canadian Experiences*, University of Waterloo, Department of Geography Publication Series No. 5 (Waterloo, Ont., 1975), 213.
7. See E. Jack Schoop, "Coastal Zone Plan Implementation," *Journal of the Urban Planning & Development Division. Proceedings of the American Society of Civil Engineers*, Vol. 104, No. UPI (May, 1978).
8. See Zigurds L. Zile, "A Legislative-Political History of the Coastal Zone Management Act of 1972," *Coastal Zone Management Journal*, 1 (1974), 235-74.
9. See, for example, James H. Purinton and Allen H. Miller, "Wisconsin's Citizens Think About Their Coast," paper presented to Coastal Zone 78 Conference, San Francisco, March, 1978.
10. The following chronology was developed from several sources, but notably from Lloyd Brooks, "The Shore Zone," paper presented to Federal-Provincial Parks Conference, 1976; Canada, Department of the Environment, Water Management Service, Atlantic Unit, *Coastal Zone: Proceedings of a Seminar held at Bedford Institute of Oceanography, March, 1972*, 2 vols. (Ottawa, 1972) – hereafter cited as *Bedford Seminar*; C. W. Raymond, "The Role of Government in Realizing the Potential of the Coastal Zone," paper presented to Institute of Public Administration of Canada, 1976; Johnston *et al.*, *Coastal Zone: Framework for Management*.
11. House of Commons Special Committee on Environmental Pollution, *Minutes of Proceedings and Evidence*, June 23, 1970, p. 3:17.
12. See *Bedford Seminar*.
13. Kell Antoft, "Interventionist Pressures in a Pragmatic Society: A Policy

Study of the Non-Resident Land Ownership Issue in Nova Scotia 1969-1977,'' M.A. thesis, Dalhousie University, 1977. Although the meeting had a greater impact on the debate over non-resident land-ownership than on the discussion of the broader coastal zone issue, it was significant as one of a series of meetings which brought together a group of officials and scientists who came to share a view of the need for some form of coastal zone management in the Atlantic region.

14. K. B. Yuen, "Some Socio-Economic Aspects of Coastal Pollution in Canada," in *Bedford Seminar*, I, 102.

15. *Bedford Seminar*, II, 24.

16. *Ibid.*, 22.

17. "Use Conflict in Marine Conservation: The Strait of Georgia," *Bedford Seminar*, I, 35.

18. *Ibid.*, II, 37.

19. See Canada-Prince Edward Island Consultative Committee on Water, Task Force on the Coastal Zone, *Report* (Charlottetown, 1973).

20. See Brooks, "The Shore Zone," p. 4.

21. See *Westwater Notes*, vols. 1- , 1972- , for a running commentary on Westwater's activities.

22. Diane Draper has effectively conveyed this aspect of the debate in "Environmental Interest Groups and Institutional Arrangements in British Columbia Water Management Issues," in Mitchell (ed.), *Institutional Arrangements for Water Management*, 119-70.

23. See Maritimes Coastal Zone Seminar, *Proceedings and Recommendations* (Halifax, 1973), 1, 2.

24. Johnston *et al.*, *Coastal Zone: Framework for Management*, vii.

25. *Ibid.*, 161.

26. *Ibid.*, 162.

27. *Ibid.*, 153.

28. *Ibid.*, 162-3.

29. G. E. Beanlands, "The Coastline of Atlantic Canada: A Diagnosis," background paper presented to Canadian Council of Resource and Environmental Ministers, Saskatoon, Sask., June 2, 1977.

30. See, for example, Ketchum (ed.), *The Water's Edge*, 215; Robert L. Bish *et al.*, *Coastal Resource Use: Decisions on Puget Sound* (Seattle, 1975), 66; The Canadian Committee for MAB, Canada MAB Report #7, Sub-program 3, *Coastal Eco-systems Research Framework* (Ottawa, 1976), 2, 7; and the report entitled *Coastal Management: The Marine Shorelands of the Capital Region* (Victoria: Capital Region District Planning Department), 12, which emphasizes the need for an administrative framework to facilitate the coordination of federal, provincial, and local responsibilities over marine shorelands.

31. A policy community consists of those government agencies concerned with a particular policy field together with their attentive publics. These latter include institutions, pressure groups, specific interests, and individuals – including academics and journalists – who are affected by or interested in the policies of specific agencies and make it their own business to follow and attempt to influence those policies.

32. Raymond, "The Role of Government," pp. 15-16.

33. *Ibid.*, pp. 14-15.

34. Beanlands, "Coastal Problems in Canada," p. 19.

35. Johnston *et al.*, *Coastal Zone: Framework for Management*, 67. The deci-

sion to divide the Service was part of a major reorganization of the Department. It is described in Johnston *et al.*, 61-70.
36. Maritimes Coastal Zone Seminar, *Proceedings*.
37. DREE, *A Proposal for a Coastal Resources Inventory and Mapping Program for the Maritime Provinces and Newfoundland presented to Dept. of Regional Economic Expansion* (Mimeo, January, 1974, preliminary draft).
38. See Johnston *et al.*, *Coastal Zone: Framework for Management*, chapters V and VII.
39. Brooks, "The Shore Zone," p. 2.
40. *Ibid.*, p. 3.
41. Brooks to author, November 26, 1976.
42. H. Mills, in *Proceedings of the 16th Federal-Provincial Parks Conference St. John's, Nfld., Oct. 3-7, 1977* (St. John's: Department of Tourism, 1978), 28.
43. Raymond, "The Role of Government," p. 5.
44. CCREM Shore Management Symposium. Presentation of the . . . Steering Committee to CCREM Executive Committee, January 23-24, 1978, p. 2.
45. J. C. Day and J. G. Michael Parkes, "Canadian Freshwater Lake-and Marine-Shore Areas: Uses and Management," paper presented to Canadian Council of Resource and Environment Ministers, Victoria, B.C., October 4-5, 1978.
46. "Notes for a Speech" CCREM, Shore Management Symposium, Victoria, B.C., October 5, 1978, p. 2.

CHAPTER FIVE

James Bay Project:
Environmental Assessment in the
Planning of Resource Development

by Robert Paehlke

The chill of autumn, 1979, saw a gradual beginning for Quebec: the official opening of the huge LG-2 dam, the first phase of the James Bay Project. The intense protest that was the chief focus of attention for the Canadian environmental movement in the early 1970's is now only rarely recalled. The James Bay Project was central in the shift of that movement's concerns from pollution to a more multi-dimensional concern with the broad and complex interrelationships between economy and ecology. The project and the objections that arose at its initiation were also significant in the development in Canada of an important administrative and planning tool: environmental and social impact assessment. This chapter seeks to reconstruct the events that took place and to analyse their meaning and importance.

The Project Emerges

The James Bay Project was made public by Premier Robert Bourassa on April 29, 1971, in a speech to a meeting of the Quebec Liberal Party. It was launched with music and multiple-screen visuals, and the words "The world begins today" echoed through the large arena. Beneath the partisan and political nature of the public birth of the James Bay Project lies a conception which may well have been equally political in both its nature and its timing. In 1970 Premier Bourassa had campaigned primarily on a stated intention to create 100,000 jobs for a Quebec economy that lagged badly behind those of Ontario and the Western provinces. By the spring of 1971 his government had gone through the trauma of the FLQ kidnappings and the declaration of the War Measures Act by the federal government. Few commentators felt that the Bourassa Liberals had come through that crisis well. The mood in Quebec at the time of the James Bay announcement is expressed well in an assessment in the *Financial Times of Canada* that, "beset by a rising tide of unemployment and a dearth of new business investment, Premier Bourassa unveiled the James Bay Project as a bold new drive to create jobs and promote economic growth."[1] The Bourassa government was seeking to recapture initiative, to appear decisive, upbeat, and dynamic.

The project itself was nothing if not bold and massive. It entailed the expenditure of $6 billion on a complex of hydroelectric, road, airport, mining, forestry, and tourist development. The centrepiece of the proposal involved the ultimate development of the hydroelectric power potential of at least eight previously unutilized rivers: the Nottaway, Rupert, and the Broadback in the southern portion of the project area and the Eastmain, La Grande, Kanaaupscow, Great Whale, and Opinaca in the north. The province's total electric-power production would be increased by fifty per cent or more. Thousands of square miles of land would be submerged under man-made lakes and the total area encompassed by the project would be some 133,000 square miles, an area larger than Great Britain. $200 million would be spent on 600 miles of roads, the longest of them heading 300 miles north from Matagami, a town itself 350 miles due north of Ottawa.

Clearly the project's political possibilities could not be realized unless it was also seen to make economic sense. To demonstrate the viability of the project three engineering studies were made public at about the time of Premier Bourassa's announcement. The first, by engineers at Hydro-Quebec, concluded, in reference to the southern phase of the project, that "the cost of producing energy [from nuclear plants] would be greater than the evaluation of the cost of the NBR complex."[2] The second study, by Rousseau, Sauvé, Warren et Associés, a Quebec consulting engineering firm, concluded similarly: "the cost of energy [from James Bay] at Montreal will be lower than that provided by thermal or nuclear energy."[3] The final study, by Asselin, Benoît, Boucher, Ducharme, and La Pointe, also consulting engineers, rejected nuclear and thermal plants as options, in large part because they felt that "pollution problems [would] render these solutions more and more complex"[4] and thereby relatively more costly. This third study also estimated that 45,000 on-site jobs would be created at the peak of construction, and that direct and indirect employment levels would see up to 138,000 jobs created by the project. These figures were later called into question, as were the overall relative-cost conclusions of all three studies.

An appreciation of the significance of the James Bay Project can be greatly enhanced by a brief look at recent Quebec history. Prior to the Quiet Revolution, Quebec could have been fairly characterized as a society that was rural-centred or at least rural-yearning, deeply religious or at least church-dominated. Until the early 1960's the Quebec economy was, by North American standards, backward; its politics, particularly in the Duplessis era, was characterized by rabid anti-communism, a bucolic mythology, an inward-looking nationalism, and corruption.[5] The situation began to alter with the rise of the Quebec Liberal Party under Jean Lesage in the early 1960's. Quebeckers came to realize that during World War II and its aftermath Quebec had become an urban and industrialized society. There was a rapid transformation of the French-language educational system, from an emphasis on classical and professional training to an acceleration in learning business and technical skills: engineering, accounting, and other first-order needs of a technological society.[6]

The Lesage campaign of 1961 focused in large part on the issue of taking over the private power companies of Quebec. The Lesage Liberals came to power and moved quickly on their promise. The new Minister of Natural Resources, one René Lévesque, oversaw the takeover which occurred in 1962, many decades after the creation of Ontario Hydro by Sir Adam Beck. Top dollar was paid to the owners of the private utilities and the bulk of the money for the purchase was borrowed from New York banks. The Quiet Revolution was neither decidedly socialist nor thoroughly nationalist in character; the creation of a large publicly-owned utility monopoly in Hydro-Quebec was rather the basis for the further industrial development of Quebec in the context of an integrated North American economy. But whatever the character of the transformation that took place in the 1960's, the creation of Hydro-Quebec and the rapid development of Quebec's electrical energy resources may well have been as central to the transformation as were the changes related to language and culture. And the two forms of change have been linked in many ways through the years: from the popularity in Quebec of a song, "La Manic," about the massive

Manicouagan power project, to the fact that Hydro-Quebec is by far the province's largest French-speaking employer.

Consideration of the development of James Bay rivers at Hydro-Quebec also began in the early 1960's. One 1964 study indicated it would not be possible to develop the area before the late 1970's. Nevertheless, throughout the rest of the decade field engineering studies went on within the utility and in 1967 Hydro-Quebec president Jean-Claude Lessard reported to the Quebec parliamentary committee on Crown corporations that the development of the James Bay rivers would be the corporation's next major project, though he did not establish a date. Little was heard of the project from that time until Premier Bourassa's 1971 announcement. Retrospective constructions have indicated that the Premier was in New York in September, 1970, attending to the financing of the project and that the Quebec cabinet was making a decision to go ahead in November, 1970, the October Crisis having occurred in the interim.[7]

After the announcement of April 29, 1971, the scene of events shifted to a more orthodox locale for major public policy decisions: the Quebec National Assembly. The Assembly debate, described by journalists in terms like "fierce" and "intense," centred primarily around Bill 50 – a bill which created the James Bay Development Corporation (JBDC) and five subsidiary companies.[8] The opposition, consisting of the badly weakened Union Nationale and the rapidly strengthening but as yet disunited indépendantistes, raised many questions. Premier Bourassa, however, arguing urgency, rushed the bill through the National Assembly in June, 1971. The JBDC was granted sweeping powers of expropriation, was seemingly exempted from regulations protecting natural resources (in Section 42 of the bill), and in effect was made the appointed government of the James Bay region, an area equal to one-fifth of the province.[9]

The opposition argued that the costs of James Bay power would be far higher than the costs of power from either Churchill Falls or Manicouagan. It was also argued that money invested in manufacturing would create ten direct jobs for each direct job created by an equal investment in hydroelectric power.[10] But the government often did not reply in detail; it merely fell back on its clear majority.

M. Pierre Nadeau, former vice-president for business development of IAC, Ltd., was appointed President and Chairman of the Board of JBDC and President of the James Bay Energy Corporation (JBEC). Nadeau was not an engineer and had no previous familiarity with hydroelectric projects. The corporation had 1,000 mining claims to process and it very shortly thereafter called for tenders on $60 million worth of access roads and airports for the remote James Bay region. The construction of access roads only made sense if one assumed project construction would proceed soon thereafter.

Although the government had released three favourable engineering studies, Hydro-Quebec authorized at least one further investigation. In June, 1971, Lionel Cahill, general manager of engineering, commissioned a study of relative costs to be done by United Engineers and Constructors, Inc., of Philadelphia. The study was completed in August, 1971, but neither its existence nor its results became known until the report was leaked in February, 1972. This report indicated that the costs of nuclear energy might well be lower than James Bay energy. The press made a considerable issue of this matter, and in May, 1972, the Montreal *Gazette* reported that Roger Warren, the author of a report which dismissed nuclear energy as a viable alternative, would not specify which nuclear system – Canadian or American – his firm had studied. Nuclear energy is nuclear energy, Warren claimed.[11] Essentially, the whole question of relative direct costs rested on an array of assumptions regarding general inflation, wage inflation, oil costs, and technological evolution. Few consulting firms made their assumptions public and no cost estimates have turned out to have been accurate.

Assessing Environmental and Social Impacts

The James Bay engineering studies of the 1960's did not encompass environmental considerations. Neither the announcement of the project nor the debate over Bill 50 mentioned environmental impacts. Technical and engineering feasibility, economic viability, and political impact were undoubtedly discussed at many levels from many points of view prior to and after the James Bay decision was made. But potential ecological, climatological, and social impacts seem not to have played a significant role in the decision-making process in either Hydro-Quebec or the Bourassa government. No environmental review was begun until July, 1971, though clearly vegetation, fish, animals, and birds will be affected both upstream and downstream from the dams and containment areas.

The major food fish of the James Bay region are littoral spawners; they lay their eggs in the shallow areas near the shore. The new inshore areas created by the flooding will be far less reliable as spawning grounds because water levels will fluctuate considerably as water is drawn down to produce power:

> Eggs of fall spawning whitefish, lake char, and brook trout will be exposed to freezing or drying by changing levels in the shallow water. Essential sources of food for larger fish, the shiners and minnows, often spawn in spring and early summer in the same inshore area.[12]

In a northern climate such as that of the James Bay region, restabilization of fish populations will be slow, taking perhaps 25-30 years – and that restabilization will be at lower levels for many species. Animal species also depend on water levels, especially in marsh areas. Moose need submerged plants as summer feed. Beaver and muskrat need stable water levels to protect lodges and burrows. Caribou migration patterns also will be affected and populations are almost certain to decline. In addition, the James Bay region provides the summer feeding and breeding grounds for many species of migratory birds, including Canada, Snow, and Blue Geese. As much as 25 per cent of the total population of some species summer in the region affected by the project. These bird species, too, are dependent on the vegetation of the near shore regions for food supply and nesting sites.

Additional serious environmental damage will result from the fact that trees will not likely be cleared from areas to be flooded. This will result in the waste of an estimated 15 million cords of black spruce. Drowned forests, particularly in cold waters, take sixty or more years to decay and throughout that period place a large BOD on the water ecosystem. A more gradual pace of development might allow for the economic use of this resource.

Finally, many experts suspect that the James Bay Project ultimately could affect the climate of an area far larger than the James Bay region. The water temperature in James Bay and Hudson Bay is related to the rate of fresh-water flow. The date of ice break-up is dependent on fresh water from the rivers – reduced flow could mean delayed break-up. This in turn might alter climatic conditions. Dr. Lloyd M. Dickie of the Bedford Institute suggested that longer winters and greater snowfalls are possible in Ontario, Quebec, and the Maritimes. Vegetation limits in the Hudson Bay region are already delicately balanced and studies have shown that slight differences in annual temperature have shifted the treeline almost 180 miles in the last 900 years.[13]

All in all, it might be said that northern ecosystems are fragile indeed. They are much like those of deserts; they are less diverse and correspondingly less adaptable than are temperate-zone ecosystems. Species have few options: if their regular food supply is altered, they decline or disappear. Everything that exists is in fine tune and any change in water, climate, or life forms is a severe change. It is difficult indeed for humans to tread lightly in such regions, and when we fail even to try our impact is doubtless severe.

Few who defend the environment do so for self-interested economic motives. They see themselves as defenders of the long-term general interest of both humanity and nature. Such an intention is something which, until the late 1960's, was uncommon in the day-to-day political process of developed economies. It is also something very difficult to demonstrate – its values and claims are less easily quantified than those that normally enter political discourse. When decisions are made on an issue-by-issue, project-by-project basis, the assertions of environmentalists can easily seem petty to hard-headed political and economic decision-makers, those individuals whom society expects and pays to balance interests and resolve differences. By way of compensation for this disadvantage, environmental interest groups may at times seem enormously self-assured regarding their cause and even self-righteous in their presentation of it. The James Bay Project was in many ways a classic example of such environmental politics.

The environmentalist cause was championed by the James Bay Committee, a small number of Montreal activists with a larger number of supporters and sympathizers throughout Canada and the United States. This committee variously described itself as being "affiliated with"[14] or having "the support of"[15] ten to twenty other major organizations. Included in this list were the major Quebec environmental organizations, the major Quebec nature and conservation organizations, many environmental organizations of regional or national scope, the major Quebec native peoples groups, and several anti-poverty or pro-employment groups. Conspicuously absent from the list were any business, civic, government, or labour organizations.

The James Bay Committee came into being in the autumn of 1971, asked the government to hold public hearings on the project, and requested copies of all government-commissioned taxpayer-funded studies and reports related to the James Bay Project.

Neither request was granted. By January, 1972, the committee had commissioned and received its own ecological study of the project written by J. A. and G. C. Spence.[16] The report was thorough though prepared without time or opportunity for extensive field work.

In March, 1972, the committee produced a position paper covering the political, economic, energy, legal, environmental, and social aspects of the project. This paper was distributed widely – for example, to the 75,000 members of the Quebec Wildlife Federation – and was published elsewhere.[17] In May, 1972, the James Bay Committee requested that it be allowed to present its views to parliamentary hearings being held in Quebec City. The request was denied. In July, 1972, the committee produced a forty-page booklet entitled *James Bay: Progress or Disaster?* The booklet called for a halt to all development activities in the region, including road building, until (1) thorough economic, environmental, and social studies were done and published; (2) the government held public hearings throughout the province; and (3) the native people of the James Bay area gave their free consent to the project. The committee also attempted to link itself with other recent environmentalist successes – the Spadina Expressway in Toronto, the Everglades Airport in Florida, the Ramparts Canyon Dam in the Yukon, and the South Indian Lake Project in Manitoba.[18] In every forum available, it attempted to remind the public of the severe negative ecological effects of other projects, especially the 1967 W.A.C. Bennett dam on the Peace River of British Columbia.

Unable to get public-sponsored hearings, the James Bay Committee held hearings of its own in Montreal in April, 1973. Witnesses came from throughout Canada and from New York State; a large majority were English-speaking. Included among the witnesses were Michel Chartrand, the Quebec labour leader, two federal Members of Parliament, and a representative of the Canadian Labour Congress. Notably absent, though scheduled to appear until the last minute, was Jacques Parizeau on behalf of the Parti Québécois. In conjunction with native people's groups the committee held major fund-raising events attended by thousands; it also ultimately published the full proceedings of the hearing as a book.[19] The hearings and many of the committee's earlier efforts were well-covered by both the print and electronic media, yet the efforts of the committee, in spite of their thoroughness, were most notable for their utter lack of impact on the decision-making process.

Environmental Impact Assessment: An Afterthought

Environmental Impact Assessment (EIA) in one form or another is now the normal course of action in many North American political jurisdictions. But the James Bay Project was announced in the same year that the federal Department of the Environment was created, the year after the passage of the U.S. Natural Environment Protection Act (NEPA). NEPA required the use of EIA on a national basis for the first time. Canadian jurisdictions have been much slower to accept the wisdom of this procedure than their American counterparts. In the early seventies in Quebec there apparently was no consciousness of the meaning and usefulness of such procedures in the upper echelons of government.

Estrin and Swaigen define EIA and identify its intended purpose as follows:

An environmental impact assessment is a study of the effects that a program, project or other undertaking might have on the natural and human environment. . . . Its purpose is to discover the problems an undertaking might cause before a firm decision has been made to go ahead with it at any cost.[20.]

EIA is designed to bring to light hidden environmental and social costs, *prior* to a decision on whether and how a given project is to proceed. EIA attempts to determine whether or not any of these costs might be prevented or ameliorated, and, if such costs are unavoidable, to decide whether they are outweighed by the potential benefits. The whole logic of EIA is preventative; it seeks to avoid both excessive corrective and remedial costs and irretrievable damage.

Effective EIA is always an expensive procedure. It requires exhaustive on-site investigations of ecology, extensive research regarding similar proposals, public hearings that seek to hear expert testimony on behalf of both proponents and opponents, and an intelligent integration of economic, ecological, social, and other viewpoints. The Berger Inquiry into the proposed Mackenzie Valley pipeline is a classic study of the potential environmental and social impacts of a large-scale project.[21] The pipeline was proposed not long after the James Bay Project; the public inquiry cost several million dollars, was highly visible, and took two years to complete. The EIA outcome altered the project but did not reject the construction of a pipeline.

In sharp contrast to that style of proceeding, the major environmental study for James Bay, a joint federal-provincial effort, was launched in July, 1971, three months after it was announced that the project would proceed. In August, 1971, the task force was given the final details of its terms of reference. Hydro-Quebec spokesman Andre Langlois told the scientists that "time constraints would not allow a detailed study."[22] No field studies of any kind were carried out. No public hearings were held at any time. No contact was made with outside experts. The total budget for the study was $30,000, some .0001 per cent (one one-millionth) of the now-estimated ultimate cost of the La Grande portion of the project. The federal and provincial scientists produced their report in early February (shortly after the JBC produced theirs).

The report itself is critical of the procedures under which the EIA was carried out, and states that "Engineering studies on the James Bay project began many years ago, but this task force was not established until after mid-1971. . . . environmental studies should be initiated much earlier – in effect, concurrent with engineering planning."[23] Weeks before the EIA was completed all but one road contract had been let and work was proceeding at an incredibly rapid and expensive pace. For example, it was reported in early March, 1972, that up to twenty-two supply helicopters were operating and were down only for darkness and servicing.[24]

Substantively, the report concluded that the only "potentially alarming" impact would be on native peoples. It reported potential negative effects of flooding and draw-down on fish, animal, and bird populations and recommended the clearing of trees and brush before flooding. One of the report's major conclusions is curious, urging that "the James Bay project be used as a large-scale natural laboratory for comprehensive multi-disciplinary research into environmental problems and studies of how ecological processes are modified by major developments at these latitudes."[25] What in effect was proposed was making a laboratory of roughly one quarter of the province of Quebec.

Native Peoples

The proposed James Bay Project was not only environmentally problematic, it was socially problematic as well, a potential threat to every means of livelihood available to the 6,000 people living in the region. The Cree Indians were long-established when Henry Hudson sailed into James Bay in 1611. They have lived with and managed the ecology of the region for centuries. Living within nature's bounds in a harsh climate for such a long period of time demonstrates that, for them, hunting and fishing are more than means of earning a living. They constitute a way of life. Their whole culture and consciousness is bound up with a particular place. For the Cree, environmental impacts and social impacts are inseparable.

Underlying the impact of the James Bay Project on the native peoples is a legal history. In 1912 the government of Canada passed an act which allowed for the incorporation of certain lands of the Hudson's Bay Company into the Province of Quebec. A huge portion of present-day Quebec passed to the province on the condition that it reach agreement with the native peoples of the region. The status of the territory thus remained ambiguous until the time of the James Bay Project. A Commission of Inquiry under Judge Henri Dorion established that the native peoples had "real and incontestable rights" over the huge tracts of land in question, perhaps a quarter of the province. Negotiations ensued directly, but in April, 1972, the talks were broken off with the province and announcement was made that the native peoples, represented by the Indians of Quebec Association and the Northern Quebec Inuit Association, would proceed to seek an injunction to halt the project. At this time the Indians also issued an appeal to federal Indian Affairs Minister Jean Chrétien to intervene. In May the provincial government, seeming to reverse itself, announced that it would proceed first with the La Grande portion of the project rather than the NBR portion. Premier Bourassa mentioned that fewer native people would be affected by that portion of the project.

Court proceedings were formally launched in December, 1972, before Superior Court Judge Albert Malouf. The JBDC was represented by C. Antoine Geoffrion, a partner in the favoured Liberal Party firm in Quebec. Judge Malouf granted an injunction. This decision was reversed by a higher court, which accepted that proceeding was economically necessary. Negotiations began again and concluded in agreement in November, 1975. Throughout the negotiations work proceeded on the project at a rapid pace.

A complex and detailed 1700-page agreement was ultimately reached. It was signed by the Northern Quebec Inuit Association, (NQIA), the James Bay Cree, the JBDC, the JBEC, Hydro-Quebec, and both the federal and the provincial governments. The Indians renounced all further land claims in an area which amounted to the northern two-thirds of Quebec. One dam on the La Grande would be moved upstream a bit. All future projects could proceed subject to environmental impact assessment, but "cannot be opposed on social grounds."[26] In return for this agreement the Indians were given some $225 million tax-free in various forms. Much of the money was to be in Quebec debentures paid to special corporations on which provincial and federal representatives would sit for ten years. The Indians were given some 6,000 square miles for "exclusive use," though expropriation and mineral rights were left with the province.

Keith Crowe, senior negotiator for the NQIA, commented afterwards that both federal and provincial government negotiators had stayed in the background and most negotiations were with the JBEC. He found this a disturbing way to proceed – in effect, the native peoples were negotiating their birthright with corporations. Other commentators pointed out that in Alaska, where a settlement was reached with native peoples prior to construction of the Alaska pipeline, there was a five-year freeze on development allowing for preparation for a settlement. Negotiations with and without bulldozers at one's door, it was often stated, are very different matters. Native peoples ultimately received approximately $1.50 per acre for lands signed away, though this amounted to approximately $10,000 for each native person in the area.

Economic Imperatives

International Aspects

It is difficult to discuss the international aspects of the James Bay Project because, while clearly they are crucial, very little of substance is known about how the various arrangements were made. There is international involvement in three key areas: financing, engineering, and electrical energy purchases. Financing for the James Bay Project is made through bond sales largely on the New York market. Interest on those bonds will amount to at least $4 billion during the construction phase of the project. On at least three occasions David Rockefeller of the Chase Manhattan Bank met with Premier Bourassa, yet nothing was disclosed about the content of their meetings. The last of these meetings was in March, 1972.

In May, 1972, Premier Bourassa announced that the bulk of the engineering work on the project would be handled by Bechtel Engineering of Quebec, a subsidiary of the U.S.-based Bechtel Corporation, by far the largest engineering firm in the world. In July, 1972, Hydro-Quebec announced it had agreed to sell power to Consolidated Edison of New York starting in 1977. The pact allows for the construction of a 765,000 volt transmission line from the Quebec border to New York City. The agreement is nominally reciprocal. It was widely reported with the announcement that New York City's peak demand comes in the summer and Quebec's in the winter.[27] However, Con Ed is only required to supply power in emergencies and at its local price, a price considerably higher than that which Hydro-Quebec charges New York for Quebec power.[28]

Also worth mentioning here is René Lévesque's famous speech to the Economic Club of New York shortly after the Parti Québécois (PQ) defeated the Liberals at the polls in 1976. Lévesque reassured the New York financial community regarding regulation of Hydro-Quebec. He stated that northern rivers would be developed to their full potential, that the financial integrity of Hydro-Quebec would continue to be backed by the Quebec government, and that power would flow "north-south."[29] The PQ's early opposition to James Bay clearly had declined as the project progressed and the party came nearer to and then attained power.

JBDC: A Struggle for Power

In May, 1972, it became increasingly clear that there was a falling-out between Hydro-Quebec and JBDC. The two corporate partners had agreed to the decision to proceed first with the La Grande rather than the NBR portion of the project. They issued separate reports offering different estimates of power potential and total costs. On May 27 the *Financial Post* reported: "It is understood the debate lurking beneath these statements is whether an international firm, such as Bechtel Corporation, will be hired to help manage the project, as Hydro would like, or a local firm . . . as [JBDC] would like."[30] On May 30 Premier Bourassa confirmed that Hydro would be given direct management control over the James Bay Project. During hearings before the natural resources committee Pierre Nadeau stated that "If Hydro-Quebec gets the total management mandate for the project I do not see what could be the future of the energy subsidiary or its president."[31] In late summer Mr. Nadeau resigned as president of JBEC, remaining as one of two JBDC representatives on the board. He was succeeded by Robert Boyd, one of the three Hydro-Quebec representatives on the board.

Hydro-Quebec moved quickly to let the major project management contract to Bechtel Corporation. Premier Bourassa made the announcement suggesting that some aspects would be contracted to Quebec engineering firms, but these aspects have proven to be minor indeed. The PQ objected to the by-pass of Quebec-based concerns in the management of the project. Most observers were left wondering why the JBDC was created in the first place.

Energy: Needs, Forms, and Costs

In retrospect one can see the dispute over the James Bay Project as a precursor of the energy-crisis politics which have come to fuller fruition since the OPEC oil-price increase of 1973. Opposition to the James Bay Project centred primarily on the damage to the ecology of the immediate region and the disruption of the way of life of native peoples. But surprisingly, from a contemporary environmentalist perspective, nuclear energy was seen to be a possible, more environmentally benign alternative to the James Bay Project.[32] There was insufficient appreciation, even among environmentalists, of the important distinction between renewable and non-renewable energy sources. However, by April, 1973, the JBC-sponsored hearings gave considerable emphasis to the potential of energy conservation as an alternative to increases in energy production capacity. In brief, one can see in the James Bay conflict the contemporary environmentalist energy position in formation. The fundamental difference between then and now is the relative lack of concern with nuclear power and the absence of Amory Lovins' elegant conception of hard-path and soft-path energy options.[33] A soft-path approach emphasizes conservation and renewable energy resources; a hard-path strategy does not.

In the contemporary perspective we can see the large-scale generation of hydroelectric power as the one energy form that does not neatly fit the hard-path or the soft-path model. It is renewable, but centralized. It can involve massive environmental damage, but it need not be catastrophically disruptive. Clearly, smaller-scale hydroelectric generation would be preferable environmentally though possibly more expensive, especially in labour time. Northern sites, it might be argued, are relatively suitable for hydro-generation since tree growth is slow and therefore potential for methanol production is limited. In evaluating the James Bay Project within a soft-path strategy one would still be left with three central concerns: (1) the relative fragility of northern ecosystems; (2) the possibility that energy could be extracted from the river systems in question in a more benign manner; and (3) the effect of pace-of-development on energy use in construction and on environmental impact.

An alternative conception of the James Bay Project might see the integration of methanol production (beginning with the clear-cutting of forests to fuel construction machinery), a larger number of smaller-scale dam sites, and wind generation on the shores of James Bay and elsewhere in the region. Such an approach, or any other integrated and environmentally more benign approach, would doubtless be more costly per unit of energy generated. It therefore would make sense only if coupled with an intensive and comprehensive energy conservation strategy. Many useful components in such a strategy were offered by the opponents of the James Bay Project, particularly by Brian Kelly, formerly of Pollution Probe and now with the Office of Energy Conservation in Ottawa.[34] A crucial factor not fully appreciated at the time of the James Bay Project, but again a key environmentalist concept-in-formation, is the relationship between employment levels and energy strategies. Clearly, a soft-path strategy is more employment-intensive than any hard-path strategy, including large-scale hydroelectricity generation.[35] Clearly, too, soft-path approaches are based on a different economic logic than presently exists in most constituencies and could only be based on a different underlying politics and political process than existed in Quebec in 1970-73.

Conclusion: Political Realities

Politics is the forum wherein competing values are weighted one against the other.[36] This process, by its nature, is an art rather than a science, and inevitably requires decision-makers to evaluate comparatively at least apples and oranges, if not cultures and bulldozers. In the case of the James Bay Project, it is difficult to imagine an effective and rational decision-making process which did not integrate and evaluate a wide range of technical possibilities in the face of several interpretations of ecological, economic, cultural, and political facts and values. In my view there were at least three points at which the political system functioned ineffectively. A short discussion of these three points will serve as a conclusion to this chapter.

Underdevelopment and Environmental Concerns

Quebec in the 1960's was very much an economic hinterland within an economic hinterland called Canada.[37] The James Bay region was a hinterland within the province of Quebec – as are the northern regions of each of Canada's provinces, excepting perhaps Prince Edward Island. A hinterland not only generally lacks economic autonomy, it also lacks political autonomy. The Inuit and Cree of northern Quebec could not opt to reject the James Bay Project in the name of cultural preservation and the ecological integrity of the region in which they had lived for millennia. Their political economy, while probably more sustainable, is so much less technologically sophisticated than ours that they simply had no power and worked as effectively as they could within our system to get some justice in terms of our values.

Quebec, relative to English Canada and the United States, is proportionately less a hinterland. But Quebeckers have developed, within their culture, a "catch-up" mentality born of many historic humiliations at the hands of English Canada. The same mentality prevails in Western Canada with regard to the East, and in the Atlantic Provinces with regard to everyone else. The desire to be as economically advanced a region as any other burns fiercely everywhere in Canada except perhaps in southern Ontario. In the face of this, ecological values are difficult to put forward when they appear to threaten economic growth prospects.

A locale which perceives itself to be "underdeveloped" will understandably confuse economic growth with economic security, outside investment with increasing wealth, and an influx of temporary employment opportunities with stable prosperity. When unemployment rates are high and few jobs are available, ecological considerations do not receive their due weight. In such a context a full range of options is foreshortened. Those who can hold out the firm prospect of economic growth and employment are not asked to modify their intentions. This is true regardless of the fact that the capital cost of each new job is massive, perhaps one million dollars for each direct (and temporary) job created at James Bay. Proposals are not often or easily adjusted or even delayed in the interest of social or ecological considerations. In short, underdevelopment can produce powerlessness, and self-consciousness regarding underdevelopment can induce hasty and irrational decision-making. The James Bay Project was created in just such a context.

Nationalism, Federalism, and James Bay

Another critical factor in James Bay decision-making is the fact that Quebec's economic underdevelopment and self-consciousness were amplified by its cultural distinctiveness. French-speaking

Quebeckers had been growing in confidence and assertiveness regarding the place of their language and culture within Confederation for at least several decades prior to 1970. The Quiet Revolution integrated these changes with a growing acceptance of Quebec as a newly urban, technologically sophisticated and industrialized society. In the hierarchy of symbolic meaning within the Quiet Revolution, hydro power and Hydro-Quebec rank high indeed. In several ways the rise of Quebec nationalism and the general fragility of Canadian federalism significantly affected the James Bay decision.

The political opposition in Quebec, the Parti Québécois, was unable and/or unwilling to sharply and continuously oppose the James Bay Project or that institution which initiated it (Hydro-Quebec). The party, in opposition, did not propose mechanisms for public review of Hydro-Quebec decision-making in spite of the fact that its decisions were involving public funds on a scale beyond those of the government itself. More importantly, neither in opposition nor in power has any party sought to impose mechanisms for strictly reviewing Hydro-Quebec's rate structure, as does the Canadian Transport Commission, for example, with Bell Canada's rates. Hydro-Quebec controls more hydroelectric generating capacity than any single entity in the world other than the whole of the Soviet Union. It is publicly owned. Yet its decisions are rarely, if ever, subject to public scrutiny or review.

As Quebec political parties were hesitant to appear to be intervening against Hydro-Quebec, so the Canadian federal government was hesitant to appear to be intervening against the Province of Quebec. Constitutionally, an intervention might have been justified, for example, under the Navigable Waters Protection Act as was recommended by Conservative MP Gerald Baldwin.[38] There is as well a federal constitutional responsibility over "Indians, and land reserved for Indians" under Section 91(24) of the British North America Act. But here the federal government allowed not simply Quebec but also the JBEC to take the dominant role in land-claim negotiations with the Cree and Inuit. In addition, an excellent case could be made for intervention on the basis of fisheries protection and especially on the basis of the protection of migratory birds under the U.S.-Canadian Migratory Birds Convention of 1916, a major treaty. All of these bases were precisely spelled out in a paper prepared with the federal Department of the Environment in May, 1972, and leaked thereafter to little avail.[39] Constitutional realities are one thing, political realities another. In the case of James Bay, coming the year following the imposition of the War Measures Act and in the face of rising Quebec sympathy for the PQ, political realities prevailed handily.

Economic Centralization and Political Process

Underlying all of the central issues associated with the James Bay Project is the broad question of expansion of the scale of technological development. That expansion is in turn associated with extension of the time-frame of project development and a tendency to centralization of capital. The lengths of time required for project development, particularly with energy projects, have now come to exceed the reasonable life expectancies for democratic tenure. Centralization of capital and project scale are inseparable twins, the chicken-egg nature of which I would not wish to begin sorting in such writing exercise as this. Nonetheless, I do suggest that the pattern we have seen unfold in the James Bay Project is a pattern that the economically and technologically overdeveloped societies of the world have not yet learned to deal with effectively.

It is not, as has been discussed above, hydroelectric power generation in itself that is environmentally problematic. What is problematic is hydroelectric power generation on a massive scale. As well, only a society with a centralized and centralizing economy and techno-structure requires the very rapid growth in energy demand which in turn seeks energy sources at the very edge of the globe. The extremely fragile ecologies of northern and other frontier regions are threatened by the rapid and careless influx of large numbers of technologically comforted, environmentally arrogant people. Threatened, too, by that influx are the very human cultures which have learned to live in and with those ecologies. It is ironic that the very group in North America most threatened by cultural hegemony and homogenization may have initiated a similar assault against the James Bay Cree.

Environmental and social impact assessment is a tool that can, to some extent, open up the political and economic decision-making processes which lie behind these large-scale technological projects. It can, as well, help to incorporate non-economic, non-partisan values into the decision-making equations before irreversible decisions are made within normal channels and institutions. In an earlier, less technologically advanced era such formal, legalistic techniques to assure both public participation and ecological integrity were less necessary. A more diverse economic decision-making process is both less politically and less ecologically threatening. Any one project that will increase by a significant fraction the hydroelectric capacity of a large, hydroelectrically super-rich province, and that involves many, many billions of dollars, may *by nature* pose a potential threat to the democratic character of decision-making and to the ecological integrity of its site. At the least the possibility of such decisions requires us to rethink the adequacy of existing institutional structures, and also to redefine the time-frame within which our political processes are conducted.

Project by project assessments may not be adequate to deal with the issues confronting contemporary technological societies. Nonetheless, with this in mind, environmental and social impact assessment and the large-scale public participation that could accompany it might prove to be a *sine qua non* of the rapid transformation of democratic decision-making that some feel cannot come in time to meet the environmental and resource challenges facing us.[40] It should also be said that no one project can irretrievably disrupt global ecology; and, that each project can be improved. The earlier that environmental sensitivity enters the decision-making process, the better is the chance that it will have a significant influence on the outcome. No one can say what might have happened at James Bay. We can only try to improve the future.

NOTES

1. Joan Fraser, "Revival Route on James Bay," *Financial Times of Canada*, October 25, 1971, p. 17.
2. *Financial Post*, February 12, 1972, p. 2.
3. *Ibid.*
4. *Ibid.*
5. The best discussion in English of the Duplessis regime is Herbert F. Quinn, *The Union Nationale* (Toronto, 1963).
6. A fuller appreciation of the Quiet Revolution can be obtained by a reading of Marcel Rioux, *Quebec in Question* (Toronto, 1971).
7. Ralph Surette *et al.*, "The Pros Grab for James Bay," *Last Post*, 3 (May, 1973), 24-30.
8. *Bill 50: James Bay Development Act*, 1971, p. 4.
9. *Ibid.*, p. 13.
10. See *Journal des Debats*, Commission Parliamenture des Richesses Naturelles, May 28-29, 1971.
11. Montreal *Gazette*, May 13, 1972, p. 7.
12. Valanne Glooschenko, "The James Bay Power Proposal," *Nature Canada*, 1 (January/March, 1972), 7.
13. *Ibid.*, 8.

14. James Bay Committee, *Position Paper on the James Bay Development Project* (Montreal, March, 1972), 2.
15. James Bay Committee, "For Immediate Press Release," Montreal, November 23, 1972, mimeo, p. 5.
16. J. A. and G. C. Spence, *Ecological Considerations of the James Bay Project* (Montreal, 1972).
17. James Bay Committee, "Position Paper on the James Bay Project," *Alternatives*, 1 (Summer, 1972), 14-21.
18. James Bay Committee, "James Bay Committee Report," April 21, 1972, mimeo, p. 3.
19. Fikret Berkes (ed.), *James Bay Forum* (Montreal, 1973).
20. David Estrin and John Swaigen, *Environment on Trial* (revised edition, Toronto, 1978), 43.
21. Mr. Justice Thomas R. Berger, *Northern Frontier, Northern Homeland*, vol. 1 (Ottawa: Supply and Services Canada, 1977).
22. Glooschenko, "James Bay Proposal," 9.
23. As reported in the Montreal *Gazette*, February 3, 1972.
24. Toronto *Globe and Mail*, March 10, 1972.
25. As reported in the *Winnipeg Free Press* in a column by Maurice Western on February 3, 1972.
26. See "The James Bay Agreement: A Summary," *C.A.S.N.P. Bulletin*, 16 (December, 1975), 4-7.
27. See Toronto *Globe and Mail*, July 27, 1972, p. B2.
28. Brian McKenna, "The Power and Glory of James Bay," *Weekend Magazine*, 27 (March 19, 1977), 8.
29. *Ibid.*, 8.
30. *Financial Post*, May 27, 1972, p. 38.
31. Toronto *Globe and Mail*, September 8, 1972, p. B3.
32. See, for example, JBC, *Position Paper*, 2-3; and P. Lind in *Save James Bay* (Toronto: Canadian Association in Support of Native Peoples, 1973), 4-6.
33. Amory Lovins, *Soft Energy Paths* (Cambridge, Mass., 1977). For Canadian soft-path studies, see *Alternatives* (Summer-Autumn, 1979).
34. Brian Kelly, untitled, in Berkes (ed.), *James Bay Forum*, 107-9.
35. Richard Grossman and Gail Daneker, *Jobs and Energy* (Washington, D.C.: Environmentalists for Full Employment, 1977). See also David B. Brooks, *Economic Impact of Low Energy Growth in Canada: An Initial Analysis* (Ottawa: Economic Council of Canada, 1978).
36. David Easton, *The Political System* (New York, 1953).
37. A good general introduction to the discussion of metropolis and hinterland is Kari Levitt, *Silent Surrender* (Toronto, 1970).
38. According to a Canadian Press story carried in most major papers on February 9, 1972.
39. Michael J. Bird, *An Analysis of Federal Interests Affected by the Proposed James Bay Hydro Development* (Ottawa, May, 1972, xerox). Copy on file with author.
40. William Ophuls, *Ecology and the Politics of Scarcity* (San Francisco, 1977).

CHAPTER SIX

Great Lakes Water Quality: A Study in Environmental Politics and Diplomacy

by Don Munton

Environmental politics often seem to reflect the worst aspects of the political process. Empty rhetoric abounds, posturing is pervasive, concrete actions come but slowly and infrequently. Why it should be so, however, appears a mystery. No one, after all, is in favour of more pollution. Particularly during the early 1970's, public awareness of and apparent concern about pollution and the environment made them issues of national and local priority. The mass media mounted an extraordinary campaign, countless environmental groups sprang up, and a new breed of scientists, the ecologists, was thrust into the public limelight. Until the faltering economies of the major industrial nations and the so-called oil "crisis" of 1973 redirected public attention, there was even talk of an emerging new environmental ethic, of a growing awareness of the delicate relationship between man and his environment. And yet, so little seemed to happen in terms of government policies.

Explanations of this apparent disjunction between public demands and expectations, on the one hand, and governmental action, on the other, are all too often overly simplistic. The gap is not solely due to collusion between political and business elites to ensure corporate profits and economic growth, or, in the pejorative if less ideological sense, to "politics" – though there is undoubtedly a degree of truth in this explanation. To understand this gap between public demand and government action it is essential, first of all, to avoid exaggerating its extent. While the public did become more aware of environmental problems, largely as a result of media coverage, the degree of personal concern about them was never great.[1] The ease with which inflation and energy came to head the polls as "most important problems" in the mid-1970's was as much a function of the environment's tenuous position in the public consciousness as it was of the dominance of economic growth on that consciousness. Also, the apparent lack of concrete political action is in part an illusion. The impact of some important, far-reaching government measures in the environmental area, such as the now-accepted process of environmental impact assessment, is becoming apparent only with the passage of time. With these two major qualifications in mind, it can be argued that the gap between public demands and government results was and is not as wide as many critics suggest. It cannot be argued, however, that no gap exists.

The reasons why results have fallen short of demands lie both in the diverse and intricate nature of environmental problems and in the uncertainties and equally intricate nature of the political process. The constraints lie not only in a lack of scientific knowledge about the actual problems and their solutions, but also in the difficulty of reconciling the competing demands, always present in the political arena, and the diverging interests of different political jurisdictions. Competing public demands and diverging political interests are tough enough to resolve within a given national government and within a federal system where the provinces or states play a major role. When an environmental problem also spans an international boundary the difficulties are multiplied. To further our understanding of the demands for and constraints on environmental policies that are both domestic and international in scope, the present essay examines the politics of Canadian and American water pollution control programs for the Great Lakes during the 1960's and 1970's. This issue is a useful one because at least a modest degree of success was achieved, as reflected by two international agreements, in the face of the full range of problems and limitations encountered with such multi-jurisdictional questions. Moreover, the political process was an extremely complex one involving federal, provincial, and state governments; a binational agency; a host of government departments, officials, and cabinet ministers; scientists, administrators, and diplomats; an aroused public; and lethargic polluters of all kinds, public as well as private, governmental as well as corporate. This complexity was compounded by scientific, social, and political changes underway before and during the negotiation of the two agreements.

Background to the 1972 Agreement

The Great Lakes Water Quality Agreement of 1972 grew directly, though not solely, out of investigatory work done under a joint Canada-U.S. "reference" to the International Joint Commission (IJC) in 1964. Prior to the 1960's, the governments of Canada and the United States twice had requested the IJC to study pollution problems in the Great Lakes region, in 1912 and 1946. In approving its 1950 report, the two countries had established a common set of water quality objectives and a bilateral monitoring board for the Lakes' connecting channels. But it was soon clear that a broader approach was needed; scientific evidence was mounting of serious basin-wide pollution problems, especially in Lake Erie.[2] After waiting seven years for the Ontario government's approval, Canada and the U.S. formally agreed on the new reference in October, 1964. This reference thus came about before increased public concern about water pollution became evident in 1965-66. Following its own established practice, the IJC appointed two joint investigatory boards (one each for Lake Erie and for Lake Ontario-St. Lawrence River) consisting mainly of scientists and engineers drawn from the various federal, provincial, and state government departments. The boards were slow in getting investigation underway, largely because of a general lack of staff and organizational capacity to do the required field research. Their interim report, based almost entirely on earlier scientific studies, emphasized the problem of nutrients, especially phosphorus, as the cause of "eutrophication" of the Lakes. The IJC passed this report on to the two countries in the fall of 1965, complete with the recommendation that measures be taken to limit phosphorus inputs. Ontario and the various American governments, however, were not yet willing to consider such measures and the report was set aside. The studies on the Great Lakes continued through 1966-67.

In early 1968 the two boards (which often met at the same place and time, since memberships overlapped) appointed a small editorial committee to draft their final report. The officials on this committee, in addition to performing regular agency duties, worked together through a lengthy series of meetings at various sites around the Great Lakes. Questions of scientific evidence, interagency differences in approach, and somewhat diverging bilateral views were eventually resolved, though the sheer job of drafting and revising the massive and complex, three-volume, 800-page report proved an equal challenge. The document was ultimately delivered to the IJC in the early fall of 1969. The commissioners were pleased, and promptly made the report public. To no one's surprise, the boards unanimously concluded Lakes Erie and Ontario and the international section of the St. Lawrence were indeed being polluted on both sides of the boundary. The report emphasized phosphates and eutrophication, and presented data showing for the first time the relative contribution of U.S. and Canadian sources of pollution. Most was from the American side. The major recommendations were that phosphate control programs be implemented immediately, that a new set of water quality objectives be set for these waters, that additional programs be adopted to meet these water quality objectives, and that a new international board be established to co-ordinate both these programs and the required monitoring and surveillance.

The IJC held public hearings on the report in eight cities around the Great Lakes during January and February, 1970. These followed closely a series of December hearings on another report into the environmental hazard posed by oil and gas drilling on the Canadian side of Lake Erie. The January-February hearings featured a heated confrontation between government and detergent industry experts over whether phosphates were indeed the problem and whether controls on phosphate levels in laundry products were needed. The general consensus by the end of the hearings was that the deleterious effect of phosphates had been argued conclusively. The detergent companies were thought to be in retreat. The IJC, recognizing what it termed the "urgency" of the situation, and also recognizing a political opportunity, decided not to wait until its final report would be ready in the fall. Instead, it forwarded a special Interim Report to the governments in April, 1970. This action may also have reflected the commissioners' recognition that the momentum toward a Great Lakes agreement had already begun to shift to the politicians, bureaucrats, and diplomats.

The years 1969 and 1970 were extremely active ones with respect to environmental policy in both countries. The Canadian parliament approved an array of environment-oriented legislation during this period, including the new Canada Water Act, which required reductions in the amount of phosphates in detergents. In the U.S., President Nixon made a point of signing the recently passed National Environmental Policy Act into effect on New Year's Day, 1970, and followed up this gesture by emphasizing pollution problems in his January State of the Union message and by sending to the Congress in February a Special Message on the

Environment. Strong doubts persisted that the White House had become genuinely committed to cleaning up pollution, but it appeared the Nixon administration wanted to avoid being left behind by the environmental bandwagon.[3] The much publicized controversy over whether or not Lake Erie was "dead" ensured the Great Lakes a prominent place in the public eye and the ensuing political debates.

In December, 1969, two trial balloons were raised about bilateral solutions for the Lakes – both by U.S. officials. One was from President Nixon's science adviser, while the other came from White House adviser Daniel Moynihan, who had been charged with rescuing an earlier proposal by Nixon for a NATO "Committee on the Challenges of Modern Society" (CCMS) – a proposal that had been met initially with considerable disinterest by other NATO members. Moynihan was determined to find CCMS "pilot projects" member countries could agree to, and Canada-U.S. co-operation on Great Lakes pollution seemed to him an ideal candidate. Ottawa's tentative response to the idea of talks, though not to the CCMS proposal, was positive. A growing number of Canadian officials had become much concerned about the extent to which largely American pollution was damaging the Lakes. They also had become convinced something more than mere pious words was necessary. Still, it took a few months before the bureaucratic machinery began to roll.

The Minister of Energy, Mines and Resoures (EMR), Joe Greene, had already proposed to External Affairs the initiation of formal talks with Interior Secretary Hickel. EMR argued strongly that work had to begin immediately toward a co-operative Canada-U.S. arrangement, including a new bilateral environmental agency and probably an entirely new bilateral environmental treaty. Such far-ranging proposals did not excite External Affairs. Diplomats, by training if not by instinct, are wary of overly formal international arrangements. Moreover, the venerable Boundary Waters Treaty and its prodigy, the IJC, had served Canada well, and the practical realities of international and U.S. domestic politics made the possibility of a similar but better treaty, from Canada's point of view, seem highly unlikely. External Affairs also received an indication from the Canadian embassy in Washington that Hickel was in disfavor and not the best Nixon administration official to approach. The two departments ultimately agreed a joint group should draft a position paper for exploratory talks with the Americans at an early date.

"The time is ripe for new initiatives," declared the paper

quickly produced by an official of EMR.[4] With the new Canada Water Act, EMR added, the government was "in a stronger position to apply pressure on the U.S. to correct pollution abuses and cooperate in new forms of water quality management." While Canada's position may well have been better at that point than months or years earlier, the successful application of pressure on the U.S. government was to prove rather difficult. When one is the lesser power, it seems, the time is seldom ripe for initiatives until the greater power sees fit and agrees to move. And, through the spring and summer of 1970, Washington did not see fit. A series of blunt, highly critical speeches by Joe Greene, a number of them to American audiences, seemed to have little effect.

The American government's inertia did not stem primarily from a lack of commitment to environmental causes or lack of responsiveness to a neighbor's concerns, though the Nixon administration was seldom accused of an abundance of either. Rather, the resistance had more to do with a lack of clear organizational responsibility and a resulting dose of bureaucratic infighting. The expected release of the IJC's Interim Report in April, 1970, had promoted the arranging of a meeting of department officials from External Affairs and the State Department, as well as plans for a ministerial-level meeting. News of this arrangement appears to have incited the interagency battles. The President's newly formed and bureaucratically ambitious Council on Environmental Quality (CEQ), headed by Russell Train, had set its sights on the Great Lakes at one of its first organizational meetings in early February. It was by no means alone. Also interested was Daniel Moynihan in the White House, who still wanted the Great Lakes issue for his CCMS project. The State Department's Office of Environmental Affairs, also newly formed, was very much interested as well. Given the international nature of the issue and of the forthcoming meetings, the State Department had at least a claim to the chairmanship of the U.S. side. Finally, the Department of Interior's Federal Water Quality Administration, which was, after all, the operating agency for federal water pollution programs, made its play for the lead role.

The meeting of department officials was postponed a month while the interagency territorial battles were played out in Washington. CEQ and Train eventually emerged the first round victors. The White House gave CEQ responsibility for the initial talks with Canada, and Train was also named head of a Presidential Task Force charged in part with drafting a U.S. response to the IJC report. Because this task force had begun to meet by early

May, 1970, the Americans went into the bilateral talks with the intent only of exchanging views, not intending to make commitments or to begin negotiation of a formal agreement.

Negotiating the 1972 Agreement

The preliminary meeting of officials proved a less than heartening experience for all but the most patient of the Canadian contingent. An ongoing, rather low-key debate among Canadian officials as to the most desirable result of the consultations was more or less resolved by the time of the May 25 meeting in favour of aiming for a formal agreement but not the establishment of a new supernational environmental agency. The Canadian delegation proposed the two countries begin negotiation of a new agreement with water quality objectives, standards, and abatement commitments. U.S. officials responded that such a scheme would be difficult, since the states, not the federal government, had the responsibility for water pollution. The Americans proposed instead what one Canadian official characterized as "the continuation of past arrangements" along with a vague proposal for the establishment of "a new institutional framework" for co-ordinating programs.[5]

The two sides also differed significantly on the basic premise underlying any abatement programs. The Canadian side argued that Article VIII of the 1909 Boundary Waters Treaty gave each side the right, in effect, to contribute pollution up to fifty per cent of the "assimilative capacity" of the waters. For the U.S., as the major polluter, acceptance of this principle would have required drastic pollution control measures, while for Canada it would have meant at most a minimun cutback. American officials thus refused to accept the argument. Article IV of the treaty, they countered, obligated both sides to control transboundary pollution. American officials also noted for their part that new federal programs were forthcoming and that the emerging consensus in Washington was that a reduction of phosphates in detergents was needed. Failing to agree on the broad political questions before them, the officials proceeded to discuss various technical issues raised in the recently released IJC Interim Report, including oil and gas drilling, ship waste, dredging, and emergency co-ordination.

Despite the evident lack of agreement between the two sides, the first ministerial-level meeting devoted to Great Lakes pollution problems in the history of Canadian-American relations took place on June 23, 1970, in Ottawa. Canadian cabinet ministers urged acceptance of the recommendations of the IJC Interim

Report and proposed the negotiation of a water quality treaty. They met with no more success than had their officials the previous month. The two sides did manage to agree that transboundary pollution existed, that most of it originated on the United States side, and that such pollution was contrary to the obligations each had under the Boundary Waters Treaty. But the American side was not yet prepared to approve the IJC recommendations nor to begin negotiations. The Canadian back-up proposal for a working group to examine the adequacy of the present effort and the need for a possible agreement, however, was accepted after a private discussion between Russell Train and Joe Greene. Throughout the summer of 1970 the Canadians cautiously maintained a degree of diplomatic pressure for further progress. In the process they secured American agreement to hold the first meeting of the Joint Working Group in late September and acceptance in principle of the approach it should take.

The American commitment to a bilateral approach for controlling pollution in the Great Lakes was not long in coming, but in the end owed little to direct Canadian pressure. On September 24, Train submitted to President Nixon the final report of his task force.[6] The report recommended a series of positive steps, including the extension of the IJC purview to "the entire Great Lakes basin," increased support for the commission's chronically understaffed U.S. section, bilateral agreement on controlling pollution from watercraft and on an oil-spill contingency plan, and establishment of a "pollution control board" under the IJC's aegis as recommended by the 1969 Advisory Board report. More importantly, the task force advocated a thorough consideration of the recommendations in the still forthcoming IJC final report, and such priority for the Great Lakes in U.S. water programs "as required to reduce pollution from U.S. sources so as to be in full compliance with the Boundary Waters Treaty . . . [i.e., the elimination of transboundary pollution] by 1972." This last recommendation, with its rather unrealistic goal and deadline, along with the others in the report, were approved by Nixon on October 1. The task force report, though never released publicly, became the basis on the U.S. side for securing co-operation from the various agencies involved in the issue.

At the September, 1970, meeting of the Canada-U.S. Joint Working Group the two sides quickly agreed on the establishment of and terms of reference for ten sub-groups (covering water quality objectives and standards, institutional matters, environmental legislation, contingency planning, the co-ordination of special programs and of research, and pollution from hazardous materials, from agriculture and forestry, and from watercraft). The sub-groups, involving approximately seventy-five federal, state, and provincial officials in all, began series of meetings toward drafting reports on their particular problems. Their work predictably took longer than expected but for the most part proceeded well.

By March, 1971, most sub-groups had reported. The unresolved issues included whether the U.S. federal government would limit detergent phosphates, the question of an IJC staff unit, vessel waste regulation, and, more generally, the nature and form of the prospective bilateral agreement. The full Joint Working Group met in April, 1971, to approve a final compromise report and recommend the scheduling of another ministerial meeting for June. The evident progress notwithstanding, Canadian officials remained apprehensive that the Nixon administration would not, in the end, undertake firm commitments and that the eventual agreement would be more talk than action.

After the largely successful work of the officials, the ministerial meeting of June 10, 1971, was a smooth and well-orchestrated affair. The Joint Working Group Report was approved and the way thus cleared for the beginning of formal negotiations. Hopes were high for an agreement by fall. An initial meeting of officials in Washington at the end of June discussed preliminary drafts produced by both sides and identified points of agreement and disagreement. But then the process stalled.

First the Canadian officials became preoccupied with the negotiation of a back-up agreement with Ontario. After several meetings, some of which were at least as difficult as any held with the Americans, the federal and provincial governments finally agreed Ottawa would provide an accelerated $173 million program of CMHC loans and grants for municipal sewage treatment facilities, while Ontario would assist in implementing the prospective Canada-U.S. agreement. Then the bilateral talks were further delayed in mid-September when what the Canadians thought was the U.S. government's slow movement toward detergent phosphate controls was abruptly reversed. Nixon administration officials warned of possible harmful effects to human health from the replacement of phosphates in detergents with the leading alternative, NTA (nitrilotriacetic acid), despite a lack of scientific evidence as to dangers, and advised the public to return to the use of phosphates. The administration was immediately and heavily criticized for having capitulated to political pressures from the major soap and detergent companies. This declaration not only sealed the fate of proposals for U.S. federal government phosphate controls, but also delayed the bilateral negotiations for months as EPA officials reassessed the U.S. ability to reduce overall phosphate loadings in Lakes Erie and Ontario without federal controls on the content of detergents.

A December 14, 1971, meeting in Ottawa of the two negotiating teams began detailed consideration of both sides' draft texts. Much of the discussion proved difficult. The U.S. draft was considerably more qualified and less specific on certain items, and was particularly lacking with respect to phosphate reductions, implementation programs to attain common water quality objectives, and new IJC responsibilities and staff office. Canadian pressure on these points was unsuccessful. The Americans also remained determined to resist the Canadian argument that the Boundary Waters Treaty ought to be interpreted as giving each country equal rights to the assimilative capacity of the Lakes. The Canadians recognized that, no matter how solid the legal basis for this claim might be, it would remain politically unacceptable to the U.S. They thus dropped the argument prior to a joint drafting group meeting in mid-January.

Canadian efforts during subsequent sessions were aimed at securing as firm as possible American commitments on implementation programs. In this they were again only partially successful. After a long discussion during an early February full negotiating meeting in Washington, the Canadians reluctantly accepted an American-proposed wording to the effect that municipal programs "would be complete *or in the process of implementation*" by December 31, 1975 (emphasis added). This phrase was to become the object of much attention in ensuing months and years when U.S. municipal treatment programs were noticeably lagging. But the U.S. side, under heavy pressure from budget officials concerned about the large expenditures involved, could agree to no more. The February meeting did manage to approve, on an *ad referendum* basis, most of the body of the draft agreement. Having yielded on two of their key points, however, Canadian negotiators were apparently less willing to be conciliatory on the two remaining ones – phosphate reductions and the proposed IJC office.

Canadian officials pushed hard to obtain what they regarded as an adequate schedule of U.S. reductions of phosphate inputs. Diplomatic pressure was also kept up during this period to overcome apparent State Department reluctance to establishing the IJC office. That task was eased when U.S. IJC section chairman

Christian Herter, Jr., on behalf of the State Department, obtained an indication of congressional support for the necessary funding. At the final full negotiating session in mid-March the Canadians accepted the latest American proposals on phosphate reductions, even though these were short of the 1970 IJC recommendations. Both sides also agreed to a provision which authorized but did not require the IJC to establish a Great Lakes regional office. Final wording changes to the text were made during the following week, and the agreement was subsequently approved by the Canadian cabinet in late March. After six years of studies and two years of intensive discussions and negotiations, the Great Lakes Water Quality Agreement was ceremoniously signed on April 15, 1972, by Prime Minister Trudeau and President Nixon during the latter's visit to Ottawa.

For many environmentalists, the agreement's provisions, if not too late, at least represented no real advance over what could be expected from both countries' existing programs. The essence of the agreement, much as originally proposed by Canada at meetings two years earlier, was a set of common water quality objectives, compatible standards, commitments on implementing programs to achieve these objectives, and procedures for monitoring subsequent progress. The target for municipal programs was the end of 1975 and special schedules stipulated required reductions in phosphate loadings to Lakes Erie and Ontario by specific dates. The agreement also gave the IJC additional responsibility for the collection and analysis of information on objectives and programs, for the verification of data, and for the publication of reports and studies. It further directed the IJC to establish a "watchdog" Water Quality Board, to supersede the old Connecting Channels Board, and a Research Advisory Board, to coordinate future scientific work.

The establishment of the former board reflected the fact that the job of pollution control, let alone of a "clean-up," had barely begun; the establishment of the latter reflected the fact that much of the needed scientific knowledge was not yet at hand. Such problems as vessel wastes, pollution of the Upper Lakes, and pollution from land use (non-point sources) had proved too contentious or too complex. While identified in the agreement, they were left for future study. Moreover, consistent with the reports of the IJC and its advisory boards, the agreement put very little emphasis on the whole area of industrial pollutants. It also made but passing reference to such problems as toxic substances and radioactivity. At the time these omissions remained virtually unnoticed, at least by outsiders. But they became dominant concerns well before the stipulated joint fifth-year review of the agreement and its renegotiation began in 1977.

Implementation of the Agreement

The Great Lakes Water Quality Agreement did not effect any change in responsibilities for implementing pollution programs; these remained firmly in the hands of the respective governments. But the programs were no longer to be carried out in semi-isolation. The International Joint Commission moved quickly to begin its new co-ordinating and monitoring functions on the Great Lakes. The Canadian and American co-chairmen and members (including state and provincial representatives) of the Great Lakes Water Quality Board and Research Advisory Board were appointed, on recommendation from the governments, within a few months of the signing of the agreement. Both boards soon established a rather complex structure of subcommittees, each charged with specific duties and composed generally of more junior officials. A number of the senior Canadian officials on these boards also were sitting simultaneously on a federal-provincial review group set up under the Canada-Ontario agreement and on a federal interdepartmental committee concerned with Great Lakes pollution. By the end of their first year of operation, both boards settled into a fairly regular pattern of four or five meetings per year. The subcommittees met at least as often, working much of the time on reports for their respective parent bodies. In July, 1973, the two boards presented the first of a series of annual reports to the IJC on the progress achieved by the governments under the agreement. The emphasis in these reports, at least the first five, was on municipal pollution problems and programs. This emphasis reflected the bias of the original agreement; it also reflected the fact that comparative data on industrial pollution problems were more difficult to obtain and to summarize. The Water Quality Board undertook various special studies as well, including one on PCB's (poly-chlorinated biphenols), and in later reports began to focus more on the problem of toxic substances, most of which are discharged from industrial plants.

In September, 1972, after consultation with the governments, the commissioners proposed Windsor, Ontario, as the location for the new Regional Office and submitted a staffing plan and budget. An American director and Canadian associate director were appointed, and the office eventually opened in early May, 1973. Despite some slowness in U.S. funding, its growth was substantial and rapid. The modest annual budget of approximately $270,000 in 1973-74 increased to over $1,000,000 within three years, and by 1978 the staff had expanded to eighteen scientific and engineering professionals (seven of them Ph.D's) and fourteen support personnel. The bulk of the Regional Office staff's work – over 90 per cent by most estimates – consists of support of and secretariat functions for the boards and their various subcommittees. Staff personnel assigned to these groups assist in writing reports and arranging meetings, and generally maintain close contact with the government officials involved. This office has also sponsored a series of technical workshops on specific pollution and abatement questions and has actively and extremely successfully pursued a public relations and interest-group liaison function. The development of the Regional Office has not been an untroubled one, however. While inadequate U.S. support, growing pains, and clashing personalities played a part, the underlying structural problem was a dispute over the Regional Office's relationship to the boards and the IJC.

The original 1972 agreement did not make clear whether the office was to serve the commission, the boards (formally under the IJC, but comprising senior government officials), or both. At the first meeting between the newly appointed government representatives to the Water Quality Board and the commissioners there was strong disagreement over whether the Regional Office was solely to serve the board and take direction therefrom or whether it would do independent monitoring of the government's performance under the agreement and be responsible to and have its own access to the commissioners. "The Board members," in the words of one participant, "didn't want any . . . damn regional office doing end runs"; the IJC, on the other hand, "didn't want to be entirely in the Board's hands."[7] The commission refused to back down or to clarify the ambiguity in the terms of reference of its Regional Office; it asked the Regional Office to try to serve both masters.

Despite the firm positions on each side, this initial disagreement did not lead to immediate conflicts, in part because the commissioners were careful not to have the Regional Office staff going out as "policemen" on a regular basis. But the issue did not fade away. Commission dissatisfaction increased over the inadequacies of existing government programs, new personalities came to both the Regional Office and the Water Quality Board, and the frictions mounted. The real problem with the Regional Office's activities and responsibilities, according to one former board co-chairman, "was more a general apprehension [on the board's part] than actual incidents." At a more basic level, the essential problem, according to a commissioner, was that "everyone was fighting for power." During 1976 a review of this office was carried out for the Water Quality Board co-chairmen by their own staff. It came to positive conclusions about the secretariat function performed for the boards and their various committees, but was very critical about its organization, its tendency to hire "overqualified" staff, and especially the ambiguity of its mandate. In what was probably a tactical mistake, neither the Regional Office management nor the IJC chose to respond formally or informally to this report. Thus began a process which was to lead eventually to the major intergovernmental – and public – controversy during the renegotiation of the agreement in 1977-78.

If institutional developments stemming from the 1972 agreement, such as the IJC boards and Regional Office, were fairly soon in coming, program developments were considerably slower. This was particularly the case on the American side. Only partly as a result, improvements in water quality were even slower. This was reflected in the annual IJC reports on Great Lakes water quality. The first two reports were highly qualified with regard to any progress or failures. "It appears," noted the commissioners' report of 1972, "that further degradation of the water quality of the Great Lakes may have already been slowed down in some respects, but there is not yet available any scientific basis to support a claim for improvement except in local areas or on some parameters, such as in phosphorus loadings."[8] The report instead diplomatically emphasized the commission's "need" – and of course, the commissioners' strong desire – for adequate funding and support of the Regional Office.

The IJC noted but did not express any undue concern over the impoundment by President Nixon of U.S. federal funds for municipal sewage treatment plants in November, 1972. Publicly at least, the commissioners attempted to avoid the heated political debate that ensued within the U.S. and that attracted Canadian observers. The IJC suggested that the need to sort out the necessary administrative regulations and arrangements was in fact the cause of U.S. delays, pointed the finger at the lack of treatment facilities in Detroit and Cleveland, and mildly urged early release of the required federal grants. Privately, however, the commissioners recognized that while it had been "a mistake to think all the problems could be solved in three years" (i.e., by the agreement's December, 1975, deadline), the lack of U.S. federal funding had indeed seriously delayed municipal programs. The IJC reports emphasized the immediate need for better data on water quality and for better and more comparable analyses of these data, and the commissioners soon strongly recommended to the governments a major monitoring and surveillance program that had been designed and, with difficulty, agreed to by the Water Quality Board's subcommittee on surveillance.

The tone of later IJC reports, based on those of its board, gradually became more firm and more critical. In the 1975 version, the commissioners underscored the board's conclusion that progress so far had been "generally slow, uneven and in certain cases, disappointing."[9] They noted among other points that the phosphorus loading reductions agreed to in 1972 were not being met. They began to identify specific geographic "problem areas" by name, and urged more forcefully the establishment of U.S. regulations on detergent phosphates. The emphasis also began to shift from municipal pollution questions. Based on improved data, reports began to focus more on industrial sources and, in particular, on toxic substances, which the commissioners suggested "may well be the most serious and long-term problem governments face in ensuring future beneficial uses of the Great Lakes."[10] The political focus shifted as well. While a few American cities continued to contribute the bulk of the municipal pollution, the two countries were a little more even with respect to sources of industrial pollution. Part of the problem, the 1976 report suggested in a fine piece of diplomatic bureaucratese, was "that both the setting of regulations and their enforcement are more flexible in Canada than in the United States."[11] "Flexibility" is often a good thing; when applied to pollution control, however, it is a diplomatic way of saying "laxity." And Canadian laxity in this case means Ontario laxity.

The degree to which attention had shifted to industries on the Canadian as well as the American side of the Great Lakes reflected not only a degree of progress in municipal programs and improved data on industrial pollution, but also what was at least perceived to be the Ontario minority Conservative government's declining political will to pressure powerful industries during a period of economic slow-down. The shift in attention was also a result of inevitable comparisons between Canadian programs for controlling industrial pollution and those established under the new U.S. Water Pollution Control Act Amendments of 1972. Ushered through an environment-conscious Congress in 1971-72, what eventually became U.S. Public Law 92-500 specified a "no discharge" goal by 1985, required the implementation of industrial plant effluent standards through a permit system, provided for substantially greater federal government involvement, and authorized huge increases in grants for municipal sewage treatment facilities. Although the Nixon administration refused in the coming years to release funds authorized by Congress, the United States now had potentially highly effective water pollution legislation and a pollution abatement policy based on effluent standards rather than water quality standards. The passage through Congress of PL 92-500 had virtually no impact on the bilateral negotiations leading up to the 1972 agreement. But its stringency and new approach were destined to have a significant impact on the fifth-year review and its renegotiation during 1977-78.

Review and Renegotiation of the Agreement

Doubts exacerbated by the impoundment of federal water pollution funds by President Nixon in the fall of 1972 prompted the Canadian government to request a series of Great Lakes "stocktaking" meetings with the U.S. Although Canadian federal officials were reluctant to level public criticisms of U.S. performance under the 1972 agreement, various Ontario politicians, Canadian newspapers, and other spokesmen were less restrained. Nor were the critics satisfied by occasional American attempts to defend their record. As a result, some U.S. officials came to believe they had "gotten a bum rap" on implementation. And, perhaps in reaction, they seem to have adopted, during their fifth-year review of the agreement, the strategy that the best defence is a good offence. The American position developed during the spring of 1977 was to press hard for what they saw as a "stronger" agreement by urging that its provisions be as consistent as possible with more stringent American domestic statutes, and particularly by pressuring Canadian officials to bring their industrial pollution programs into line with PL 92-500.

A senior review group on the agreement was established early in 1977 with representatives from all U.S. agencies concerned with Great Lakes water quality. Three sub-groups and a number of working groups were activated to review water quality objectives and surveillance, phosphorus, point source discharges, hazardous substances, radioactivity, and research. The sub-group reports were then used as the basis for a series of public meetings held in early June in four cities along the American side of the Great Lakes. The report of Sub-Group A proved particularly controversial. It suggested two major changes. One was that industrial pollution programs on both sides of the Great Lakes should be in accordance with U.S. Public Law 92-500. The other was that the International Joint Commission's Windsor Regional Office should be "disestablished" with the staff and functions being transferred to the two countries' respective environmental agencies. The argument for this change was based not only on the existing uncertainty as to the Regional Office's mandate, but also on the rather exaggerated fear that its continued functioning would result in an "erosion of the sovereign authority" of the governments.[12]

Of these two proposed changes, the second was by far the more controversial with American environmental public interest groups represented at the sparsely attended public meetings. Most of these groups were in favour of a tightening of both industrial and municipal pollution programs in the Great Lakes basin. One representative, though, did note that it seemed unfair to insist that Canada adopt a system not yet proven effective in the U.S. Virtually all the environmental groups, however, strongly opposed the demise of the Regional Office. While the purpose of the sub-group reports was in part to stake out an extreme bargaining position for the future negotiations with Canada, the "disestablishment" proposal seems to have been a serious one, and the public opposition seems to have forced its reconsideration. Over the summer, concerned officials met with key congressmen, and then much more quietly (and rather slowly) went about preparing the formal American negotiating position.

On the Canadian side, discussions were held in late 1976 and early 1977 under the auspices of a senior review committee. Similar to its American counterpart, it established a number of task forces of a mostly technical nature (e.g., water quality objectives, surveillance, toxic chemicals, airborne pollutants, etc.). The committee work seems to have been largely the preserve of Environment Canada officials; External Affairs representatives mainly confined their focus to the question of the International Joint Commission and its Regional Office and to the basic principles of the agreement. The Canadian officials considered but ultimately rejected the idea of pushing for the agreement to be turned into a formal treaty. As had their American counterparts, federal and Ontario authorities staged public hearings – in Toronto and Thunder Bay in early July. Almost forty briefs were presented and about 240 people attended, but many were obviously confused about the nature of the agreement and the respective roles of the various governments and the IJC. Overall, the mass media and public seemed to have been less than fired with excitement by what had been dubbed "Water Quality Week."

The first formal meeting of the Canadian and American negotiating teams took place on April 13, 1977, just one day before the end of the fifth year of the 1972 agreement during which it was supposed to have been reviewed.[13] The Canadians were not prepared to be distracted prematurely from their own review and were opposed to using a joint working-group format similar to that followed in 1970-71. The two sides agreed only to exchange "shopping lists" of items for eventual consideration, to develop drafts independently, and then to compare these drafts. This meeting itself lasted but a few hours, the major debate having been over whether the official public communique on the session should or should not refer to "strengthening" the agreement. If the Canadian side had been in any doubt up to this point concerning the differences that were to be negotiated, these doubts were firmly dispelled as a result of a May 16, 1977, "joint steering group" meeting in Chicago for which the Canadians were provided a copy of the U.S. sub-group reports.

The differences separating the two sides were substantial. From the Canadian point of view, there were three major objections to the American position. The first was with respect to whether U.S. Public Law 92-500 would, in effect, be applied to the Canadian side of the Great Lakes. This American proposal, what one official termed "a fine example of imperialistic thinking," was rejected in part on the legal principle that American law should not be applied, extra-territorially, to Canada. The proposal was also rejected on the more political argument that there was "less need" for similar effluent standards on the Canadian side because it contributed less total pollution. The application of such standards was also politically unlikely. It would have meant a tightening of industrial pollution requirements in Ontario, and these would have to be enforced by a Conservative government that had never shown itself eager to confront industry in such fashion.

The second major Canadian objection concerned the American proposal for adopting basin-wide as opposed to boundary water standards – a proposal that would have broadened the scope of the agreement to include all tributaries flowing into the Great Lakes in addition to the boundary waters, those through which the international boundary runs. The Canadian position against including tributaries was in part based on the question of sovereignty; since these tributaries are entirely within the respective countries, it was argued, they are a domestic not an international matter. A second argument, which also applied to the proposal for effluent standards, was that the concept of water quality standards – the basis of the 1972 agreement – was "more appropriate" in this context and ought to be retained. The overall water quality objectives approach is, of course, much more compatible with the Canadian position on the two countries' "equal rights" to the use of the Great Lakes than is the effluent standards approach. The latter would require similar source-by-source reductions despite the disparity in the total amounts of pollutants from each side. The Canadians, therefore, argued each country should be responsible for taking such measures as necessary to ensure both together met the common water quality standards in the boundary waters. The third major Canadian objection concerned the U.S. proposal to eliminate the IJC Regional Office. While sympathetic to the idea of redefining its role, they were not, as one noted, "disestablishmentarianists."

Canadian and American officials spent the fall and winter of 1977 refining their draft texts of the new agreement and clearing these through all departments involved. One of the major issues fought out within each government, pitting the respective environmental agencies against nuclear power industry interests, was over whether or not new and tougher radiation standards would be included. The two sides exchanged drafts during February, 1978. The U.S. version now called for a major reorganization, not the "disestablishment," of the Regional Office, but was otherwise very similar to the proposals produced by Sub-Group A. A plenary negotiating meeting on March 30 in Ottawa found the American side pushing hard their arguments on effluent standards and tributaries. The Canadian side resisted, and ultimately was successful. After a lengthy debate, the meeting settled in principle both these questions. More junior officials from each side then held a series of meetings on the wording of the text. A final plenary negotiation meeting on May 11, 1978, resolved almost all remaining differences. A number of additional points, though, had to be settled eventually by the heads of the respective negotiating teams, Richard Vine of the State Department and Russell McKinney of External Affairs, and over long-distance telephone by other External Affairs and State Department officials.

The major unresolved issue was the IJC Regional Office. After considerable discussion of alternative structural arrangements and operating responsibilities, the negotiators agreed to specify the functions of the Regional Office, where this had not been done in 1972, and limit these to providing (1) administrative and technical support for the boards, and (2) a public information service. In the former function, the Regional Office would be responsible to the boards (not the IJC); in the latter it would be responsible to the Joint Commission. It was on hearing of this arrangement that the Canadian section of the IJC became concerned about the fate of its beleagured Regional Office. Maxwell Cohen, the chairman of the IJC's Canadian section, made forceful representations with the Department of External Affairs and its minister, Don Jamieson, and with the Prime Minister's office.[14] Cohen's most basic objection was that the commission's ability to review independently the governments' progress under the agreement depended on its direct link with the Regional Office. What government officials claimed was a matter of management and staffing had for the commissioners, at least on the Canadian side, clearly become a matter of principle and of the governments' commitment to pollution control programs in the Great Lakes.[15] The issue became a highly sensitive one, and, according to an American official, "the Canadian side backed off." A compromise provision was ultimately arranged, stipulating that the two governments, with the IJC's help, would undertake a special review of "the staffing of the Office." At a meeting in Toronto arranged for the IJC, on June 2, 1978, External Affairs and State Department representatives assured the commissioners the governments were prepared to be "flexible." A "gentleman's understanding" was reached that this review would encompass both staffing and functions – as the commission wanted.

This resolution of the matter evidently did not satisfy everyone, however. At the annual mid-July IJC public meeting on Great Lakes water quality, one of the Canadian commissioners, Keith Henry, who was leaving the IJC in a few months, strongly criticized what he saw as "a disguised but effective emasculation of the IJC."[16] Henry's public outburst, a rare event for a commissioner, was roundly applauded by representatives of environmental groups who were present at the meeting. The two federal governments were defended by representatives from the State Department and External Affairs who argued that "90-95 per cent" of the new agreement was the result of the work of the Joint Commission (and its boards) and that the proposed review of the Regional Office should not in any way be taken to imply a lessening of their commitments.

Whether because the new agreement followed the lines of the 1972 version, because it was even more technical than its predecessor, because officials had kept in close touch with their ministers, or because environmental matters generally evoked less political concern in 1978 than in earlier years, the text was approved by the Trudeau cabinet in mid-July almost without discussion. Final American acceptance, however, did not come for five months. Once again, as in 1972, the White House's fiscal overseer – the Office of Management and Budget (OMB) – needed much convincing that there were no financial commitments in the agreement beyond those already required by existing American domestic environment programs. OMB eventually gave its approval in mid-autumn. The Great Lakes Water Quality Agreement of 1978 was rather quietly signed into effect in late November during a busy Ottawa visit by Secretary of State Cyrus Vance.

While the basic structure of the 1972 document was maintained, the specific substantive changes were in some cases crucial. The two countries agreed that municipal and industrial pollution abatement and control programs would be completed and in operation no later than the end of 1982 and 1983, respectively. The former deadline was in effect the day on which American officials expected the sewage treatment facilities for Detroit finally to be "on line." The new agreement also set out a new, more stringent set of overall phosphorus-loading reductions for each of the Great Lakes, but left the actual division of loadings between the two countries – a highly contentious matter – to be negotiated within eighteen months. The Canadian position here, based on the principle of "equal rights" of the two countries, was that the U.S. should be allowed no more than one-half of the permissible loadings. The Americans, of course, still disputed this interpretation and insisted the allowed loadings should take into consideration the larger U.S. population. The agreement further called for the discharge of toxic chemicals to be largely eliminated and specified approximately 350 "hazardous polluting substances" to be banned from the Lakes. It also included a new surveillance program and revised water quality objectives, including much tougher standards for radioactivity. The agreement thus reflected the consensus of officials on both sides of the border that municipal pollution programs were well underway, that industrial pollutants now represented the major problem requiring attention, and that the agreement itself had to be expanded to cover a range of problems not previously foreseen or simply not covered in the 1972 version.

Conclusion

Obviously, the political processes involved in negotiating and implementing pollution control programs for the Great Lakes are highly complex. Also, the short-term results have not been spectacular. The water quality of the Lakes is only beginning to improve in some ways as a result of these programs, although the agreements of 1972 and 1978 put into effect the basis for substantial long-term progress. What the foregoing analysis suggests is that the slowness of the political process and the initial lack of improvement in the Great Lakes is not solely or even mainly the result of supposed government disinterest in environmental issues, of obviously inadequate government programs, or of "politics" in the pejorative sense. To be sure, the governments' interest could have been greater and longer-lived, the programs could have been implemented earlier and more forcefully, the funds could have been spent faster and in greater quantities, and the degree of political manoeuvring could have been less. But the practical constraints that enter into environmental politics in all political systems must also be recognized in any realistic assessment of these agreements. Aside from the sheer physical fact that the size and condition of the Great Lakes ensure noticeable improvements cannot occur overnight, the constraints are at least three.

First of all, much of the scientific knowledge required for pollution abatement programs was and still is lacking. Faced with highly complex issues, governments do not usually – and should not – make decisions without a reasonable effort to identify the nature of the problem at hand and to gauge the effects of possible alternative solutions. In the case of Great Lakes pollution, the lengthy 1964-1970 IJC study successfully established the facts of the pollution problems perceived at that time. It soon became apparent, though, that these were only some of the problems, and perhaps were not the most serious dangers. Moreover, while the solutions for some specific problems were obvious (e.g., eliminate inputs of mercury or PCB's), the effects of other policy measures, and thus the desirability of these measures, have been matters more of informed speculation than of hard scientific evidence (e.g., the effect of reducing phosphate loadings).

Second, environmental problems obviously are not the only ones on the political agenda. Pervasive and strong public demands for other government actions – for example, to ensure a healthy economy and reduce unemployment – often conflict with environmental demands. Especially in the case of large water bodies like the Great Lakes there are the competing interests of many different types of users. It is consequently extremely difficult even for the most committed bureaucrat or politician dealing with environmental problems to win all the political battles that must be fought over scarce government resources with other bureaucrats and politicians equally committed to different concerns. Thus, there are always limitations on how much money can be spent on building sewage treatment plants, hiring more scientists to do more studies on other possible problems, and so on.

Third, differences and complications will inevitably emerge when two or more governments with partially differing interests at stake are involved. The notably unsuccessful discussions that have taken place over pollution in the Mediterranean and in various international rivers provide ample evidence of the extraordinary difficulties encountered in such multi-jurisditional situations. If the participants include, as in the case of the Great Lakes, not only national jurisdictions but also two or more levels of government within each, all with some interest and responsibility, then the federal-provincial and federal-state dimensions added to the bilateral dimension further complicate the mix. Being human, politicians tend to avoid assuming responsibilities perceived as less than urgent or politically essential; when they do move, they tend to try to share with other politicians and levels of government as much of the burden and as little of the credit as possible. Part of this is electoral politics, but part is common sense. Few tax-paying citizens want their government to accept a larger portion of pollution control expenditures or stiffer regulations than the "other guy" or than "necessary." The multiple jurisdictions of the Great Lakes area, and the political and socio-economic differences among them, ensure different approaches to pollution control and different definitions of what is the fair share of clean-up effort by each. These differences, as we have seen, take much time and effort to reconcile.

The most fundamental bilateral disagreement during the negotiation of both the 1972 and 1978 agreements concerned whether the two countries have "equal rights" to the "use" of the waters, and thus each to control sufficiently so as to contribute no more than one-half of the "allowable" pollution, or whether the two have a mutual responsibility to take equivalent measures to control pollution. The Canadian and Ontario governments, reflecting the country's position as the contributor of less pollution, advanced the "equal rights" argument and opposed the establishment of uniform, basin-wide control measures. Rigid effluent standards, they said, are less necessary on the less populated, less industrialized Canadian side. The American government, on the other hand, advanced the "equal responsibility" argument. It staunchly opposed any suggestion that its greater population and industry require a considerably greater, more rigid control effort than that on the Canadian side. This basically political disagreement was not resolved by the negotiations; it will continue to surface in bilateral environmental relations.

The two sides did agree, though, to adopt pollution control measures which compromise neither side's position on the central principle yet identify the degree of mutuality in the two sides' somewhat opposing interests. It might also be noted that there were, in the Great Lakes case, other than strictly bilateral differences to resolve. On a less fundamental level, compromises were made to reconcile the diverging interests of various governmental departments and agencies involved. Compromises were also reached between the somewhat differing priorities and interests of the governments and the International Joint Commission, a process that dominated the later stages of the 1978 negotiations.

There is a degree of truth in the oft-repeated refrain that "no one is in favour of pollution." It is a mistake, though, to conclude that the process of environmental policy-making ought therefore to be relatively simple and straightforward, and that if it is not then the bureaucrats and politicians must be at fault. To be sure, no one – politician, bureaucrat, or average voter – is entirely blameless for the slow pace of environmental efforts. But to look first for such a scapegoat is to ignore the considerable constraints on government environmental policies, among them the lack of relevant scientific knowledge, the competing demands of the political arena, and the problems posed by the presence of different political jurisdictions with differing interests and priorities. In a modern industrial society like Canada, such constraints lead seemingly inescapably to a complex and usually slow policy process and to less than dramatic policy results in dealing with many problems. The effort to deal with environmental issues, themselves the products of socially and technologically complex societies, is not merely representative of this pattern. In many ways it is the archetypal contemporary public-policy conundrum.[17]

NOTES

1. A number of studies have suggested that the public's concern about environmental problems in the early 1970's was superficial and perhaps even ar-

tificial, having been induced by extensive mass media coverage rather than by personal observation and understanding. See, for example, Gilbert Winham, ''Attitudes on Pollution and Growth in Hamilton, or 'There's An Awful Lot of Talk These Days About Ecology,' '' *Canadian Journal of Political Science*, 3 (1972), 389-401; J. W. Parlour and S. Schatzow, ''The Mass Media and Public Concern for Environmental Problems in Canada, 1960-1972,'' *International Journal of Environmental Studies*, 13 (1978), 9-17; and D. Munton and L. Brady, ''American Public Opinion and Environmental Pollution,'' Research Report, Behavioral Sciences Laboratory, Ohio State University, 1970.

2. A number of key scientific studies on the Great Lakes during the late 1950's and early 1960's demonstrated the historical trend toward serious pollution levels. The key role of phosphates, although a matter of some dispute until approximately the mid-1950's, was generally accepted by scientists in the mid-1960's, at least by those not in the employ of the soap and detergent industry. Various IJC reports list references to this research.

3. The consensus of U.S. officials interviewed by the author was that President Nixon was personally indifferent, if not opposed, to serious efforts for more effective pollution control measures. For a defence of the Nixon administration's policies, see John Quarles, *Cleaning Up America: An Insider's View of the Environmental Protection Agency* (Boston, 1976); and John D. Whitaker, *Striking a Balance: Environment and Natural Resources Policy in the Nixon-Ford Years* (Washington D.C., 1976).

4. Letter and attached draft, E. Roy Tinney to K. Wardroper, March 16, 1970, Department of External Affairs files, 25-5-2-Great Lakes 4, Volume 1 (declassified).

5. ''Report on Meeting of Canada-United States Officials on Great Lakes Pollution,'' May 25, 1970, Department of External Affairs files, 25-5-2-Great Lakes 4-2, Volume 1 (declassified).

6. Memorandum for the President from Russell Train, Chairman, Council on Environmental Quality, ''Task Force on the Improvement of the Effectiveness of Water Quality Control on the Great Lakes – Final Report,'' September 24, 1970, Department of State files (declassified).

7. These and other personal comments quoted below were obtained from confidential interviews with participants, conducted during the summer of 1978 and the spring of 1979.

8. International Joint Commission, *Report on Great Lakes Water Quality for 1972*, 21.

9. *Ibid.* (1975), 1.

10. *Ibid.*, 3.

11. *Ibid.* (1976), 2.

12. Memorandum, George R. Alexander, Chairman of Sub-Group A, to Ms. Barbara Blum, Chairperson, U.S. Senior Review Group, Environmental Protection Agency, May 16, 1977 (unclassified).

13. The IJC was only peripherally involved in the negotiations. An IJC report on the 1972 agreement, sent to the governments in early March, contained few specific suggestions regarding changes in the text of the agreement. It did suggest the IJC's jurisdiction should be expanded to cover various joint activities, such as contingency plans and vessel waste, not under its jurisdiction in the original agreement. The commissioners also urged the governments to revise the water quality objectives, to set firm target dates for both municipal

and industrial pollution programs, and to consider including some references to land-use planning. The bulk of their report, however, concerned operations and progress under the existing agreement.

14. Confidential interviews, June 15 and 22, 1978. Personal relationships may or may not have played a part here. Cohen is known to be an acquaintance of Pierre Trudeau. The then Director of the IJC Regional Office was a brother-in-law of ex-External Affairs Minister Don Jamieson.

15. It was also a matter of authority and power politics. "The fundamental question," for one commissioner, was "who runs the system." (Confidential interview, February 8, 1979.)

16. Personal notes, July 19, 1978. In a later interview on CBC Radio's "As It Happens," Henry said that he was "mad as hell" about the new agreement because, by extending the Board's authority over the Regional Office, "the governments are taking away our inspectors." Given that the Regional Office staff had only very rarely been used in such a manner by the commissioners, Henry was presumably referring more to potential service than past practice. It is not yet clear (as of mid-1979) what effect the government's review of the office will have on the way in which and extent to which the IJC can undertake independent surveillance and verification on the Lakes.

17. The research for this essay was made possible by a leave fellowship from the Social Sciences and Humanities Research Council, and by part of a collective grant to the Centre for Foreign Policy Studies at Dalhousie University by the Donner Canadian Foundation.

CHAPTER SEVEN

Policy, Pipelines, and Public Participation: The National Energy Board's Northern Pipeline Hearings[1]

by John B. Robinson

The Background

The discovery of oil in Prudhoe Bay, Alaska, in 1968 was the occasion for both hope and fear on the part of the Canadian government. The hope was that similar discoveries would soon be made in the Canadian Arctic, thus opening the North to development, a persistent theme in Canadian politics at least since John Diefenbaker's "Northern Vision." The fear was that the transportation of Alaskan oil south would reduce the market for Canadian oil exports to the United States. At this time energy supplies were thought to be abundant[2] and the major policy problem for the Canadian government was to try to assure sufficient markets for domestic production.[3] The National Oil Policy of 1961, which partitioned the country into two halves, the eastern half to be served only by imported oil, had ensured that the export of Canadian oil to American markets was crucial to the economic viability of oil production in western Canada. As a result, early plans for frontier development in Canada centred on the construction of an export-oriented oil pipeline up the Mackenzie Valley intended to ship both American and Canadian oil to the United States.[4]

Unfortunately for Canadian plans, not oil but natural gas was discovered in the Canadian Arctic. Consequently, the emergence of the Trans-Alaska pipeline proposal to deliver Alaskan oil by pipeline and tanker to the U.S. west coast and the refusal of the American government to consider Canadian counter-offers for a Mackenzie Valley oil pipeline shifted official attention toward the possibility of a natural gas pipeline up the Mackenzie Valley. Although official hopes for an oil line existed as late as 1974, the government was heavily involved in gas pipeline planning by 1970.[5] As with the plan for an oil pipeline, the initial purpose of government involvement was the promotion of increased exports. Not only were increased gas exports considered good *per se*, they also were felt to help the chances of increasing oil exports. When the National Energy Board approved 6.3 trillion cubic feet of gas exports to the United States in 1970, this decision was linked explicitly to the question of Canadian oil exports in the accompanying government press release: "The Government, in its consideration of these matters, has proceeded in the expectation that . . . access for Canadian oil to the United States will be satisfactory."[6]

Preliminary industry submissions concerning a Mackenzie Valley natural gas pipeline had been made to the federal government as early as 1969, and when the government's Northern Pipeline Guidelines were issued in August, 1970, a formal application was expected by 1972 at the latest. However, little progress was made until 1972, partly because of the industry's experience in Alaska, where a protracted court case and regulatory problems were delaying official approval of the Trans-Alaska pipeline, and partly because of the rivalry between the two industry "study groups" examining the pipeline issue. In June of that year, at government insistence, the two groups merged to form the Gas Arctic-Northwest Project Study Group, which became known by the name of its service corporation, Canadian Arctic Gas Study Limited (CAGSL). By this time, the prospects for early advancement and approval of an export-oriented gas pipeline were diminishing as it became apparent that Canadian supplies of oil and gas were not as abundant as had been thought.[7] In February, 1973, the government imposed oil export controls; by the end of that year the OPEC oil embargo, price hikes, and a gas shortage in the U.S. had confirmed the shift in official perspective from perceptions of abundance to expectations of future shortfalls.

If anything, however, this shift only strengthened government support for a Mackenzie Valley pipeline. In both government and industry circles, the rationale for a pipeline simply was switched from the promotion of increased exports to the provision of gas to meet future domestic requirements. Once touted as desirable in order to increase exports to the United States, the Mackenzie Valley pipeline was now to be described as necessary to avoid imminent shortages in Canada.

Another event also had an impact on the preparation of the pipeline applications. In September, 1974, one member of

CAGSL, Alberta Gas Trunk Line Limited, left the consortium to form a rival group, Foothills Pipelines Limited, which proposed an alternative "all-Canadian" pipeline up the Mackenzie Valley. Unlike the CAGSL proposal, which involved bringing both American and Canadian gas south to markets in Canada and the United States, the Foothills "Maple Leaf" line would carry only Canadian gas from the Mackenzie Delta south to markets in southern Canada. Foothills aggressively promoted the nationalistic nature of its project, and began to prepare an application for the National Energy Board. The result was to further delay the Arctic Gas application, the first volumes of which reached the National Energy Board (NEB) in March, 1974. Supplementary material was filed in late 1974 and early 1975, at the same time as the formal submission of the rival Foothills application.

During the course of the subsequent hearings by the National Energy Board it became apparent that the Foothills application could not be sustained because sufficient gas had not been found in the Mackenzie Delta to support a pipeline.[8] The result was the development of the Foothills (Yukon) proposal by the Foothills group, submitted to the Board in August and September, 1976, and amended in February, 1977. This proposed a pipeline to transport only American gas from Prudhoe Bay, running parallel to the Alaska Highway through Alaska and the Yukon to British Columbia and Alberta and thence to the United States.

The irony of Foothills, the proponent of the "all-Canadian" Maple Leaf Project, submitting a proposal for a pipeline to carry only American gas to American markets was not lost on the participants in the NEB hearings or on the NEB itself, but events were to prove the Foothills decision wise since it was the Foothills (Yukon) proposal that eventually was approved.[9]

The decision-making process on the northern pipeline applications took place in the context of this confusing welter of rival proposals and shifts in policy perspective. Clearly, the extent of government involvement in the pre-hearing process of pipeline planning not only had a great impact upon the development of the pipeline proposals but also resulted in a predetermination of the desirability of a frontier pipeline before any of the formal decision-making processes had begun. Between March, 1971, and January, 1974, at least five federal Cabinet ministers, including Prime Minister Trudeau, gave speeches endorsing the idea of a frontier gas pipeline. Perhaps the most explicit was Jean Chrétien, Minister of Indian Affairs and Northern Development, who said in early 1974 that "This government, after weighing all the factors involved very carefully, has come to the conclusion that a gas pipeline down the Mackenzie Valley is in the public interest.''[10] This conclusion was reached before any formal pipeline proposals had been submitted and before any of the hearings related to these proposals had begun.

The existence of such predetermination was important for three reasons. In the first place, the government's attitude was crucial in maintaining the momentum of the pipeline applications throughout the changes in policy perspective and the industry rivalries described above. The statements and actions of the government provided the assurance that the industry needed in order to proceed with the lengthy and expensive application process. Secondly, this predetermination meant that the most important decision concerning the pipeline proposals, the decision as to whether any pipeline was needed, was made in a way that involved no participation by interests outside the federal government and the oil and gas industry. That is, a "closed" decision-making process was in operation for several years prior to the formal regulatory and hearing process; during these years many of the preliminary questions surrounding frontier pipelines were thrashed out in private. The point is not so much that the government created such a closed process but that representatives of the oil and gas industry appear to have had free access to it.[11] Finally, the government's predetermination could be expected to have a significant influence on the National Energy Board hearings on the northern pipeline applications.

The Decision-Making Process

Officially, the most important part of the formal decision-making process was the set of public hearings to be held by the National Energy Board. The NEB, formed in 1959, is the key federal agency involved in decision-making on major oil and gas project applications. The Energy Board has two statutory functions: to advise the federal government in energy policy and to regulate those aspects of the energy industry that are subject to federal jurisdiction. Under the NEB Act, any proposal for the interprovincial or international transfer of oil or natural gas must be approved by the NEB, which then issues a certificate of public convenience and necessity. If a certificate is granted then the application is referred to the federal Cabinet for final approval. If the Board refuses an application, however, its decision is final. This statutory requirement for NEB approval of major certificate applications, together with the Board's practice of holding full public hearings on such applications, meant that the Board's northern pipeline hearings were generally expected to be the crucial component of the federal decision-making process on the pipeline issue.

It is important to recognize that, prior to the beginning of the hearings and the exercise of its regulatory functions, the NEB was extensively involved, in pursuance of its advisory duties, in the government activities concerned with planning and expediting the Arctic Gas pipeline proposal. The major vehicle of this involvement was the Task Force on Northern Oil Development, of which the NEB chaired the Pipeline Committee and the Marketing Committee and participated on two of the others: the Economic Impact and Transport Committees. As Dosman remarks, "the Energy Board . . . was at the centre of northern pipeline construction from the start."[12]

And NEB involvement was not limited to its participation in the task force. As of 1975, it participated on twenty-eight interdepartmental committees and task forces, at least five of which were or had been directly involved in planning or evaluating the northern pipeline proposals.[13]

The most significant example of this prior involvement with the pipeline proposals, however, occurred with the appointment of Marshall Crowe as chairman of the National Energy Board on October 15, 1973, and subsequently as chairman of the NEB panel hearing the pipeline applications. Before becoming chairman of the NEB, Crowe had been active in the field of pipeline policy. As Deputy Secretary to the Cabinet and the Deputy Clerk of the Privy Council Office from 1969 to 1971, he was involved directly in pipeline planning.[14] However, it was as president, and eventually chairman, of the government-owned Canadian Development Corporation (CDC), from 1971 to 1973, that Crowe was most directly involved with the pipeline applications. During Crowe's tenure as president, the CDC became a member of the Gas Arctic-Northwest Project Study Group and Crowe himself became a member of the Management Committee of the Study Group. He continued in this role until his appointment to the NEB in October, 1973.

Crowe's involvement with the early government activity regarding northern pipelines and his participation in the Gas Arctic-Northwest Project Study Group illustrate the close government-industry connections characteristic of the pipeline planning process. His subsequent appointment as chairman of the government agency hearing the applications was no doubt seen as the logical culmination of his extensive involvement in northern pipeline issues. In this case, however, the courts did not agree. A challenge to Crowe's participation in the hearings by several public interest groups was first referred to the Federal Court of Appeal, which sided with the NEB.[15] Three of the public interest groups appealed the decision to the Supreme Court of Canada, which ruled, on March 11, 1976, that Crowe should step down from the NEB panel hearing the pipeline applications on the grounds of "reasonable apprehension of bias."

The hearings, delayed for more than five months, were forced to restart in their entirety after the Supreme Court decision, and the Crowe case had a significant impact on their outcome. Had the original hearings continued as scheduled, there would not have been time for the Foothills (Yukon) proposal to emerge. Given the lack of drilling success in the Mackenzie Delta, and the NEB findings regarding the need for frontier gas, the result would undoubtedly have been the approval of the Arctic Gas application.

One final aspect of the Energy Board's pre-hearing activities with respect to northern pipelines should be mentioned. In the fall of 1974, the NEB, under its advisory powers, held a hearing on the supply and demand of natural gas in Canada. This hearing occurred in the context of the shift in policy perspective regarding gas supply and demand described above. In its report, issued in April, 1975, the NEB concluded that frontier gas would be needed almost immediately to offset looming domestic shortages, thus providing corroboration for the new arguments of the pipeline proponents.[16] In effect, this decision meant that the need for a frontier pipeline was established before the pipeline hearings started and that, in the absence of overwhelming evidence to the contrary, this need would be considered a given in those hearings.[17]

Although NEB approval represented the major regulatory requirement, a successful pipeline applicant also would need to be granted approval for a pipeline right-of-way from the federal Department of Indian Affairs and Northern Development (now the Department of Indian and Northern Affairs). Initially, there was strong resistance within the government to the idea of holding a separate set of hearings on the right-of-way issue. However, the combination of increased opposition to the pipeline among native groups and environmentalists and pressure by the NDP upon the then-minority Liberal government resulted in the appointment, on March 21, 1974, of Mr. Justice Thomas Berger of the British Columbia Supreme Court to hold a public inquiry, under the Territorial Lands Act, into the environmental and socio-economic terms and conditions that ought to be attached to a right-of-way permit for a Mackenzie Valley pipeline.

At first glance, the Berger Inquiry was to be only a minor component of the pipeline decision-making process, in no way as important as the NEB's northern pipeline hearings. The NEB, after all, had been involved from the beginning in northern pipeline planning. It was a permanent federal agency with broad regulatory and advisory powers, and its approval was required before a pipeline could be built. Furthermore, it had the authority to examine all issues surrounding the pipeline applications, including the question of need for a pipeline and the economic and engineering viability of the proposals and their national and regional socio-economic and environmental impacts. The Berger Inquiry, on the other hand, was a one-time public inquiry set up by a reluctant government under political pressure. It had very limited terms of reference, being instructed only to consider environmental and socio-economic terms and conditions that might be attached to a Mackenzie Valley pipeline, the need for which would presumably be dealt with elsewhere. In addition, the Berger Inquiry had only advisory powers, reporting to the Minister of a Department that had been actively involved in promoting the concept of a gas pipeline. Yet, in the end, it was the Berger Inquiry that captured the imagination of the Canadian public, that garnered by far the most publicity and sparked the most controversy, and that arguably was the single most important factor in determining the final decision.

This curious difference between statutory power and political authority was matched by a significant difference in the style and substance of the two sets of hearings. The Berger Inquiry represented a more open process than the NEB hearings. It offered a much greater opportunity for extensive and effective public participation and by its wide scope and broadly interpreted terms of reference it encouraged such participation. The existence of these differences, together with the similarity of the subject and timing of the two sets of hearings, means that the Berger Inquiry serves as a useful basis for comparison in examining the NEB hearings. This is particularly true of those areas where discretion existed with respect to the conduct and style of the hearings, precisely the area where the greatest contrast existed.

The Hearings

The NEB hearings on the northern pipeline applications began on October 27, 1975. Because of the disqualification of Marshall Crowe, however, the hearings were terminated and began anew on

April 12, 1976. These second hearings consisted of 214 days of testimony and produced over 37,000 pages of transcripts. The hearings ended on May 12, 1977, and the NEB report was released on July 4, 1977. Of the total of 106 companies, governments, associations, and individuals who participated in the northern pipeline hearings, the majority were from the oil and gas industry (42) or were industrial consumers of gas or potential suppliers of labour or materials to a northern pipeline (28). The rest were provincial governments or agencies (5), intervenors from the Northwest Territories or the Yukon (19), public interest groups (9), and individuals (3). Of these, 33 supported Arctic Gas, 14 supported Foothills or, later, Foothills (Yukon), 29 supported both applications, 19 opposed both, and 11 took no position.

While most of the intervenors were of a type familiar to the NEB, "non-conventional interests"[18] also participated: native groups, public interest groups, and individuals. While most of the northern intervenors participated only in the NEB's brief visits to the North (totalling twelve hearing days), the northern pipeline hearings witnessed the most extensive involvement of public interest groups in NEB history. The non-conventional intervenors contributed to the hearings in two main ways. In the first place, as a result of the scale of their involvement and the co-ordination of their case, these intervenors were able to participate actively and regularly in cross-examination and to present a fairly coherent and detailed argument to the Energy Board. Early in the hearings a number of public interest groups banded together to form a group, called the Public Interest Coalition, for the purpose of co-ordinating their case against the pipeline proposals. This coalition also published a pipeline newsletter sent out to approximately 900 civil servants, politicians, public interest groups, individuals, and media personnel. In addition to their substantive contribution to the pipeline hearings, the non-conventional intervenors also raised a number of procedural questions concerning the conduct of the hearings and of the energy decision-making process itself. The most important of these actions was the challenge to Marshall Crowe, but several of the groups, notably the Canadian Wildlife Federation, were active in raising other procedural questions of major importance. One of these will be further discussed below.

The pipeline hearings were divided into four phases dealing respectively with engineering and cost data; contracts and financial matters; socio-economic, environmental, and other public interest matters; and supply and demand. The time allotted to each phase decreased radically as the hearings progressed, from about four months for Phase 1 to about two weeks for Phase 4. In addition, throughout the course of the hearings, the Energy Board lengthened the hearing day from an original four hours to an eventual eleven and a half hours for some periods at the end of the hearings. Both of these changes occurred as a result of the NEB desire to speed up the proceedings, apparently in order to keep in step with the American decision-making process on the pipeline applications.

The Energy Board decision turned down the Arctic Gas and Foothills applications and approved, subject to certain conditions, the amended Foothills (Yukon) application. Yet, even in the Board's own words, the "eleventh hour filing" of the amended Foothills (Yukon) application "suffered from a lack of detailed assessment of the potential socio-economic and environmental impacts."[19] Given this lack of socio-economic and environmental evidence in the Foothills (Yukon) application, there is rich irony in the reasons given by the Energy Board for the dismissal of the Arctic Gas proposal:

On the evidence before it, and having regard to all relevant matters taken into account, *including particularly the environmental and socio-economic problems*, the Board is not satisfied that a certificate should be issued.[20]

This irony is further compounded when it is remembered that the environmental and socio-economic evidence together took up less than a month of the hearings (out of over twelve months of hearings) at a time when their progress was highly disorganized and the NEB was making strong efforts to speed up the entire process.

Part, perhaps much, of the reason for the Energy Board's decision may have been the great impact of the report by the Berger Inquiry, released three days before the end of the NEB hearings. Because of the great publicity surrounding that inquiry, Berger's categorical rejection of the Northern Yukon pipeline route proposed by Arctic Gas and his recommendation that no pipeline be built in the Mackenzie Valley for ten years had the effect of making the Arctic Gas proposal politically unacceptable. Moreover, unlike the NEB, Berger had spent most of his time examining the environmental and socio-economic evidence.

The Berger Inquiry started its hearings in March, 1975, a year after Justice Berger was appointed and seven months before the NEB hearings began. The hearings ended on October 15, 1976, after 283 days of testimony that involved 1,700 witnesses and resulted in over 40,000 transcript pages. The Berger report was tabled in the House of Commons on May 9, 1977, about two months before the NEB report was released.

The procedure followed by the Berger Inquiry differed quite substantially from that of the NEB hearings. A division into "formal" and "community" hearings allowed the expert evidence to be presented with normal (though relaxed) rules of evidence and rights of cross-examination, while the evidence of the people to be most directly affected by a pipeline could be presented informally, "in their own language and in their own way."[21] One of the most important procedural differences between the Berger Inquiry and the NEB hearings had to do with the issue of funding for intervenors. The NEB has consistently refused to fund public interest intervenors appearing before it although there is no apparent statutory bar to such funding.[22] Before the northern pipeline hearings began an application was made by several public interest groups to the Minister of Energy, Mines and Resources for funding to participate in the NEB hearings. After some delay the group was informed, just before the hearings began, that no funding would be available.

The position of the Berger Inquiry on this issue was quite different. On the recommendation of Mr. Justice Berger, funding was provided by the federal government to native groups, environmental groups, northern municipalities, and northern businesses "to enable them to participate in the hearings on an equal footing (so far as that might be possible) with the pipeline companies – to enable them to support, challenge, or seek to modify the project."[23] Subject to meeting certain criteria of need, interest, commitment, and accountability, funds were provided to intervenors in the above categories with no strings attached as to how the money was to be spent.

A final difference between the Berger and NEB hearings was in the different attitudes of Berger and the NEB in interpreting their mandates. The NEB traditionally has adopted a low public profile, denying that it has a significant policy-making influence and preferring to cloak itself in the anonymity of a civil service agency.[24] Thus, the broad authority of the Energy Board to make policy is never made explicit and its decisions tend to be cast in terms of narrow technical issues.[25] Berger, on the other hand, interpreted his terms of reference in the widest possible fashion, examining the issue of northern development as a whole and the impact of modernization and western values upon the North. Perhaps most importantly, Berger cast the pipeline issues in terms of a choice of conscience, of morals, and of alternative concepts of human development. A greater contrast with the NEB's approach can hardly be imagined.

Problems and Issues

1. Independence of the Board

Obviously, the federal government was firmly committed from an early date to the approval of a Mackenzie Valley natural gas pipeline and members of the NEB were deeply involved in the process of pipeline planning before the hearings started. It appears that the cause of much of this prior involvement by the NEB was the dual functions vested in the Energy Board by the NEB Act in 1959. One obvious problem caused by the existence of both regulatory and advisory powers in the NEB is that Board members may, as in this case, become directly involved in planning or assessing specific proposals before the formal regulatory process begins, thus compromising their independence as the regulatory agency hearing those proposals. Even when such specific involvement does not occur, senior Board members engage in ongoing consultation with the Minister and the industry in fulfilment of their advisory duties. As the NEB has acknowledged, "The policy dispositions and empirical findings resulting from the review and advisory activities of the N.E.B. constitute the framework within which the Board examines applications in the context of Section 44 of the NEB Act."[26]

These considerations suggest that the National Energy Board functions more as a kind of semi-detached policy-making arm of the executive branch of the government than as an independent regulatory agency.[27] Such a conclusion is borne out by other studies of the regulatory process in Canada, which indicate that the dominant interpretation of regulatory behaviour developed in the United States, whereby such agencies tend to become "captured" by the industry they regulate, is not applicable in Canada. Rather, Canadian regulatory agencies, including the NEB, tend to be "managerial" in nature, reflecting the dominant influence of the government. As Lucas and Bell note, "Rather than speculate about industry capture, it is probably more significant to observe that the Board more often views the world through the eyes of the executive branch of government than of industry."[28]

This judgement takes on additional significance in light of the increasing tendency of the federal government to explicitly prejudge the merits of proposals that will later be heard by the NEB. Since the northern pipelines decision, the government has announced its position with respect to a proposed extension of domestic gas pipelines to Quebec and the Maritimes, with respect to the proposed Alaska Highway oil pipeline, and with respect to the scheme to "pre-build" the southern part of the Alaska Highway gas pipeline system. In such cases, the NEB, which has yet to rule on any of these proposals, appears more and more to be reduced to the status of a policy technician, dealing with the mechanics of how a predetermined decision is to be implemented rather than with whether such a decision is desirable.

2. The Openness of the Hearing Process

For several reasons, NEB hearings do not represent a very "open" decision-making process. The first reason arises directly out of the analysis above: the close nature of the relationship between the Energy Board and government and industry tends to make the reception offered to non-conventional interests chilly at best. A further reason relates to the information upon which NEB decisions are made. Because of its advisory functions and the large amount of industry and government consultation, the Board often has access to a great deal of information related to a specific application that is not yet on the hearing record. This information is often derived from, and shared with, government and industry sources who thus have access to information unavailable to other intervenors. This issue was raised during the northern pipeline hearings.

On May 6, 1976, two motions were presented on behalf of the Public Interest Coalition requesting (1) access to all information concerning the pipeline applications which had been or would be made available to the NEB as a result of its advisory functions, and (2) a list of all government studies related to the pipeline applications. In responding to these motions, the Energy Board both asserted that it was not legally required to release the contents of "ministerial communications" and indicated that the concept upon which they felt the motions to be based was "unthinkable and may well be considered frivolous or vexatious."[29] Notably, the Board did not deny the existence of ministerial communications or the suggestion that its decisions were based upon more than the record of the hearings. Given the history of this issue, that is hardly surprising. The characterization by the NEB of the concept underlying the coalition's motions as unthinkable, frivolous, and vexatious, however, indicates how non-conventional intervenors can expect to be treated when they raise questions concerning the rationale of the decision-making process itself.

Two other factors also work toward restricting public participation in NEB hearings. These are the amount of money necessary for successful participation in Board hearings and the necessity to conform to relatively strict legal rules of conduct. These constraints serve to deter all but the most determined individual intervenors, while lengthy hearings tax the resources of even the most wealthy public interest groups.

3. Procedural Matters

A number of procedural issues were highlighted by the conduct of the National Energy Board during the northern pipeline hearings. The first of these relates to the Board's use of its ability to control the day-to-day operations of hearings. As indicated previously, the NEB rulings in respect to hearing hours and to the order of hearing sub-phases had a detrimental effect on the quality of the hearings. Altogether, the order of sub-phases was changed many times, while the hearing hours were extended five times (once temporarily) for a total hearing day, in some cases at the end of the hearings stretching from 8:00 in the morning to 7:30 at night. The result was confusion, disarray, and a considerable decline in the quality and quantity of cross-examination. All intervenors were required to submit written direct evidence, in question and answer form, in advance of the appearance of their witnesses, upon which those witnesses were cross-examined. Before Christmas, potential cross-examiners had several weeks to read the evidence of individual intervenors, and each evening had the opportunity to review the morning's transcript and prepare cross-examination for the next day, but by the end of the hearings some panels were appearing with little warning, at times catching other participants by surprise, and at such a hectic pace that adequate preparation was impossible. Indeed, counsel for various participants often could be seen in March and April rapidly skimming the written direct evidence of panels as they were being sworn in.

A second procedural issue relates to the deadlines for the submission of this written direct evidence. At the beginning of the hearings, the deadline for the submission of evidence in the ''public interest'' sub-phases was set for a time that turned out to be seven months in advance of the eventual hearing of that evidence. In response to a request by public interest groups for an extension of the deadline, the Board ruled that the deadline for the three sub-phases in which the public interest groups were presenting virtually all of their evidence would be extended by seventeen days. At that point the deadline for submission of Phase 2 evidence (to be presented by the applicants) was over one month later than the deadline for the public interest sub-phases even though these latter, as part of Phase 3, were not heard until after Phase 2 evidence was presented. In other words, the applicants, with many times greater resources, were given much more time to prepare and present their cases than were the public interest groups.

Public Participation: Some Conclusions

In a recent review of energy decision-making in the United States, C. O. Jones has noted that the number of actors involved in the decision-making process has increased markedly during the last decade, as "cozy little triangles" of bureaucrats, legislators, and clients are replaced by "sloppy large hexagons" reflecting the advent of public interest groups, politicians, and international participants to the energy decision-making process.[30] Though different in detail, the same general process is also visible in Canada. Here, too, a cozy relationship between regulatory agencies and relevant governments and industry has been increasingly challenged by outside interests, in this case consisting primarily of non-conventional interests, including public interest groups.

With respect to the NEB, the result of this process has been a great increase in non-conventional participation in its deliberations. The most important function of such participation has been to introduce issues and concerns that would not otherwise have been addressed by the Board. This may be done in any of three ways. A non-conventional intervenor may challenge existing proposals in terms of broader or different criteria than those traditionally applied by the Board; it may suggest policy alternatives other than those proposed by industry applicants; or it may challenge the scope or procedures of the decision-making process itself. Examples of all of these can be found in the northern pipeline hearings. The result is that non-conventional intervenors help to serve as what Doern calls "countervailing constituencies" at NEB hearings, broadening the focus of the deliberations beyond the interests only of the federal government and industry applicants.[31]

The increase in non-conventional participation in NEB hearings has not gone unchallenged. A common criticism of such participation is that it often consists merely of ill-informed opposition to any large-scale energy project. The record of non-conventional participation in the NEB's northern pipeline hearings does not support this charge. In the Board's own words,

Public interest groups have made major contributions, not only in the cross-examination of the applicants, but also in the presentation of their evidence on the need for, and the timing of, a pipeline and in particular on the socio-economic and environmental consequences of having one.[32]

A more substantial criticism of increased participation by non-conventional interests in NEB deliberations has to do with the question of "regulatory lag." Industry spokesmen, in particular, have become increasingly vocal about the transaction costs of delays in decision-making. This has been particularly evident in Ontario, where extensive government review of and citizen opposition to specific Ontario Hydro proposals led Robert Taylor, the chairman of Hydro, to compare the energy planning process to the game of snakes and ladders and to complain bitterly about the number of snakes (i.e., delays) in the decision process.[33]

In fact, however, far from always increasing the inefficiency of the energy decision-making process, "regulatory lags" may often serve a useful purpose. As Helliwell notes, "the often decried lags in getting approval for large new energy projects have performed a valuable function in reducing the extent to which supply is likely to overshoot demand in the 1980's."[34] In other words, delays in the decision-making process will often permit flaws and weaknesses in the arguments supporting a particular proposal, that otherwise would not have been apparent until after approval was received, to become visible in time to be considered in the decision. Obviously there are limits to the length at which any proposal can be examined. Nevertheless, recent experience suggests that the costs of a hasty approval may well be substantially greater than those resulting from a thorough review.

Although increasing non-conventional participation in NEB activities may be desirable for the above-mentioned reasons, the Board's reaction to such participation and its actual impact to date remain disappointing. Virtually all commentators on the NEB have noted that non-conventional intervention appears to have had little impact upon Board decisions.[35] Despite the Board's plaudits for non-conventional intervenors in the northern pipeline hearings, for example, it is unlikely that their submissions had a significant effect on the eventual decision. It is more likely, given the circumstances surrounding the Board's decision, that these interventions, insofar as they related to socio-economic and environmental matters, were used as cover for the Board's essentially political decision to turn down the Arctic Gas application. More recently, substantial involvement from public interest groups in the Energy Board's 1978 hearings on both oil and natural gas supply and demand had no visible impact upon the Board's conclusions.[36] While the NEB appears ready to grant intervenor status to anyone interested in participating in its hearings, this apparently does not imply that the submissions of these intervenors will be seriously considered.

Moreover, despite the increase in non-conventional participation in NEB hearings, a number of serious obstacles remain to discourage such intervention. Briefly, these are: (1) the excessive formality of Board hearings and notices; (2) the high cost of effective participation in hearings; (3) the discouraging attitude of Board members and the habit of extensive *ex parte* consultation of Board staff and members with government and industry representatives; and (4) the Board's secrecy regarding internal studies and the results of consultations with government and industry that are relevant to specific hearing issues.

One result of these obstacles is that, in practice, participation in NEB hearings is almost always limited to a small number of relatively well-informed and financially strong public interest groups which tend to become deeply involved in particular issues. The problem is that participation by these groups does not reduce, and may actually serve to reinforce, the reality of a closed decision-making process for other groups and individuals. The fact that there are some outside interests able and willing to participate in public hearings does not increase the chances of less wealthy and knowledgeable groups and individuals. Moreover, because some groups are able to participate, decision-makers can point to such participation as evidence of the openness of the decision process.

If public participation is to be encouraged in the energy field, it is clear that the decision-making process must be opened up to a greater degree than at present. This could be accomplished in the following ways: (1) the funding of groups and individuals intervening in public hearings, subject to their meeting such conditions as those applied at the Berger Inquiry; (2) the relaxation of the formal rules of practice and procedure in public hearings; (3) the deliberate attempt to encourage public involvement through increased publicity; (4) the initiation of broad-ranging public inquiries on selected energy topics at regular intervals; and (5) the release of background studies and other information relevant to particular issues to interested groups and individuals. It seems likely that such changes would be resisted by conventional participants in the energy decision-making process. A final glance at the Berger Inquiry indicates why this should be so. As suggested above, the great popularity and impact of that inquiry resulted primarily from Berger's decision to open up his inquiry to non-conventional interests and to interpret his mandate in the widest possible sense. Success in these goals, however, had the effect of diminishing the relative importance of the conventional participants in the pipeline decision process, and of the government itself. Thus, open hearings like those of the Berger Inquiry are a direct threat to the authority of the traditionally important actors in the policy arena.

At the same time, such participation appears to be increasing. While it is still too early to tell if this trend will continue, the history of the northern pipelines decision suggests strongly that, in some cases at least, the energy decision-making process is better served by "sloppy large hexagons" than by "cozy little triangles."

NOTES

1. I want to thank François Bregha for his assistance and comments in the preparation of this paper. The reader is referred to Mr. Bregha's book, *Bob Blair's Pipeline* (Toronto, 1979), for further discussion of the events and issues surrounding the northern pipelines decision.
2. National Energy Board, *Energy Supply and Demand in Canada and Export Demand for Canadian Energy – 1966 to 1990* (Ottawa, 1969).
3. J. G. Debanné, "Oil and Canadian Policy," in E. Erickson and L. Waverman (eds.), *The Energy Question: An International Failure of Policy*, vol. 2 (Toronto, 1974).
4. E. Dosman, *The National Interest: The Politics of Northern Development, 1968-75* (Toronto, 1975).
5. *Ibid.*
6. Department of Energy, Mines and Resources, "Press Release," September 29, 1970.
7. The first indications, in late 1972, came with respect to oil supply. See National Energy Board, *Potential Limitations of Canadian Petroleum Supplies* (Ottawa, December, 1972).
8. Because the Arctic Gas line was also to contain American gas from Prudhoe Bay, the disappointing results of exploration in the Mackenzie Delta were not crippling to the CAGSL application.
9. After receiving official approval from both the U.S. and Canadian governments in 1977, the Alaska Highway pipeline has been significantly delayed by

the debate over natural gas price deregulation in the U.S. as well as by financing issues, including the question of whether the southern portion of the pipeline should be built first to provide an early cash flow from new Alberta exports. As of November, 1979, plans were to have the whole pipeline built and operating by late 1984, two years later than originally expected.

10. Jean Chrétien, "Speech to the Legislative Dinner on the Occasion of the Opening of the 51st Session of the Council of the Northwest Territories," Yellowknife, N.W.T., January 18, 1974.

11. See Dosman, *The National Interest*, 83, 113, 217-8.

12. *Ibid.*, 67.

13. A. R. Lucas and T. Bell, *The National Energy Board – Policy, Procedure and Practice*, prepared for the Law Reform Commission of Canada (Ottawa: Supply and Services Canada, 1977), 175-6.

14. Dosman, *The National Interest*, 70-1.

15. In response to the challenge to his participation in the hearings, Crowe remarked: "It need hardly be stated that I and my fellow members of the panel propose to assume and to discharge our duties and exercise our powers, on the evidence and in the public interest." ("Memo to Interested Parties and New Intervenors," October 17, 1975.) This statement, with its belief in the *unquestionable* propriety of Energy Board actions, accurately reflects NEB attitudes toward any questioning of its activities.

16. For a discussion of the close historical correlation between NEB forecasts and industry export and pipeline proposals, see J. Robinson, "Elastic Gas," *Ontario Report*, 3 (February, 1979).

17. Evidence concerning the existence of a substantial gas surplus was presented to the Energy Board before the hearings were over, but its findings were that frontier gas would be needed for domestic markets by the mid-1980's at the latest. Within six months, this forecast was obsolete. Current expectations are that Canada has sufficient gas in non-frontier areas to last until at least the early 1990's. See National Energy Board, *Canadian Natural Gas – Supply and Requirements* (Ottawa, February, 1979).

18. The term is from Lucas and Bell, *The National Energy Board*, 67.

19. National Energy Board, *Reasons for Decision – Northern Pipelines* (Ottawa, June, 1977), 1-57.

20. *Ibid.*, 1-165. Italics mine.

21. T. R. Berger, *Northern Frontier, Northern Homeland*, The Report of the Mackenzie Valley Pipeline Inquiry, vol. 2 (Ottawa: Supply and Services Canada, 1977), 226-7.

22. Lucas and Bell, *The National Energy Board*, 155.

23. Berger, *Northern Frontier*, vol. 2, 225.

24. Lucas and Bell, *The National Energy Board*, 35.

25. For discussion of a recent example, see J. Robinson, "Policy by Default," *Ontario Report*, 3 (August, 1979).

26. National Energy Board, In the Supreme Court of Canada on Appeal from the Federal Court of Appeal, *Factum of the Respondent* (1976), 32.

27. A number of commentators have suggested that the Energy Board may function as a kind of depoliticization mechanism, deflecting public criticism of energy policy away from the government. See B. Fisher, "The Role of the National Energy Board in Controlling the Export of Natural Gas from Canada," *Osgoode Hall Law Journal*, 9 (1971), 578, 595; Dosman, *The National Interest*, 202-3; R. Foulkes, "The Regulatory Function of Government: The National Energy Board," M.A. thesis, Carleton University, 1977, pp. 18, 21.

28. Lucas and Bell, *The National Energy Board*, 41. See also G. B. Doern (ed.), *The Regulatory Process in Canada* (Toronto, 1978), 28.

29. National Energy Board, "Decision on Motion," May 18, 1976, p. 10. This ruling confirmed a similar ruling in the 1976 Hydro export hearings.

30. C. O. Jones, "American Politics and the Organization of Energy Decision-Making," *Annual Review of Energy*, 4 (1979), 105.

31. Doern (ed.), *The Regulatory Process*, 27-8.

32. National Energy Board, *Reasons for Decision*, 1-59-60.

33. Robert Taylor, address to the Royal Commission on Electric Power Planning, Toronto, November 19, 1976.

34. J. Helliwell, "Canadian Energy Policy," *Annual Review of Energy*, 4 (1979), 223.

35. See, for example, Fisher, "Role of National Energy Board," 130-1; Lucas and Bell, *The National Energy Board*, 60.

36. National Energy Board, *Canadian Oil – Supply and Requirements* (Ottawa, September, 1978); NEB, *Canadian Natural Gas – Supply and Requirements* (Ottawa, February, 1979).

CHAPTER EIGHT

Arctic Seas: Environmental Policy and Natural Resource Development
by Edgar J. Dosman

Introduction

Environmental policy in Canada's Arctic seas – that vast arc of ice-infested waters from the Beaufort Sea in the west to the Labrador Shelf in the east – was neither a regional nor a national issue until 1968.[1] That year continues to serve as a convenient benchmark in Arctic development: the discovery of large oil and natural gas reserves on the Alaskan North Slope acted as a catalyst for accelerating interest in hydrocarbon exploration in Canada's North also. Since most promising geological structures lie offshore, this could only mean that Arctic waters would soon be faced with offshore exploration, with accompanying industrial development, and therefore with the risks of major environmental disasters such as oil blowouts and spills.[2]

Second, 1968 also witnessed Humble Oil's (now Exxon) decision to proceed with the famous SS *Manhattan* trials of 1969 and 1970. If the Alaskan discoveries stimulated a new era of penetration and economic development, particularly in offshore areas, the *Manhattan's* voyages served notice that Arctic waters were navigable. The prospect of commercial shipping in what until now was almost universally regarded as a closed and frozen zone could no longer be excluded. Thus, in transportation as well as resource exploration, a conceptual break-through had occurred. With the emergence of a new maritime and territorial frontier, government circles were forced to confront the multi-dimensional challenge facing Canada, including such basic issues as northern sovereignty and the limits of Canadian jurisdiction in Arctic waters.[3] Not unnaturally, environmental policy formed part of a broader strategy as well as a response to potential hazards resulting from the production and transportation of natural resources.

Arctic Seas and High Arctic Development

The origins of the Arctic Waters Pollution Prevention Act, the centrepiece of the many instruments now in place to regulate shipping in Arctic waters, illustrate the complexity of environmental policy-making in an environment that is changing so rapidly. That act, passed by Parliament in April, 1970, empowers the Canadian government to establish shipping safety control zones up to one hundred miles of the nearest land, and all ships are prohibited from entering the zones unless they comply with regulations regarding their design, construction, manning, and equipment. Ships entering Arctic waters are also required to provide evidence of financial responsibility for any pollution damage they may cause.

Prime Minister Trudeau, speaking to the House of Commons in support of the Arctic Waters Pollution Prevention Act, underlined the gravity of the pollution threat to the Arctic environment and stressed that Canada, rather than violating international law, was in fact merely in advance of it, acting creatively in the legal no-man's-land created by new marine technology and thereby spurring the international community to seek multilateral solutions to major pollution hazards. Some observers even hazarded the opinion that the legislation revealed a unique Trudeau approach to Canadian foreign policy, a unique sensitivity to Canadian international responsibility created by the opening of the Arctic waters.[4] Indeed, his defence of the Arctic Waters Pollution Prevention Act still stands as perhaps the most eloquent environmental statement of the risks of pollution in this area:

The Arctic ice-peak has been described as the most significant surface area of the globe, for it controls the temperature of much of the northern hemisphere. Its continued existence in unspoiled form is vital to all mankind. The single most imminent threat to the Arctic at this time is the threat of a large oil spill . . . [which] . . . would destroy effectively the primary source of food for Eskimos and carnivorous wild life throughout an area of thousands of square miles . . .; because of the minute rate of hydrocarbon decomposition in frigid areas, the presence of any such oil must be regarded as permanent. The disastrous consequences which its presence would have on marine plankton, upon the process of oxygenation in Arctic North America, and upon other natural and vital processes of the biosphere, are incalculable in their extent.[5]

But did this apparent sensitivity to potential marine threats signal a unique approach to environmental policy in Arctic waters in general? The answer here is no. While the act and its regulations (1972) impose rigorous standards on *vessels* and their owners, offshore drilling, which poses formidable environmental challenges, is much further advanced in Canada than in any other circumpolar nation. The Soviet Union, with the probability of extensive reserves, has not yet initiated an offshore drilling program; drilling off Greenland's western coast turned up dry holes and has been abandoned. In Alaska, Exxon has been drilling offshore near Prudhoe Bay since October, 1978, and against heavy local opposition. But in Canada major industrial offshore activity is currently under way in the Beaufort Sea and the Sverdrup Basin in the Arctic Islands, as well as in the eastern Arctic, with grave concern being expressed both within and outside government circles about the adequacy of contingency planning to cope with a blowout or major pollution emergency.[6]

In fact, the apparent paradox of extremely restrictive shipping controls in the Arctic Waters Pollution Prevention Act on the one hand, and the same Government's willingness to accept risks associated with offshore drilling on the other, dissolves when the former is seen in its political context; it was a clever response to a direct but rather clumsy U.S. challenge to Canadian sovereignty. Anti-pollution legislation gave Canada an internationally persuasive method of extending jurisdiction over Arctic waters.[7] But when a pipeline rather than tanker mode was chosen to market Alaskan North Slope oil, the northern sovereignty crisis eased, and the memory of the primary motivation for the legislation likewise faded. It is now readily acknowledged that Trudeau's forceful statements and support of the Arctic Waters Pollution Prevention Act were based not on conclusive research findings but rather on intelligent hunches regarding the vulnerability of Arctic waters.[8]

As a public issue the environmental quality of Arctic seas has gone through three distinct stages since 1968: (1) There was first the 1968-70 period when Canada was fascinated both by the voyages of the *Manhattan* and by the northern sovereignty challenge; (2) this interest was quickly replaced by an almost all-encompassing concern about pipeline construction in the western Arctic; and (3) as the pipeline debate climaxed in early 1977, industry interest in offshore activity again began to accelerate. This last period, however, has coincided with diminished public interest in the northern environment. The Mackenzie Valley pipeline debate of the mid-1970's was an event of profound importance for the environmental movement in Canada, and a rallying point for a broad coalition of interests that ranged from native organizations, church and public interest groups, and university research organizations to elements of the Canadian business community. The one-man commission of Justice Thomas Berger to investigate the impact of the pipeline system proposed by Canadian Arctic Gas Pipelines Ltd. (CAGPL) provided a national focus for an interested public eager to learn about the people and lands of the North. Opening hearings on March 3, 1975, in Yellowknife, this first open environmental impact assessment project in the North frankly captured the imagination of the country. When Berger presented the first volume of his report in April, 1977, the pipeline application was effectively dead (although it faced so many other problems by this time that it may well have collapsed under its own weight in any case).[9]

But it was catharsis. Almost as incredible as the wave of emotion that accompanied the Berger Inquiry was the speed with which the Canadian public thereafter lost interest in the North and resumed its parochial pastimes: unemployment, national unity, prices, and complaining in general. It is therefore a peculiarity of the post-Mackenzie period that there is little public attention to the perhaps more important environmental issues raised by Arctic offshore activity. This is balanced somewhat by the increasing strength and legitimacy of the native communities and their organizations, and by an increased awareness by both government and industry of the dangers and risks of working in this extraordinary environment where southern technological solutions often fail to work, yet the fundamental environmental issues confronting Arctic seas remain much less well-known than those affecting northern pipeline development. Public interest groups are finding it difficult to develop sufficient expertise and credible objectives to arouse an energy-conscious public that has had its northern fling, so to speak, during the Berger Inquiry.

Nevertheless, a brief summary of industry initiatives in the High Arctic gives an indication of the range of activity that is now taking place.

1. *Dome Petroleum: Offshore Drilling in the Beaufort Sea.* In the spring of 1976 the federal Cabinet gave approval to a new phase of Beaufort Sea exploration in the deep offshore by Canadian Marine Drilling Ltd., a wholly-owned subsidiary of Dome Petroleum Ltd. of Calgary. It has initiated a unique exploratory drilling program in the Canadian North, using ice-strengthened drill-ships and a growing fleet of supply boats, ice-breakers, and ancillary equipment. It is the costliest drilling in the world. Its program, hampered by an extremely short drilling season, has produced nine wells so far, with optimists predicting commercial production by 1985. Should a breakthrough occur in the Beaufort Sea with a major oil discovery, the whole shape of development in the High Arctic would be decisively affected.

2. *The High Arctic.* In the Arctic Islands, Panarctic Oils Ltd. of Calgary (47 per cent controlled by Petro-Canada) has drilled 144 exploratory wells and increasingly is moving offshore where the most promising geological structures have been located. After more than a decade of disappointing activity it recently has announced (May 15, 1979) a major find of offshore natural gas that could double its established gas reserves of 12.8 trillion cubic feet.[10]

3. *The Arctic Pilot Project.* The geographical location of High Arctic natural gas reserves has stimulated interest in an LNG (liquefied natural gas) transportation system as a potential option for marketing northern natural gas. In late 1976 industry discussions culminated in the Arctic Pilot Project, a proposal to transport 250 million cubic feet of LNG a day from Melville Island to southern markets with two giant LNG carriers. Sponsored by Petro-Canada, Alberta Gas Trunk Line Co., and Arctic Petrocarriers, a consortium of Canadian shipping companies, the concept envisages year-round transportation from Bridport Inlet on Melville Island through Lancaster Sound to an eastern Canadian terminal. This would introduce year-round navigation in Arctic waters for the first time. Currently before the National Energy Board, the proposal, if accepted, would initiate a new era in Arctic shipping.[11]

4. *The Eastern Arctic.* Drilling already has begun south of 60° off the Labrador Shelf, using drill ships and semi-submersible rigs. In the 1979 drilling season, Imperial Oil and Aquitaine completed an exploratory drilling program off the southeast corner of Baffin Island. Although an application to drill in Lancaster Sound has been turned back, the geological structures of the entire offshore region from Lancaster Sound to the Labrador Shelf are considered very promising by industry and will attract increasing attention in the future.

5. *Oil Tanker Traffic.* Although Panarctic's tantalizing Benthorn discovery on Cameron Island did not yield commercially viable reserves, the possibility of oil tanker traffic through the Northwest Passage in the next decade does exist. In anticipation of discoveries in the Beaufort Sea, Dome Petroleum of Calgary is already preparing plans for oil delivery by 1985. Similarly, conceptual planning for the delivery of Alaskan North Slope oil by tanker has been initiated, although implementation of such a system appears to lie some distance in the future.[12] Oil tankers in Arctic waters would present a clear environmental hazard, requiring detailed attention to terminal and loading facilities, navigational systems, the regulations of the Arctic Waters Pollution Prevention Act, ice-breaking capabilities, and contingency planning.

6. *Ice-breaking Bulk Carriers.* Subsequent to government approval of the Nanisivik lead-zinc mine at Strathcona Sound, the *MV Arctic*, a 28,000-ton bulk carrier, was constructed by Port Weller Drydocks (St. Catherines, Ont.) and operated by a consortium of Canadian shipping companies led by Federal Commerce and Navigation. The first bulk carrier of ice-class II strength in the world, the vessel completed her first season in 1978. Recently, Cominco has expressed serious interest in developing its lead-zinc property on Little Cornwallis Island, deep in the islands of the Canadian Arctic archipelago, a development that would extend bulk shipping further into Arctic waters, presumably using the *MV Arctic*. However, it is not likely that a sister ship to the *MV Arctic* will be developed for some time.

7. *Polar Ice-Breaker Construction.* Canada currently does not possess polar ice-breakers – the aging fleet is primarily designed for assisting ship movements during the short summer and more particularly for the St. Lawrence River and the Gulf. However, developments in international marine technology, the demands of northern sovereignty, and the increasing pace of resource exploration all foreshadow polar ice-breaker construction for Canadian waters within the next decade. Dome Petroleum has plans for an Arctic class X ship, the Arctic Marine Locomotive, although currently it is constructing an experimental ice-class IV vessel. For its part the federal government has currently approved the design stage for an Arctic ice-class X nuclear ice-breaker.[13]

These developments, taken together, signal a new era for Arctic waters. They can no longer be seen merely as isolated agents of change, but must be viewed within the future context of the High Arctic. As development proceeds, and particularly if hydrocarbon production systems are put in place, the region will experience a quantum jump in activity. The cumulative impact of this change, both in socio-economic and environmental terms, forms the primary focus for environmentalists concerned with the future of Arctic waters.[14]

Northern Objectives: The Approach to Environmental Policy

Since the High Arctic–the waters and islands of the Canadian Arctic archipelago–confronts a threshold of irreversible change, the first order of business is to determine how environmental priorities relate to national objectives in the Arctic. In fact, *Canada's North 1970-80*, the 1972 federal document intended as a policy framework for northern development, has a stated order of priorities which emphasizes environmental protection. They are:

a) to put into rapid effect the agreed guidelines for *social improvement*;
b) to maintain and enhance the natural environment;
c) to encourage and stimulate the development of *renewable resources*;
d) to encourage and assist strategic projects in the development of non-renewable resources and in which joint participation by government and private interests is generally desirable;
e) to provide necesssary support for non-renewable resource projects of recognized benefit to Northern residents and Canadians generally.[15]

Thus, maintaining environmental quality is the priority, ahead even of renewable resource development.

There also have been other encouraging developments for environmentalists. In 1970 the creation of the Department of the Environment established a mechanism for co-ordinating the numerous environmental programs within northern-oriented agencies and departments; three and a half years later, in December, 1973, the Cabinet agreed to establish a formal environmental assessment and review process.[16] Interdepartmental committees and regulations for the management of northern waters have proliferated, to the near despair of observers and participants alike.[17] The approval process, for example, involves an estimated twenty-eight different codes and regulatory instruments. The real question, however, concerns the meaning in practice of the priorities set out in *Canada's North 1970-80*. This is far from simple, for since 1972 new imperatives have entered the scene.

Two distinct elements – the shock in late 1972 of discovering that Canada faced future energy shortages, and the requirements of "technological sovereignty" (the technological capability to support national sovereignty)[18] – came together by July, 1973, to produce the announcement of a new Canadian oceans policy by the Minister of State for Science and Technology:

Canada must develop and control within its own borders, the essential elements needed to exploit offshore resources by:
(1) stimulating development and effective participation of Canadian industry in the plan to see that Canada controls the essential industrial and technological ingredients to exploit offshore resources.
(2) emphasizing a wide range of marine science and technology programmes relating to management of marine environment, renewable and non-renewable resources. . . . achieving, within five years, world recognized excellence in operating on and below ice covered waters . . . equal or superior to foreign governments or large multinational corporations.[19]

This announcement is now perceived as having been unduly optimistic – the five-year period is long since passed and world-recognized excellence remains a target only. Experts agree in fact that decisive action at every level is required to ensure Canadian technological leadership in the Arctic offshore.[20] The point here, however, is the potential conflict with the priorities set out in *Canada's North 1970-80*; the key objective of Canada's new oceans policy is to prepare for and to facilitate offshore hydrocarbon exploration.

As well, the emerging energy crisis resulted by 1976 in a "need to know" policy, which provides lucrative financial incentives to shore up faltering exploration in frontier areas, including Arctic waters. The objective of the policy is "to double, at a minimum, exploration and development activity in the frontier regions of Canada over the next three years, under acceptable social and environmental conditions."[21] Large write-off allowances as well as the active participation of Petro-Canada, the state oil company, have played a major and perhaps decisive role in maintaining exploration activity. In fact, afer the first blush of optimism, 1968-73, frontier oil and natural gas drilling in the Northwest Territories, the Arctic Islands, and the east coast offshore declined for five consecutive years. Panarctic's successful Whitefish H-63 gas discovery of May 15, 1979, probably would not have materialized without Petro-Canada's initiative.

It would be unrealistic to evaluate industrial activity in Arctic waters without reference to defence and strategic needs as well.[22] Since major oil and natural gas discoveries would drastically alter the strategic significance of the High Arctic and commercial shipping in Arctic waters, Canada must develop sufficient capabilities to control the pace and timing of development in this sensitive region, and this implies year-round navigational experience, independent of or in conjunction with commercial operations.[23] Yet, relentlessly, such activity also will affect the Arctic marine environment. Lancaster Sound, for example, is a biological miracle, but unfortunately it is and will remain the main marine route into the central Arctic and the Northwest Passage. Year-round movement of ships in this body of water will inevitably bring unintended and unexpected environmental consequences in the future as polar ice-breakers and commercial carriers enter Arctic waters.

In short, there is no environmental *policy*, much less any performance criteria, which could put meaning into the priorities of *Canada's North 1970-80*. Essentially, a decision has been taken to initiate and sustain offshore development in Arctic waters; it is acknowledged that environmental risks exist, but that *in balance* the need to locate energy reserves is worth these risks. The assumption is that non-renewable resource development in Arctic waters, particularly oil and natural gas exploration, will continue and accelerate. As one observer has recently put it, "our main interest is to ensure that the development of non-renewable resources does not swamp either the renewable resources or the native population and the way of life of the first North Americans."[24] Most environmental groups assume that development will proceed, and restrict themselves to minimizing negative impacts and improving the regulatory process.

Non-renewable resource development is, in practice, the first priority among the numerous parallel federal responses to particular pressures in the High Arctic. These pressures include Inuit land claims, national parks and other conservation initiatives such as the International Biological Program, resource development, scientific and research programs, and territorial interests. So far, the regulatory structure set up to guide the "safe development" of Arctic waters does not permit a holistic approach in which basic questions of objectives are focused. For example, should portions of the area such as Lancaster Sound be permanently set aside, even though the geological structures beneath them are some of the most promising in the entire Arctic? What role should cultural values play in the timing of development? These basic questions bring into focus the fundamental conflict of values affecting the future of our Arctic waters, and the questions are not currently being addressed.

For many Canadians, the strength of the Berger Inquiry was its attempt to come to grips with basic developmental objectives in the western Arctic. In the High Arctic this exercise has not taken place either in a similar inquiry or in parliamentary or territorial debates. As the years pass, decisions are made by default: the industrial integration of the High Arctic in the Canadian and North American economies is now predictable. When points of no return are reached the issues also become redefined, and become narrower; they emphasize the capabilities needed to ensure that offshore development is in the national interest. But what we cannot lose sight of is that this vast region is experiencing *fundamental* change.

Environmental Management in Arctic Waters

In practice, environmental "policy" in Arctic waters focuses on the regulatory regimes established for particular activities and the structures and procedures for project approval, monitoring, and evaluation.

Environmental threats to the Arctic marine environment arise from various activities: (1) transportation and ice-breaking; (2) other marine operations (defence, research, oceanography, etc.); (3) energy exploration and exploitation (offshore oil and gas drilling, production, platforms, vessels, etc.); and (4) land-based pollution (industry tailings, ports, community disposal sites, natural seepages, etc.). Given the current low level of mining and land-based discharge, shipping and offshore drilling have attracted the most attention of environmentalists, and the discussion here will focus on these activities.[25]

The Canada Shipping Act and the Arctic Waters Pollution Prevention Act give Transport Canada authority and responsibility to regulate navigation and prevent pollution *from ships*. Essentially, Part XX of the Shipping Act is replaced by the Arctic Waters Pollution Prevention Act in the Arctic. The sixteen shipping safety control zones (in order of escalating severity) provide a framework for highly restrictive and comprehensive regulations for all ships navigating in the Arctic.[26] There are no powers of exemption, and any change must be submitted as an amendment to the regulations. Drill-ships and mobile drilling rigs are treated as ships when navigating. Under the Arctic Waters Pollution Prevention Act and its regulations, owners of all vessels navigating in Arctic waters are liable for costs of cleanup or loss or damage resulting from ship-related pollution such as the deposit of wastes. The Canadian Coast Guard monitors vessels approaching Arctic waters to ensure evidence of financial responsibility.

Another aspect of Arctic navigation relates to the unified traffic control system to ensure an effective Arctic-wide information service for ships regarding weather, ice conditions, ice-breaker support, or emergencies. NORDREG Canada (the Arctic Canada traffic system) was introduced officially by the Canadian Coast Guard in July, 1977, and is centred at Frobisher Bay. Commercial shipping, of course, is very limited, restricted to the summer months and then only with extensive ice-breaker support. In 1978, for example, forty commercial ships in the Eastern Arctic were provided with ice-breaker escort. (Ten Coast Guard ice-breakers were deployed.) In total, more than fifty vessels were active in resupply and resource traffic.[27]

It is resource traffic, particularly the prospect of year-round oil and LNG shipments as High Arctic production systems are put in place, that raises fears. In this sense, the Arctic Pilot Project proposal now before the National Energy Board has provided an arena for a review of the adequacy of existing regulatory instruments in this area.[28]

Contingency Planning in High Arctic Development

Protection of the living resources of Arctic waters in areas of offshore drilling depends on technologically advanced *preventive* and *clean-up* measures: (1) to prevent accidents by ensuring the integrity of the drilling system and of operational procedures; and (2) to ensure that if and when accidents do occur the oil is contained immediately without severe damage.[29] In Arctic waters, by an accident of geology, the most promising areas for offshore hydrocarbon exploration usually coincide with the most biologically productive. The approval of offshore drilling has witnessed rapid developments to improve technology in both areas, and it also has produced a major five-year federal study entitled AMOP (Arctic Marine Oilspill Programme).[30] Developed by the Environmental Protection Branch of the Environmental Protection Service, AMOP reflects the two basic industry-government assumptions regarding contingency planning: first, despite much progress, there is a current lack of adequately proven countermeasures to deal with major oil blow-outs; second, there is now a major commitment on all sides to meet the challenge.

Actually, to speak of "the Arctic marine environment" is artificial and oversimplifying. Generalizations are of little use in so complex an area and in one having such startling regional differences. Therefore, in analysing the environmental conditions confronting offshore drilling, it is best to identify distinct regions.

1. *The Beaufort Sea.* Here the average open-water season is about four months, with ice landfast to 20 metres depth during winter. The ice cover further out is made up of relatively large first-year and multi-year floes. If a subsea blow-out occurred near the end of the open-water drilling period, oil and natural gas could be discharged under the pack ice. Only one major operator, Dome/CANMAR, is involved in deep offshore drilling, but this has been a high profile area with the accompanying federal interest at the highest level. In general, the hazards of drilling from artificial islands are not considered as great as from drill-ships.[31]

2. *The Arctic Islands.* The average open-water period varies from 0-3 months; during winter the ice is all landfast. Again, there is one primary offshore operator, Panarctic Oils Ltd., which has developed thickened ice-pads as drilling platforms. The remote area, extremely thinly populated, is believed to be richer in natural gas than in oil, and consequently the Arctic Islands are considered the least hazardous from the point of view of a major oil blow-out.

3. *The East Coast.* Here, both above and below 60°N, the open-water period varies widely (the Labrador Sea has been included in AMOP), from three months in the North to nine in the South and further offshore. Winds and southern currents (storms may fetch as far as Portugal) create a dynamic, fast-moving ice pack. Icebergs offer an additional hazard. Moreover, the southern waters are adjacent to some of the richest fishing grounds in the world. A recent study of the probability of an oil blow-out resulting from exploratory drilling in the Labrador Sea concludes that the danger here is four times greater than in the Beaufort Sea.[32]

In moving ice, the most common condition, no relief well drilling is possible. According to AMOP, "our present knowledge and capability regarding the cleanup of oil in moving ice is poor, and there is great potential for improvement."[33] In this situation there are admitted risks, although there is much disagreement as to the risk levels for any area. Blow-outs of exploratory wells are rare, but they do occur – most recently, in June, 1979, a blow-out off the

Yucatan Peninsula poured 30,000-45,000 barrels of oil a day into the Gulf of Mexico.[34] And this Mexican blow-out could not be shut off for several months.

Contingency planning is therefore of enormous importance, and both industry and government are aware that a major accident could be fatal in terms of public opinion. AMOP is one reflection of this; more stringent regulatory requirements for offshore drilling is another. Improved co-operative arrangements between operators and the Marine Emergency Office of the Canadian Coast Guard is yet a third. In the eastern Arctic, unlike the Beaufort Sea where there is a single major operator, a number of operators have formed an Eastcoast Oil-Spill Co-operative to select oil spill equipment and agree on procedures. Under the supervision of the Canadian Coast Guard and in consultation with the appropriate federal and provincial agencies, the project is designed to maximize response preparedness in the event of an emergency.[35] Details of contingency planning have been shared with Danish officials, who of course are very much interested in the effectiveness of contingency planning because the only operators currently drilling are on the Canadian side of the offshore international boundary. Government and operator requirements regarding contingency planning are different. By regulation, the company is responsible for countermeasures to deal with small accidents; in the case of a major blow-out, requiring all possible capabilities, the Canadian Coast Guard would lead and conduct the response.

The following specific areas related to contingency planning require immediate national attention:

1. *Research.* Programs such as AMOP and groups such as the Centre for Cold Oceans Research and Engineering (C-CORE) are providing valuable leadership in research in the critical categories: the physical environment; resource utilization; blow-out probability; the behaviour of oil as it rises to the surface and interacts with ice; the environmental prediction and logistics capability for specific Arctic regions; and Canadian response capabilities. Far more work, however, is required, given the magnitude of the task. This will be even more the case if production systems are initiated.

2. *Government-Industry Co-operation.* Given the many unknowns, both government and industry must ensure both short- and long-term co-operation in research and countermeasures. The three BREX (Beaufort Response Exercises) carried out so far by the Marine Emergency Office and Dome/CANMAR have been very useful, for example, in clarifying procedures. The recent for-

mation of a high-level industry-government committee to review
long-term environmental research needs is another.

3. *Training.* A recent Environmental Protection Service publication, *Probabilities of Blowouts in Canadian Arctic Waters,*
found that human error (rather than environmental or equipment
risk factors) offered the greatest hazard on drill-ship and artificial
island systems.[36] Adequate personnel training is therefore a crucial
element in the protection of Arctic waters.

4. *The Emergency Office of the Canadian Coast Guard.* This is
a new (1971) and understaffed organization.[37] With a current
country-wide personnel of thirty-six including headquarters staff,
and with escalating responsibilities for the world's longest coastlines, the organization requires far greater support and resources if
it is to respond to major Arctic disasters.

The Regulatory Process

Concern has been expressed regarding the regulatory process required for the approval of major Arctic offshore projects. Some
comments are specific to the mandate and procedures of the Environmental Assessment Review Process. For example:

> The Federal Environmental Assessment and Review Office
> (FEARO) is appended to the Department of Environment with
> no legislated mandate and with no legal status. The EARP of-
> fice and this panel have only an advisory function. They advise
> the Minister of the Environment who can then in turn advise the
> Minister of Indian and Northern Affairs (or other proponent
> departments as appropriate). In conducting the review process
> this panel has no power of subpoena, no rules of evidence, no
> clear onus of proof, and no fixed procedures. Hence there is no
> assurance of procedural fairness and no indication that the rules
> of natural justice would be followed.[38]

Other criticisms involve the fragmentation of authority in assessing industry proposals and enforcing the standards of projects; the
limited non-discretionary opportunities for public involvement in
the process; the lack of involvement of native interests in High
Arctic development regulations; and the role of the National
Energy Board.[39]

A broader range of questions involves the current lack of appropriate consideration of "first-order" issues before individual
projects are assessed. Industry as well as academic concern has

been directed at this problem because industry does not want to repeat the Mackenzie experience where, after an investment of tens of millions of dollars, the application was rejected. Instead, some recommendations for change have suggested that a forum be created fairly early on for the consideration of fundamental land-use issues in relation to the proposed project. At this point social, environmental, and other national policy implications could be weighed. If rejected, the proposal would fall, but at least all parties would know where they stood. If accepted in principle, the next stage in the approval process would deal with second-order questions such as timing and standards.

Increasingly, industrial activity in Arctic waters involves national priorities as well, particularly in energy policy. The future of the High Arctic as a region of Canada therefore must be clarified. Moreover, the separation of the three components in the current regulatory process for offshore drilling–environmental, socioeconomic, and technical–is essentially artificial. The *total* environment is changing.

Conclusions

No study of environmental policy in Arctic waters would be complete without the standard recommendation for more and better environmental impact studies. This shop-worn comment does have a continuing validity in certain areas of Arctic marine studies, however, and particularly in major long-term studies modelled on the Eastern Arctic Marine Environmental Studies, without being project specific. The compilation of basic data on the High Arctic should be perceived as a national responsibility, and the data as a potential national resource that is fundamental to the understanding of our environment. The essentially short-term perspective on research of Ottawa policy-makers in the last decade has served the country badly. Truly major phenomena, such as the natural richness of Lancaster Sound, are simply not yet understood, but drilling programs are already being prepared.[40]

Furthermore, it is no longer tolerable for Canada to approve offshore drilling programs without year-round ice capabilities. While it is true that drilling is confined to what are considered safe periods of the year, same season relief well capability is increasingly essential; a polar ice-breaker would not ensure this capability, but it would at least be a necessary first step. In general, unless a year-round navigational capability is achieved vital research needs cannot be met.

Offshore industrial activity and transportation in Arctic waters are still in their infancy, but as they intensify the circumpolar dimension will be increasingly evident. In the Beaufort Sea and the eastern Arctic, bilateral relations with the U.S. and Denmark have been affected, and in the latter case a whole new dimension has been created. The Arctic environment shows little regard for the sector theory or any other territorial claim, and Arctic coastal zone management inevitably will be not only a major national but also an international concern. The pattern of Canadian-U.S. co-operation in the Beaufort Sea since 1976 and the Canadian-Denmark Marine Environment Committee foreshadows the emergence of a "northern foreign policy."[41]

According to a recent study by the Science Council of Canada,

Canadians have alternatively, and occasionally simultaneously, viewed the North as a cornucopia of resources, an important strategic military locale, the native peoples' last refuge, a barren wasteland, and as a natural laboratory for biological, physical, oceanographic, and social science.[42]

This comment presents the dilemma facing Canada as her third coastline is progressively tied into the Canadian and world economies. If past experience is any guide, the rapid advance in technical aspects of Arctic environmental management will continue, but coastal zone management in Arctic waters confronts Canada with a challenge the magnitude of which is only now becoming apparent.

NOTES

1. The Labrador Sea, although not strictly speaking part of Arctic waters geographically, faces similar ice and weather conditions and is normally included for practical purposes in the definition. For example, it has been included as a study area in the Arctic Marine Oilspill Programme (AMOP).
2. According to Panarctic Oils Ltd., the offshore area is expected to contain the major portion of natural gas reserves in the Canadian Arctic islands.
3. See Edgar J. Dosman (ed.), *The Arctic in Question* (Toronto, 1976).
4. A. E. Gotlieb and C. Dalfen, "National Jurisdiction and International Responsibility," paper presented to the First Annual Conference of the Canadian Council on International Law, October, 13, 1972.
5. House of Commons, *Debates,* April 15, 1970.
6. See, for example, B. R. Ledrew and K. A. Gustajtis (eds.), *An Oil Spill Scenario for the Labrador Sea,* C-CORE, Technical Report, March, 1978.

Reprinted in *C-CORE News,* Vol. 3, No. 2. Also see *A Study of Environmental Concerns: Offshore Oil and Gas Drilling and Production* (Ottawa: Environmental Protection Service, 1978).

7. Dosman (ed.), *The Arctic in Question,* particularly chapter 3.

8. An interesting symptom is the western offshore boundary respecting the Arctic Waters Pollution Prevention Act; the sector principle is utilized.

9. This point is made in Mr. Justice Thomas R. Berger, *Northern Homeland, Northern Frontier,* The Report of the Mackenzie Valley Pipeline Inquiry, vol. 1 (Ottawa, April 15, 1977). See also D. J. Gamble, "Is Arctic Offshore Drilling for the Birds?" paper presented to the 44th North American Wildlife and Natural Resources Conference, Toronto, March 24-28, 1979.

10. The effect of the Whitefish H-63 discovery between Melville and Lougheed Islands was to rekindle interest in the Polar Gas project, hanging fire since 1972.

11. For details of recent marine developments in Arctic waters, see Research Report No. 48, *Marine Transportation Policy Project,* University of Toronto/York University Joint Programme in Transportation, May, 1978.

12. François Bregha, "Petroleum Development in Northern Alaska," Symposium on Marine Transportation and High Arctic Development, CARC, March 21-23, 1979.

13. D. E. Evans, "The Proposed Canadian Coast Guard Class X Nuclear Icebreaker," paper presented to the American Association for the Advancement of Science, Houston, Tex., 1979.

14. Dr. E. F. Roots, "Environmental Aspects of Arctic Marine Transportation and Development," Symposium on Marine Transportation and High Arctic Development, CARC, March 21-23, 1979, p. 25.

15. *Canada's North 1970-80* (Ottawa: Department of Indian Affairs and Northern Development, 1972), 28.

16. *A Guide to the Federal Assessment and Review Process* (Ottawa: Environment Canada, 1977).

17. Albery, Pullerits, Dickson and Associates, *Marine Transportation of Oil and LNG from Arctic Islands to Southern Markets* (Ottawa: Transport Canada, 1978). A special chapter is devoted to institutional obstacles to project approval.

18. Josef Kates, "Technological Sovereignty," *Canadian Research* (July-August, 1977), 25.

19. *New Oceans Policy* (Ottawa: Ministry of State for Science and Technology, 1973).

20. Pallister Resource Management Ltd., *Steering a Course to Excellence; A Study of the Canadian Offshore Oil and Gas Industries* (Ottawa: National Research Council of Canada, 1977).

21. *An Energy Strategy for Canada* (summary) (Ottawa: Energy Mines and Resources, 1976), 25.

22. Franklyn Griffiths, *A Northern Foreign Policy,* CIIA, Wellesley Papers, 1979.

23. Edgar J. Dosman, "Strategic Issues in Canadian Arctic Waters," *Navy International* (October, 1978).

24. Max Dunbar, "Science Policy and Arctic Marine Transportation," Symposium on Marine Transportation and High Arctic Development, March 21-23, 1979.

25. Currently there is only one functioning mine in Canada's High Arctic, Nanisivik at Strathcona Sound on Baffin Island.

26. Research Report No. 48, *Marine Transportation Policy Project,* esp. pp. 171-91.
27. *Submission to the Lancaster Sound EARP* (Ottawa: Transport Canada, 1978) gives a useful summary of the mandate and role of that federal agency in Arctic waters.
28. See A. Lucas *et al.,* "Regulation of High Arctic Development," Symposium on Marine Transportation and High Arctic Development, CARC, March 21-23, 1979.
29. Eastern Arctic Marine Environmental Studies – Outline of a Programme (Ottawa: Department of Indian Affairs and Northern Development, 1977), 5. See also Arctic Petroleum Operators Association, *Proceedings of Seventh Annual Environmental Workshop* (1978), 102-17, for an interesting discussion of current technology in the field.
30. AMOP, Experimental Oilspill Programme, Draft Document (Ottawa, January 19, 1979).
31. F. G. Bercha and Associates, *Probabilities of Blowouts in Canadian Arctic Waters* (Ottawa: Environmental Protection Service, 1979), 55-71.
32. Ledrew and Gustajtis (eds.), *An Oil Spill Scenario,* 7.
33. AMOP, Experimental Oilspill Programme, 3.
34. Toronto *Globe and Mail,* June 9, 1979.
35. *Eastern Offshore News,* Vol. 1, No. 1 (Eastcoast Petroleum Operators Association, Calgary, Alta.).
36. Bercha and Associates, *Probabilities of Blowouts,* 59.
37. *National Marine Emergency Plan* (Ottawa: Canadian Coast Guard [Transport Canada], May 5, 1977); and *Joint Canada-U.S. Pollution Contingency Plan* (June 20, 1974).
38. *Presentation* to Lancaster Sound EARP Hearing, CARC, p. 2.
39. Lucas *et al.,* "Regulation of High Arctic," pp. 59-60.
40. Dunbar, "Science Policy," p. 3.
41. Griffiths, *A Northern Foreign Policy,* particularly pp. 99-112; and *Interim Canada-Denmark Contingency Plan* (May 5, 1977) with its *Operational Annex* (February, 1979).
42. Science Council of Canada, *Northward Looking; A Strategy and a Science Policy for Northern Development* (Ottawa, 1977), 40.

CHAPTER NINE

West Coast Oil Pollution Policies: Canadian Responses to Risk Assessment

by W.R.D. Sewell and N.A. Swainson

On February 23, 1978, Canada's Minister of State (Environment), the Honourable Len Marchand, announced on behalf of the Government of Canada that it saw no need for a west coast oil port at that time, "or in the foreseeable future,"[1] and thus, in effect presaged the end of a much publicized West Coast Oil Ports Inquiry. The inquiry had been established eleven months earlier in response to growing concerns about the implications of large-scale tanker movements along the coast of British Columbia. It had involved extensive public hearings and a very considerable investment of public funds. Yet it was brought to an end when its work was far from complete, when some of the basic questions it had set out to deal with had not been resolved, and in a manner which disappointed the proponents of a proposed tanker off-loading facility at Kitimat, B.C., some of the opponents of that project, the Government of British Columbia, and the commissioner himself.

Why this happened will be the subject of a good many case studies in the years to come. That it happened is a reflection of two of the most outstanding characteristics of contemporary policy-making. One of these concerns the way in which items appear on the public agenda, and what happens to them once they have reached it. As Anthony Downs has noted, policy issues tend to pass through at least five distinct stages, beginning with their "discovery" by a few individuals, followed by their recognition by a larger public, and ending with a subsequent decline in their relative and perhaps absolute importance[2] (Figure 1). Of particular concern here is the extent to which shifts in public values, the "institutionalization" of issues, or deliberate action by political actors result either in issues acquiring a permanent though highly variable place on the agenda, or in their total disappearance from it. A second characteristic of our policy-making which this event underscores relates to the increasing complexity of some issues as they pass through the issue-attention cycle. This is especially characteristic of questions relating to natural resources and the environment, which involve a wide range of social values whose weights are subject to significant change over time. Inevitably, society has had to design both institutional mechanisms, in the form of laws, policies, and administrative arrangements, and patterns of political behaviour, which enable it to respond to this complexity. At the same time, each generation has had to respond to the additional challenge of making these mechanisms and forms of behaviour flexible enough to reflect not just changes in the level of complexity and changes in placement on the public agenda, but flexible enough, also, to deal with changes in the very nature of the policy problems themselves. Generating appropriate structural and behavioural changes had become crucial to producing legitimate policy decisions in the seventies.

The purpose of this essay is to describe the evolution of the west coast oil pollution issue within the framework of these two broad concepts. Thus it will be concerned with tracing the variable position of the issue on the Canadian public agenda, the manner in which it became increasingly complex and changed otherwise in the course of a decade, and the responses to it that emerged both in the lay community and in the various levels of government in Canada. The essay concludes with some suggestions as to what the implications of the Canadian experience with this policy question are for Canadian policy analysis.

Origins and Evolution of the Issue

Experience in various parts of the world over the past decade has shown that coastal zones face an increasing prospect of major environmental disruption as the result of the expansion of oil tanker traffic. The probabilities of such a disruption are especially high off shorelines which are indented and subject to severe storms. Such is the case with the west coast of Canada. Nevertheless, until the late 1960's there was almost no public concern about the prospect of a major oil spill in that area despite the fact that, until the

Figure 1: The Issue-Attention Cycle.
(*Illustration by Ian Norie and staff,
Department of Geography, University of Victoria.*)

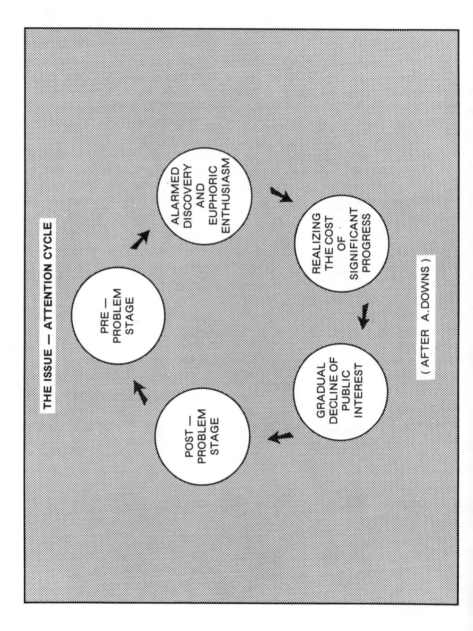

mid-1950's, virtually all of the petroleum consumed in British Columbia and Washington State was brought in by tanker, and much of this petroleum, when refined, was distributed by water along the northwest coast of the continent.

Three factors combined to put the matter of potential west coast oil spills on the Canadian political agenda. First, it became clear during the 1960's that, of necessity, the United States was becoming progressively more dependent on imports of oil. Secondly, in Canada as elsewhere, there was mounting awareness and anxiety about the environmental effects of resource development and utilization. By the end of the decade, accidents elsewhere had served to emphasize not only the likelihood of a major oil spill on the west coast, but also the nature and magnitude of its consequences. A third factor, linking the first two, was the discovery in 1968 of large deposits of oil on the north slope of Alaska. After an intense examination of other transportation routes, the companies involved proposed that the oil be moved to the south shore of Alaska by pipeline, and thence by tanker to the continental United States (Figure 2).

The responses in Canada to the emerging possibility of greatly increased west coast oil tanker traffic appear to have moved through five distinct phases. These phases reflect the oscillation of the place of this question on the Canadian political agenda, and the varying complexity of the institutional response to it.

Phase I: First Reactions

Initially, the threat of west coast maritime pollution captured the attention of only a limited number of Canadians. Most of these were environmentalists or journalists; a few were politicians anticipating the emergence of this agenda item, or deliberately moving it up the attention cycle. They had to sensitize an unconcerned public, and the governments of Canada and B.C., whose instinct, even after the question was officially recognized, was to generate cautious *ad hoc* responses to it.

Of the various actors involved, David Anderson, MP, was probably the one most responsible for getting the oil spill question directly on to the Canadian agenda. Elected to Parliament in 1968, he quickly sought to publicize the issue, in part via the process of having a special committee of the House of Commons established on environmental pollution. The committee, with a membership including several MP's from British Columbia, quickly addressed this question, and in its third report (June 21, 1971) concluded that

Figure 2: Proposed Tanker Routes and Terminals.
(Illustration by Ian Norie and staff,
Department of Geography, University of Victoria.)

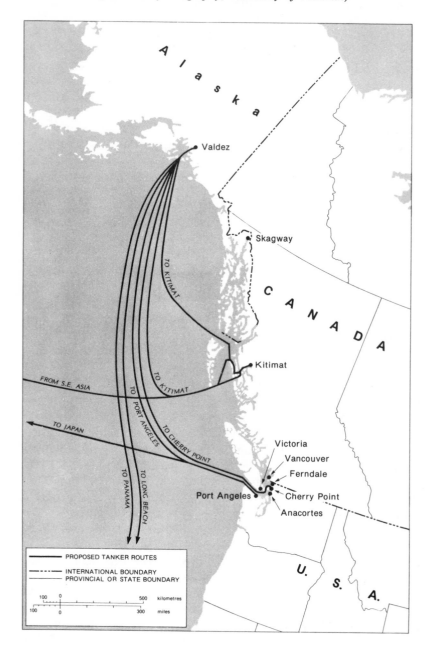

a new tanker route from Alaska south (Alaska was already an oil producer) would be detrimental to Canada's national interest and should be opposed by its government.[3] Much earlier in 1971, however, it had become evident that the matter was already on the federal cabinet's agenda. The Secretary of State for External Affairs, the Honourable Mitchell Sharp, revealed as much in statements to the House of Commons in January and February. The Minister of Energy, Mines and Resources, the Honourable Joe Greene, made it clear that he had relayed the Canadian government's concern over and opposition to expanded marine oil haulage on the west coast while in Washington, D.C., in March, and, furthermore, that he had invited American oil companies to apply to the National Energy Board (NEB) for permission to build an oil pipeline across Canada to the heartland of the United States. Meanwhile, on February 4, 1971, B.C.'s legislature unanimously endorsed by resolution precisely the position advanced four months later by the federal parliamentary Committee on Environmental Pollution.

Actually, between 1971 and 1973 inclusive, members of the federal cabinet appear to have been more than willing to echo the sentiments of Messrs. Sharp and Greene, although they do seem to have had difficulties in putting together a comprehensive policy on the subject. The cabinet ministers were well aware of the fact that in opposing seaborne exports from Alaska they were incurring some responsibility for helping the Americans find an alternative solution to their problem; hence the oil pipeline proposal. But they clearly had problems within their own ranks over assessing the value of the pipeline to Canada, and over the priority to be given to forestalling marine transportation of Alaskan oil. They had difficulty also over the 1971-72 winter with their colleague Mr. Anderson, who pushed them vigorously on the oil tanker question, and, on his own initiative and in conjunction with the Canadian Wildlife Federation, carried his opposition to the tankers to Washington, D.C., where he became a party to some of the legal actions launched to emphasize the environmental significance of the proposed Trans-Alaskan pipeline, minimally to delay it, and to forestall it if possible.

Some members of the Canadian cabinet, such as Minister of Communications Eric Kierans, resisted the proposal to ship Alaskan oil across northern Canada by pipeline. Others, such as the Honourable Jack Davis, the Minister of the Environment, while vigorously opposed to the west coast route, insisted that a decision not be made on a pipeline pending a major environmental assessment of its impact. At the same time, as the decade advanced, the Canadian cabinet seems to have become increasingly conscious of the fact that, insofar as the crucial decision was focused almost entirely on the movement of Alaskan oil and barring almost immediate action on a Canadian overland pipeline, the crucial decision on this question was likely to be made in Washington. The Nixon administration appears to have been well-briefed on the possibility that getting a clearance in Canada for a joint pipeline would likely face a complex mix of Canadian environmentalist, autarkic, native land claim, and nationalist opposition. In addition, as the decade advanced the U.S. government made little secret of its inclination on economic and security grounds to support the Alaska pipeline plus tanker distribution system.

If there was any real chance of delaying a formal commitment by the United States to the Trans-Alaskan pipeline, it was largely eliminated when, on May 11, 1972, United States Secretary of the Interior Rogers Morton announced that the line would be approved and a right-of-way permit granted. Still, some possibility of delaying or reversing this decision was provided by the continued strength of American environmentalist opposition to the U.S. government's decision, and the Canadian government did take advantage of it. In the spring of 1972, it tried, unsuccessfully, to get the American government to agree to a study by the International Joint Commission of the risks associated with tanker traffic on adjacent Canadian and American waters on the west coast. Late in that year, and again in 1973, it offered to guarantee the supply of Canadian oil to American refineries in Washington State (at least, the major one at Cherry Point) if the United States would refrain from shipping Alaska oil to them by sea. A favourable response to this proposal was not obtained. In 1973, the Trudeau government also renewed its invitation to the American oil companies to apply to build a Mackenzie Valley pipeline.[4]

In some ways the most interesting Canadian proposal on the subject in 1973 came from the new NDP premier of British Columbia, the Honourable David Barrett. Mr. Barrett, in March, drew upon the work of a group of Queen's University professors to propose, on a visit to Washington, D.C., trans-shipping Alaskan oil by a combined pipeline and railway system which would run through his province, and thus make unnecessary increased west coast tanker traffic. His proposal was greeted skeptically, but served to emphasize (as he did not hesitate to point out on his return) the uncertainties in or indecisiveness of Canada's energy policy at that time.[5] Whatever the explanation for the hesitancy of the Canadian government to this point, the first phase of Canadian policy-making came to an end when the OPEC oil embargo applied during the October, 1973, Arab-Israeli war forced a reassessment of energy policies in nations around the world, and the U.S. Congress finally passed the roadblock-clearing Trans-Alaska Pipeline Act. With the last hurdles on that project removed, work on the line began in April, 1974.

Phase II: Deflection of Attention

The second phase of Canadian policy-making began after the clearance given to the Alaska pipeline and the announcement of a new National Energy Policy for Canada by the prime minister in December, 1973. It spanned approximately two years. The first phase had been marked by a gradual appreciation, especially among government personnel in Canada, that the early solutions to the problem advanced from the Canadian side had been simplistic, and that there were no evident answers to the problem that did not involve for Canada some environmental, social, economic, and political costs and risk. What answers there were, of course, also involved potential benefits in some situations. This gradual impression was heightened in governmental circles during the second phase. On the other hand, during this phase the policy question moved well down the public agenda from the very considerable position it had reached between 1971 and 1973. It did not disappear, and demanded increasing attention by some governmental personnel. But its prominent place on the agenda was taken, in a sense, by the proposals of the Canadian Arctic Gas consortium and then of the Foothills Pipeline Ltd. consortium to build northern gas pipelines, as well as by the appointment in 1974 of the Berger Royal Commission, and its subsequent hearings.

There were two distinctive features to the manner in which the breadth of the policy problem expanded, and its complexity was heightened during this period. One of these concerned the way in which changes in Canadian energy policies were to have almost immediate effects on west coast tanker transportation. In 1974, the Canadian government announced that it intended progressively to phase out its oil exports to the United States, which averaged 920,000 barrels per day (bpd) between 1971 and 1974. Late in 1975, it decided to accelerate the pace of these export reductions; shortly thereafter, the National Energy Board projected that Canadian exports of light crude would cease after 1980, and exports of heavy crude, down to 77,000 bpd by 1981, would decline to 26,000 bpd by 1986.[6]

There were two direct consequences of this Canadian action for the west coast. One was that the five major American refineries on Puget Sound had to turn quickly to alternative imported oil to meet their requirements of approximately 280,000 bpd. Whereas in 1972 some 90 per cent of this oil was provided from Canada by pipeline, in 1977 it all had to be brought in by tanker, from Alaska, Indonesia, and the Middle East. The other consequence was that in the Northern Tier states apart from Washington (Montana, North Dakota, Minnesota, Wisconsin, and Michigan), a crude oil shortage also began to develop as a consequence of the cut-off of Canadian supplies. Washington and Michigan do have access to alternative sources – via sea or pipeline – but the other states' refineries faced an almost immediate need to accelerate product shipments from refineries elsewhere, to build new pipelines to alternative sources, or to sponsor the reversal of flows in some existing lines.

The second feature of the changing dimensions of this policy question stemmed from the gradual appreciation in Canada of the fact that a significant portion of the forthcoming oil from the north slope of Alaska would be surplus to west coast American requirements. This had not been anticipated earlier, and was only partly a function of a limited capacity of west coast refineries to handle the heavier higher-sulphur north slope crudes. What this meant, of course, was that the Alaskan oil producers would be looking, almost from the moment the Trans-Alaskan line began to operate, for trans-shipment points whereby they could divert this surplus to the oil-deficient areas in the interior of the United States. Thus, the impending tanker traffic from Alaska along the west coast could be expected to serve directly some west coast needs, and indirectly those of the continental heartland.

Canadian federal and provincial authorities watched the American oil companies, and their state, local, and federal governments, wrestle with the Alaska surplus problem. They saw up to a dozen different schemes emerge. Some, such as an offshore oil port on the Washington coast, were abandoned as infeasible after exhaustive technical analysis. Some, such as shipment around Cape Horn, turned out to be excessively expensive. Others examined included trans-shipment via the Panama Canal to Gulf of Mexico ports (now utilized), and the building of new pipelines across Guatemala and from northern California to Nebraska. By 1975, one of the most seriously sponsored proposals was that of the Standard Oil Company of Ohio (Sohio) to build a trans-shipment and off-loading facility at Long Beach in southern California, whence by a combination of new and existing pipelines Alaskan oil would be moved to Midland, Texas, and connected there to a major pipeline network.

Phase III: The Emergence of New Options

The third phase in the Canadian decision-making covered, roughly, the year 1976. It was highlighted by still further broadening of the issues at stake, and, most importantly for Canada, by the rapid advance of planning for three projects which, while primarily designed to deal with Alaskan oil surplus and American import requirement problems, were to be of immediate concern to Canada. During this period, the segment of the Canadian public and of Canadian departmental/agency personnel concerned with the implications of tanker traffic, and especially tanker traffic beyond that required to service the domestic needs of Washington State, became increasingly conscious of the fact that the Trans-Alaskan pipeline was due to be completed by mid-year, 1977. As a consequence, the threat of west coast oil pollution moved upward on the Canadian agenda before December, 1976, but only slightly. On the whole, it remained a matter of relatively low political visibility.

One of these new proposals was the plan of the Northern Tier Pipeline Company, which was to become the subject of intensive examination by American authorities stretching over several years (Figure 3). The heart of it is a pipeline from the Pacific Northwest across the Northern Tier states to Clearbrook, Minnesota – a major pipeline junction. As originally projected, this line would have commenced at one of the American refineries on Puget Sound, and thus would have meant a major increase in tanker traffic through the islands of this region. This plan subsequently was modified to involve a terminal at or west of Port Angeles on the Strait of Juan de Fuca. A second proposal to surface was jointly that of the Trans Mountain Pipe Line Co., whose facility links Vancouver and Puget Sound with Edmonton, and the Atlantic Richfield Co., the owner of a major refinery at Cherry Point in Washington State. The essence of their plan was that the Cherry Point terminal would be expanded to handle an increased flow of offshore crude, which would be pumped to Edmonton on Trans Mountain's line, and then distributed to the Northern Tier states by existing and under-utilized pipeline facilities. The Trans Moun-

Figure 3: **Major Existing and Proposed Crude Oil Pipelines.**
(*Illustration by Ian Norie and staff,*
Department of Geography, University of Victoria.)

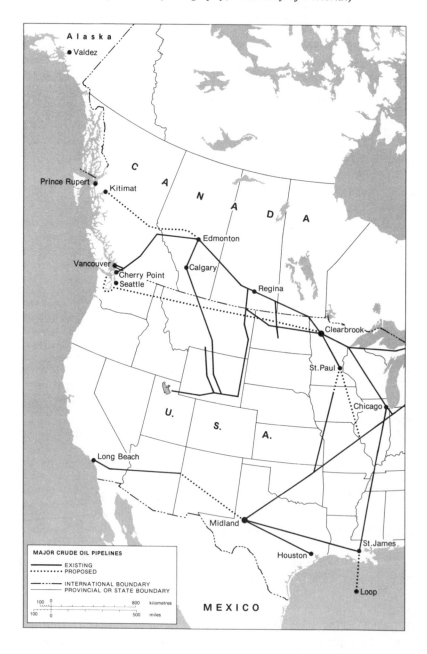

tain line, as proposed, would in fact handle alternating flows at different times in the month, with Vancouver's refineries still drawing Alberta crude from it.

Finally, another proposal emerged in 1976, that of Kitimat Pipe Line Ltd. (KPL), ultimately a consortium of five American oil refineries in the Northern Tier states, and the Canadian firm, Interprovincial Pipe Line Ltd. This group proposed to construct an off-loading terminal at Kitimat, British Columbia, at the head of Douglas Channel, a long west coast fiord, as well as a 753-mile-long pipeline to Edmonton, where this line would connect with existing distribution networks. The KPL facility was to have an initial capacity of 420,000 and a final design capacity of 650,000 bpd. The two major market areas its proponents anticipated serving were the Northern Tier states (plus some states to the south), and Canadian refineries in southern Ontario and Montreal. While the planning of the first two of these proposals had been the subject of considerable public controversy in Washington State for some time, it was the filing by KPL of an application with the NEB for permission to proceed with its project which, at the end of Phase III, was to raise the implications of west coast tanker movements to a significant place on the public agendas of British Columbia and Canada. The proposed KPL project would either bring into play, or intensify, the activities of the branches of government responsible for dealing with it.

Inevitably, the institutional arrangements involved in Canada and the United States played an important role in determining both the nature and timing of the governmental responses. On the whole, the Canadian arrangements relating to the regulation of oil shipments and the location of tanker terminals are simpler than those in the United States. In many ways, the primary Canadian federal agency is the National Energy Board, with responsibilities relating to energy transmission and a major concern (shared with the Department of Energy, Mines and Resources) about Canada's energy supplies. Jurisdiction over tankers, however, is mainly in the hands of the Department of Transport and the National Harbours Board. In addition, the Department of Fisheries and the Environment has a direct interest in marine pollution questions. In British Columbia, on the other hand, the provincial government appears to have only limited powers with respect to the siting of oil port facilities, especially if the area in question has been brought under the national Harbours Board Act. KPL, for example, never applied for a permit from British Columbia's Pollution Control Board. The province's ownership of Crown land in some cases might provide it with the required jurisdictional leverage, but this consideration, in the Kitimat case, was offset by the fact that much of the foreshore and the bed of Kitimat Arm were owned by the Aluminum Company of Canada, and were, in any case, just possibly subject to expropriation by the NEB. It has been argued that the provincial cabinet under B.C.'s Environment and Land Use Act can require by order-in-council the preparation of environmental assessments prior to the issuance of provincial or municipal development permits. To date, however, this power has not been invoked on this question.[7]

In and adjacent to the State of Washington in American waters, the jurisdictional mix is different. There, all four levels of government (including the counties) have planning and control powers that bear on shoreline development, although the powers of the counties and municipalities vis-a-vis energy-related facilities appear to have been largely pre-empted by a state creation, the Energy Facilities Site Evaluation Council (EFSEC). The members of EFSEC, apart from the chairman, are primarily the heads of a broad range of state agencies (or their designees). As a consequence, EFSEC frequently has been able to generate a consensus on various economic, social, and political questions, both within its ranks and among the Washington State community. Its certification decisions go to the governor, who makes the final decision to approve or reject applications. All this is not to suggest that the jurisdiction of EFSEC is clear; actually its relationship with other state agencies has been the subject of controversy for a number of years.

The interface between the powers of EFSEC and those of the American federal government is also clouded. The views of a number of federal agencies concerned with fish, wildlife, and water quality, for example, also have to be taken into account in siting decisions, not just by the Corps of Engineers (COE), the most crucial federal instrumentality in this decision-making process. An environmental impact statement must be prepared for every major federal action that could significantly affect the environment. A COE permit is required for virtually every shoreline development, and will only be issued after the views of the public and of agencies at all levels of government have been ascertained. The COE must be satisfied that any project is in the public interest, and will not issue a permit if state or local agencies have denied authorization – unless, of course, it is convinced that such action reflects an overriding national interest. Other federal agencies as well, such as the Environmental Protection Agency (EPA), the Department of Transportation (with its interest in pipeline routing), and the U.S. Coast Guard (with its controls of ship navigation and construction standards), have responsibilities that bear on siting decisions. Still others have powers of another sort dealing with questions of energy pricing, use, conservation, and the like. Under some circumstances the EPA can override COE permit approval. In short, the road to American energy-facility siting and energy-transmission decisions runs through a very considerable although not impenetrable thicket.[8]

When Kitimat Pipe Line Ltd. filed its application with the NEB in December, 1976, it also deposited a six-volume submission with the Canadian Ministry of Transport to confirm that it was complying with the TERMPOL (Terminal Policy) Code prepared earlier in the decade by a number of federal departments, including the Ministries of Transport and the Environment. By invoking a voluntary procedure, the TERMPOL Code provides for a logically ordered evaluation of the navigational and pollution and general environmental risks associated with proposed marine terminal systems. The KPL application, indeed, was the first to which it was applied.[9] When the application was received an "in-house" TERMPOL Co-ordinating Committee of federal government personnel was established to assess the submission and report within four and a half months. The company was notified of a considerable list of deficiencies in its submission in February, 1977, and the TERMPOL assessment, along with the Kitimat Company's replies to the February requests for additional answers, were published in May of that year.

Phase IV: The Thompson Inquiry

While this institutional in-house response to the KPL application got under way, however, the Canadian cabinet had to wrestle with a crucial question in view of the place this issue now had on the public agenda – the extent to which broad public participation should be invoked in the preparation of a policy response to the Kitimat proposal. The applicant companies for some time had made no secret of their belief that time was short, that their expected customers faced real supply difficulties, and that the costs of delay were great. Their assumption was that the mandatory hearings on the application conducted by the NEB would be the venue of any required broad-spectrum public input. But the very considerable opposition to the Kitimat project in B.C. thought otherwise, coming especially as it did from environmental groups and those connected with the west coast fishery, and strongly demanded a public inquiry. As it turned out, 1977 was to be a vintage year for the utilization of this device, and the federal cabinet decided to opt for its application to this proposal.

On March 10, 1977, Dr. Andrew Thompson was appointed as a one-man commission to examine the social and environmental implications of the proposed tanker route and shore-based terminal, while the NEB was expected to continue with its assessment of the land-based dimensions of the KPL proposal. Dr. Thompson's terms of reference were as follows:

(a) to inquire into and concerning and to report upon:
   (i) the social and environmental impact regionally (including the impact on fisheries) that could result from the establishment of a marine tanker route and construction of a marine terminal (deep water oil port) at Kitimat, B.C.;
   (ii) navigational safety and related matters associated with the establishment of a marine tanker route and construction of a marine terminal at Kitimat, B.C.; and
   (iii) the broader concerns and issues related to oil tanker movements on the West Coast as might be affected by the proposal; and
(b) to report upon representations made to him concerning the terms and conditions which should be imposed, if authority is given to establish a marine terminal at Kitimat, on the size, construction and operation thereof and on the size, construction and operation of tankers in the approaches thereto.[10]

He was authorized to hold hearings in British Columbia, and to adopt such procedures as he felt were expedient. Federal government departments and agencies were directed to assist and co-operate with the inquiry, and Dr. Thompson was to report to the Minister of Fisheries and the Environment and the Minister of Transport, by December 31, 1977. The government also made it clear that it was going to provide for participant funding.

During the early organizational stage of his inquiry's work, Dr. Thompson made a number of crucial planning decisions. One, for example, was to use a good deal of the participant funding to stimulate sustained, informed evidence from combinations or coalitions of the main groups desiring to be heard (specifically those speaking for the native peoples, fishermen, and environmental organizations), rather than from sub-units of these broad categories. He decided also that his commission's counsel would be responsible for calling witnesses and generating evidence to ensure that all sides of the question were heard and all relevant data obtained, but that, in contrast to traditional practice before regulatory commission hearings in Canada, the counsel would not carry the main burden of interrogating witnesses. This role was to be left to counsel for, or spokesmen for, the participants themselves. Perhaps most important of all, Dr. Thompson opted for a broad interpretation of his terms of reference, to include an examination of oil supply and demand considerations. Six phases for the formal hearings were projected to focus on (1) opening statements, statutes, and regulations; (2) implications of supply and demand for west coast tanker traffic; (3) facilities and marine operations; (4) environmental impacts; (5) fishing industry impacts; (6) social and economic impacts. Not the least of his decisions involved provision for the widest possible dissemination of information generated in the course of the inquiry to participants and other interested parties. Provision was made for formal and much more informal community hearings.

During the early stages of the Thompson Inquiry a number of unanticipated developments were to alter its scope significantly, and at the same time were to have a varying impact on the complexity of the issues facing the Canadian government. One of these was the filing of an application with the NEB on May 30, 1977, by Trans Mountain Pipe Line Ltd., requesting permission to go ahead with its alternative flow project. Inherent in this proposal, it will be remembered, was a major expansion of the off-loading facility at Cherry Point, in Washington State. A second development followed on June 1, 1977, when Kitimat Pipe Line Ltd. moved to place its NEB application in abeyance and to support the Trans Mountain scheme as a means of attaining a good many of its own objectives at considerably reduced expense. Here, certainly, was a complication. Dr. Thompson's initial reaction was to argue that as the Kitimat application was only in abeyance, and as the Cherry Point expansion was the subject of intense environmental opposition in Washington State, his inquiry should continue as planned. For a while, indeed, it did. But he did go to Ottawa, where, on June 30, his commission was renamed the West Coast Oil Ports Inquiry and received modified terms of reference. Section (a) iii of his instructions now required him to inquire into and report on "The broader Canadian concerns and issues related to oil tanker movements on the west coast as might be affected by

Kitimat Pipe Line Ltd., Trans Mountain Pipe Line Ltd., and other proposals."[11]

With this broadened mandate (which included an examination of the likely impact of the Northern Tier proposal), the inquiry's formal hearings opened in July, 1977, in Vancouver, and were followed immediately by informal community hearings. Phase I of the formal hearings began on September 26 and lasted until October 13. After a week of community hearings Phase II of the formal sessions, designed to examine the supply and demand background to projected west coast tanker traffic, commenced on October 24 and continued until an adjournment on November 4. Once again, external events were to have a major impact on the inquiry's progress. On October 5 the United States Congress approved the so-called Magnuson amendment to the Marine Mammals Protection Act, which amendment had the effect of foreclosing any chance that there could be a major expansion of tanker traffic into Puget Sound waters. Thus, on October 31, 1977, it was the Trans Mountain Company's turn to announce that its NEB applications should be placed in abeyance. This, in the broadest of terms, was the background to the rather extraordinary situation in which Dr. Thompson and the federal cabinet found themselves. They had established an inquiry before which there were now no active proponents. The result was considerable confusion, and not a little uncertainty; speculation emerged almost at once that the Kitimat proposal would be revived, and pressure mounted in Washington and Ottawa to accelerate the decision-making process. Pressure was mounted in B.C. also, from among the supporters of the Thompson Inquiry, for its continuance. Convinced that further investigation should precede any final governmental policy decision, and that no emergency existed which would justify bypassing this process, Dr. Thompson, after meeting with federal cabinet ministers, announced the indefinite postponement of his inquiry on November 9, on the understanding that it would be reconvened, that the December 31 deadline for the submission of a final report would be lifted, and that he would present an interim Statement of Proceedings before March 31, 1978. This he did on February 23, 1978, after receiving suggestions concerning it from his counsel and the inquiry participants at three days of hearings on December 13-15. Also in December, a revised federal order-in-council made it clear that in the event of a new serious application for a marine terminal on the west coast of Canada (note the projects thus excluded), the two directly involved federal ministers were committed to consulting with Dr. Thompson concerning the extension or re-creation of his commission.

By January, 1978, however, some very real doubts clearly had emerged within the federal cabinet concerning the utility of the Thompson Inquiry. Funding for participants in the inquiry was not extended into the first quarter of 1978. And when a revised application for an expanded Kitimat terminal and pipeline was filed with the NEB on January 9, 1978, by a consortium that now included Sohio – Alaska's major producer – the Cabinet moved to change the nature and locale of the debate. On January 16 Energy Minister Alastair Gillespie asked the NEB to investigate and report under Section 22 of the National Energy Board Act on

... a range of possible oil supply situations that might occur over the next 10 to 15 years and the import dependency which might develop for British Columbia consumers as well as for eastern Canadians. Where significant imports are required, [he went on] your views on the size, location and timing of petroleum ports of entry are requested.[12]

Convinced that his inquiry still had a major role to play, Dr. Thompson argued the case for its revival when he filed his Statement of Proceedings in February. Indeed, he suggested that "The applicant, Kitimat Pipe Line Ltd., is entitled to better treatment," as he emphasized the cost and delay involved in an on-again, off-again inquiry process, and the need to acquire more information. By now, however, the federal cabinet's mind was made up, and on February 23, 1978, immediately following their receipt of Dr. Thompson's report, Mr. Marchand issued the statement mentioned at the beginning of this paper. On the same day, Prime Minister Trudeau told a press conference that the proposal could be revived to meet domestic needs, and went on to observe, ". . . if it is just for the Americans my off hand attitude is why don't they build a port on their west coast if they want to bring oil for themselves."[13]

Phase V: The National Energy Board Reference, 1978

The NEB conducted its investigation into the oil import requirements of Canadians and the relative merits of locating additional import facilities on the west as opposed to the east coast of Canada under far different circumstances from those which had existed a year earlier. With the Cabinet veto of the Kitimat project, at least in the immediate future, and the closing of the door on the Thompson Inquiry, the question of west coast oil pollution moved down the public agenda almost as rapidly as it had moved upward at the end of 1976. In its hearings, which began in May, the NEB received submissions concerning a number of projects that would involve increased oil tanker movement on the west coast. One was from the new Kitimat consortium, and another from the Trans Mountain Pipe Line Company, which drew attention to the way off-loading facilities at Roberts Bank just south of the Fraser River's estuary could play the role earlier projected for Cherry Point (Figure 2). Two proposals advanced by the Foothills consortium involved plans to import Alaskan and possibly other offshore oil at either Haines or Skagway, Alaska, and to pipe it via a new line utilizing the proposed Alaska Highway gas pipeline corridor to the existing pipeline networks running south and east from Alberta. All of these projects were presented primarily as means of servicing American markets, but also as mechanisms that could help meet a variety of Canadian needs as well. The major environmental groups which had appeared before the Thompson Inquiry, and the Government of British Columbia, all expressed concern to the NEB over the likely impact of increased west coast oil traffic.

The NEB came to a crucial conclusion in its September, 1978, report. This was to the effect that insofar as Canadian needs were concerned, "There should be no need for augmenting existing oil importing capability through 1995," and was derived, as its chairman pointed out, from a changed outlook which "reflects a lower anticipated increase in demand as well as an improved supply forecast, particularly in oil sands development."[14] Based on this conclusion, the Board came to a further one: that it simply was not necessary to discuss the relative merits of new import facility sites on the two coasts. Hence, further consideration of that question was bypassed, for the short run at least, and the fifth phase in Canada's decision-making on this subject had come to an end.

West Coast Oil Pollution and the Public Agenda

Accounting for the rise and the subsequent agenda experience of policy issues is not easy, beyond making the obvious references to changes in public values and to the manner in which institutional responses to the issues themselves may serve to keep these matters on the agenda as well as to remove them from it. Reflection on Canada's experience with the threat of west coast oil spills, however, does suggest some hypotheses which may be helpful in probing these questions.

A critical factor in explaining why some issues are constantly on the agenda is the nature of the problem. If it involves the provision of a public good, as a well-protected environment does, and if the affected public is jurisdiction-wide, then it is probable that the issue will remain on or close to the political agenda. Canada's experience with the oil spill threat certainly indicates that although environmental issues command support that varies over time, this support has a residual strength, which suggests that the question itself is unlikely to disappear entirely from the political agenda in the near future. The intensity with which some values are held, and the capacity of the concerned citizens to articulate their views, are also definitely related to agenda placement. Obviously there are thresholds involved in determining the impact of the intensity with which values are held, and these are functions, sometimes, of changes in the perceived scale of a problem. The manner in which British Columbians' perceptions of the risk of oil spills oscillated during the 1970's is a case in point.

Clearly relevant also to appearance on and placement on the agenda is the question of issue complexity, although its impact can be variable. Complex issues may rise slowly to the agenda, as they are by definition associated with uncertainty. Once they get there, however, their very complexity may keep them there, as society finds it difficult to produce effective institutional responses to them. If an issue does not possess an escalating complexity it is much easier to generate an institutional response to it, which takes it off the agenda or lowers its visibility thereon.

Problem complexity, of course, has several possible dimensions. The larger the number of such dimensions (or of dimension subsets) involved, the greater the likelihood an issue will command attention and be difficult to resolve. The oil spill problem clearly demonstrates this. Technology is one such dimension. The technology of tanker construction, for example, has produced major increases in tanker size and operating efficiency, along with corresponding increases in the consequences of a tanker-related accident, should one occur. Assessing the significance of such developments, along with the technical dimension of ship operation and navigation, of accident frequency prediction, of spill containment and clean-up, are all obvious parts of this decision-making, and all questions to which specialized agencies of the Canadian government gave much attention during the 1970's. Equally pertinent are the various technologies associated with overland oil transportation in North America, with the capacity of refineries to handle only certain categories of crude oil, and now with the production of synthetic oil.

A second feature of problem complexity concerns the nature and number of systems that policies may affect. In this case, complex social as well as physical/biological systems were directly involved, a fact well-illustrated when, before the Thompson Inquiry, a spokesman for the native people of B.C. advanced the claim that they are the owners of and have jurisdiction over the marine resources of the west coast, and hence have a right to be able to protect these resources from supertankers.[15] A third major source of complexity derives from the number of values directly associated with policy options, and even more importantly, from the value conflicts that emerge within as well as between individuals. Our policy question here, for example, involved a direct face-off between environmental values and the values we place on our relations with our neighbours, as well as on the place of energy in our lives. In addition, there certainly is a dimension of complexity associated with the number of jurisdictions of government (and their subdivisions) which respond to policy questions. The point has already been made that, to date, harmonizing the roles of the governments of Canada and British Columbia has not been too difficult on the west coast oil production question. Rather more challenging has been the need to co-ordinate the different institutional responses of two federal systems, and further still, the approaches of the three major federal Canadian departments involved: Transport, Fisheries and the Environment, and Energy, Mines and Resources. Jurisdictional issues, of course, have turned out to have a major bearing on the capacities of national governments to regulate tanker traffic beyond the confines of the territorial sea.

Other considerations may affect the relationship between an issue and the public agenda. Issues, for example, may warrant and receive a place on the agenda in times of domestic equanimity, only to be shunted off it when a crisis narrows the attention span of the political system. It is evident, for example, that in the early 1970's there was general concern about environmental disruption and also political support for action to deal with it. The oil crisis following the Arab-Israeli war, and problems of the economic downturn in the seventies, however, have resulted in attention being deflected away from environmental issues to other matters the policy-makers believe are even more urgent.

External developments, such as wars or the occurrence of a major disaster, may move items on or off political agendas, and may certainly add immensely to the complexity of the policy formation process. As well, the efforts of political actors other than those in government may frequently put new items on the agenda or have the effect of keeping "old" ones there. Again, public inquiries (like legislative debate), by deliberate intent, are mechanisms designed to keep issues on the public agenda, perhaps at a predetermined level, while the political system pursues further insight and engages in a search for the moving compromise that lies at the heart of successful policy-making. In this process, of course (as seems to have happened with the Thompson Inquiry), issues may be kept at a higher level of visibility for a longer period of time than the sponsoring government originally intended.

All of the factors mentioned on the immediately preceding pages have had a bearing on the way in which the risk of west coast oil pollution has been handled. Because of the increasing complexity of the problem, resulting from its economic, political, social, and jurisdictional dimensions, and because of the weight Canadians continue to give to the values involved, the question appears likely to remain on the public agenda. It appears likely, also, to evoke further appeals for further recourse to the mechanisms of direct democracy. Both the federal and the provincial levels of government have seen extensive experiments in this connection, and more doubtless lie ahead of us. "Involving the public" has become for some the obvious road to legitimate decisions; for others, however, it appears to have imposed high costs on the polity, and often to have estopped the decision-making process.

Recently, the public inquiry itself has attracted much attention. It is widely asserted that this mechanism can facilitate the emergence of a social consensus, either by generating the broadest possible analysis of sensitive environmental questions or simply by confirming the comprehensive nature of the government's response to them. The inquiry as a viable forum also may help coordinate the perspectives of branches of government representing conflicting values, may educe information not normally available to government agencies, and permits a unique degree of sustained attention on a single problem. On the other hand, some see the inquiry as an oversold device that often stimulates an asymmetric debate and recognition of the values involved; in other words, some would argue that the inquiry is not ideal for dealing with highly technical problems, that it does not necessarily produce the meeting of minds so often claimed for it. In short, its critics argue, the public inquiry is not a panacea, and must be considered side-by-side with other devices, such as task forces, workshops, opinion surveys, public meetings, and still other types of hearing. None of these mechanisms, they also claim, can be allowed to displace the legitimate role of representative government in this age of the mass society.

The issue of public involvement also emphasizes the problem of time. However desirable the canvassing of the widest possible array of viewpoints is, it is time-consuming and expensive. And in some circumstances it may be counter-productive, particularly when a valuable opportunity for social improvement is lost. Thus the challenge to institutional designers is severe. They must reflect the complexity of emerging issues in appropriate responsive mechanisms on the one hand, and, at the same time, simplify the decision-making process to keep it manageable on the other. They ignore at their peril the discipline of Occam's razor. In Canada we have not yet worked ourselves out of the dilemmas this state of affairs evokes. The responses generated to the Thompson Inquiry by late 1977 serve to illustrate the point. A good many of the intervenors who were opposed to the KPL application in the first place were delighted at the comprehensive approach the inquiry was taking and not at all perturbed over the fact that by November, 1977, only one and one-half of the six projected phases of it had been covered. The delay in decision-making to them was a positive gain. The reaction of the project proponents, however, was just the reverse, as they were concerned about the measured pace of the exercise (the twenty-seven days devoted to formal hearings, and five devoted to community hearings, in the course of nine months), and skeptical, to put it mildly, about the inquiry's capacity to evoke and assess comprehensively the technical data reflecting all the values involved. Indeed, their greatest concern by late 1977 was their claim that Dr. Thompson had fundamentally misread his terms of reference in getting into a comprehensive assessment of Canada's future oil supply and demand at all. As we have seen, the federal government itself became concerned at the cost of the inquiry (over $1 million), and at the way in which adversarial positions taken before Dr. Thompson did not seem to be producing a domestic consensus on the issue. Above all, the federal cabinet was concerned at the way in which the disagreements between participants in the inquiry were being reflected back on it, while its own capacity to move was being attenuated.

It is obvious that the institutional mechanisms involved face still other challenges than the overall paradox just mentioned. One is the need to be able to absorb the impact of – and to generate adequate responses to – the unpredictable event that so often acts as a triggering mechanism producing a major change in the position of an issue on the public agenda, or effecting a major change in the options open to government. The point, of course, is that the external and unpredictable events frequently call for major changes in direction requiring some internal legitimization, which may come easily or with great difficulty. In a sense, for example, the passage of the Magnuson amendment by the U.S. Congress in October, 1977, was such an external event, for by foreclosing any possibility that U.S. inland waters beyond the Strait of Juan de Fuca would be subjected to additional risk from enhanced tanker traffic, it made the political costs to a Canadian government which accepted such a risk in similar Canadian waters (when the energy needs involved were largely American) very much greater. The interim conclusion reached by the Thompson Inquiry served to illustrate this point. The matter may be looked at in another way. The Canadian government took advantage of the Magnuson amendment, and another unexpected event, some major improvements during 1977 in the Canadian supply/demand equation, to simplify its decision-making. The legitimacy of a new Canadian west coast oil port was determined, in short, by insisting (as had not been the case in 1976) that it be assessed solely in the context of direct Canadian energy need. Whether or not the rejection here of a continentalist perspective minimizes environmental risk over time and distributes it equitably along the west, east, and south shores of North America is itself a major policy question, one which Canadians may well have to re-examine in the years to come.

As noted earlier, the question of west coast oil pollution is once again low on the Canadian public agenda. But it has not disappeared. Over 500 tankers a year now pass through the Strait of Juan de Fuca inbound for refineries in the Ferndale-Anacortes and Cherry Point areas. Many more passages of smaller tankers and barges are being made annually to distribute the products of Canadian and American refineries along the west coast. By statutory enactment, administrative action, and moves to invoke international conventions, the Canadian and American governments are acting to further regulate the movement of these vessels to minimize the risk of accident, to clarify responsibility should it occur, to ensure the provision of compensation in such an eventuality, and to prepare contingency oil spill clean-up plans.

The question has not gone away in another sense because the supply requirements of the Northern Tier states have not evaporated, and in the winter of 1978-79 the U.S. energy picture was greatly complicated by another external event, the political upheaval in Iran. There is a very real possibility that the United States may decide in the near future to establish a new oil import terminal on its northwest coast. If it is located at or near Port Angeles, in spite of continuing opposition from the local municipality and adjacent Clallam County, the result will be a major expansion of tanker traffic into the Strait of Juan de Fuca and a heightened need for close co-operation between Canadian and American authorities. If either of the Alaskan ports mentioned earlier should be selected, the risk to Canada of the expanded traffic would be minimized. One problem with this last proposal, apart from the costs involved, seemed at the end of 1978 to be the very indeterminate state of the Alaska Highway gas pipeline project, and hence its corridor route to the centre of the continent. And a direct consequence of the hold-up on the Foothills gas pipeline project was the renewed serious consideration being given to shipping Alaskan natural gas to Valdez by pipeline and transporting it in liquefied form by tanker to markets farther south. Thus, at the beginning of 1980 the possibility existed that an American off-loading terminal might be established in the Strait of Juan de Fuca which would be attracting both bulk crude and liquefied natural gas tankers!

The concerns expressed by Canadians in the early 1970's at the threat of west coast oil pollution certainly produced results other than the Trudeau government's veto of the Kitimat oil port proposal. When the U.S. Congress passed the Trans Alaska Pipeline Authorization Act in 1973, for example, it expressly provided in two ways for compensation for residents of Canada injured as the result of a spill derived from tankers travelling between Valdez and another American port. Accidents on both coasts (and elsewhere) have prompted the Canadian government to tighten up its statutory provisions relating to liability and compensation for marine pollution, although enforcement difficulties still remain. The clean-up responsibilities of several federal government agencies have also been clarified. Vessel equipment and watch-keeping standards have been strengthened, and effective collaboration between the Canadian and American coast guards has been established, not least over the routing of marine traffic.

As Canada entered the 1980's it was not possible to predict how this country was likely to respond to the uncertainties ahead. (Some of these, by the way, stem from the fact that the oil and gas reserves of Alaska were not supplemented by major new finds during the 1970's, as earlier had been expected.) In 1980, indeed, it was not possible to write off completely any of the west coast oil import proposals advanced in the preceding decade, save for Sohio's Long Beach plan, which was abandoned in the late spring of 1979. During 1979, American authorities continued with their comprehensive assessment of the Northern Tier proposal, anchored on a Port Angeles terminal. A revised Trans Mountain import scheme, based on an off-loading facility at Low Point, some twelve miles west of Port Angeles, incorporating a tie-in with the American Puget Sound refineries as well as with those in Vancouver, and now involving a new pipeline paralleling the existing line between Vancouver and Edmonton, also remained the subject of intensive study in both Canada and the United States. Both Trans Mountain and Foothills applied to the NEB in 1979 for permission to go ahead with their proposals, although the Foothills application was withdrawn on November 15 of that year. In mid-February, 1980, the NEB called for further marine and general environmental studies in connection with the Trans Mountain project.

A major new development in this policy-making, however, saw President Carter give the American government's approval to the Northern Tier plan on January 17, 1980, subject to that company's raising the required financing within one year. The president made it clear that he was rejecting the Foothills proposal the Canadian government had supported, and that, if the Northern Tier's sponsors did not meet the condition he had established, then he favoured going ahead with the Trans Mountain scheme. This decision notwithstanding, hearings on the Northern Tier proposal were expected to continue before the EFSEC of Washington State well into 1980, and it was clear that the Northern Tier group faced major difficulties in proving the financial viability of their plan. Thus, there was a real prospect that the Trans Mountain option was the one which might be selected after all. Finally, to complete and complicate the record, it is only fair to add that, at the beginning of the new decade, some modest support had begun to re-emerge in British Columbia for the Kitimat plan, in the context of a reappraisal of the environmental risk associated with a great increase in Strait of Juan de Fuca traffic, which both the Northern Tier and Trans Mountain schemes would entail.

Much will depend on the operative ideals, the values of the 1980's, the discovery or development of new sources of energy, the location of these sources, the policies of new administrations, and the place of other items on the agenda. Thus far, the responses to the threat of west coast oil pollution have emphasized the operative, technical, and research aspects of the problem. The challenge in the next decade will be to generate effective responses to new oil import proposals and to the crises that may emerge if the scale of oil transfers on the west coast continues to rise. The experience of the 1970's suggests that some of our existing institutions may serve us well as we seek the necessary synthesis of social values, and as we seek decisions widely regarded as legitimate. In some circumstances, different approaches to these same institutions may be required. It seems inevitable, however, that some new institutional arrangements will be needed, as well, to meet the conditions of the future.

NOTES

1. *The Vancouver Sun*, February 24, 1978, p .1.
2. Anthony Downs, "Up and Down with Ecology," *The Public Interest*, 28 (Summer, 1972), 38-50.
3. House of Commons, *Debates*, June 21, 1971, p. 7268.
4. John Saywell (ed.), *Canadian Annual Review of Politics and Public Affairs* (Toronto, 1974), 227-8.
5. *Ibid.*, 228.
6. U.S. Department of Energy, "Crude Oil Supply and Demand Issues Bearing on West-to-East Pipeline Projects," prepared for presentation to the West Coast Oil Ports Inquiry, October 28, 1977, pp. 14-15; William Perrine (Ashland Oil Company), "Statement," for the West Coast Oil Ports Inquiry, September, 1977, pp. 5-8.
7. For a useful summary of the Canadian jurisdictional situation, see "Interim Submission of Commission Counsel: West Coast Oil Ports Inquiry," pp. 43-9, 51-76.
8. See Marc J. Hershman, "The Legal Framework for Energy Facility Siting in Washington State," prepared for presentation to the West Coast Oil Ports Inquiry, September, 1977.
9. Andrew R. Thompson, "Statement of Proceeding," West Coast Oil Ports Inquiry, February, 1978, pp. 93-5.
10. *Ibid.*, 112.
11. Order-in-Council 1977-1980, June 30, 1977.
12. National Energy Board, *Canadian Oil: Supply and Requirements* (Ottawa, September, 1978), 207.
13. *The Vancouver Sun*, February 24, 1978, p. 2.
14. NEB, *Canadian Oil: Supply and Requirements*, 1, 2.
15. See "Interim Submission of Commission Counsel," pp. 47-9; and West Coast Oil Ports Inquiry, *Record of Proceedings*, Vol. 1, pp. 13-15.

CHAPTER TEN

Resource Development in Northern Ontario: A Case Study in Hinterland Politics

by Geoffrey R. Weller

Northern Ontario now faces major resource development and environmental problems. In any region the types of environmental problems and the precise mix of public policies used to combat them are heavily dependent upon the nature of the regional economy. Not only are the major threats to a region's environment determined by its economic structure but so also is the line-up of interest groups on what might be termed the "development" to "pristine wilderness" continuum. It is therefore important, before analysing the nature of public policy relating to resources development and the environment of northern Ontario, that the characteristics of the regional economy be specified, the nature of the major environmental threats be delineated, and the patterns of demand imposed upon the government of Ontario by northern interest groups be clarified. In this regard, the resource development and environmental problems of northern Ontario can best be treated as a case study in "hinterland politics."

Northern Ontario as a Hinterland Region

Northern Ontario consists of roughly that area of the province covered by the Canadian Shield. This amounts to 90 per cent of the total land area of Ontario. The sheer size and the geology of the region determine, to a large degree, the resource-based nature of its economy. The mining industry is important throughout the northern part of the province, although markedly more so in northeastern Ontario and especially around Sudbury. The forest industries are also important throughout the northern part of the province, although notably more so in northwestern Ontario and especially around Thunder Bay. Because of the need to export bulk commodities from the region and because the region straddles Canada's east-west transportation corridor the transportation industry is also a vital element in the regional economy. This is true particularly of Thunder Bay, placed as it is at the head of the Great Lakes and at one end of the St. Lawrence Seaway with its grain elevators, coal terminal, ore dock, and railway yards. Partly because resource industries are very heavy consumers of power, what might be termed the power industry is also of importance in northern Ontario. The geography of the region directly creates another important industry, namely tourism. The vast expanses of the north with its many rivers and lakes attract not only the sports fisherman, the hunter, and the skier but also the less energetic tourist out to see some scenery considerably more dramatic than that in southern Ontario. There are few secondary manufacturing industries and only the Algoma Steel plant in Sault Ste. Marie and the Canadian Car plant in Thunder Bay represent major variations from the regional norm. There is also very little agriculture in northern Ontario and very little opportunity for development in this sector because of the region's geography and climate.

The nature of the region's economy largely determines the total size of its population and the pattern of settlement of that population. Resource industries are very capital-intensive and becoming increasingly so, and this helps to keep the region's population low. In 1978 it amounted to some 806,000 out of Ontario's 8.2 million, with 225,000 living in northwestern Ontario and 581,000 in northeastern Ontario. The population of the northeast is declining slightly while that of the northwest is increasing very slightly. The resource-based nature of the regional economy has also meant that few major cities have developed. There are only three of any size (Sudbury, Sault Ste. Marie, and Thunder Bay) and even these do not have very diversified employment bases. Apart from a few towns of moderate size, such as Timmins and North Bay, the remaining population of the region lives in small, often very small, isolated, one-industry towns.

The geography of the region and the nature of the regional economy have combined to create a lack of regional cohesiveness. The "north" is clearly divided between the northeast and northwest and, moreover, there isn't even a great deal of cohesion within each of the two regions. The economy is itself not a particularly "coherent" one because, as J. Benidickson has put it, "southern Ontarions had their own view of northern development which contrasted sharply with the possibility of an integrated and self-reliant regional economy."[1] The lack of regional cohesiveness is also seen in the division of the population between whites and native peoples and then again in the divisions within each of these population groups. The white population is divided between French-speaking and English-speaking. The native population is divided in four ways: two language groups, Metis, and non-status Indians. The lack of cohesiveness in the population is further accentuated by the fact that the native population has either not wanted to participate or has been excluded from participation in the major industries of the region. There is a rapid rise in this population, which means there will be a rapid increase in the proportion of the regional population that will be Indian. This, combined with the fact that the land will only support a very limited proportion of the Indian population in their traditional ways of life, will mean an intensifying of problems in the social environment that will increasingly spill over into white communities, in the manner that it has in Kenora,[2] unless Indians are included in the economic development of northern Ontario.

The nature of the economy and the consequent population characteristics and lack of regional cohesiveness all clearly reveal that northern Ontario is a hinterland region of southern Ontario; thus, all arguments about development or environmental protection are coloured by this fact. Many in the region are alienated and aggrieved because they feel the region is being exploited by southern Ontario and by the industries located in the north. The north is seen by a great many of its residents as having its natural resources, people, and money extracted from it to serve the interests of the south, which in return gives little or no thought to either balanced northern development or the proper protection of the northern environment.[3] Partly because of this sense of grievance arguments about development and environmental protection take on a rather polemical and bitter tone, as we shall see. This tone is also, however, partly the result of a feeling of frustration on the part of many regional residents and groups at their lack of political clout. The region only has fifteen provincial representatives and ten federal members of parliament and no political boundaries of its own. One illustration of this frustration is the recent creation of the Northern Ontario Heritage Party, which initially pushed for separate provincial status for northern Ontario but now restricts itself to trying to get a better deal for the region.

Resource Development and Environmental Problems

Although many may still regard northern Ontario in a rather romantic light as a wilderness of clear skies and clean waters, the major industries of the region have created a rather different reality and many feel that if rapid action is not taken the situation may become far worse. In this section the nature of the damage done to the northern environment and the threats posed by the major industries will be delineated.

The single largest threat to the environment of northern Ontario comes from the forest industry, which includes not only pulp and paper mills but also the often forgotten lumbering operations. At its present stage of development, the industry represents a danger to the environment; any expansion would simply enhance this danger, which can be seen in at least three main respects: it denudes the forests, pollutes the water, and pollutes the air. The forests of northern Ontario are being cut at a rate which makes full regeneration impossible and thus the forests are presently being utilized essentially as if they were a non-renewable resource.[4] It is estimated[5] that of the huge areas being logged, one-third are left untreated and are not likely to regenerate, one-third are left untreated but are likely to regenerate, and one-third are treated with only a 50-60 per cent chance of success. Unless something fairly drastic is done soon this aspect of the industry looms as far more significant than the air or water pollution created by pulp and paper mills.

The air and the waters of northern Ontario have been and are being seriously polluted by the forest industry. The single best known example of this is the contamination with mercury of the English-Wabigoon Rivers near Kenora, which achieved the proportions, with the filming in the region by Philippe Cousteau, of a major international environmental scandal.[6] Mercury pollution is not only a problem in the Kenora area. In fact, it affects the whole region, for in the eastern part the Timmins-Kirkland Lake area is spotted with lakes contaminated by mercury. The effluent from pulp and paper mills also contributes to the increasing pollution of the Great Lakes and constitutes a threat to drinking water in many places. Thunder Bay's water supply, for example, is threatened by the effluent from the concentration of four large pulp and paper mills in that city. Air pollution from pulp and paper mills is usually readily apparent even to the layman because of the distinctive stench that is likely to greet him in a large number of towns throughout the region.

The second largest threat to the environment of northern Ontario comes from a mining industry that also creates both water and air pollution in significant quantities. Water pollution stems from many sources. Some of the lakes around the Elliott Lake area, for example, are used as tailing dumps for local uranium mining operations resulting in radioactive contaminants in the waters of the Serpent River basin. Heavy metals and arsenic contaminate a number of lakes in the Sudbury area. In addition, the mining industry in the United States has also produced some significant pollution that affects northern Ontario. The asbestos residue dumped into Lake Superior from the taconite plant at Silver Bay in Minnesota contaminated Lake Superior on the Canadian as well as the American side. Air pollution created by the mining industry also stems from many sources and is of various kinds. It relates not only to the scars on the landscape in Sudbury and the layer of red dust that covers Atikokan but also to the arsenic breathed in by gold miners, the exposure to radioactive dust at Elliot Lake, and the ingestion of asbestos fibres by workers in many locations.

The transportation industry is also responsible for some pollution in northern Ontario, although by no means on the same scale as with the forest and mining industries. Significant amounts of grain dust, for instance, are released into the atmosphere in Thunder Bay, and this used to constitute the major local source of emissions. The exact effect of this on the general population and on workers in the industry is subject to dispute. Many people in Thunder Bay also worry that a newly constructed terminal for handling coal destined for southern Ontario will also create a large amount of air pollution when it goes into full operation, even though a great many protective measures have been taken at the terminal. Another worry stems from the passage of products through northern Ontario. Fears have been expressed about the effect of the proposed Polar Gas pipeline from the Arctic.[7] Another source of fear is the very high rate of train derailments in the region. Although only one large accident has occurred, the derailment of a train load of acid in Thunder Bay in 1978, the possibility for further, more serious ones exists. More particularly, concern has been expressed about the possible shipment by rail of nuclear waste material to depository sites that may soon be constructed.

Perhaps the most serious potential threats to the environment of northern Ontario come from what might be termed the power industry. The major policy actor in the power industry as it affects northern Ontario is Ontario Hydro, but other policy actors include the Polar Gas Consortium, Atomic Energy of Canada Ltd., and major private firms such as Acres Planning and Research Ltd. The region is affected by the power industry not only because of its own demand for power, although this is indeed large and growing, but also because it is seen as a sizeable source of energy for other regions, an area through which gas from the far north has to be piped, and because it is regarded by some as a suitable site for disposing of nuclear waste materials.

The region's own demand for power is enormous, largely because of the nature of the industries located within it. Pulp and paper mills and smelters consume vast quantities of energy. Northern Ontario, contrary to popular belief, is now a net importer of energy from other regions and indeed from other provinces, for considerable purchases have to be made from Manitoba. Simply to keep up with demand Ontario Hydro is having to build a number of power stations in the north. Some of them are very large, such as the 800 megawatt station being built at Marmion Lake near Atikokan, which, it is estimated, will cost a billion dollars to build. Conventional power stations of this magnitude can cause considerable air and water pollution within a wide radius around them. Many groups, ranging from the Indians near Atikokan to the United States authorities (who fear the pollution of nearby American territory), have protested strongly that inadequate safeguards are being taken at Marmion Lake.[8]

Possible rather than actual threats to the environment in northern Ontario stem from the potential many feel the region possesses as a source of power generation for other regions. This potential lies in the possibility of developing a great deal of hydroelectric power from several rivers draining into James Bay and Hudson Bay and from the suitability of the shoreline areas of the northern Great Lakes for the location of several large nuclear power stations. Studies have already been undertaken into the feasibility of tapping the energy potential of the Severn, Winisk, Attawapiskat, Albany, and Moose river basins.[9] If ever undertaken the utilization of these resources would be an even vaster enterprise than the James Bay development. Some versions of the ideas for development involve large-scale water diversions. The potential for enormous human, ecological, and perhaps even climatic damage is evident. The Director of Design and Development for Ontario Hydro has been reported as having stated that northern lakeshores, especially those around Lake Superior in northwestern Ontario, are highly suitable for the location of nuclear power stations because of the abundant clean water and building space.[10] He thought such a development might come about if Ontario decided to produce nuclear energy for export, which, in his view, was better than shipping out uranium fuel to foreign generating stations because of the jobs that would be created in Canada. Perhaps significantly, Acres Ltd. has already presented a plan to the Porter Commission on electrical generation in Ontario whereby nuclear stations in northern Ontario would produce power for the Detroit area.[11] Also, a high capacity tie-line to northern Ontario from southern Ontario is being built. Such large-scale development of nuclear power stations inevitably would create all the environmental hazards they do elsewhere.

Another potential threat to the northern environment from the power industry stems from the possibility that a pipeline will be constructed across part of the region to bring Arctic natural gas down to southern markets. The Polar Gas Consortium has already proposed that such a pipeline be built. This raises the same fears that pipelines do everywhere, namely, the effect of construction on both the natural and human environment, the possibility of leakages, and the possible effect on such things as animal migration patterns. As well, an even more immediate fear is that northern Ontario will become the dumping ground for nuclear waste materials. This fear was precipitated by a recent agreement reached between the federal and Ontario governments to jointly develop a nuclear waste repository by 1985; a great many of the most favourable sites for such a repository were indicated to be in northern Ontario, especially northwestern Ontario. The possibility of the construction of such a facility raised not only fears of leakage from the site or during shipment to the site, a fear heightened by the large number of train derailments experienced in the region, but also resentment at the thought that the region should be regarded as a dumping ground.

The Structure of Policy Demands

An analysis of the demands placed upon the government relating to economic development in northern Ontario and its effect on the environment reveals that there exist within the region various views, on a continuum ranging from those for development at all costs to those for no further development and even a return to a pristine wilderness. For the purposes of the present analysis, the groups that comprise this continuum are roughly placed into two categories, those for further economic development and those against. An attempt will be made to assess the relative resources for political influence available to these sets of interests.

Proponents of Development

The groups supporting further development in northern Ontario range from those who argue development should take place at all costs to those who argue it should come about only if the environment is protected. Those that support development constitute both withinput and input groups. Basically, however, the major line of division is between those who support more of the same kinds of development that exist already, and hence see no need to change the hinterland status of the region, and those who, while not necessarily opposing more of the same kind of development, also want development that will change the hinterland status of northern Ontario by diversifying the employment base.

The groups that support essentially more of the same kind of development are the forest industry, the mining industry, the municipalities, and, on the withinput side, the Ontario Ministry of Northern Affairs, the federal Department of Regional Economic Expansion, Ontario Hydro, and various other ministries and agencies of the Ontario government. The forest and mining industries are especially strong advocates of development in northern Ontario and their point of view is strongly supported by most of the smaller local chambers of commerce, many of whom would agree with the sentiments expressed by the Timmins-Porcupine Chamber of Commerce that "we wish to live in a community of life and vitality, not a ghost town. Therefore we encourage the exploration and development of resources."[12] Many of the municipalities in Ontario's north are strong advocates of development. This is largely because development brings more jobs, a broader tax-base, and thereby the possibility of more or better municipal services. That numerous agencies of the Ontario government are strong advocates of economic development for northern Ontario is revealed by the submissions they made to this effect to the Hartt Commission.

The groups wishing for the kind of development that will change the hinterland status of the region are the chambers of commerce of the larger cities, the Northern Ontario Heritage Party, and some labour spokesmen. The Chambers of Commerce of Sudbury and Thunder Bay are especially keen to see not only the development of resource-based industries but also the development, on a significant scale, of secondary manufacturing industries to widen and stabilize their employment bases. The Sudbury Chamber of Commerce felt so strongly about the matter that it precipitated a violent exchange with the provincial government by replying to the government's stated plans[13] for the northeastern region with a brief entitled *A Profile in Failure.* This brief, prepared in 1976, said the government plans "represented the pinnacle of intellectual bankruptcy of the Southeastern Establishment in even analysing the problems of the north, let alone dealing with them effectively" and also represented "colonial exploitation of the natural resources of northern Ontario for the benefit of the Golden Horseshoe."[14] Darcy McKeough, the Treasurer of Ontario at the time, is reported to have stated, "I got so mad I couldn't finish reading it."[15] Later he also reportedly said, "We are just not going to see in my lifetime a motor vehicle assembly plant in Sudbury or a refrigerator plant in Thunder Bay."[16]

Although all these groups might not always quite see eye-to-eye on the precise nature of the development that should take place in the north, they do constitute very powerful political forces. The forest and mining industries have considerable resources for influencing policy. The Ontario Forest Industries Association and the Ontario Mining Association represent very large companies, some of which, such as Reed and Inco, rank as world-scale multinational corporations.[17] These industries have large financial resources at their disposal and are able to promote their views in ways not generally possible for those groups that oppose development. In addition, they employ large numbers of people throughout the north, and even the larger cities are heavily dependent for their economic well-being on the employment created by these industries. Moreover, the resource industries generate about $5 billion worth of goods and services annually, which, since most of this production is exported, is "an enormous asset in the balance of payments for Ontario and for Canada as a whole, in international trade."[18] The major municipalities and chambers of commerce have relatively easy access to government, and those withinput ministries and agencies that support development are among the most influential ones in the provincial government. In short, there is an extremely powerful nexus of interests supporting the development of northern Ontario.

Opponents of Development

Groups opposing further development in northern Ontario range from those perhaps not opposed to development *per se* but doubtful of the current adequacy of environmental safeguards to others that really would prefer the north to be essentially a wilderness area. Those that oppose development come only from input groups, and these consist of various native groups, environmental groups, some unions and tourist organizations, and the Ontario Professional Foresters Association.

The two major Indian treaty groups in northern Ontario, Treaty 3 and Treaty 9, have both expressed serious doubts about the very concept of development as understood by white society. Not only have Indian organizations been dubious about the nature of white development philosophy,[19] they also have opposed many of the specific developments, such as the Marmion Lake Generating Station,[20] and plans for development, such as the diversion and damming of the mâjor northern rivers.[21] It should not be thought, however, that native peoples organizations oppose development as such, but development in their view would have to meet two absolutely fundamental requirements. First, there would have to be rigorous environmental safeguards; second, Indians would have to be allowed to participate fully in development and the benefit from it.[22] This latter condition makes a great deal of sense because development without significant native participation, as is the case now, tends to destroy the traditional bases of their life without replacing them with anything. This leads to societal breakdown, horrendous social problems, and a degeneration of Indian-white relations leading to radicalism and violent protest (as at Anicinabe Park)[23] on the part of some Indians and racism on the part of some whites.[24]

A large number of environmental groups oppose northern economic development, at least in the manner it has so far been conducted or seems likely to be conducted in the near future. Some of them are province-wide organizations, such as the Ontario Public Interest Research Group and Pollution Probe, while others are essentially creations of northern residents themselves, such as the Dam the Dams Campaign, the Anti-Mercury Ojibway Group, the Citizens Committee Studying Nuclear Waste, and Environment North. The degree of concern for the environment varies considerably, from those who simply wish to see stronger pollution control legislation to those, such as the Coalition for Wilderness, that argue that "the best use [for land] often may be no use"[25] and that large areas of the north should be left completely untouched. Labour unions have often shown concern for northern environment, and Clifford Pilkey, the president of the Ontario Federation of Labour, said before the Hartt Commission, "unions will not be blackmailed into jobs at the expense of the environment."[26] Tourist organizations also have spoken against development. The Northern Ontario Tourist Outfitters Association, for example, has complained of the effect of logging on the shorelines of many lakes and of the bad effects on them of pollution generally.[27] Another group that has opposed what it regards as irresponsible development is the Ontario Professional Foresters Association (OPFA). This organization has spoken out very strongly, as indicated by former president John Blair's statement to the Hartt Commission that

the provincial record of forest management has resulted in a serious depletion of the forest resources and forest land base south of 50°. For this reason the Ontario Professional Foresters Association is opposed to the expansion of forest harvesting and land use operations north of 50° under existing forest policy, statutes, programs and practices.[28]

The groups opposing development do not have anything like the same resources for influencing policy as those supporting development. They are organizationally fragmented and financially weaker, and have no tradition of easy access to a receptive government. Not only are the Indian groups fragmented, they are still dependent to a degree on white advisers because the number of Indians with the appropriate education or experience is small. The environmental groups are often philosophically as well as organizationally fragmented, and many are relatively short-lived. Most of them also are financially weak, depending on charity or assorted small government grants. Moreover, the whole environmental issue seems to be losing its political saliency and concern for economic growth has risen considerably. OPFA, however, has had a substantial impact on policy-makers despite its small size because of its skill base and willingness to speak out publicly. In August, 1976, OPFA held a two-day seminar at Lakehead University's School of Forestry for some forty MPP's and cabinet ministers and made its points concerning what it regarded as government mismanagement and neglect rather bluntly.

Patterns of Policy Responses

The pattern of group demands that has just been delineated places the Ontario and federal governments in an invidious position. Although the pressures from those in favour of development are undoubtedly the strongest, the governments cannot afford to ignore opposing points of view. The result has been the promotion of development in a piecemeal fashion and the passage of piecemeal legislation to lessen the environmental impact of such development. This approach contains the risk of pleasing neither sets of interests.

Two factors, other than the pattern of group demands, also mitigate against the development of coherent policy. These are the large number of governments involved in the policy process and the large number of agencies concerned within each level of government. Both the federal and Ontario governments have policies for the economic development of northern Ontario and both have policies for the protection of the region's environment. There is confusion and, indeed, conflict in federal-Ontario relations in both areas. Moreover, the government of the United States has also become involved because of international attempts to clean up the Great Lakes and because of its objections to specific developments in northern Ontario, such as the Marmion Lake Generating Station. Also, a vast number of departments and agencies within each level of government deal with various aspects of economic development and environmental protection in northern Ontario. At the provincial level most of the line ministries and many agencies, such as Ontario Hydro, have some responsibilities in the north, but then there are also co-ordinating ministries like Treasury, Intergovernmental Affairs, and Northern Affairs which have northern responsibilities that cut across those of the line ministries. It is not clear which ministry, if any, has overall planning authority for northern Ontario.

Policies to Promote Economic Development

Both levels of government have strongly endorsed the need for greater economic development in northern Ontario. Provincial economic development policies largely emanate from three sources, the Ministry of the Treasury, the Ministry of Industry and Tourism, and the Ministry of Northern Affairs. Federal economic development policies emanate largely from the Department of Regional Economic Expansion (DREE). The policies adopted have been of three types: the funding of infrastructure development, the provision of incentives to industry, and the creation of a provincial Ministry of Northern Affairs.

A great deal of emphasis has been placed on infrastructure development as a means of promoting the economic development of northern Ontario by both the federal and provincial governments. Responsibility for economic planning in Ontario clearly resided with the Ministry of Treasury, Economics and Intergovernmental Affairs (TEIGA) until 1978. In that year the Ministry was split into the Ministry of the Treasury and the Ministry of Intergovernmental Affairs. TEIGA had a regional planning program that produced two reports entitled *Design for Development* for the northwestern and northeastern regions.[29] Both reports basically recommended the indirect promotion of economic development by means of funding infrastructure projects. The Ontario Economic Council stated, in relation to the northwestern Ontario study, that it "may be characterised as basically concerned with providing a climate and framework, through public responsibility for infrastructure that would tend to induce expansion of the private sector in the designated centres."[30] The Regional Priorities Budgets of the Ministry were one of the major means of implementing this objective. DREE's approach has reflected the emphasis of *Design for Development* on infrastructure projects, with the vast majority of its money being spent on such things as sewage system improvements and access roads. DREE's involvement in northern Ontario began with the signing of a General Development Agreement with Ontario in February, 1974, and a Northwestern Ontario Subsidiary Agreement in the following year. Total DREE outlays in northern Ontario amounted to about $120 million by the end of 1978.

The two TEIGA reports and the general approach have been heavily criticized. The Sudbury Chamber of Commerce remarked of the *Design for Development* report for northeastern Ontario that it was nothing more than a pablum of policies, a restatement of innocuous motherhood objectives based upon impressionistic descriptions of the problems, and the reprinting of published data on expensive paper.[31] This criticism of the report may have been partly motivated by the fact that Sudbury had not been designated the "primate centre" (*sic!*) for the northeast as Thunder Bay had been for the northwest. Many felt this was a politically motivated omission reflecting the fact that Sudbury was an NDP stronghold. The Ontario Economic Council has remarked of the general approach of both the federal and provincial governments that

in the effort to generate growth, the objective was consistent with the development of large-scale private resource projects encouraged by the public provision of infrastructure and services, the acceptance of the provision of relatively few permanent jobs because of the capital intensity of these industries, the absence of real diversification of the industrial and employment base and continued reliance on demand external to the region.[32]

This policy is of benefit to what were earlier identified as the most influential interest groups, namely the major industries located in the region. It is not likely to promote the sort of economic development wanted by the chambers of commerce of the larger cities and by the other groups that want to eliminate the region's hinterland status by developing a wider industrial and employment base.

In early 1980, both the federal and Ontario governments announced that very large incentive grants will be made to the forest industry. The total sum to be provided until 1985 to the industry in northern Ontario alone will amount to between two and three hundred million dollars. The governments have argued that such support is needed to stimulate the expansion and modernization of the industry. Both levels of government fear that if modernization does not take place a good part of the industry will vanish with disastrous consequences for the economy of the region.

Both the federal and Ontario governments have established a set of incentive measures in support of secondary manufacturing, service industries that support manufacturing, and the tourist industry. One of the Ontario agencies supplying incentive funds is the Northern Ontario Development Council, established in 1970 and located in the Ministry of Industry and Tourism. Similar funds are provided by DREE under the Regional Development Incentives Act. Although not without significance, the use of incentives has been heavily criticized. Much of the money is given to low-wage industries such as tourism or to industries closely related to the forest industry. This approach to economic development also has been accused of being relatively ineffective in that it tends to be capital-based and often results in windfall gains to firms that would have gone ahead with expenditures anyway. It is not an approach likely to create the kind of economic development desired by the chambers of commerce, nor is it likely to change the north's hinterland status.

In 1977 the Ontario government began a new approach to northern economic development with the creation of the Ministry of Northern Affairs. This represented an attempt to overcome the negative feelings in the north with regard to the adequacy of the existing programs; it also attempted to consolidate under one roof most of the northern programs that had grown up throughout the bureaucracy.

The negative feelings toward the government's policies were reflected in the fact that the Conservatives for a long time had not had the support they felt they should have had in the north. The Conservative Party therefore has had a long-standing desire to win the region back into the party fold and, essentially, away from the NDP. One way to do this was to create a special ministry for the north, thereby illustrating the government's concern for the region, and to give that ministry a high profile in the north. Premier Robarts had been unwilling to create a separate northern department, or even many special programs for the north, for fear of balkanizing the province. This reluctance diminished gradually under Premier Davis, and in 1977 he created the Ministry of Northern Affairs with Leo Bernier as Minister. Bernier made sure, in organizing his department, that it had a high profile in the north. He not only appointed many northerners but he structured the ministry on a highly regionalized basis, with assistant deputy ministers located in Kenora and Sault Ste. Marie and a total of twenty-nine offices throughout the north. Only 30 per cent of the ministry's staff are located in Toronto. It may well be that the announcement of the creation of the ministry just prior to a provincial election did have something to do with the loss of three seats in the north by the NDP.

A number of Conservative MPP's from the north, including Bernier, Rene Brunelle, John Rhodes, and John Lane, had long argued within the party that there was a need to consolidate all northern programs under one roof as well as create a political focus for the north. They also had argued the need for further economic development in the north. To their voices from within the party were added those from outside, such as regional chambers of commerce, municipalities, and the Northern Ontario Heritage Party. The creation of the ministry was also the logical result of developments that had taken place within the Ontario bureaucracy. Even though Robarts had been worried about possible balkanization he did start the Northern Ontario Development Corporation (NODC) and then under Davis the Ministry of Mines developed a series of northern branches, TEIGA set up regional priorities budgets, and various other ministries set up special programs for the north. Thus the Ministry of Northern Affairs might be seen as a logical development based upon what other ministries had already been doing in a disjointed fashion. This is reflected in the fact that the new ministry has taken over the Ontario Northland Transportation Commission; NorOntair; the Isolated Communities Assistance Fund; the twenty-five northern offices of the Ministry of Natural Resources; the northern roads capital construction budget from the Ministry of Transport; and the regional priorities budget from what was TEIGA. The ministry would also no doubt like to take over the NODC from the Ministry of Industry and Tourism.

It is not yet clear that the ministry will be a powerful force for balanced development although there are a number of factors indicating that it might well become so. The ministry apparently is well-staffed and has a great deal of support within the region from the groups that favour development. Moreover, as Minister of Northern Affairs, Leo Bernier is a member of all three policy field committees of Cabinet and a member of the management board of Cabinet. This gives him unusual access and may well translate into considerable influence. An indication that influence is already being exerted might be the fairly rapid growth of the ministry's budget even in a period of restraint. On the other hand, the ministry suffers from severe handicaps. It took over what might be described as a rag bag of policies from all kinds of sources and may have difficulty developing a cohesive ministerial structure and imposing its own "grand strategy" for economic development. In the latter regard it is not aided by the absence of an overall provincial plan. The ministry also is a "horizontal" one by no means fully in control of all northern programs, and it will have to co-operate with "vertical" ministries over northern policy. This may not prove to be an easy task. It is too early in its life to pass any judgements; all that can be said is that, whatever the motives behind the establishment of this ministry, it has an opportunity to become a powerful force for balanced and integrated economic and social development in northern Ontario.

The infrastructure development approach and the incentives approach do not amount to a comprehensive set of regional development policies or anything that might be termed a "grand strategy" because they do not encompass items such as transportation and housing nor do they form part of an overall economic strategy for the province. For all that the programs are frequently presented as a plan, they are "indicative of a piecemeal approach which is not as conducive as it might be to the development of northern Ontario."[33] In fact, they reveal that the two governments' commitment is only to a fairly slow expansion of industry and is, moreover, only a commitment to expand resource-based industries and not to change the very nature of the economy to eliminate the region's hinterland status. The creation of the Ministry of Northern Affairs, however, at least should have the effect of enabling the pursuit of present objectives in a more coherent manner. In time, it may lead to the generation of an overall economic strategy for the region.

Policies to Protect the Environment

The policies enacted by both the federal and Ontario governments to protect the environment via their respective environment ministries have been as piecemeal as those related to economic development. Two major types of legislation affect the environment of northern Ontario. First, distributive legislation provides benefits from general taxation via such things as incentives and subsidies to specific industries or groups. Second, regulatory legislation places restrictions on specific industries and groups in the name of the public interest.

In the first category, Premier Davis took a hard line in 1971, stating that polluters would have to pay for the protective measures needed. The federal government took a similar hard-line position in the early seventies, but neither level of government has stuck to this position and both have initiated a large number of distributive policies in recent years. Both have given tax write-offs to various industries in the region and have given grants for the installation of air and water pollution abatement equipment. Money is available for this purpose from numerous sources at both levels of government.

Much of the pressure for programs of this kind has come from the major industries of the region, many of which have argued that they need support, especially in view of the estimated $230 million needed by the pulp and paper industry to meet the Ontario Ministry of the Environment's pollution control objectives over a ten-year period.[34] The Ontario government has chosen to disagree with the conclusions of a 1976 report,[35] which stated that with the then existing tax concessions and other distributive policies the expenditure of this large sum of money was unlikely to cause serious hardship for the industry. Instead, it favoured the conclusion of a report written by officials in the Ministries of the Environment, Treasury, Natural Resources, and Northern Affairs after talks with company and union officials.[36] This report recommended the government spend at least $27 million a year for seven years to help the pulp and paper industry. The total of $189 million bears a striking resemblance to the $180 million the report estimated was necessary to meet the Ministry of the Environment's then outstanding pollution control orders. And the money would not necessarily be used for pollution controls because it was recommended the industry receive it in the form of a general corporate tax reduction and grants that would apply to plans for modernization as well as pollution control.

One of the major subsidies to northern industry is the Ontario government's responsibility for silviculture in the province. In 1962 the Crown Timber Act was amended to give the provincial government control of forest regeneration because the forest industry had not been performing an adequate job in the government's view. As Kari Lie has put it, "the industry was understandably delighted with this new policy."[37] The policy was indeed a massive subsidy to the industry, or it would have been if the government had attempted to fully regenerate the forests. As noted earlier, the government only attempts to regenerate roughly half of the cutover areas requiring treatment and then only has a 50-60 per cent success rate. It also has been pointed out that this arrangement has led the industry to take a very short-term exploitative approach to logging that is destructive in the long run. Some thought has been given to passing the responsibility back to the industries but that has not happened. In December, 1978, a further large subsidy was given to the industry in the form of an agreement between the Ontario Ministry of Northern Affairs and the federal Department of Regional Economic Expansion.[38] This five-year, $71.5 million agreement is aimed at accelerating the building of roads, primarily in the far north, to stands of mature timber. The companies will suggest where the government-financed roads should be built. Some of the money will be spent on improving forest regeneration practices.

Both levels of government also have come to the assistance of the major municipalities of the region with distributive policies related to their need to upgrade sewage and water facilities. In fact, a great deal of money has been used on such projects, with over $30 million being spent on sewers in Thunder Bay alone. Part of the reason for these large-scale expenditures is that they meet both the needs of economic development, because they are useful infrastructure projects, and of environmental protection.

Regulatory policies also have been used to protect the environment of northern Ontario, essentially in the form of provincial standards for air and water pollution and in the requirement that mandatory environmental assessments be made of major projects. Regulations are largely enforced by fines. Ontario standards are determined in consultation with Ottawa and then the provincial government negotiates individual compliance schedules with each major polluter. The compliance schedules vary, therefore, from polluter to polluter within the same industry and they vary from industry to industry. The Minister of the Environment, H. Parrott, argues that this is a logical way to proceed because uniform standards, as applied in the United States, do not take account of the fact that there are different plant conditions within an industry.[39]

Although there have been regulatory measures, neither level of government has consistently given the impression that it takes the need for environmental protection as seriously as the need for economic development. Federal Energy Minister Alastair Gillespie suggested at the time of large-scale layoffs by Inco in Sudbury that Ontario should water down its air pollution standards to save mining jobs in the area. Although Premier Davis called this statement "incompetent"[40] his own government on occasion has denied the need for regulation in areas where many of those affected would have welcomed it. When it was feared Thunder Bay's drinking water might be being polluted by asbestos fibres from the Silver Bay, Minnesota, taconite plant the government belittled data gathered by Lakehead University and the Minister of the Environment simply denied there was a problem. Also, the government's continual downplaying of the effects of mercury pollution in the English-Wabigoon system probably was a good part of the reason it became the international scandal that the government was seeking to avoid. The Ontario government not only illustrates its weak commitment to protection of the environment relative to its commitment to economic development by downplaying or denying the need for regulation in many areas. It also illustrates this weak commitment by the fact that it occasionally has exempted certain projects from mandatory environmental assessments, has relaxed pollution control orders on some companies, and has imposed only low or minimal penalties.

The Marmion Lake generating station project was exempted from mandatory environmental assessments in the fall of 1976. The government argued that the project was too advanced to come under consideration of the then new Environmental Assessment Act, and anyway it was essential that it be built if brown-outs were not to occur in northwestern Ontario in the future. Since that time the provincial government has refused requests from Indian groups, local white residents, and even the U.S. government to refer the project to the International Joint Commission. In 1978 it was learned that the Environmental Protection Agency in the United States was conducting an environmental impact study of its own on the power station because it is felt it will adversely affect the Boundary Waters Canoe Area in Minnesota. The provincial government has not budged on this matter, nor agreed to install scrubbers, despite representations from many groups and the involvement of the American Vice-President and Secretary of State.

Individual compliance orders can be relaxed at the discretion of the Minister of the Environment. In 1978 the provincial government relaxed two pollution control orders relating to Inco in Sudbury and Reed Ltd. in Dryden. In doing so it earned the ire of the opposition parties, both of which called it a sellout and argued this was just another example from many of how the provincial government had either not even bothered to enforce legislation or had relaxed orders made to companies. An example of lax enforcement was that after establishing pollution standards for the pulp and paper industry in 1969, a 1976 report[41] indicated that of the thirty-one mills in the province only three had met the biochemical oxygen demands and only six were meeting the standards for the elimination of solids before they were dumped into lakes and rivers. Mr. Miller, the Provincial Treasurer, admitted in late 1978, when announcing his support of a report calling for more tax concessions and grants to the industry, that the pulp and paper companies had not exactly leaped to bring in pollution control equipment, even when ordered to do so. He said quite bluntly that the orders "have not worked in the past."[42]

In many instances the fines levied against companies for polluting the environment have been minimal, and they can hardly be said to constitute a serious deterrent. In 1977, for instance, Reed Ltd. was fined only $5,000 on five counts. The biggest fine ever levied in Canada for pollution of the Great Lakes is $64,000 against the American Can Company located in Marathon on the north shore of Lake Superior. This contrasts markedly with some American fines, such as a $4 million fine against the U.S. Steel Corporation at Gary, Indiana, and a $1.6 million fine against Ford for pollution at its River Rouge plant.

The preferred policies for protecting the northern environment are clearly distributive rather than regulatory. Distributive policies have had a relatively high degree of success in cleaning up municipal pollution but relatively little success in cleaning up industrial pollution. In relation to the clean-up of the Great Lakes, Ontario is ahead of the United States in cleaning up municipal waste but, according to a report of the International Joint Commission,[43] lagging in efforts to control industrial waste, especially that created by the pulp and paper industry. This fact does not mean that the Ontario government is likely to increase regulatory controls on the industry, for the Minister of the Environment is reported to have said:

I think we have got to become much more cooperative-that doesn't mean nicer-to the pulp and paper industry. I don't think the only approach is tougher and tougher orders. I think standards have to rise, but you can't always discipline a kid by hitting him. Sometimes he will need a good kick in the pants, but sometimes he will need assistance. What form the assistance will take I can't yet say.[44]

The Hartt/Fahlgren Commission: An Exercise in Symbolic Politics

Another response of the Ontario government to the patterns of economic demands and environmental concerns has been the appointment of a Royal Commission on the Northern Environment. Pressure for the creation of such a commission began when Mr. Bernier, Minister of Natural Resources, announced to the provincial legislature in 1976 that a "memorandum of understanding" had been signed between the government and Reed Ltd. for the granting of timber rights to a 19,000 square-mile area of northwestern Ontario. Liberal leader Stuart Smith called for a legislative committee of inquiry but Opposition Leader Stephen Lewis of the NDP and Patrick Reid, Liberal-Labor member for Rainy River, called for a Berger-type inquiry. The issue rapidly became a *cause célèbre* and considerable criticism was leveled at the government. Partly in an attempt to stave off some of this criticism, Mr. Justice Patrick Hartt of the Ontario Supreme Court was appointed in December, 1976, as chairman of a Special Environmental Assessment Board that would study the proposed agreement. Considerable pressure was still applied on the government, particularly by Treaty 9 Indians and the NDP, and in early 1977 the terms of reference were widened to include the likely impact of development on the native peoples. Hartt implied he would indeed undertake a Berger-type inquiry and obtained a great deal of public money to award to groups to allow them to make presentations to the inquiry. Then, in July, 1977, the inquiry became transformed into a full-scale Royal Commission. This occurred when the Liberals and New Democrats said they would tack onto the bill setting up the inquiry the condition that it begin only after sport fishing had been banned on the English-Wabigoon river system. To avoid this the government dropped the bill and appointed Hartt a royal commissioner under a cabinet order-in-council.

The Royal Commission and Judge Hartt started out with great plans and great hopes, and were much heralded in the press. The concentration on the Reed project had gone and the main focus of the inquiry was clearly to be an overall strategy for the development of the northern part (north of the 50th parallel) of northern Ontario. Throughout 1977 the commission and a large retinue held hearings throughout the north and received presentations from a remarkably wide variety of groups with a similarly wide range of views. As time progressed it became clear that the commission either was finding the terms of reference too broad or did not wish to deal with such broad terms of reference. It also became clear that the commissioner and many of his staff were feeling not only overwhelmed by the task at hand but were cooling to the whole enterprise. The suspicion began to arise among many northerners that a southerner and a staff of young southern "whiz-kids" simply did not understand the problems of the north despite all the analysis and the hearings.

What had such brave beginnings in late 1976 began to collapse in early 1978 with the publication of the commission's interim report.[45] The interim report was variously described as a "vacuous anti-climax" and "a disappointment."[46] The report made only six recommendations in its forty-one pages and was generally described as wishy-washy and vague. At a press conference it became clear that Hartt had become disillusioned with the whole enterprise. He said the terms of reference were too wide and the commission's role should be limited to two functions, an environmental assessment of the proposed Onakawana lignite mine and a review of the planning process in the West Patricia area (the area that includes the proposed Reed timber limits). It also was suggested that a small task force (eight to ten persons) headed by a respected northerner be set up to investigate ways of involving northerners more in government decisions. Premier Davis promptly rejected this, pointing out that he had only just created a Ministry of Northern Affairs. Hartt also said that he, as a southerner, could never hope to understand fully the concerns of northerners and said he would prefer to return to the Ontario Supreme Court.[47] The report also called for the creation of a committee to guide negotiations between the federal and provincial governments and the Indians. Shortly after the appearance of the interim report Hartt became chairman of the committee dealing with Indian negotiations, formally titled the Indian Commission of Ontario, and the Toronto office of the Hartt Commission disintegrated with most employees going elsewhere.

In August, 1978, Ed Fahlgren was appointed commissioner. Mr. Fahlgren is a mining executive from Red Lake with Conservative political affiliations. Largely because of his background, Chiefs

Kelley and Rickard of Treaties 3 and 9 have been critical of the appointment, and indeed called for the abolition of the commission. Mr. Fahlgren, however, has pushed on, appointing his own staff and shifting the centre of his operations from Toronto to Thunder Bay, with a satellite centre in Timmins. He states he is his own man, and he argues his objectives are those of involving northerners in the making of decisions which affect their lives, weighing resource and economic development against adverse social and environmental repercussions and developing a range of alternative scenarios for the future of the north. He states that he hopes to submit his report to the provincial government by December, 1981. Given the nature of the origin of the Hartt/ Fahlgren Commission and the history of its activities to date, it is hardly reflective of any particular policy approach, and unless Mr. Fahlgren can recover a great deal of lost ground it is unlikely to have much impact.

Conclusions

The institutional structure of the policy-making system as it has affected resource development and environmental policy in northern Ontario over the past decade or so has exhibited some signs of moving toward greater concentration and integration, although this is more clearly seen among environmental policy institutions. Prior to 1972, water pollution was the responsibility of the Ontario Water Resources Commission and air pollution the responsibility of the Air Management Branch of the Department of Energy and Resource Management. Since 1972, both have been the responsibility of the Ministry of the Environment, and its effectiveness is often questioned and the leader of the Liberal opposition says the ministry appears to be a ship lacking direction and a rudder.[48] Even if this is the case, at least a structure is in place that could lead to better direction than was previously possible.

This is more than can be said at present of the institutional structures responsible for development. Prior to 1977 most of the responsibility rested with TEIGA. The creation of the Ministry of Northern Affairs clouded matters somewhat and further diffusion occurred with the splitting of TEIGA into two departments in 1978. It is to be hoped that an integration and concentration of institutional structures will occur again, presumably the logical focus being the Ministry of Northern Affairs. Yet, even if the responsibility for development matters eventually focuses on the Ministry of Northern Affairs, there will be no real institutional mechanism for making trade-offs between development concerns and the environmental concerns institutionalized in the Ministry of the Environment. The policy outputs of the Ontario government have been piecemeal in both the areas of development and of environmental protection in northern Ontario, and there is no real plan for either, let alone a grand strategy integrating the two. Environmental policy has been primarily distributive rather than regulatory and development policy clearly has favoured a fairly slow expansion of largely resource-based industries by means of infrastructure construction and incentives. The nature and balance of these policies clearly indicate the dominance of development over environmental concerns and the dominance of resource-based development over the sort intended to create a more balanced economy. This, as we have seen, mirrors the pattern of policy influence and demands.

NOTES

1. J. Benidickson, "Northern Ontario: Problems and Prospects, Past and Present," *Alternatives*, 7 (Autumn, 1978), 5.
2. See E. M. Jacobsen, *Bended Elbow* (Kenora: Central Publications, 1974).
3. See D. Scott, "Northern Alienation," in Donald C. MacDonald (ed.), *Government and Politics of Ontario* (Toronto, 1975), 235-48; and G. R. Weller, "Hinterland Politics: The Case of Northwestern Ontario," *Canadian Journal of Political Science*, 10 (1977), 727-54.
4. See K. Lie, "The Plight of Ontario's Northern Forests" *Alternatives*, 7 (Autumn, 1978), 17-25; and K. W. Hearnden, "Growing the Second Forest in Ontario – A Political and Professional Challenge," speech given to the OPFA Seminar for MPP's on the status of Ontario's forests, Lakehead University, Thunder Bay, August 30-31, 1976.
5. Lie, "Plight of Northern Forests," 19.
6. See Warner Troyer, *No Safe Place* (Toronto, 1977); G. Hutchison and D. Wallace, *Grassy Narrows* (Toronto, 1977); J. Harding, "Mercury Poisoning," *Canadian Dimension*, 11 (October, 1976), 14-23; Ontario Public Interest Research Group, "The Dryden Story," *Last Post* (December, 1976), 33-40; and Ontario Public Interest Research Group, *Quicksilver and Slow Death* (Toronto, 1976).
7. See J. MacPherson and G. Thompson, "Polar Gas: A Premature Pipeline," *Alternatives*, 7 (Autumn, 1978), 34-9.
8. See Peter Kelley, "Marmion Lake Generating Station: Another Northern Scandal?" *Alternatives*, 7 (Autumn, 1978), 13-6.
9. See D. H. Pimlott, "The Water Equation," *Alternatives*, 7 (Autumn, 1978), 26-9.
10. See *Lakehead Living*, June 14, 1978; and Thunder Bay *Times-News*, May 26, 1978.

11. Thunder Bay *Times-News*, May 26, 1978.
12. See Royal Commission on the Northern Environment, *North of 50*, No. 2 (December 21, 1977), 2.
13. Ontario, Ministry of Treasury, Economics and Intergovernmental Affairs, *Design for Development. Northeastern Ontario: A Proposed Planning and Development Strategy* (Toronto, 1976).
14. Sudbury and District Chamber of Commerce, *A Profile in Failure* (Sudbury, 1976), 1, 7.
15. See Toronto *Globe and Mail*, May 10, 1977.
16. See Thunder Bay *Chronicle-Journal*, May 20, 1977.
17. See J. Swift, *The Big Nickel: Inco at Home and Abroad* (Kitchener: Between the Lines, 1978).
18. Hon. Leo Bernier, Minister of Northern Affairs, "Remarks to the Federation of Northern Ontario Municipalities," Parry Sound, April 29, 1977.
19. See, for example, the Treaty 3 brief to the Royal Commission on the Northern Environment in *North of 50*, No. 2 (December 21, 1977), 16.
20. Kelley, "Marmion Lake."
21. See *Thunder Bay Chronicle-Journal*, August 13, 1976.
22. See Chief Andrew Rickards presentation to the Royal Commission on the Northern Environment in *North of 50*, No. 2; and Chief John Kelley's presentation in *ibid.*, No. 1 (November 29, 1977), 16, and No. 4 (March 23, 1978), 18-20.
23. J. Gallagher and C. Gonick, "The Occupation of Anicinabe Park," *Canadian Dimension*, 10 (November, 1974), 21-40.
24. See Jacobsen, *Bended Elbow*.
25. See *North of 50*, No. 1, 15.
26. See *North of 50*, No. 4, 10.
27. See Thunder Bay *Chronicle-Journal*, September 8, 1978.
28. See *North of 50*, No. 1, 27.
29. Ontario, Department of Treasury and Economics, *Design for Development: Northwestern Ontario Region* (Toronto, 1970); and Ontario, Ministry of Treasury, Economics and Intergovernmental Affairs, *Design for Development: Northeastern Ontario Regional Strategy* (Toronto, 1977).
30. Ontario Economic Council, *Northern Ontario Development* (Toronto, 1976), 10.
31. See *A Profile in Failure*.
32. *Northern Ontario Development*, 11.
33. *Ibid.*, 12.
34. See Pimlott, "The Water Equation."
35. J. A. Donnan and P. A. Victor, *Alternative Policies for Pollution Abatement: The Ontario Pulp and Paper Industry* (Toronto: Ministry of the Environment, 1976).
36. As reported in the Toronto *Globe and Mail*, December 6, 1978.
37. K. Lie, "Plight of Northern Forests," 19. For an analysis of the government's policy, see F. J. Anderson, "Ontario Reforestation Policy: Benefits and Costs," Lakehead University, Department of Economics: Staff Discussion Paper No. 78-04, 1978.
38. As reported in the Thunder Bay *Chronicle-Journal*, November 23, 1978.
39. As reported in *ibid.*, November 30, 1978.
40. See Toronto *Globe and Mail*, December 10, 1977.
41. Donnan and Victor, *Alternative Policies*.
42. As reported in the Toronto *Globe and Mail*, December 6, 1978.

43. As reported in the Thunder Bay *Chronicle-Journal*, November 30, 1978.
44. *Ibid.*
45. Ontario, Royal Commission on the Northern Environment, *Interim Report and Recommendations* (Toronto, April, 1978).
46. See, for example, the Thunder Bay *Chronicle-Journal*, April 8, 1978.
47. See the *Ottawa Citizen*, April 5, 1978.
48. As reported in the Toronto *Globe and Mail*, October 14, 1978.

CHAPTER ELEVEN

The Mercury Problem: An Examination of the Scientific Basis for Policy-making
by Fikret Berkes

Introduction

The Problem

The mercury problem is defined in this essay as having two components, an industrial pollution component and an environmental mercury component. Industrial pollution occurs in a few well-defined pockets in parts of Canada and no doubt also affects surrounding regions to some extent by atmospheric transport. This is the better known component of the problem and most public interest and regulatory action has focused on this aspect. While some of the parties affected by mercury pollution remain dissatisfied, it may be said in general that the situation is under control, at least in the sense that sources of pollution have been inventoried and quantified and the single largest source (from chloralkali plants) effectively eliminated by 1975.

By contrast, the environmental mercury component of the problem has proved perhaps more difficult than the first for policy-makers, and is by no means under control. The environmental mercury problem affects large areas, rather than being confined to a few pockets. Mercury bioaccumulates in large, long-lived predatory species of freshwater fish over vast areas of the Canadian North; many marine mammal species; some species of large, active, long-lived marine fish such as swordfish and tuna; and, of course, the people who eat these animals.

There is scientific controversy over a number of key issues that affect policy: the relative importance of atmospheric transport of mercury pollution as compared to natural geological sources of mercury, the significance of moderately elevated mercury concentrations in animals, and the significance of moderately elevated human blood mercury levels in many communities, almost all of them in the North. My purpose is to evaluate the scientific basis of policy-making rather than the policy process itself, focusing primarily on the environmental mercury component of the problem. In particular, the role of assumptions, facts, interpretations, and uncertainties will be examined as they affect policy. The essay will discuss how the availability of technical-scientific evidence has influenced the evolution of policy on mercury.[1]

Evolution of Policy on Mercury

That mercury is an occupational health hazard was said to be known to Pliny in the first century A.D. Commercial use of such organic mercury compounds as seed dressings began during the First World War and led to a number of outbreaks of methylmercury poisoning, most notably in Iraq. Fish contaminated by methylmercury from a chemical plant were the cause of an epidemic of poisoning in Minamata, Japan, beginning in the 1950's. To 1974, 107 persons died in Japan and many others subjected to a high-dose exposure were shown to have suffered irreversible neurological disorders, kidney and liver dysfunction, and probably teratogenic and mutagenic effects. In Iraq during 1971-72, 459 cases of hospital deaths were attributed to mercury poisoning.

In the mid-1960's, some Canadian scientists asked federal authorities to undertake a survey of mercury in fish, but such action was not taken, presumably because there were no organic mercury discharges from chemical plants in Canada.[2] In 1967, however, Swedish scientists showed that inorganic mercury can be converted by bacteria in sediments into toxic methylmercury which can bioaccumulate. In 1969, a university biologist produced first public evidence of mercury-contaminated fish in Canada, from Lake St. Clair, downstream from a chloralkali plant. The federal government then started an extensive survey of mercury levels in Canadian waters.

Commercial fishing was banned by Environment Canada in 1969 in the South Saskatchewan River, and in April, 1970, newspaper headlines across Canada read "Fish poisoning stops $4 million-a-year Lake Erie fish catch." Federal government action

(Department of Agriculture) also included a ban on the production and sale of seed-dressing products made with mercury. A guideline of 0.5 ppm for fish and fish products sold in Canada was established by Health and Welfare Canada in 1970. Enforcement of the guidelines is through the Fish Inspection Regulations, specifically section 6(1), which states that "No person shall import, export or process for export any fish that is tainted, decomposed or unwholesome or otherwise fails to meet the requirements of these Regulations." The definition of "unwholesome" includes substances toxic or aesthetically offensive to man. Export covers shipping from one province to another.

In 1972 Environment Canada issued regulations for the chloralkali industry, restricting mercury in the water effluent to 0.005 pounds per ton of chlorine produced per day. Chloralkali Mercury National Emissions Standards Regulations were drawn up under the Clean Air Act, and the compliance date for these regulations was July 1, 1978. The establishment of special committees to deal with the mercury issue began in 1973 with the formation of the Standing Committee on Mercury in the Environment, a federal body. Tripartite federal-provincial-native committees were established, starting with Ontario in 1975, Manitoba, and Quebec. Provincial task forces were established in 1975 to review the problem in northwestern Ontario and northwestern Quebec.

Health Hazard of Mercury: Facts, Assumptions, and Interpretations

In Canada the health hazard of mercury is controlled in three ways.[3] The first is a preventive measure by the use of a 0.5 parts per million (ppm) mercury standard. It is assumed here that by far the greatest public exposure to mercury comes from eating fish. The figure of 0.5 ppm is taken from the World Health Organization. Some other nations, including Japan, Sweden, and more recently the United States, employ a less strict standard of 1.0 ppm. The standard of 0.5 ppm, if used alone, is deficient on two major counts: (1) no distinction can be made between the industrial mercury component and the environmental mercury component of the problem; and (2) no allowance is made for the consumption level.

Second, guidelines are established for the consumption levels because the standard for fish is arbitrary in the sense that the actual human intake of mercury depends on the amount eaten as well as on the mercury content of fish. Thus, the key factor is the human intake level of mercury. The problem here is that the calculation of intake levels is complicated, and the regulation of consumption levels is very difficult. In Canada, the allowable intake level is 60g fish/day at 0.5 ppm mercury. It should be noted that these assumptions logically lead to allowable intake levels of 30g fish/day at 1.0 ppm, and, furthermore, 15g fish/day at 2.0 ppm, even though no country allows this. Hence, a major problem for policy implementation is that one cannot simultaneously regulate both the fish mercury level and the consumption level. If the fish mercury level is regulated standards are simplified and implementation is made easier, but this does not make allowances for the amount eaten. On the other hand, if the consumption level is regulated, this is biologically and medically sound. But the regulatory agency finds itself, for example, setting two different standards for the sport fisherman, who may consume much only in the short term, and native fishermen, who may have a higher average yearly consumption of the same fish.

Banning the sale of fish with more than 0.5 ppm mercury is no doubt an effective control of mercury exposure for much of the Canadian population, even in the absence of a program to educate the public about mercury. For the average consumer, the figures indicate that fish such as tuna and swordfish at 0.5 ppm cannot possibly be damaging because the consumption levels are too low. Even at higher levels of mercury, a strong case can be made, as indeed the U.S. swordfish industry has argued, that the average consumer does not ingest hazardous levels of mercury.

For people who catch and eat their own fish, however, the situation is more difficult to control, and consumption levels may also be much higher than the average Canadian intake. Two groups of people may be recognized here: sport fishermen and native people who obtain food from local domestic (or subsistence) fisheries. Where sport and domestic fisheries exist side by side, the scientifically logical practice of attempting to set two different standards has created problems. In the case of northwestern Ontario, the Indian people could see non-native tourists catching and eating fish, even after the native people were told not to do so. This appeared to contradict the government teaching and elicited suspicion among the Indian people.

Third, the mercury health hazard is controlled by the use of human blood and hair mercury concentration standards. Established and implemented by Health and Welfare Canada, these standards specify the following blood mercury levels in parts per billion (ppb): (a) less than 20 ppb in blood: normal acceptable range; (b) between 20 and 100 ppb: proportionately increasing risk; (c) more than 100 ppb: high risk. In practice, all individuals with over 100 ppb in the blood (equivalent of 30 ppm in hair) are encouraged to undergo detailed clinical examinations. The blood mercury testing program in Canada is extensive. As of late 1978, the data set included over 30,000 test results from about 300 communities across Canada and was growing at a rate of about 1,000 per month. Most of these data are available in the form of Health and Welfare Canada press releases.[4]

Controlling the health hazard of mercury is hampered by problems unrelated to biological and medical science and the regulatory process. The concept that a substance may be dangerous at some levels of concentration but not at other levels is difficult to comprehend. Even in English, the concept strains the meaning of the word "pollution" as it is commonly used. With many of the native languages, the problem is compounded. The eastern Cree Indian language, for example, does not have a word for pollution; there are only words for poisoning, which refers to acute poisoning, and for disease, which refers to contagious disease.

Even with the best of intentions, therefore, a control program on mercury, properly translated, can still lead to misunderstanding, bewilderment, and distrust in a northern native community. Apparent contradictory action by two different government departments would increase the confusion. When the educational campaign is supplemented with a Minamata horror film, chances are good that the audience will experience considerable stress, and some people will reject all of the information offered.[5]

Perhaps the most serious drawback for the control programs of mercury exposure concerns the lack of agreement among experts regarding the seriousness of the problem. The Canadian public in general and the native peoples in particular have received conflicting information regarding the interpretation of symptoms of mercury poisoning, the significance of observed mercury levels in animal and human tissues, and the exact sources of mercury. These uncertainties have undermined the credibility of government action and information. The difficulty is that there appears to be no easy solution to the uncertainties, and this in turn has ramifications for the formulation of policy.

Policy Implications of Scientific Uncertainties

Is There Mercury Poisoning in Canada?

Perhaps the most heated and emotional arguments regarding mercury in Canada revolve around the question of the interpretation of mercury disease symptoms. Such symptoms have been observed by Barbeau *et al.* and Harada and in a few other fragmentary studies.[6] As Shephard puts it, "one of the problems in assessing mercury poisoning is that the signs and symptoms, at any rate in the early stages, are nonspecific and few can be attributed with certainty to mercury poisoning." Harada's surveys on eighty-nine individuals in northwestern Ontario have led him to conclude that "the neurological symptoms observed are characteristic of mercury poisoning. However, the symptoms were relatively mild, and many of them were thought to be caused by other factors." When such statements are converted into newsworthy material, the tendency has often been to overlook the qualifications offered by the investigator.

The balance of medical opinion in Canada does not seem to accept the evidence as clearly showing mercury poisoning. The position of Health and Welfare Canada is consistent with this interpretation. According to Dr. B. Wheatley, Health and Welfare Canada has not been able to confirm cases identified by some investigators as showing mercury poisoning; in particular, the findings of the Japanese investigators in northwestern Ontario have not been confirmed.[7] Medical arguments of this nature are difficult to translate conceptually, and many media reports and popular books have emphasized only the evidence *for* mercury poisoning. Governments have done little, however, to dispel these uncertainties and to educate the public.

Significance of Moderately Elevated Blood Levels of Mercury

Over large areas of the North, moderately elevated blood mercury levels have been discovered in areas with no obvious mercury pollution. The number of communities so affected is potentially very large and each new survey seems to be finding new problem areas. For example, according to a Health and Welfare Canada news release dated August 22, 1978, a total of 732 blood mercury samples were tested from 27 communities across Canada. Of these, "51 showed mercury levels in excess of 100 parts per billion (ppb) above which an individual is regarded as being at risk; 439 were between 0 and 19 ppb which is the normal human range and 244 results were between 20 and 99."

The question is, if 0-19 ppb is regarded as normal, what is to be done with the 20-99 ppb group and the group over 100 ppb? The reporting of the results often creates more questions than it answers.[8] What is the "risk"? The highest blood mercury value reported in Canada was 649 ppb in July, 1975, in northwestern Quebec. Yet there have been no officially recognized cases of mercury poisoning in Canada. The Health and Welfare Canada definitions of "high risk" and "proportionately increasing risk," therefore, add up to a dilemma in the minds of many people: if there is such a risk at those levels, then there must be people suffering from poisoning; or else if there are no people suffering from mercury disease, there cannot be the risk that is claimed.

Such an appraisal of Health and Welfare Canada policies is unreasonably harsh, however, because the intention doubtless is to maintain a "safety margin," especially in view of the possibility of chronic damage at low dose; this is difficult to diagnose because of the lack of specificity in symptoms. Further, the experience in Japan cannot easily be used to generate safe levels because there are still uncertainties about the analytical methods and the way in which tissue levels were reported. Most technical literature on the subject refers to 200 ppb as the lowest level at which symptoms have been observed, but this must also be considered a controversial conclusion.

Bakir and associates related blood mercury to the incidence of symptoms, based on the experience of Iraq. The range of 0-100 ppb was associated with 5 to 9.5 per cent incidence of three neurological symptoms, but the authors believed that at this range the symptoms were caused by factors other than mercury. The 101-500 ppb range was associated with incidence of 5 per cent of two symptoms. Above 500 ppb the incidence of symptoms sharply increased in direct proportion to the blood concentration. Concentrations exceeding 3000 ppb were associated with deaths, 17 per cent at 3001 to 4000 ppb, and 28 per cent at 4001 to 5000 ppb.[9]

It is not clear how appropriate these findings are in the Canadian context. As explained below, answers are being sought by the use of an epidemiological study:

The numerous studies already carried out across Canada and in Quebec in particular have not been able to determine which neurological signs and symptoms are due specifically to mercury contamination and which are due to other factors combined with mercury contamination, such as the abuse of medications, the presence of disease, or malnutrition. For this reason, an epidemiological study is needed to identify specifically the effects of methylmercury intake on populations exposed to pollution by this toxic substance, by comparing them with a control group that has not been so exposed.[10]

Significance of Moderately Elevated Mercury Concentrations in Animals

The expansion of the mercury problem from a few pockets in industrialized parts of Canada to the vast area of the Canadian North raises new questions. One of the key questions is whether the moderately high levels discovered in tissues of northern animals are due largely to man-made pollution or to natural background levels of mercury that were historically present in the environment. If the latter is the case, such mercury should technically not be referred to as pollution, and the problem for the decision-maker becomes different. In placing the question in perspective, it should be emphasized that there is a clear difference between mercury levels in fish in the few polluted pockets as compared to those from the vast northern area from Labrador-Ungava to the Northwest Territories. In polluted areas, predatory fish almost always contain more than 3 ppm. In Clay Lake (1970) mean levels were pike 9.2, walleye 12.1, and whitefish 3.6 ppm. These are among the highest levels recorded anywhere in the world; the mean concentrations in Minamata at the time of the outbreak were about 11 ppm.[11]

By contrast, in areas that do not directly receive mercury pollution, most fish have less than the standard of 0.5 ppm. Some of the large predatory fish, however, may reach or even exceed 1 ppm, but values approaching those quoted above have not been found. Several species of large predatory marine fish, such as swordfish and tuna, contain on the order of 0.5-1 ppm. Based on findings of high levels in museum specimens, the balance of scientific opinion since the mid-1970's is that there have been no significant increases in mercury in these marine fish that can be attributed to man-made sources.[12] With respect to northern Canadian lakes, however, no scientific consensus has emerged.[13]

Some studies in the Great Lakes region of the U.S. suggest that even in these areas, with some waterborne as well as airborne mercury pollution, there has been little historical change. Recent and museum specimens of walleye, adjusted to a standard length, showed no statistically significant increases over the past forty years in four of seven localities tested; contamination in western Lake Erie had increased by 27 per cent over the historical concentrations.[14] Also, researchers have found no systematic change in the mercury content of Greenland ice cores over the past 150 years.[15] Such findings suggest that in areas of the Canadian North, more than 500 to 1,000 kilometres from the nearest industrial source of mercury pollution, moderately high levels in fish cannot readily be explained on the basis of atmospheric fallout.[16]

Nevertheless, there have been two divergent views among officials and specialists with regard to dealing with this problem. These arguments may be summarized as follows. (1) The high background levels are "natural" and northern natives have always eaten these fish. They may also have developed a tolerance because in historical times their intake levels were even higher. The "normal" blood standards as applied to southern Canadians are therefore meaningless in the case of these people who depend on local resources for their food. As bush food in these areas is indispensable and irreplaceable, care should be taken not to disrupt their way of life and patterns of nutrition. (2) Whether or not mercury is of industrial or natural origin makes no difference; the chemistry is the same and the effect is the same. All persons, no matter who they are and where they are, face an increasing health risk at blood mercury levels above 20 ppb. Given the possibility of sublethal low-dose effects, first priority should be given to reducing blood mercury levels, over and above other considerations.

Both of these positions certainly are valid even though there clearly is a contradiction between the two in terms of the action that should be taken. There are adherents to each of the two positions from both medical sciences and natural sciences, so that the division in opinion is not along disciplinary lines. In practice, however, there is evidence that the two views have been evolving toward a common middle ground.

Implementation of Fish Consumption Guidelines

Formal statements of policy on mercury in remote areas are not available as these policies, according to Health and Welfare Canada, have to be flexible enough to accommodate variations by area, and to evolve as information becomes available. The following is a description of the general approach of Health and Welfare Canada, as provided by Dr. B. Wheatley:

> . . . the policy is that when significantly elevated blood mercury levels are found, the close cooperation of the people affected should be sought in finding a method to modify, rather than radically disrupt, the eating patterns and lifestyle so as to achieve a level of mercury intake which will not take an individual's blood mercury level out of the normally accepted range. Within this general approach, specific allowance is made

for special "at risk" groups such as pregnant women and small children. Advice is, of course, also concentrated on those recognized as being heavy fish eaters or who, in certain areas, are fishing guides and thus more exposed to large intakes of fish because of their occupation.[17]

An example of local solutions devised by the regional offices of Health and Welfare Canada is Dr. R. D. P. Eaton's description for the Northwest Territories:

In a few communities, chief among them being Tuktoyaktuk, we have instituted a policy of routine antenatal hair testing with the aim of identifying any individual whose blood mercury level might be expected to be at 100 ppb at some time during her pregnancy. If such a person were to be identified, and so far this has not occurred, she would be advised to reduce consumption of sea mammals for the remainder of her pregnancy and during suckling. This of course relates to the Inuit coastal communities.

In the case of Indian communities we have turned up very few remarkable levels, but in the case of Fort Good Hope we had a lead from one sample from an elderly lady who took fish from a lake different from anyone else in the survey sample. . . . Follow-up by examining fish from the lake in question revealed some moderately high levels in predator fish, up to about 1.5 ppm. We have advised that pregnant mothers not eat predators from this lake and that in general it would be advisable to eat such fish no more than once a week.[18]

Policies dealing with the reduction of blood mercury levels in the Northwest Territories have been changing since 1971. At that time, the Inuit were advised to lower their seal meat intake to levels that some experts considered unrealistically low. In particular, some medical experts concerned with nutrition pointed out that deterioration of health that would accompany abandoning traditional food sources would likely be more serious than the perceived hazard of mercury from these sources, and further challenged the implicit assumption that environmental mercury in these remote areas had increased significantly beyond its historical levels. The Inuit themselves also challenged the directives, arguing that they have always eaten a great deal of seal meat for many generations, without ill effects. Dr. R. D. P. Eaton added the following information with regard to

. . . the previous directive issued to reduce seal meat consumption. This was done in the Keewatin about 1971 at a time when the first assays of seal and whale meat and liver were made and the directive was given on the basis of total mercury levels. *It was not realised at that time that the bulk of the mercury in seal liver was inorganic and non-absorbable.* This directive, though never formally countermanded has long since been allowed to lapse.[19]

Implementation of policies to control exposure to environmental mercury has changed with the changing perception of the nature of the hazard. At the community level, these changes have frequently caused confusion. If part of the blame for this confusion lies with the media, it should also be remembered that media reports are more or less exclusively based on press releases from Health and Welfare Canada.[20]

In March, 1977 headlines in major Canadian Newspapers and a furore in the local press, radio and TV proclaimed "dangerously high mercury blood levels found in Tuktoyaktuk!" This led either to head shaking disbelief and loss of credibility of Medical Services – the prevailing reaction in Tuktoyaktuk, where residents pointed out that they had participated in a hair, but no blood mercury sampling program, and that the Minister must have mixed up things – or anxiety and panicky reactions of some Inuvik, and a minority of Tuktoyaktuk residents, who demanded to be examined for "mercury poisoning".[21]

Dr. O. Schaefer, quoted above, also pointed out that hair samples collected from the Inuit in 1969 had shown, in fact, higher levels than those collected in 1976. Yet no attempt was made to put the situation in perspective.[22]

Similarly in northern Quebec, the Cree people stopped eating fish temporarily following the initial mercury scare in 1970-71. Following the extensive mercury testing of 1975-76 they stopped once more, not only in the Waswanipi area where the polluting chloralkali plant was located, but as far north as Great Whale River, more than 700 kilometres from the source of pollution. These events have made some northern natives skeptical about the reality of the problems and have forced some to question the motives of the government, especially in the face of increasing southern interests in northern resources. A researcher has quoted an Inuk as retorting: "How do you know that mercury was not always there and the seals and the whales and the fish and we got used to it?"[23]

Solving the Problem?

The Industrial Pollution Component

Regarding industrial pollution, the response has been rapid. The main sources were identified within a year, once the problem was recognized.[24] Government action in stopping this pollution, however, proved to be less effective, no doubt due to reluctance in jeopardizing the economic status of chemical industries. Vast quantities of mercury were still being dumped into Canadian waterways in the 1970's. Between May, 1972, and April, 1975, major chemical companies were unable to account for up to 65 per cent of the mercury purchased; one chloralkali plant attached to a pulp mill in northwestern Quebec "lost" 7,437 of 11,248 kg mercury purchased during the period.[25] By virtue of regulations drawn up under the federal Fisheries Act in March, 1972, mercury losses from chloralkali plants to the water effluent were brought down from an estimated 67,000 kg in 1970 to less than 460 kg in 1975.[26] The fact that alternative, mercury-free processes are available for chloralkali production made it possible to reduce the largest industrial source of mercury pollution. Controlling other sources may prove more difficult. According to data compiled by Environment Canada, there are many other sources of mercury emissions, most notably the combustion of fossil fuels. The burning of coal and petroleum released to the environment about 27,000 kg of mercury in 1970.[27]

According to the *Policies and Poisons* report, "inorganic mercury, once released into the air, can be transported great distances and be deposited with acid rain in distant regions where methylation readily occurs because of high acidity. . . . Thus, mercury contamination illustrates the interaction of environmental factors with man-induced activities to produce a higher level of risk."[28] If one takes into account also the atmospheric drift of mercury and acid rain to Canada from the U.S., it may be seen that fossil fuel mercury is more difficult to control than chloralkali pollution: not only is there no ready alternative to coal and oil, but also the larger problem, in effect, is pollution from a non-point source.

There also has been evidence that the reduction in pollution loads, in some cases, resulted in the reduction in mercury in organisms. Hence, in the well-publicized case of Lake St. Clair, for example, recovery of the environment was relatively rapid. Between 1970 and 1976, the mean mercury level in walleye (adjusted to a standard fish size of 40 cm) fell from 2.1 to 0.56 ppm, a 73 per cent reduction.[29] A number of Great Lakes fisheries, initially closed in 1970, have been permitted to reopen after mercury levels declined. These included the yellow perch fishery in Lake Ontario (reopened in 1972) and the lake trout fishery in Lake Superior (1974).

In the case of the two chloralkali plants in northwestern Ontario and Quebec, large amounts of mercury continued to be discharged until 1975; as of 1979 there was no published evidence that mercury levels in fish were decreasing. The lack of government action in these two pollution areas, in turn, prompted action by native organizations. The National Indian Brotherhood established a mercury program in 1974, started to exert pressure on the government regarding the northwestern Ontario case, and received considerable support from the media, scientists, environment groups, and Japanese mercury experts. Meanwhile, the Grand Council of the Crees of Quebec in November, 1976, filed suit for $8 million damages against fifteen companies, including the chloralkali plant and a number of mining and smelting companies. With evidence provided by Japanese experts and the Barbeau report, the media, citizens groups, native groups, and scientists such as many of those involved in the Science Council of Canada panels on *Policies and Poisons* all started to demand tighter standards and controls on pollutants.

The Environmental Mercury Component

One of the consequences of increasing pressure, starting in 1975-76, was increased blood mercury testing by Health and Welfare Canada and tightening of informal fish and marine mammal consumption guidelines in remote northern communities with no obvious mercury pollution. No new scientific information had become available between 1971 and 1976 to suggest a health problem due to mercury in these remote northern settlements, and as has been seen there was considerable information to the contrary, yet the focus of government and media concern suddenly turned to these communities.

In terms of reducing blood mercury levels, Health and Welfare policies may be said to have been effective. Once the Inuit and Indians stop eating fish and marine mammals, their blood mercury, in the space of several months, goes down. No evidence, however, indicates that the reduction of blood mercury levels has resulted in an improvement of health conditions for those people. On the other hand, there is good evidence that native peoples go back to eating the fish and marine mammals after a year or so following a mercury scare. This has happened on two occasions, once following the 1970 scare and again following the 1976-77 scare in parts of the North. The reason for this is economic. Bush food is free for hunters and fishermen, while store-bought food, especially in remote northern regions, is prohibitively expensive. There is increasing concern among some officials and scientists that the nutritional and cultural cost of not eating bush food may outweigh the presumed benefits of reducing blood mercury levels.[30]

Government policy is intended to minimize disruption to the native economy, but in practice such policy does not work as originally intended. A good illustration of the situation at the community level comes from a case study of Wemindji (pop. 600), a Cree community on the James Bay coast.[31] Blood mercury levels, individually reported by Health and Welfare Canada, showed that there had been seven people at 50 ppb or more, the maximum being 87 ppb. Interviews indicated that all of those people were middle-aged or older, and had eaten fish from inland lakes. The only common predatory fish in the area, with levels known to be around 1 ppm, was pike. On the coast all fish tested had been under 0.2 ppm. The people had been shown a film on Minamata and had been supplied with a news clipping from a southern paper singling out Wemindji as a mercury-risk area. The item had been taken out of context from a Health and Welfare Canada press release and there had been no attempt to put the issue in perspective, to point out, for example, that mercury levels at Wemindji in fact had been below those in most other James Bay communities and bore no resemblance whatever to the mercury levels in Minamata victims. The excitement and concern in the community were such that all fishing activity had ceased; there was a rush on store food, mainly "junk" food. Ironically, the people were spending money on canned tuna at the local store with mercury levels probably approaching 0.5 ppm while refraining from catching the fish at their doorstep with levels below 0.2 ppm. Clearly, if there was indeed a mercury problem at Wemindji, the solution was to reduce the intake of the major source of mercury, pike, and not to discourage all fishing activity. This approach became the gist of the subsequent guidelines on consumption of fish published by the Grand Council of the Crees of Quebec.[32]

Conclusions

The industrial pollution component of the mercury problem in Canada may be said to have been under control since about 1975. There are areas, such as Grassy Narrows-White Dog in northern Ontario, where solutions to the tragic situation may never be found, and there are still major sources of pollution, such as the burning of fossil fuels, which will prove to be extremely difficult to control. But in the context of natural sources of mercury some man-made sources may not be very large. Emissions of 27 tons of mercury from coal and oil combustion in Canada in 1970 may be compared to the yearly discharge of 16.7 tons from one river in Alaska in a mercury-rich geological region.[33]

The information covered in this essay leads to a conclusion that the mercury problem in the late 1970's in Canada is no longer mainly a pollution problem but an environmental mercury problem. The people primarily affected are northern natives of many remote communities whose social, cultural, economic, and nutritional well-being are being further eroded as a result of the elimination of some native food sources from their subsistence economy. This is happening inadvertently through government policy and regulations established in the absence of any reasonable evidence that these peoples' health is endangered by the mercury they ingest from their local food sources.[34]

The environmental mercury component of the problem is more difficult to regulate than the pollution component because of many uncertainties; some may be solved in the coming years but others probably will remain resistant to technical solutions. In this regard, the mercury problem has parallels: "For example, although $2 billion and 30 years have been spent studying the biological effects of ionizing radiation, acceptable exposure levels are still debated."[35] Similarly, with respect to mercury, establishing a uniform set of acceptable levels either in food or in human blood will prove very difficult because there probably is no "threshold level" as such. The regulatory process is therefore forced into making difficult choices: if the response is uniform but arbitrary across the nation, it will not be taking into account the unique situation in each area; if it is tailored to local needs, then it risks the criticism of using double standards.

One major reason for the mercury problem (or non-problem) in many northern native communities in areas of no obvious pollution is that, spurred by public pressure, southern standards of blood mercury levels have been applied to these communities. As Dr. O. Schaefer puts it, "first of all we have to inform them [northern natives] of the exact findings and facts relating to their specific situation and not use translations and deductions derived from quite different sources and profoundly different situations."[36] Dr. Schaefer further notes the need to distinguish pollution from the natural background levels of a substance, in this case mercury:

> We must be overcautious and must tend to err on the safe side whenever concerned with a new element or factor affecting our food or environment. We must on the other hand be extremely conservative and reluctant to upset long existing balances and adjustments if encountering factors and elements long established and not recently introduced by modern man.[37]

Similar views have been expressed by others as well. Comar, for instance, maintains that two kinds of efforts are required as a basis for decision-making: one is the estimation of the actual risks; the other involves a value judgement, namely, the judgement of the acceptable level of risk.

This leads to a risk/benefit approach. The *benefit* from the local food sources for northern native peoples may be partially quantified by calculating the replacement value of the food and employment benefits from guiding and commercial fishing. While the cultural and psychological values of fishing may not be readily calculated in monetary terms, the total benefit of fishing perhaps may be indirectly approached by considering how much more public funds might have to be diverted to support native communities which are closer to being totally dependent on government assistance for food and which have fewer employment opportunities and greater social problems than they now have.

The *risk* of exposure to low-dose chronic methylmercury in the local food sources may be more difficult to calculate. Mercury may be producing harmful effects not detectable epidemiologically. Symptoms may be attributable to other dietary factors; there may be factors in the diet, such as selenium, which counteract possible harmful effects of mercury; and there may be mercury tolerance among some native peoples. All of these are possibilities the acceptance or rejection of which may take a long time.

NOTES

1. Analysis of the actors in the mercury problem and the jurisdictions involved has already been done by others; therefore no extensive review is attempted here. Two federal departments have been involved: Health and Welfare Canada (concerned mainly with the human health aspects of the problem) and Environment and Fisheries Canada (concerned with analyzing mercury levels in the environment and with issuing regulations to reduce air and water pollution). The Department of Indian Affairs and Northern Development was criticized for inactivity by such observers as Charlebois. At the provincial level, the Ontario Ministry of the Environment was active in analyzing mercury in the environment and in issuing fish consumption guidelines. In Quebec, the equivalent ministry was inactive while Ministère des Affaires Sociales was active in the area of health. For further elaboration, see C. T. Charlebois, "An Overview of the Canadian Mercury Problem," *Science Forum*, 59 (1977), 17-36; and G. B. Doern, *Regulatory Processes and Jurisdictional Issues in the Regulation of Hazardous Products in Canada* (Ottawa: Science Council of Canada, Background Study No. 41, 1977).

2. For further information, see Charlebois, "Canadian Mercury Problem"; and *Policies and Poisons* (Ottawa: Science Council of Canada, October, 1977).

3. For details, see, for example, *Health Implications of Contaminants in Fish* (Toronto: Ontario Ministry of the Environment, 1978).

4. The analysis of these data had not been completed when this paper was written (Dr. B. Wheatley, Health and Welfare Canada, Ottawa, personal communication, October 3, 1978). Much of the existing data on mercury in Canada can be found in I. G. Sherbin, *Mercury in the Canadian Environment* (Ottawa, Environmental Protection Service, Fisheries and Environment Canada, 1979).

5. A film showing victims of mercury poisoning in Japan had been made available to the various native organizations, including the Grand Council of the Crees of Quebec and Treaty Three in Ontario. For the Ontario case, see I. E. La Rusic, "A Report on Mercury in the Environment in the Communities of White Dog and Grassy Narrows: The Dietary Aspects and Problems of Communicating with the Local Populations," prepared for the Medical Services Branch, Health and Welfare Canada (Ottawa, 1973).

6. A. Barbeau, A. Nantel et F. Dorlot, *Étude sur les effets médicaux et toxicologiques du mercure organique dans le nordouest Québécois* (Quebec: Ministère des Affaires Sociales, 1976); M. Harada, "Epidemiological and Clinical Study of Mercury Pollution on Indian Reservations in Northwestern Ontario, Canada," in *Science for a Better Environment*, Proceedings of the International Congress on the Human Environment, Kyoto (Oxford, 1977), 867-75; D. A. E. Shephard, "Methylmercury Poisoning in Canada," *Canadian Medical Association Journal*, 114 (1976), 463-72.

7. Dr. B. Wheatley, Health and Welfare Canada, Ottawa, personal communication, October 18, 1978.

8. Results of mercury tests are reported back to individuals by letter. The policy is also that the letter should be delivered, by hand, by an individual able to advise the person receiving the result on its significance and any action which needs to be taken (Dr. B. Wheatley, January 3, 1979). In the author's own

experience in northern Quebec, the advice often received is that the people should avoid eating fish. Even for those in the 0-19 ppb range, the reporting of results often causes much confusion and anguish.

9. F. Bakir et al., "Methylmercury poisoning in Iraq," Science, 181 (1973), 230-40.

10. The excerpt is taken from a Health and Welfare Canada press release, February 27, 1978. The study in question was undertaken jointly by Health and Welfare Canada, Québec Ministère des Affaires Sociales, and The Donner Canadian Foundation, in co-operation with the Cree regional and local governments in northern Quebec.

11. An Assessment of Mercury in the Environment (Washington, D.C.: National Academy of Sciences, 1977), 83.

12. Ibid., 44.

13. Possibility of high geological background levels of mercury may not be a problem unique to Canada. According to Prof. P. Nuorteva (Dept. of Environmental Conservation, University of Helsinki, personal communication, October 20, 1978), Finns have "recently observed the same situation in large areas in the eastern part of [their] country." The origin of these high levels is still a mystery, and the mercury content of snow and rain is being monitored to determine if the levels are due to atmospheric transport.

14. T. M. Kelly, J. D. Jones, and R. G. Smith, "Historical Changes in Mercury Contamination in Michigan Walleyes (Stizostedion vitreum vitreum)," Journal of the Fisheries Research Board of Canada, 32 (1975), 1945-54.

15. Assessment of Mercury in Environment, 28.

16. Lake trout in the Great Whale River area, northern Quebec, some 700 km from the nearest industrial source, contain about 1 ppm. Interviews with a Cree fisherman from Great Whale, a man who had the highest recorded value at the time, revealed that his blood level of 242 ppb was fully explainable on the basis of his normal bush diet, which included the equivalent of a medium to large lake trout every three days. See F. Berkes and C. S. Farkas, "Eastern James Bay Cree Indians: Changing Patterns of Wild Food Use and Nutrition," Ecology of Food and Nutrition, 7 (1978), 155-72.

17. Dr. B. Wheatley, Health and Welfare Canada, Ottawa, personal communication, October 3, 1978.

18. Dr. R. D. P. Eaton, Health and Welfare Canada, Northern Medical Research Unit, Edmonton, personal communication, November 10, 1978.

19. Ibid. Italics mine.

20. A Health and Welfare Canada press release dated August 22, 1978, implicated marine mammals for high blood levels in Sugluk, northern Quebec, and the Inuit were instructed by the local nurse to reduce intake or stop eating these animals. The official letter had advised pregnant women to avoid seal liver altogether, but had not restricted seal meat.

21. Dr. O. Schaefer, Health and Welfare Canada, Northern Medical Research Unit, Edmonton, personal communication, September 23, 1977.

22. Ibid.

23. Dr. O. Schaefer, personal communication, October 10, 1976.

24. Charlebois, "Canadian Mercury Problem," 31.

25. "Missing Mercury Mystifies Government," Ottawa Citizen, October 16, 1975.

26. Status Report on Compliance with the Chloralkali Mercury Regulations—1975 (Ottawa: Environmental Protection Service, Fisheries and Environment Canada).

27. *National Inventory of Sources and Emissions of Asbestos, Beryllium, Lead and Mercury. Summary of Emissions for 1970.* EPS 3-AP-74-1 (Ottawa: Air Pollution Control Directorate, Environment Canada, 1974).

28. *Policies and Poisons,* 19.

29. *The Decline in Mercury Concentration in Fish from Lake St. Clair, 1970-1976.* Report No. AQ573-3 (Rexdale: Ontario Ministry of the Environment, 1977).

30. C. S. Farkas, University of Waterloo, writes: "Central to the effect that mercury contamination has had on the health of the native populations in these areas is whether it is possible to isolate the health effects of mercury toxicity from the coexisting complex problems present in these northern communities." Personal communication, November 14, 1978.

31. F. Berkes, unpublished field notes from Wemindji, northern Quebec, February, 1977.

32. *Current Information on Mercury in Fish in the James Bay Territory; Recommendations on Eating Fish, Using the Results of Mercury Tests on Fish Collected in the Summer of 1976* (Montreal: Grand Council of the Crees of Quebec, 1977).

33. H. Nelson, B. R. Larsen, E. A. Jenne, and D. H. Sorg, "Mercury Dispersal from Lode Sources in the Kuskokwim River Drainage, Alaska," *Science,* 198 (1977), 820-4.

34. A parallel case might be cited with respect to the Atlantic coast swordfish industry. Following the effective termination of the Canadian fishery in 1971 because most swordfish exceeded 0.5 ppm, the U.S. fishery rapidly expanded to take advantage of the reduced fishing effort and the high market demand. In the absence of any reasonable evidence that swordfish is a health hazard, the federal Minister of Fisheries finally lifted the ban on swordfish on June 24, 1979. The Canadian fishery has started up again, but the competitive position of the Canadian industry has perhaps been permanently lost. See J. F. Caddy, "A Review of Some Factors Relevant to the Management of Swordfish Fisheries in the Northwest Atlantic," Environment Canada, Fisheries and Marine Service, Technical Report No. 633, 1976.

35. C. Comar, "Environmental Assessment: A Pragmatic View," *Science,* 198 (1977), 567.

36. Dr. O. Schaefer, Health and Welfare Canada, Northern Medical Research Unit, Edmonton, personal communication, September 23, 1977.

37. *Ibid.*

CHAPTER TWELVE

Canada's Nuclear Commitment: A Challenge in Technology Assessment

by Ted Schrecker

In the Canadian context, the commitment to nuclear energy raises a broad range of questions related to reactor safety, public health, economics, and environmental impact. Despite a number of public inquiries, many of these remain unanswered. There is a risk that technical disputes, vitally important though they are, may obscure social and political questions which are at least as relevant to the nuclear debate. On what basis ought we, as a society, to decide that we need nuclear electricity? What institutions do we have, if any, that are adequate for the kind of risk/benefit balancing involved in such a decision? What possible effects on social structure will accompany a large-scale nuclear commitment? And what are the economics of nuclear electricity, and indeed of continued high primary energy growth in general? Are there real alternatives to the nuclear commitment?

Policy decisions about nuclear power and about energy policy, like most public policy choices of any significance, are not value-free. In the nuclear debate one must maintain a healthy skepticism about "expertise." In particular, one must not allow fundamental normative decisions about the future directions of our society to be camouflaged as, or reduced to, technical decisions. Proponents of nuclear power, in particular, have largely failed to observe this caution.[1]

The combination of extreme technological complexity and major policy choices makes the nuclear commitment the greatest challenge in technology assessment we will face in the near future.

The rubric of technology assessment is a useful one; if interpreted broadly enough it encompasses consideration not only of the impacts (physical, social, economic) of a technology, but those of alternatives to the technology. Reflection on the desirability of certain effects can then feed back into policy choices. For instance, new conclusions about the biological effects of low-level radiation, coupled with the position that there are alternatives to the nuclear option, could lead to the reconsideration of policies that entail further development of nuclear energy.

Acknowledging the need to develop technology assessment implies the realization that technologies and their diffusion have not been assessed in an equitable or even systematic way. Technological decisions since the Industrial Revolution have been largely economic ones as well, and the pattern of technological development has followed priorities congenial to the interests of the most powerful sectors of society. This is true both of the broad directions of technological change (e.g., expenditures on new and esoteric military technologies; the rise of "product development" in the consumer goods industries) and of specific design and application decisions.[2] The scale of new technologies and their effects has begun to introduce a new dimension to the problem. When possible disasters affect entire ecosystems (e.g., an oil well blowout in the Canadian Arctic) or much of the globe's population (e.g., through nuclear holocaust or the depletion of the ozone layer) policy questions related to assessing the impacts of technology assume a new urgency.[3]

A study of the Canadian nuclear commitment must take into account a number of striking features. A very limited group of actors and factors has been involved in assessing this multi-billion-dollar commitment. Developing sound technology assessment is extremely difficult in situations, such as the nuclear debate, where proponents command resources vastly superior to those of opponents or skeptics. (The nuclear question is not, of course, a unique example of such a situation, or even a particularly extreme one.) The possible consequences of a large-scale nuclear commitment provide cogent reasons for developing far more sophisticated techniques and institutions for technology assessment. Such developments are essential, too, if decisions about technologies for the future are to be made in a way which gives the diffuse goal of government by the people any meaningful content.

Nuclear generation of electricity is very much a part of our present energy supply. Canada has about 15,000 megawatts (MW) of nuclear generating capacity operating, committed, or under construction, all but about 1,800 MW in Ontario. Ontario's nuclear stations supply more than 30 per cent of the province's electricity. (As recently as 1960, hydroelectric generation supplied 99 per cent of the province's needs.) Quebec and New Brunswick utilities also have made a commitment to nuclear plants, and exports of CANDU reactors are being aggressively promoted.

Official sources project a rapid increase in the importance of nuclear energy in Canada. Atomic Energy of Canada Ltd. (AECL) foresaw, in 1978, that between 60,000 and 100,000 MW of nuclear capacity would be installed in Canada by the year 2000.[4] This is equivalent to thirty to fifty stations the size of Ontario Hydro's Pickering A plant (2,000 MW). The most recent projection from the Department of Energy, Mines and Resources states that 70,000 MW of nuclear capacity could be installed by the year 2000, and sees nuclear energy accounting for 15 per cent of Canada's primary energy supply in 2000, as against 1.75 per cent in 1976.[5] In Ontario, Hydro's expansion plans are based on a mix of two-thirds nuclear and one-third fossil-fuelled new generating capacity, and the provincial government is actively defending Hydro's long-term commitment to nuclear construction.

Many factors contribute to the attractiveness of nuclear power for policy-makers. Nuclear electricity (produced from uranium, a fuel indigenous to Canada) looks better and better, for reasons related to security of supply and balance of payments, as Canadian conventional oil reserves dwindle and imported supply becomes increasingly uncertain and expensive. Electricity, it is argued, can be substituted for many uses of oil, allowing oil to be reserved for those applications where it is hardest to replace (vehicle fuels, petrochemical feedstocks). CANDU reactor technology represents one of Canada's few successful attempts to develop high technology for both domestic use and export. Much of the Canadian hinterland remains dependent on resource extraction; the expansion of uranium mining (in Ontario for Ontario Hydro's use, in Saskatchewan for consumption outside the province) is an attractive prospect for regional economies in the north of those provinces. Corporate interests in the nuclear industry are an important, though seldom considered, factor: there is no "anti-nuclear industry."

Safety, Health, and Environmental Issues

Some of the most intractable problems occur at the so-called front end of the nuclear fuel cycle: the mining, milling, and refining of uranium itself.[6] Storage and disposal of tailings from uranium mines, and from the refining process, must prevent hazards to the public arising from the leaching of radium out of tailing piles into ground water or watercourses, and from radon gas emissions from the tailings. The problem of tailings disposal will likely prove a difficult and expensive one, simply because of the huge volume of material that has to be contained. These hazards, unlike those of reactor accidents or reactor waste disposal, are already part of our Canadian experience. Radioactive contamination of watercourses in the Elliot Lake area, including the Serpent River, is a legacy of uranium mining and milling in the 1950's and 1960's. Wastes from the Eldorado Nuclear refinery in Port Hope, Ontario, were used as landfill, resulting in unsafe radon gas accumulations in many houses and other buildings in the area.[7]

A related concern is the health of uranium miners. A 1976 Ontario Royal Commission report[8] pointed up a long history of regulatory confusion in this area, and the lowering of allowable radiation exposures was implemented only after increases in lung cancer incidence had been conclusively demonstrated. There is growing concern that the "linear hypothesis," which assumes that the relationship between dose levels and the number of radiation-induced cancers is more or less direct, may not provide the margin of safety once assumed – that is, that the risk of cancer may be proportionately *greater* from low-level radiation than from higher exposures.[9] A further lowering of allowable occupational radiation exposures could have serious consequences for an expanded nuclear program, especially as regards uranium mining and reactor maintenance.

Every thermal generating plant generates approximately two units of waste heat for each unit of electrical energy. This waste heat has to be removed somehow; all of Ontario Hydro's current and committed multi-unit stations use the waters of the Great Lakes for this purpose. Ontario Ministry of Natural Resources officials have argued that the Great Lakes are already very fragile, and that the subtle ecological effects of changes in the Lakes' temperature may be undetectable for many years, until the accumulated damage is irreversible.[10]

The highest-profile area of public concern has been the possibility of radioactive releases from nuclear reactors, either in normal operations or as the result of an accident. The performance record of CANDU reactors seems to have been laudable, both with respect to accidents and routine emissions. Yet a number of unsettling problems have arisen. It was revealed in 1978, for instance, that the Emergency Core Cooling System (ECCS) in Ontario's nuclear plants, necessary to prevent overheating in case of loss of normal reactor cooling, could not live up to its original design performance targets. Ontario's Royal Commission on Electric Power Planning noted in its interim report that a breach of containment (containment systems being the "last defence" against radioactive release in case of a major mishap) had gone undetected for eighteen months at the Pickering A generating station. Ontario Hydro technical reports, made public for the first time during hearings of the Ontario legislature's Select Committee on Hydro Affairs in the summer of 1979, show frequent minor mechanical breakdowns, breaches of containment, and procedural oversights. And there is always the spectre of operator error: that, despite intensive training, an operator will do the wrong thing, or simply will have to respond to a situation that the designers of the equipment or of his training program had not anticipated.

Nuclear proponents tend to regard the fact that such problems have not resulted in dangerous accidents as proof of the basic safety of the system – a conclusion perhaps premature, given the relatively few years of reactor operating experience in Canada. However one regards those problems, they do point up the importance of how the likelihood and consequences of a nuclear accident are estimated, and of what level of risk is considered acceptable. Many recent arguments for the safety of nuclear energy have been based on a document known as WASH-1400, or the Rasmussen Report. Commissioned by the U.S. Nuclear Regulatory Commission (NRC), the study used a technique known as event-tree analysis to calculate the probability of serious reactor accidents. Based on its estimate of the consequences of a major nuclear accident, it compared the risks with a number of more commonplace accident situations – car accidents, aviation crashes, and the like. Its conclusion was that nuclear generating stations impose a probability of accidental death on the public far lower than risks we routinely accept.

Nuclear critics have raised a host of objections to the Rasmussen study, ranging from accusations of simple arithmetical error to the impossibility of identifying all relevant accident sequences.[11] An NRC review group has now supported many of the critics' reservations, accepting the basic methodology as sound but harshly criticizing the report's statistical procedures. The review group noted: "We are unable to determine whether the absolute probabilities of accident sequences in WASH-1400 are high or low, but we believe that the error bounds on those estimates are, in general, greatly understated."[12]

Although Rasmussen's results have been cited by both AECL and Dr. Rasmussen himself as being broadly applicable to Canadian as well as American reactors, they are not used in reactor licensing. The approach to licensing in Canada involves separation of reactor systems into process, safety, and containment systems. Allowable frequencies for failures involving one and two kinds of systems (single-mode and dual-mode failures) are set by the Atomic Energy Control Board (AECB), along with maximum allowable radiation releases in the event of such accidents. The licence applicant must demonstrate to the satisfaction of AECB that the design will meet these requirements. Since the process, safety, and containment systems are designed (at least in principle) to be totally independent, estimates of accident frequency are arrived at simply by multiplying the failure probabilities of systems or independent sub-systems.

This procedure for demonstrating compliance with AECB criteria is tremendously complex; AECL has noted that, since the approach is based on "guidelines," a considerable exercise of judgement by AECB is called for.[13] And critics have cited a number of shortcomings in the Canadian safety approach. For one thing, technical assumptions made by proponents are not subjected to independent or adversary scrutiny at public hearings. The outcome of accident frequency calculations can be dramatically changed by minor changes in a number of different assumptions. (This is a feature common to most multi-step arithmetical calculations.) The assumption that systems are independent means that multi-mode failures – involving the simultaneous or successive failure of a number of systems, either at random or as a result of some particular event, are inadequately considered. According to AECL:

Sequences which cannot be quantified a priori – for example, common mode failures – inherently occur very rarely. In Canada, it has long been believed that such events make a relatively small contribution to public risk when care is taken in the design and operation of the plant. Separation of control and safety systems from each other, both logically and physically, helps a lot. So does separation of the safety systems, one from another.[14]

The history of nuclear accidents, however (apparently including Three Mile Island), involves enough highly improbable accidents[15] to cast some doubt on the assumption that "sequences which cannot be quantified" need receive relatively little attention.

"In nuclear safety, risk is defined as the probability or frequency of an event times its consequences."[16] This is *one* definition; although implicit or explicit in almost all regulatory discussion of nuclear risk, it may not accurately reflect how people subject to that risk define the concept.[17] The consequences of major releases of radioactivity may be considered so objectionable that *no* frequency is acceptable. This definition of risk represents an example of the extension of "expertise" to camouflage value choices. It also has serious consequences for the licensing process. When accidents below a certain level of calculated probability need not be designed against (a decision in which this idea of risk is at least implicit), consideration of most common-mode failures is ruled out, despite potentially disastrous consequences.[18] A study of the possible consequences of a catastrophic (though very low-probability) accident at a major Canadian nuclear generating plant has never been undertaken.

The wastes from CANDU reactors remain extremely radioactive for a few hundred years, during which they decay fairly rapidly; slower decay occurs for a period of some hundred thousand years. At present, spent fuel from reactors is stored on site, a method which can be used for many years by building additional storage bays. The currently favoured technology for ultimate disposal of reactor wastes, either before or after reprocessing (see below), involves burial deep within the rock of the Canadian Shield.

The issue of waste disposal has been subjected to at least two separate evaluations in Canada,[19] in addition to AECL's ongoing research program. The lack of a demonstrated workable solution to the problem has prompted the comment that continued commitment to nuclear power represents a "leap of faith,"[20] a leap many argue is justified in light of the past history of technological progress. Ontario's Royal Commission on Electric Power Planning nevertheless recommended in its interim report that a moratorium on new nuclear construction be considered if progress is not made toward solving the waste disposal problem by 1985, a recommendation that at least partly begs the question, since the problem of spent fuel disposal is already very much with us, and will be a much larger problem by 1985.

The question of the contribution of the spread of nuclear technology to weapons proliferation has arisen not only with respect to CANDU reactor exports, but with respect to the export of uranium. This issue was brought forcefully to public attention in 1974, when India exploded a bomb using materials from a Canadian-built research reactor. Arguments by nuclear proponents have focused on Canada's safeguards provisions in contracts for reactor sales, and on the fact that CANDU reactors are uneconomic and inefficient means of producing weapons-quality materials. Counter-arguments are that the reliability of any contractual safeguard is dubious, and that military programs are not bound by the same economics as are civilian power programs. There no longer seems any reasonable doubt that "peaceful uses" increase somewhat the risk of nuclear weapons proliferation. The real question is how much increased risk (if any) is ethically justifiable, what the corresponding benefits are (jobs for Canadian workers; development of Canadian industrial competence), and whether the decision of one country will have significant impact in a world where, to use Lovins' metaphor, the nuclear genie is already very much out of the bottle.

The current CANDU fuel cycle is a so-called once-through fuel cycle. But reprocessing spent fuel for further use in advanced fuel cycles can significantly extend the life of uranium supplies. Disadvantages of reprocessing include high costs and the dangers associated with handling large additional volumes of very highly radioactive wastes. AECL is committed to a major research and development initiative on fuel reprocessing, but there has been little or no public discussion in Canada of the long-term implications of a commitment to reprocessing on a commercial scale.

A number of nuclear critics have noted that nuclear power, especially if reprocessing is involved, will either be conducive to or will actually require a long-term centralization of political power. The ability to mobilize vast sums of capital, to limit certain forms of political activity, and to restrict access to information *may* be essential to maintaining safety and security in a nuclear future.[21] The concern, however well-founded, illustrates the need in assessing technologies like nuclear energy to include consideration of the effects on social structure and on the changing distribution of power that will be involved.

A number of studies have attempted to compare the risks of nuclear power (including mining, refining, etc.) with the risks attendant on coal- or oil-fired electric generation,[22] and at least one study (AECB's *Risk of Energy Production*) has attempted comparison of nuclear risks with those of other, non-electric energy sources.[23] At least three factors limit the usefulness of such comparisons drastically. First, premises about the effects of radiation and the likelihood and effects of specific nuclear accidents must be valid; as we have seen, precision in these areas is hard to attain. Second, such comparisons assume the "risk equals probability times consequences" definition. Third, the coal-versus-nuclear comparison assumes that these are the only relevant alternatives for supplying required end-use energy. This is not necessarily the case. *Risk of Energy Production* (or the "Inhaber report," after its author) raises as well the issue of whether it is reasonable to compare the risks of technologies at various stages of development, some of which (e.g., nuclear) pose the possibility of consequences on a massive scale, while others (e.g., solar heating) pose more diverse and smaller-scale risks. Inhaber has also been charged with numerous arithmetical errors by at least one critic;[24] the charges have not at this writing been rebutted.

The Politics of the Nuclear Debate

Even during the Second World War, when the principal objective of the nuclear research in which Canada was involved was military, many of the key figures in the program saw nuclear technology as a key to Canada's post-war development.[25] Many of the industrial assets acquired or built up by government during the war were sold off, but a high level of public sector involvement continues to characterize the nuclear program. Only uranium mining, fuel fabrication, and the manufacture of components for generating stations lie within the private sector. This is in contrast to other jurisdictions, like the United States, where not only station design but many of the utilities operating nuclear plants are within the private sector. And it may well be that public ownership of much of Canada's nuclear establishment has served to blunt criticisms of its decision-making power.

A number of key institutional actors can be identified among those involved in Canada's nuclear politics.[26] The Atomic Energy Control Board was established in 1946 with a broad mandate, including the promotion of nuclear research in Canada as well as the licensing and regulation of nuclear facilities. Atomic Energy of Canada was established as a Crown corporation in 1952 for the active development and promotion of CANDU technology for commercial purposes. AECL designs and promotes nuclear power reactors, but does not build or operate them. The latter is the domain of provincial utilities; to date, Ontario Hydro has been by far the most active utility in the nuclear field. Ranked on the basis of assets, Ontario Hydro is the country's largest corporation. Also in the public sector, Eldorado Nuclear is involved in uranium refining for fuel fabrication. (Eldorado was taken over by the federal government during the war, to ensure secure supplies of refined uranium.)

A number of private corporations, of course, are actively involved in the nuclear program. The Canadian Nuclear Association (CNA), a trade association with both corporate and government members, is in practice the voice of Canadian nuclear manufacturers, and, of course, an active supporter of further nuclear development. CNA members' nuclear-related sales totalled more than $600 million in 1976.[27] As noted earlier, uranium mining corporations (Rio Algom and Denison Mines in Ontario; Amok Ltée., a consortium of French-based companies, in Saskatchewan) are major beneficiaries of the nuclear commitment, though it is hard to estimate their degree of direct influence on the debate.

Another layer has been added with the creation of federal and provincial ministries responsible for energy, with these departments presumably being responsible for developing overall energy policies of which the nuclear program is only one component. And public unease about nuclear energy has led to a number of government inquiries, all of them in an advisory role: the Cluff Lake Board of Inquiry in Saskatchewan; the Royal Commission on Electric Power Planning and lengthy hearings of the Legislative Select Committee on Hydro Affairs in Ontario. Plans for a federal parliamentary inquiry are in limbo following the defeat of the Conservative government, and plans for a commission of inquiry in British Columbia are similarly uncertain after the provincial government's decision to declare a seven-year moratorium on uranium exploration and development in February, 1980. Such public hearings have provided the principal forum for the public articulation of arguments against a major Canadian nuclear commitment.

The terms of the nuclear debate in Canada have very largely been determined by the proponents of the technology. The nuclear establishment developed in an atmosphere of wartime secrecy: "25 years ago, nuclear energy was still an esoteric, rather secret business and decisions were reached largely on the basis of discussions between Dr. C. J. Mackenzie, President of the National Research Council, and C. D. Howe, Minister of Trade and Commerce and Dr. Mackenzie's friend and former professor."[28] The tendency is reinforced by the fact that AECB is essentially a regulatory agency rather than a body charged with assessing the overall impacts of nuclear technology.

G. Bruce Doern has characterized AECB as conforming to a model he terms "professionally open" ("characterized by minimal reporting requirements and few public hearings") rather than "democratically open."[29] AECB is not required to hold public hearings, does not do so, and has told citizens' groups that its mandate does not allow it to do so. The response of AECB to the "democratically open" model is best illustrated by this excerpt from a letter to a citizens' group in 1977 from J. H. Jennekens, then Director of Licensing for AECB:

> Involvement of the public in detailed licensing and safety questions has the potential of being counter-productive to the interests of safety. The public perception of the importance of safety-related issues could be quite different from that of the industry, AECL in this case, and the regulatory authority, the AECB in this case. Industry already expends considerable effort and resources in justifying to AECB the design, construction and operation of nuclear power plants. If the public were to become involved in what would be a three-way discussion, the available resources of industry and probably the AECB could become concentrated on a few specific issues which are believed to be important to the public or to certain groups of the public. Such a development, cases of which we have observed in other countries, could reduce the available effort on other safety-related matters of equal or greater importance, individually or collectively, and overall could result in a lower achievement of safety than would otherwise be the case.[30]

Jennekens is now head of AECB. Legislation that would have "opened up" the functioning of AECB was introduced by the Liberal government in 1978, but was allowed to die on the order paper and has not been reintroduced.

Doern, in documenting the "historic coziness" of the AECB-AECL relationship, has noted that A. T. Prince, appointed in 1975, was the first head of AECB without direct links to AECL; until 1974, the presidents of AECL and Eldorado Nuclear (principal AECB licensees) were automatically members of AECB. Again, the nuclear industry serves as a major source of personnel and technical advice to AECB, and until 1975 the Board was also the major source of funding for nuclear research in Canada.[31] (In 1975 this function was transferred to the National Research Council.) Doern's work shows that the nuclear establishment in Canada has demonstrated a very high degree of cohesion. And the scarcity of neutral, or at least unattached, technical expertise is a real block to the development of competent criticism of Canada's nuclear community.

The limited size of AECB's staff leads it to rely on advisory groups which–like AECB–do not meet in public and whose independence is at least sometimes open to question. Of the eight members of the Board's Inter-Organizational Working Group, set up to review reactor safety standards, five represented AECB licensees. And the one meeting of the Board's Reactor Safety Advisory Committee for Ontario whose minutes have become public[32] was attended by eleven representatives from Ontario Hydro and eighteen from AECL – not necessarily an indication of bias, but a demonstration of the closed nature of the regulatory process.

Ontario's Environmental Assessment Act provides the potential for a much more open assessment of nuclear technology. Guidelines under the act, passed in 1975, require that assessments of projects include examination of the need for the project and alternatives to the project as well as of environmental impacts. The act is unfortunately weakened by ministerial discretion clauses, which were used to exempt the Darlington nuclear generating station (now in its early construction stages) from the act in 1977. And Ontario Hydro has indicated that it will seek amendments to the act to eliminate the need to demonstrate need for the project and alternatives to it, arguing that the assessment of a specific project should not overlap with overall policy decisions made at the ministerial level.[33]

Access to information is another illustration of the closed nature of nuclear regulation. Until summer, 1979, when the Ontario legislature's Select Committee on Hydro Affairs demanded that literally tons of technical documentation be made available to the public, almost all of the first-hand information available in Canada on the actual performance of CANDU reactors came from documents "leaked" from within AECB or AECL. The information problem takes another, more basic form: the financial and institutional resources of nuclear proponents allow the production of vast amounts of technical, "objective" material on energy policy and nuclear power. In the absence of a countervailing viewpoint argued with comparable resources, a view of the issues that is highly selective (though not deliberately misleading) becomes accepted as neutral, or at least as "expert." It is interesting to conjecture about the degree to which this monopoly on information directly and indirectly influences policy-makers in their conceptualization of the issues in the nuclear debate. Particularly in the Canadian context where, as Hooker and van Hulst have argued, publicly-owned corporations behave like private corporations in other jurisdictions because of an analogous perception of their function,[34] it is worth acknowledging that "it seems unfair to criticize citizen intervenors, for example, for not representing a 'real public interest' without recognizing explicitly that the utilities and vendors [of nuclear equipment] do not represent that interest either."[35]

In the public-hearing process, the disparity of resources comes into sharp focus. A number of inquiries have established a significant and useful precedent by providing funding for citizen interventions. But the $300,000 or so the Royal Commission on Electric Power Planning spent on intervenor funding during its hearings must be compared with the more than $1 million a year Ontario Hydro (just one of several pro-nuclear intervenors) is reckoned to have spent on the hearings by observers of the commission. Too often, *no* intervenor funding is provided for public hearings in Canada, a fact which drastically limits the usefulness of attempts to develop technology assessment of worthwhile quality.

The Need for Nuclear Electricity

A few days after the Three Mile Island accident, an editorial in the Toronto *Globe and Mail* noted: "If we are to preserve our standard of living, which is based in every aspect on heavy use of energy, we need nuclear power."[36] Similarly, *Energy Futures for Canadians*, the most recent general statement of federal energy policy, argues that doubling Canada's primary energy use between 1975 and 2000 will be necessary to maintain our economic well-being:

> The rates of growth . . . are the lowest which, by this assessment, are consistent with satisfactory economic performance, from now to the year 2000, and from 2000 to 2025. 'Satisfactory' economic performance in this context means that work is available for those who want it; annual productivity increases are not lower than two per cent, and the level of real income and its distribution generally contribute to social harmony and personal well being. 'Satisfactory economic performance' contrasts with the situation of the past 2 or 3 years when the lower growth in energy consumption in Canada and abroad can be associated, in large part, with failure to achieve 'satisfactory' economic performance.[37]

A number of dubious assumptions are evident here, including the identification of GNP as a reliable measure of well-being and the substitution of continued GNP growth for addressing the problem of distribution of national wealth (and of the social costs of producing it). The most immediately relevant error, shared by most arguments for high energy growth, involves the coupling of GNP and primary energy growth: the assumption that only minor changes are possible in the ratio of GNP per unit of energy. There is mounting evidence that this relationship is by no means as immutable as the advocates of high energy growth would have us believe – an argument buttressed by comparisons of the energy consumption of countries with comparable GNP per capita, which show wide variations in energy use per unit of output.[38]

The coupling of energy and GNP stems in part from an incomplete understanding of the difference between primary energy (energy at source), secondary energy (energy as delivered at the end-use point, minus losses in refining, transmission, and generation), and the energy actually *needed* for the task at hand – for instance, the energy used for space heating minus losses due to inadequate insulation, etc. It is largely immaterial, from a physical point of view, whether we satisfy the demand for increasing amounts of end-use energy by expanding primary supply, leaving the efficiency of energy use unchanged, or whether we modify our end uses to get more energy "use value" out of each unit of primary energy consumed. This is "raising the productivity of energy utilization" – in more ordinary terms, energy conservation.[39]

Despite expanding interest in and study of energy conservation, it remains largely ignored as a serious policy alternative to increased supply investment. Energy policy still looks almost exclusively at expanding primary supply. The commitment to nuclear electric generation can be seen as a direct consequence of this supply-side orientation: as fossil fuels become scarcer and more expensive, and imported supply raises serious economic and security problems, the assumptions of rising end-use demand and little change in efficiency of use create an anticipated supply shortfall, a gap on the graph, for which electricity generated by nuclear stations seems a ready-made, "logical" answer. But is it the only one?

We have not up to now, in making energy policy decisions, compared the costs per unit of end-use energy of building new tar sands plants and of insulating houses, or of building nuclear stations and of designing or retrofitting commercial buildings for efficient energy use. These comparisons must become an automatic step in energy policy formulation; in all probability, they will usually show conservation as a far preferable investment, in simple economic terms, until our overall efficiency of end-use improves strikingly.

Conventional energy supply technologies, unlike conservation initiatives (and renewable resource development), have historically received large-scale subsidies like oil and gas depletion allowances and subsidized nuclear research and development. Shifting these subsidies to conservation, if done on a significant scale, would fundamentally alter the comparative economics of alternative energy choices. There is not space here to make a detailed case for conservation and the so-called "soft" energy technologies like solar heating and fuel from biomass.[40] The essential point is that the evaluation of alternatives to the nuclear commitment has been grossly incomplete, and that these alternatives must be looked at in detail before the "need" for nuclear energy is assumed. Many evaluations of energy conservation possibilities have shown that in the short term there is little effect on economic growth, and sometimes positive effects on employment. In the longer term, there are clear implications for GNP growth (though *not* necessarily for well-being) in limiting energy growth, as improvements in energy efficiency become harder to achieve.[41]

Asking how much energy "we" "need" in the long term is very much like asking about the size of the proverbial fish. At *some* level of energy demand, we may require nuclear electricity. The assessment of that need must be made in light of the distinctions between primary and end-use energy, or else we must be quite explicit about the symbolic value we attach to thermodynamic inefficiency, and must know the consequences of that choice. We also must have the resources available to make intelligent comparisons between nuclear electricity and other (e.g., renewable) energy sources as directions for the future. At present, policy relating to nuclear energy in Canada meets neither of these criteria.

Conclusions and Afterthoughts

Ross Campbell, then chairman of AECL, characterized the nuclear debate in 1977 as follows:

[A] handful of highly articulate anti-growth, anti-'the present way of life' groups have caused governments to hesitate in their nuclear programs and sown widespread apprehension among the public. In short, we have lost two years of lead time that could have been used in putting the Western World's energy economy on a more secure footing.[42]

Despite his siege mentality, Campbell was right about one thing: the urgency of decisions about future energy supplies. As supplies, particularly of crude oil, get tighter in Canada over the next few years, it can be expected that the sense of urgency attached to energy supply will increase. So will the corresponding tendency to grasp at whatever straws are within easiest reach or most bureaucratically convenient. But these factors make assessing future energy technologies more, rather than less, important. I have tried to argue that the potential costs of nuclear power are of such magnitude that all alternatives should be examined. This we simply have not been doing. And without a major change in the present imbalance of resources in the nuclear debate, we cannot expect that examination to take place with the speed and competence now necessary.

A number of recent projects–for instance, a study of the alternatives to nuclear expansion in Ontario based on economically competitive improvements in end-use efficiency[43]–suggest promising progress in assessing nuclear technology. But without institutional changes, this kind of assessment will probably continue to be the isolated and largely ignored exception rather than the rule. The proponents of nuclear power in Canada represent a well-defined establishment–a term used not in a derogatory sense, though in a cautionary one. The limits to the debate on nuclear power in Canada's future have been set by that establishment, and it is becoming clear that those limits are too narrow for sensible consideration of the nuclear commitment.

NOTES

1. For instance, R. G. Hart of Atomic Energy of Canada writes: "No quantitative study that I am aware of indicates that we *need* to make a drastic change in the way we live." (*Sources, Availability and Costs of Future Energy*, AECL-5816, August, 1977.) Now how could a quantitative study answer a question like that?

2. See Joseph Coates, "Science, Technology and Social Choice," in Walter Baker (ed.), *Shaping the Future: Canada in a Global Society* (Ottawa: Center for Policy and Management Studies, 1979).

3. See J. Gordon Parr, "The Escalation of Technological Danger," *Alternatives*, 7 (Winter, 1978).

4. S. R. Hatcher, *Nuclear Power in Canada: Status and Prospects*, AECL-6173, May, 1978.

5. J. E. Gander and F. W. Belaire, *Energy Futures for Canadians* (Ottawa: Energy, Mines and Resources Canada, EP 78-1, 1978).

6. For a clear outline of the basics of the nuclear fuel cycle, see *A Race Against Time*, interim report of Ontario Royal Commission on Electric Power Planning (Toronto, 1978), chapter 4.

7. A brief history of the Port Hope contamination is given in *An Overview of the Ionizing Radiation Hazard in Canada* (Ottawa: Science Council of Canada, 1979), 161-75.

8. *Report of the Royal Commission on the Health and Safety of Workers in Mines* (Toronto, 1976).

9. See, for example, *Radiation Standards and Public Health: Proceedings of a Second Congressional Seminar on Low-Level Ionizing Radiation* (Washington, D.C.: Environmental Policy Institute, 1978).

10. See the Ministry's submissions to the Royal Commission on Electric Power Planning, May, 1976 and April, 1978.

11. See Appendix A in Amory Lovins, *Non-Nuclear Futures* (Cambridge, Mass., 1976); R. B. Hubbard and G. C. Minor (eds.), *The Risks of Nuclear Power Reactors* (Cambridge, Mass.: Union of Concerned Scientists, 1977).

12. H. W. Lewis *et al.*, *Risk Assessment Review Group Report to the U.S. Nuclear Regulatory Commission*, NUREG/CR-0400, September, 1978, p. viii.

13. J. A. L. Robertson, *Final Argument Relating to the Canadian Nuclear Power Program*, a brief to the Royal Commission on Electric Power Planning, AECL-6200, 1978, p. 39.

14. *Ibid.*, pp. 46-7.

15. See Hubbard and Minor (eds.), *Risks of Nuclear Reactors*.

16. Robertson, *Final Argument*, p. 36.

17. See P. Slovic, B. Fischhoff, and S. Lichtenstein, "Rating the Risks," *Environment*, 21 (April, 1979).

18. Robertson, *Final Argument*, p. 47.

19. A. M. Aikin, J. M. Harrison, and F. K. Hare, *The Management of Canada's Nuclear Wastes* (Ottawa: Energy Mines and Resources Canada, EP 77-7, 1977); R. J. Uffen, *The Disposal of Ontario's Used Nuclear Fuel* (Toronto: Ontario Hydro, 1978).

20. Comment by Allan Blakeney, Premier of Saskatchewan, in Bill Harding, *Uranium Mining in Northern Saskatchewan: Correspondence with the Premier* (Regina: Group for a Non-Nuclear Society, 1979).

21. See *The Unfinished Agenda*, a task force report sponsored by the Rockefeller Brothers Fund (New York, 1977), 57-8.

22. See H. B. Newcombe, "Public Health Aspects of Radiation," in *Nuclear Power: The Canadian Issues*, a submission to the Royal Commission on Electric Power Planning, AECL-5800, 1977.

23. Herbert Inhaber, *Risk of Energy Production*, AECB-1119/Rev 2, 1978.

24. J. P. Holdren *et al.*, *A Critique of the Inhaber Report*, Report ERG-79-3 (Energy and Resources Group, University of California, Berkeley, 1979).

25. See D. Torgerson, "From Dream to Nightmare: Historical Origins of Canada's Nuclear Electric Future," *Alternatives*, 7 (Fall, 1977).

26. See G. Bruce Doern, *Regulatory Processes and Jurisdictional Issues in the Regulation of Hazardous Products in Canada* (Ottawa: Science Council of Canada, Background Study #41, 1977).

27. See Hatcher, *Nuclear Power in Canada*.

28. J. S. Foster, a former President of AECL, "Closing Remarks," at AECL's "Seminar: Proposed Canadian Fuel Cycle Program" (mimeo, 1977).

29. G. Bruce Doern, *The Atomic Energy Control Board* (Ottawa: Law Reform Commission, 1977), 33.
30. Letter reproduced in Appendix 4-2 of Ralph Torrie, *Half-Life: Nuclear Power and Future Society,* Ontario Coalition for Nuclear Responsibility, 1977.
31. Doern, *Atomic Energy Control Board.*
32. Minutes of the RSAC (Ontario), AECB, August, 1976. This was one of several documents "leaked" to the Canadian Coalition for Nuclear Responsibility in June, 1978.
33. Ontario Hydro, submission to the Royal Commission on Electric Power Planning on "The Decision-Making Framework and Public Participation," 1979.
34. C. A. Hooker and R. Van Hulst, "The Meaning of Environmental Problems for Public Political Institutions," in W. Leiss (ed.), *Ecology versus Politics in Canada* (Toronto, 1979).
35. S. Ebbin and R. Kasper, *Citizen Groups and the Nuclear Power Controversy* (Cambridge, Mass., 1974).
36. "Confidence Melts Down," Toronto *Globe and Mail,* April 2, 1979.
37. Gander and Belaire, *Energy Futures,* 75.
38. See L. Schipper and A. J. Lichtenberg, "Efficient Energy Use and Well-Being: The Swedish Example," *Science,* 194 (December 3, 1976); J. Darmstadter, J. Dunkerley, and J. Alterman, "International Variations in Energy Use: Findings from a Comparative Study," *Annual Review of Energy,* 3 (1978).
39. See L. Schipper, "Raising the Productivity of Energy Utilization," *Annual Review of Energy,* 1 (1976); R. H. Socolow, "The Coming Age of Conservation," *Annual Review of Energy,* 2 (1977).
40. See Amory Lovins, *Soft Energy Paths* (New York, 1979).
41. See David Brooks, "The Economic Impact of Low Energy Growth in Canada," Discussion Paper #126 (Ottawa: Economic Council of Canada, 1978).
42. "Opening Remarks," at AECL's "Seminar: Proposed Canadian Fuel Cycle Program" (mimeo, 1977).
43. Peter Middleton Associates, *Alternatives to Ontario Hydro's Generation Program* (Toronto: Royal Commission on Electric Power Planning, 1977). See also *Creating Jobs through Energy Policy,* Hearings before the Subcommittee on Energy, Joint Economic Committee, U.S. Congress, March, 1978.

CHAPTER THIRTEEN

Issues in Canadian-American Environmental Relations
by O. P. Dwivedi and John E. Carroll

Introduction

The genesis of Canadian-American environmental relations may be traced back to the 1890's, when two irrigation congresses were held at Denver and Albuquerque and the Canadian delegates introduced a resolution urging the United States government to appoint an international commission to adjudicate conflicting rights having an international character.[1] That early concern, which finally resulted in the signing of a Boundary Waters Treaty of 1909[2] and the subsequent creation of the International Joint Commission, is a testimony to the perceptive work of the Canadians and the timely co-operation of the Americans. It should be realized, though, that that was a period marked by an emphasis on securing mutual benefits from industrial growth and the exploitation of natural resources. It is not surprising, then, to find that the Boundary Waters Treaty of 1909 was not directed toward any ecological considerations, although a passing reference to water pollution was inserted, mainly at the behest of the Canadian delegation. Notably, one of the first tasks of the International Joint Commission was to examine the question of pollution in the boundary waters; however, further references were not given to it until the end of World War II.

The period between 1946 and the late 1960's, which has been referred to as the "period of maturing continental partnership," is clearly marked by a broadening scope of joint action and joint responsibility in various fields, including boundary water and environmental questions.[3] During the end of this period the rapid increase in public awareness of ensuing danger to environmental quality brought into sharp focus the need not only for domestic environmental legislation and policies but also for concerted action in certain cases of pollution in the boundary areas. The international ramifications of such transboundary environmental cases required immediate attention and effective action on the part of Canada and the United States. This resulted in a strengthening of the existing institution as well as in the creation of other bilateral bodies. This period, the late 1960's and later, also opened up those questions of the past which had been settled by other than ecological considerations. Figure 1 illustrates areas of environmental conflicts.

At present, the environmental relationship between Canada and the United States appears to be based on two approaches: (1) where the goals of both countries seem to be fundamentally in harmony, for example, the case relating to restoration of water quality in the Great Lakes, the disputed subject matter is referred to the International Joint Commission or to a new structure such as the International Saint John River Water Quality Committee; (2) where the national interest of one country is unable to accommodate the opposing viewpoint because of economic or other domestic considerations, the question is left to be resolved by the lengthy and sometimes frustrating system of diplomatic negotiations and consultations. This chapter explains how these approaches have been employed by the two countries by analyzing existing mechanisms and selected case studies and assesses the effectiveness of these mechanisms.

Institutional Mechanisms

The resolution of environmental conflicts between Canada and the United States could take several routes. Some of these include diplomatic channels, the International Joint Commission, the Saint John River Water Quality Committee, administrative understanding reached between a province and a state sharing common environmental and resource management problems, and the role of public interest groups.

The Diplomatic Channel

Canada has traditionally (and perhaps logically) treated its affairs with the United States as the most important of its diplomatic relationships. And, unlike the United States, Canada considers these

Figure 1: Where to Draw the Line on Pollution.
Reprinted, by permission, from National Parks & Conservation Magazine,
March, 1978.

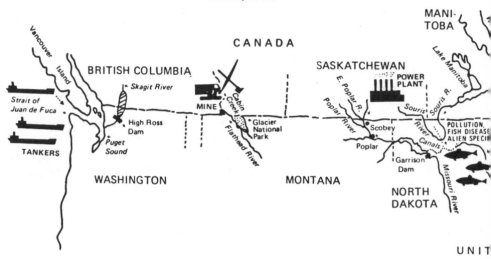

relations to be of central rather than peripheral importance. The amount of manpower, dollars, and overall effort Canada devotes to the United States reflects this centrality and importance. While the United States relegates Canadian affairs to an office staffed with a small contingent of professionals of lower foreign service rank than their Canadian counterparts, Canada has recently enlarged and upgraded its whole U.S. contingent from divisional to bureau status and its transboundary environment contingent from section to division status. The U.S. bureau of the Department of External Affairs has a professional complement of about twenty-five in comparison to five U.S. diplomats at the Department of State, for a ratio of five to one. Needless to say, the officers in charge at Canada's U.S. bureau outrank their American counterparts at the Department of State. The Canadian Transboundary Environment Division has a professional staff of five to the U.S's one environmental officer, maintaining the five to one ratio of the large units. These five are divided geographically and functionally. One officer is assigned to British Columbia and the Maritimes, reflecting common problems on the two marine coasts. One is assigned to Quebec and Ontario, reflecting the common nature of air and water quality problems in this heavily industrial

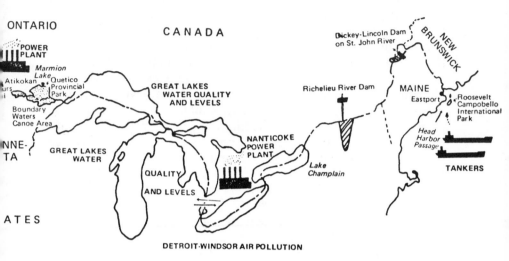

ONTARIO
POWER PLANT
Marmion Lake
Atikokan Quetico
urs   Provincial
         Park
Boundary
Waters
Canoe Area

CANADA

GREAT LAKES
WATER QUALITY
AND LEVELS

NNE-
TA   GREAT LAKES
        WATER

QUALITY
AND LEVELS

ATES

DETROIT-WINDSOR AIR POLLUTION

Dickey-Lincoln Dam
on St. John River

NEW BRUNSWICK

Richelieu River Dam

NANTICOKE
POWER
PLANT

Lake
Champlain

MAINE
Eastport

Roosevelt
Campobello
International
Park

Head
Harbor
Passage

TANKERS

region. Another is assigned the prairie region. The Arctic region and functional responsibilities relative to the International Joint Commission, environmental tasking of consulates, certain treaty matters, and other functional responsibilities are divided within the group of five, depending on interest and time. It should be remembered that all of these responsibilities are handled by *one* officer at the State Department (though with part-time assistance from the legal office).

In U.S. constitutional law the responsibility for the conduct of foreign relations rests exclusively with the federal government. This precept is taken seriously in the United States and guarded by the State Department, leaving the states with little say or influence in the conduct of U.S.-Canada relations. (While the governor of at least one state, Maine, maintains a full-time Canadian affairs adviser on the state payroll, the post is largely oriented to business relations and economic development rather than to "issues" between the state and Canada.) A small amount of Canadian concern can be found in a few governors' officers and within a few state environmental quality bureaucracies, but the federal government clearly dominates the field.

In Canada, however, the provinces play a much more important role, both directly, given their official powers and ownership of resources, and indirectly via their great influence over federal decision-making. Hence, the Department of External Affairs must defer to a degree to the provincial governments and involve them in the decision-making. Each provincial government generally has a Ministry of Intergovernmental Relations to handle this responsibility in conjunction with the Ministry of the Environment and/or the Ministry of Natural Resources. There is a corollary, then, between the intergovernmental affairs people (diplomats of a sort)[4] and the environmental or natural resources people (water or air resource professionals) not unlike the federal-level relationship between External Affairs and Environment Canada (or the relationship between a state and the Environmental Protection Agency in the U.S.). Perhaps the best example of provincial involvement on the Canadian side in U.S.-Canada environmental negotiation has been the very active and continuing involvement of the Ontario Ministry of the Environment along with the federal bureaucracy in the Great Lakes water quality issue. Ontario had a substantial role in provincial-federal negotiations prior to the opening up of Canada-U.S. negotiation on this issue. There is no provision for negotiation in the formal diplomatic sense between Washington and a state government, but there certainly is a great deal of such negotiation in Canada, and there undoubtedly will continue to be more as the provinces appear to be moving toward a greater and greater role in federal decision-making.

The International Joint Commission

Of all the mechanisms[5] created between Canada and the United States, "none has a broader mandate, greater independence, or a longer or more impressive record of accomplishment than the International Joint Commission."[6] It was created under the Boundary Waters Treaty of 1909 to prevent disputes regarding the use of boundary waters and to settle all questions between the two countries involving rights, obligations, or interests of one in relation to the other along their common frontier.[7] It actually came into being three years later when it held its first organizational meeting in January, 1912. The IJC was given a specific mandate to exercise jurisdiction over the use, obstruction, or diversion of boundary waters where the use on one side of the boundary would affect the level of the waters on the other side (Article III), and where the level of the waters would be raised in the upstream country by construction downstream in the case of rivers crossing the boundary (Article IV). In each case, an application for approval of the project must be made to the IJC before any work may be undertaken.[8] While deliberating applications for approval of projects, the commission is directed to give precedence to domestic and sanitary needs, navigation uses, and power and irrigation uses.[9] The Joint Commission is also authorized to order that suitable and adequate compensation be paid to all interests who may be adversely affected by the project.[10]

The other authority given to the IJC under the treaty relates to general matters which may be submitted to it by the two governments for its examination into and subsequent report upon the facts and circumstances. Recommendations are made jointly to both governments, though they have no binding status on the governments concerned.[11] It is under this referral authority that the Joint Commission increasingly has been asked to examine the cases of transboundary pollution. The IJC also has been empowered to arbitrate with binding decision any dispute submitted to it jointly by the two governments.[12] However, this power is yet to be invoked.

Questions relating to pollution and the preservation of the environment did not attract much public attention during the treaty negotiations. With some reluctance, a declaratory reference to pollution was inserted into the treaty: "It is further agreed that the waters herein defined as boundary waters and waters flowing across the boundary shall not be polluted on either side to the injury of health or property on the other."[13] Despite the fact that low priority was given to the question of pollution under the Boundary Waters Treaty, since then several water pollution cases have been referred to the commission for investigation. During the very first year of its operation, the IJC was requested (in August, 1912) to determine the extent, causes, and location of polluted waters that may have caused the typhoid fever. Investigations covered transboundary waters from the Rainy Lake area to the Saint John River. The final report, dated August 12, 1918, recognized the presence of pollution, mostly in the Detroit, Niagara, St. Clair, St. Mary's, and St. Lawrence Rivers. Sewage from vessels, cities, and industries was found to be the major cause of pollution. The commission recommended: ". . . it is advisable to confer upon the International Joint Commission ample jurisdiction to regulate and prohibit this pollution of boundary waters and waters crossing the boundary."[14] However, neither government was interested in providing the commission with any enforcement authority.

When the IJC receives a request for pollution investigation, it also is given the authority to draw on the services of engineers and other specially qualified personnel from the two federal and the related provincial or state governments. As well, it is authorized to seek such information and technical data as may be necessary during its investigations. It generally appoints international boards of equal numbers of professionals drawn from each country. The boards submit their findings to the IJC, and these generally are released to the public for comments. The IJC then schedules public hearings in each country, in the particular areas concerned, during which individuals and governmental agencies may present their briefs. Proceedings are kept informal. Based upon the evidence produced during the public hearings and on the initial report submitted to it by the joint board, the IJC then prepares its own report and makes recommendations to the two governments. If governments accept some of its recommendations, it may be further asked to continue surveillance over the implementation of these recommendations through international control boards.

With the exception of three cases, when the commission was divided along national lines, its reports have been based on impartial judgement and a search for the common interest.[15] The following statement made about fifty years ago by Lawrence J. Burpee, a secretary to the Canadian Section, still seems to be the guiding principle of IJC deliberations:

The Commissioners have not approached these questions as two distinct groups of national representatives, each jockeying for advantages for its own side, but rather as members of a single tribunal, anxious to harmonize differences between the two countries, and to render decisions which would be substantial justice to all legitimate interests on both sides of the boundary, and particularly to those of the common people.[16]

The commission's record in the past has been commendable. It has been successful in dealing with a remarkable number of references involving a wide range of problems, including some included in the treaty. Examples are the three air pollution references and the Point Roberts study, which involves political, recreational, economic, and social questions. The IJC has preserved its impartiality, thus earning the respect of all parties concerned, because of its emphasis on achieving and maintaining objectivity in evaluating the issues of each case. "As a result, matters that might otherwise exacerbate the relations between Canada and the United States are dealt with in an informed and dispassionate manner calculated to ensure a full consideration of the interests of both nations."[17] The commission's deliberations have been helped by the presence of conscientious professionals seconded to it by the two federal and various provincial and state governments who were brave enough to point an accusing finger to their respective governments, if the occasion so demanded.

Notwithstanding its impressive record, the IJC is not permitted under the treaty to initiate any investigation or study. With respect to air and water pollution references, however, it was asked to draw the attention of the two governments to similar pollution problems elsewhere along the common border. Although national interests and the question of sovereignty may not permit the commission to have any enforcement power with respect to transboundary pollution, to be more useful as an international environmental advisory body it should be allowed to request a reference so that a problem can be investigated before it becomes unmanageable and so the attention of the two governments can be caught in advance of a crisis, rather than subsequent to it. Finally, the power given to it under the Great Lakes Water Quality Agreement to publicize its findings should be extended to all cases referred to it so that the public interest may be served.[18] Structural reforms needed in the IJC will be considered in the concluding section of this paper.

The International Saint John River Water Quality Committee

Pollution of the Saint John River, which crosses the Canada-United States boundary between the Province of New Brunswick and the State of Maine, has resulted from three main sources: paper and pulp mills situated at Edmundston, N.B., and Madawaska, Maine; solid wastes associated with the potato industry on both sides of the boundary; and the untreated (or partially treated) municipal and industrial wastes being discharged in the Aroostook-Prestile Basin, with a larger input from the State of Maine. The pollution problem was identified earlier by the downstream public of New Brunswick who became concerned about the polluted state of the Saint John River. As a result of public concern, the Canadian federal government approached its counterpart with a proposal to establish some mechanism acceptable to all parties. Also, on the twentieth anniversary of the North Atlantic Treaty Organization in 1969, NATO established a Committee on the Challenges of Modern Society (CCMS) to consider specific problems of the human environment.[19] One of the methods adopted by the CCMS for achieving environmental cooperation among its member states was the "pilot country project" in which one country would take the responsibility for a project the CCMS has decided is worth doing. Another member country could then join as a "co-pilot." Canada undertook to act as a pilot country for a project relating to inland water pollution and it identified the Saint John River Basin as one such project. The United States government joined in as "co-pilot" of the project with France and Belgium associating themselves as interested parties. Being a CCMS project, the Saint John River pollution case could not be submitted to the IJC for investigation. Consequently, a different institutional mechanism was created when Canada and the United States signed an agreement on September 21, 1972, thereby establishing a "Canada-United States Committee on Water Quality in the Saint John River" with the following objectives: (1) to review periodically progress in the conduct of water quality planning on both sides of the boundary with a view to facilitating progress toward enhancement of water quality; (2) to exchange information about plans, programs, and actions that could affect water quality in the Basin; (3) to assist in coordination and consultation among appropriate authorities on matters and actions affecting water quality; and (4) to make appropriate recommendations to relevant authorities on both sides of the boundary and to the International Joint Commission regarding the improvement of water quality in the basin.[20]

The Saint John River Committee submitted its recommendations to the IJC in September, 1975. The commission subsequently held public hearings on this report, and through its report of February 17, 1977, recommended that a joint water quality agreement, akin to the Great Lakes agreement, be negotiated; that no new power projects should start without a complete environmental assessment; and that a new reference be given to the IJC to identify the best water uses for each segment of the river, to monitor municipal and industrial waste treatment programs, and to review various steps taken by respective governments to improve water quality. Actions on these recommendations have not yet been taken. As of November, 1978, the committee continues to meet in order to discuss the best ways of implementing the IJC recommendations. However, officials on both sides of the river do not appear to be interested in giving the IJC the authority to monitor the sewage treatment situation.[21] At the same time, both federal governments are taking time to decide whether to keep the committee as a permanent mechanism with the authority to monitor and supervise the water quality of the Saint John River.

Provincial-State Administrative Understandings

Both in Canada and in the United States, the actual implementation of environmental quality standards generally rests with the provincial or state governments. In certain instances, regional environmental problems require more regional co-operation than national co-ordination. The following three cases of regional environmental co-operation between Canada and the United States are worth mentioning: (1) Ontario-Michigan understanding concerning matters arising out of the Great Lakes Water Quality (GLWQ) Agreement, (2) the Garrison Diversion Project involving Manitoba and North Dakota governments, and (3) New Brunswick-Maine efforts to control pollution in the Saint John River Basin.

An administrative understanding between Ontario and Michigan was prompted mainly because of the realization by the Michigan government that unless international and congressional pressure was brought to bear upon the Nixon administration, delays would occur toward the compliance of the GLWQ Agreement deadline of December 31, 1975. A joint communique issued by the Premier of Ontario and Governor of Michigan, on April 10, 1974, stated that

> Michigan and Ontario are making significant progress in pollution control but objectives shared by Canada and the United States are being jeopardized by impoundment of U.S. funds and bureaucratic delays. The Governor and the Premier urged that greater priority be placed on preservation of the Great Lakes.[22]

This joint communique has been brought to the attention of the Canadian Department of External Affairs and the U.S. Department of State. The communique further added that, with respect to transboundary air pollution, the IJC should be asked to assume responsibility for monitoring pollution. The State of Michigan feels that it will fall short of Ontario efforts to control water and air pollution along the common boundary.

The proposed Garrison Diversion Project is a huge irrigation project being pushed by the U.S. Bureau of Reclamation. People in Manitoba feel that resultant drainage will dramatically increase the salinity of water flowing into Manitoba in the Souris and Red Rivers. It is also feared that the biological balance of Lake Winnipeg could be affected because of the possibility of aquatic viruses, bacteria, and rough fish species from the Missouri River system reaching Manitoba waters through the irrigation canals. The Manitoba government has been pressed by environmentalists and the provincial political parties to do everything in its power to stop the project. Consequently, it approached the Canadian federal government, which expressed its concern (through a diplomatic note dated October 23, 1973) and suggested a meeting of senior officials of both countries to reach an understanding regarding Canadian rights and interests. Meanwhile, the Governor of North Dakota asked for a direct talk with the Premier of Manitoba on this controversy. On February 25, 1974, these two met, and the question of compensation for environmental damage also was raised. By October, 1975, both federal governments agreed on a joint reference to the IJC, asking it to report on the transboundary implications of the Garrison project. The commission reported in January, 1977, and concluded that it would have adverse impacts on water-use in Manitoba. The Province of Manitoba continued to seek co-operation and support from its counterpart in North Dakota. As of January, 1980, negotiations are still continuing between the parties on this contentious issue.

Another example of provincial-state environmental co-operation relates to the efforts being made by the governments of New Brunswick and Maine. The question of the pollution of the Saint John River Basin, examined earlier, has resulted in a team approach between the two federal and state-provincial environmental agencies. On June 28, 1973, the Premier of New Brunswick and the Governor of Maine signed an agreement calling for the maintenance and fostering of close co-operation in all areas of concern consistent with such Canadian and United States federal policies as may apply in the fields of environment, energy, trade, tourism, and transportation.[23] Although such executive understanding may be interpreted as nothing more than political intent rather than legal agreement, an atmosphere of good will and mutual appreciation of transnational problems appears to have been created between Maine and New Brunswick.

In addition to the above examined three cases, other co-operative efforts are made by provincial and state governments on matters related to environment, for example, the clean-up of Lake Memphremagog by the Province of Quebec and the State of Vermont. Another example is the agreement between the State of Washington and the Province of British Columbia to establish (in 1973) legislative committees to co-ordinate pollution control methods, especially oil pollution from tankers. This agreement is strengthened by a similar federal joint contingency plan. It appears that neighbouring states and provinces may be better off by using this direct approach to resolve problems instead of waiting for their national governments, which may take some time to reach a meaningful understanding. But initiative for such action would have to come from this lower level of the governments.

The work of the Canada-U.S. Interparliamentary Group now looking more closely at environmental issues should be mentioned here. The 1977 meeting held in Victoria, B.C., addressed at least half a dozen current issues of transboundary pollution, Great Lakes levels and water quality, and bilateral implications of the 200-mile limit. According to the published Senate report of this meeting,

The basic authority for U.S. participation . . . is contained in Public Law 86-42. Under provisions of this law, not to exceed 24 Members of Congress (12 from the Senate and 12 from the House of Representatives) are appointed to meet annually with representatives of the Canadian Parliament for discussion of common problems in the interest of relations between the United States and Canada.[24]

Addressing the subject of this institution, the Canadian Senate's Standing Committee on Foreign Affairs considers "that no other interparliamentary link is nearly as important to Canada as the Canada-United States Inter-Parliamentary Group." This committee further urged ". . . the selection of delegates . . . who are carefully chosen as to individual areas of expertise and adequately briefed in order to put Canada's case in the most effective possible manner to American legislators."[25] It is unclear whether the United States Senate equally considers the work of this group to be important.

Role of Environmental Groups

It would be misleading to conclude any discussion on environmental issues without mentioning the increasingly large impact of private citizens' organizations on this process, especially in the United States. Well-known American national conservation and environmental organizations especially active in transboundary issues include the National Audubon Society, the Wilderness Society, Friends of the Earth, and the Sierra Club. The National Parks and Conservation Association has been especially vocal on the Atikokan and Cabin Creek issues and on acid rain. Given that the Boundary Waters Canoe Area, Superior National Park, Voyageurs National Park, and Quetico Provincial Park are all threatened by Atikokan, and Glacier National Park and the Flathead Wild and Scenic River are threatened by Cabin Creek coal mining, NPCA's involvement is understandable since the organization's central and traditional aim is to influence the public and legislators and lobby government for the protection of national parks and similar types of reserves. Its principal tools are its widely read magazine, *National Parks and Conservation* (which has given more coverage to the Atikokan and Cabin Creek issues than any other magazine in the United States), and its direct lobbying in the Congress and in the National Park Service and other agencies. The National Audubon Society has been especially involved and particularly effective on the Garrison issue. Being outspokenly opposed to the project largely on the grounds of its domestic wildlife and other environmental damages, the Audubon Society has used its popular magazine *Audubon* and other channels to rouse the American public (and Canadians, too) against the project. The Audubon Society has also sued directly in court to enjoin the continuation of the project and has been quite successful in these endeavours. The Wilderness Society through its magazine *The Living Wilderness*, the Sierra Club in its *Sierra Club Bulletin*, and Friends of the Earth in its newspaper *Not Man Apart* have focused at various times on these issues, the Skagit-High Ross Dam issue, Great Lakes water quality, and various other transboundary environmental problems. In truth, however, virtually no attention has been given by these organizations to the totality of such issues, simply to single issues on an individual basis.

In addition to these national organizations, countless numbers of regional, state, and local organizations are involved for short periods of time on individual problems having local impact. Some of these organizations are coalitions put together hastily to focus public attention on a particular threat (or perceived threat), only to wither when the threat dies down or disappears. The central thrust of these groups is to quickly educate the people of the region to the impact of the project as they see it, and to influence elected officials and agency bureaucrats to stop the threat or negate its impact. Occasionally, their aim is direct litigation in court, if they have necessary financial means and talent. The American judicial system differs from the Canadian system in one very important area: to litigate is an infinitely easier task for an organization in the American system than in the Canadian system. Thus, American environmentalists, when organized, are potentially more effective than their Canadian counterparts. And, for reasons of ease of access to the courts, American groups are much more likely to use this vehicle to achieve their ends than are Canadian environmentalist groups, which tend to be more oriented to education and less to direct action.

The principal national environmentalist organizations in Canada with interests in transboundary environmental issues are the Canadian Nature Federation (CNF), based in Ottawa, and the National and Provincial Parks Association, based in Toronto. CNF publishes a magazine, *Nature Canada*, which often highlights the types of problems described in this book, and does maintain liaison with various American groups on these issues. In general, however, the citizens' environmentalist movement in Canada is small, weak, and poorly organized in comparison to its American counterpart. It also lacks the sophistication now beginning to characterize the behaviour of some of the larger, more activist U.S. groups. Canada does have a few well-organized and effective regional and local groups such as Pollution Probe in Toronto, SPEC (Scientific Pollution and Environmental Control Society) in Vancouver, and a few Sierra Club chapters, in Calgary, Victoria, and elsewhere. But these groups engage basically in piecemeal activity relating only to individual issues rather than encompassing the full national scope of the problem.

In the early 1970's the first weak moves were made by citizen environmentalists in both countries to unite to attack common problems afflicting the North American environment, including all problems which were by definition transboundary. Stewart Brandborg of the Wilderness Society in Washington and Ted Mosquin of the Canadian Nature Federation in Ottawa drew together a wide number of environmentalist organizations on both sides of the border in 1974 into a coalition to be known as the Canada-United States Environment Council (CUSEC). CUSEC was not to be a new organization, *per se*, but was rather to be a coalition of the leaders of a large number of already existing groups, including virtually all national and a few regional groups. Because of the association of CUSEC's founders, the Wilderness Society and CNF were to chair the new coalition and meetings were to be held annually and were to alternate between Washington and Ottawa. According to a memorandum dated September 21, 1976, the mission of CUSEC is to enable major United States and Canadian conservation and environmental groups to "get acquainted, exchange information, review issues of bilateral and international importance and to cooperate in executing environmental action."[26] CUSEC has issued joint U.S.-Canada resolutions on such diverse issues as gas pipelines; the Cabin Creek, B.C., coal stripmining issue; Arctic offshore drilling; border wildlands protection; the Dickey-Lincoln hydrodam in Maine; Porcupine caribou herd migration; the Champlain-Richelieu flooding question; energy conservation; spruce budworm spraying; harp seals; whales; nuclear energy; west coast oil tanker ports; tar sands development; acid rain; the Garrison Diversion; and the proposed Skagit nuclear power plant. All of its positions have been along the lines of traditional environmental protection viewpoints regularly espoused by the leadership of member organizations domestically in their own countries.

CUSEC seeks to represent over fifteen organizations in both countries with a combined membership of over one million. Though well-conceived on paper, the Canada-U.S. Environmental Council has had major problems of maintaining interest and providing sufficient funding to insure that its meetings in Washington and Ottawa are held. The few meetings which have thus far taken place have been poorly attended (largely due to insufficient travel funds), while the Canadian and American co-chairmen have been immersed in higher priority domestic activity to such a degree that little time can be devoted to CUSEC matters. If the organization is to be anything more than a paper coalition it will have to achieve far more financial support (and manpower) than heretofore. The promise is there, but remains essentially unfulfilled.

Traditionally, involvement in international environmental differences was reserved to the formal channels of government. Today, however, we are witnessing an increasing involvement of organized private citizens, notably national and regional environmental groups, in these matters. These groups, "somewhat to the consternation of their governments, do not recognize international boundaries, their loyalty generally being more to the ecological health of the environment rather than to the political or economic position of their nation."[27] Beyond the increasing number and complexity of transboundary environmental issues, perhaps the biggest growth aspect of Canada-U.S. environmental relations is this involvement of private citizens through the vehicle of non-governmental organizations, organizations which undoubtedly will play a greater and perhaps critical role in the future. Whether this ultimately will be for good or ill of U.S.-Canada relations remains to be seen, but it certainly will result in greater focus on the health of the natural environment and North American man's place within this environment.

Selected Issues Examined

Among the various issues which have brought the two countries together in search of better environmental understanding, the pollution of the Great Lakes emerges as the most important. However, this case has been thoroughly examined by Don Munton in an earlier chapter of the book. Three other illustrative cases are therefore presented here.

The Eastport Tanker Route

The threat of international oil pollution has increased with the expansion of coastal traffic on both sides of the continent. Oil continues to be transported in large quantities through Puget Sound and the Strait of Georgia. On the east coast, although there exists no such traffic, the threat to Passamaquoddy Bay and the Bay of Fundy will be potentially greater if a deep-water port and refinery are built at Eastport, Maine. As the tanker traffic is generally meant for the United States refineries, any oil spill strains the Canadian-American relationship. Spilled oil is a graveyard for species of animal and plant life. Birds are especially vulnerable. The adverse effects of oil spills also can be traced in the food chain. Further, an oil spill presents a substantial danger to the total marine environment. The problems associated with oil spillage were amply demonstrated by the grounding of the *Torrey Canyon*, which resulted in Great Britain and France spending about $12 million in clean-up operations.[28] Although the *Torrey Canyon* disaster was viewed with distant concern by Canadians, the point was brought home sharply when the tanker *Arrow* sank off the Nova Scotia coast in February, 1970, and later when another tanker sank near the Cherry Point refinery in the Strait of Georgia in June, 1972. In the case of the steam tanker *Arrow*, the Canadian government appointed a Royal Commission presided by Mr. Justice Gordon L. S. Hart of the Nova Scotia Supreme Court.[29] The ship ran aground on February 4, 1970, in Chedabucto Bay near Port Hawkesbury, Nova Scotia, within Canadian waters. Efforts to save it did not succeed and finally, on February 12, 1970, it sank with a resultant large escape of oil. The Royal Commission Report observed:

Apparently no real lesson was learned from *Torrey Canyon* disaster or the major oil spills that preceded it. The attitude that it can't happen here prevailed and the voices of those who called out, warning of the dangers of pollution were ignored. There was virtually no preparation in Canada for such a marine disaster.[30]

Realizing the gravity of the situation, the Minister of Transport appointed a task force on February 20, 1970, to clean up the oil and prepare a report for future reference. By September, 1970, the operation was completed at a cost of $3 million. Subsequent to the Royal Commission Report, an amendment to the Canada Shipping Act was introduced in the House of Commons on October 19, 1970, which included provisions for prohibiting the discharge of pollutants. The government now has power to remove and destroy ships that are discharging or are likely to discharge a pollutant and can impose a fine of up to $100,000.[31]

With the case of the *Arrow* as an east coast precedent, environmentalists from both sides of the border have joined battle against the plan to transport offshore oil in super tankers to a proposed refinery complex at Eastport, Maine. The Pittston Company plans to build a billion dollar refinery, the largest refinery ever proposed in the United States. The passage to Eastport is through a narrow and deep channel entirely within Canadian waters. This passage contains one of the world's most fantastic fish feeding areas. Building of the refinery also may preclude any development of tidal power because the refinery would necessitate the creation of the largest, most expensive ship lock in the world.

Despite official Canadian objections, the Pittston Company has sought approval from the U.S. Environmental Protection Agency for an air emission licence, and from the Maine Board of Environmental Protection for discharges into the sea water. The Maine Board gave permission for smaller tankers subject to the company to seek approval of Canadian authorities for passage through Canadian waters. The government of New Brunswick objected formally to the Maine Board, and the Canadian federal government views opposing such permits were made known to the State Department. The Canadian government, however, has not formally banned tankers from using the passage; instead, it has relied on the pressure from such environmental groups as Friends of Eastport to exhaust the U.S. domestic process. The issues were not yet settled by 1979. American supporters of the refinery in Eastport point out that Canadians are simply waiting for a chance to have the Pittston facility built somewhere in the Maritime Provinces, and if that happens it could be an economic and strategic loss to the U.S.

The Garrison Diversion

As mentioned earlier, the State of North Dakota wants to irrigate some 250,000 acres of land in its north-central region. For this purpose, a project is underway to divert Missouri River water from behind the Garrison Dam in North Dakota into Lake Audubon whence it will flow by gravity through a series of supply works and reservoirs to the north-central region. The irrigation return flows will accrue to three river systems: the Souris, the Red, and the James Rivers. But the first two flow into Canada. Canadian concerns relate to water quality degradation from return flows, transfer of non-native fish, fish parasites, and fish diseases from the Missouri River system into Lake Winnipeg, and eventually to the Hudson Bay drainage. Another concern relates to the protection of the commercial sport fishery in Lakes Manitoba and Winnipeg. Canadians fear that the added nutrient reaching Canada through these two rivers will accelerate the eutrophication of Lake Winnipeg. Besides diplomatic notes, Canada informed the United States in 1973 that the diversion would violate Article IV of the 1909 Boundary Waters Treaty. Later, Canada, at the request of Manitoba, called for the establishment of a Garrison Diversion Study Board under the IJC. This reference was different from others in that it was to study a potential pollution source that was yet to be completed. The IJC study, including other similar studies, confirmed that major transboundary environmental and resource damage from the completed Garrison Dam would occur. Again, in this issue, the Canadian cause was greatly supported by the domestic environmental groups of the United States. The project size has been reduced to less than 100,000 acres, but the problem of transfer of non-native fish biota remains, as does strong Canadian opposition.

The Skagit River-Ross Dam

The case of the Skagit River controversy is an example of how the lack of foresight excluded environmental considerations at the time of signing of a bilateral agreement and of how changing social values have affected the application of this agreement. The growing needs of Seattle made it imperative for the Seattle City Light and Power Company to increase the hydro output, which was possible only by raising the level of the Ross Dam, one of the biggest dams on the Skagit. As this involved flooding of the Canadian territory, the Seattle power company, in accordance with Article IV of the Boundary Waters Treaty of 1909, applied to the International Joint Commission on May 26, 1941, for the authority to raise, by stages, the natural water level of the Skagit River 130 feet, to elevation 1,725 feet above main sea level at the international boundary, by progressively increasing the height of the Ross Dam on the Skagit River. The International Joint Commission conducted public hearings in which the representative of the Province of British Columbia interposed no objection to such an application if reasonable and appropriate compensation was made to the province and to any private interests for damage to lands in Canada. On January 27, 1942, the IJC, while approving the application, set the following condition:

> The City of Seattle shall adequately compensate the Province of British Columbia, and any Canadian private interests that may be affected, for any damage caused in British Columbia as the result of any increase in the natural water levels of the Skagit River at and above the international boundary; provided that the Ross Dam shall not be raised beyond the height at which the water impounded by it would reach British Columbia unless and until a binding agreement has been entered into between the city of Seattle and the Government of British Columbia providing for indemnifying British Columbia and private interests.[32]

This particular method adopted by the Joint Commission in approving a work subject to a binding agreement between the affected parties has created confusion about the legal validity of such an order. Under Article VIII of the Boundary Waters Treaty, the IJC is empowered, as a condition of its approval, to require "that suitable and adequate provision, *approved by it*, be made for the protection and indemnity of all interests on the other side of the line which may be injured thereby."[33] Instead of approving any final settlement, the IJC delegated to Seattle and British Columbia the right to work out the terms of compensation. Some Canadian critics feel that such a slip on the part of the Joint Commission has made its order invalid, and therefore, the City of Seattle has no legal ground to proceed with the raising of the level of the Ross Dam.[34]

As the level of the reservoir was to be raised by stages, annual agreements between Seattle and B.C. were concluded until 1967 permitting flooding across the boundary to elevation 1,600 during those years. Finally, on January 10, 1967, a 99-year formal agreement was reached, which provided that the Province of British Columbia would agree to allow the valley to be flooded for an annual payment of $34,566.21 per year in cash or in equivalent electric power.[35] Subsequently, in February, 1970, the B.C. government announced plans to establish a 3,700 acre provincial park in the Skagit Valley and to create a 32,900 acre recreation area to take advantage of the water provided by the proposed raising of Ross Dam. Meanwhile, Seattle City Light and Power Company applied to the U.S. Federal Power Commission for a licence to raise the dam.

Until then, public awareness of the need for maintaining environmental quality and wilderness value was not widespread. It was later that the gravity of environmental pollution and the need to save natural habitat became apparent. It took some time for the concerned people of Greater Vancouver to realize they were going to be deprived of one of the last remaining unspoiled wilderness areas within a three-hour drive and well-suited to human use. Public pressure was mounted on the Canadian federal government, which took the initiative to the U.S., and finally the IJC was requested on April 7, 1971, "to investigate the environmental and ecological consequences in Canada of the raising of the Ross lake . . . taking into account relevant information about environmental and ecological consequences elsewhere on the Skagit River . . . ."[36] However, the Joint Commission's terms of reference were made very restrictive, as it was particularly directed:

> to make recommendations . . . not inconsistent with the Commission's Order of Approval dated January 27, 1942, the Agreement required thereby between the City of Seattle and the Province of British Columbia dated January 10, 1967, and the purposes for which such Order of Approval was granted.[37]

The IJC estimated that direct loss to Canada was in the order of one million dollars. Needless to say, the findings were a disappointment to the concerned people of British Columbia. Meanwhile, the Social Credit government in B.C. was defeated by the New Democratic Party, which declared its opposition to the flooding. This political reality, coupled with continuous public pressure in the province, strengthened the resolve of the Canadian federal government to transmit to Washington, D.C., its opposition to the flooding. This is further reflected in a unanimous resolution adopted by the House of Commons on November 2, 1973:

That the House of Commons of Canada is unalterably and unanimously opposed to the flooding of the Canadian Skagit River Valley which will result from the proposed City of Seattle project to raise the height of the present Ross dam situated in the state of Washington and downstream from the Canada-United States border.[38]

The State Department was promptly made aware of this strong action taken by the Canadian House of Commons, but believing in its legal superiority in the case and undaunted by such Canadian feelings, the U.S. Federal Power Commission (FPC) opened its hearings on the application by the Seattle City Light and Power Company. The FPC, in July, 1978, finally approved the company's application, thus paving the way for the company to proceed with structural changes in the dam. As of January, 1980, a case brought by conservationists from the State of Washington is before a U.S. federal court. It seems that further legal battle in the U.S. courts may only delay the inevitable.

The Skagit case reveals a basic flaw in the decisions rendered by international institutions. The IJC should be permitted to review its own decisions, should such decisions be perceived to create environmental damage at a later date. The case also demonstrates many of the difficulties surrounding the development of resources in an atmosphere of rising environmental concern.

Conclusions

Reform in the International Joint Commission

While several entities have considered environmental issues between the two nations, the IJC is the oldest such institution, and has acquired prestige for its objective decisions. Only the IJC has a standing mandate to investigate any environmental matter referred to it, and also, to alert both nations to foreseeable problems that may cause difficulty even before references to them by both governments have been decided upon. Yet, compared to the approaches taken by the European Common Market countries, Canada-United States institutional framework appears to be incomplete. The Common Market has been approaching a quasi-federalism, albeit slowly, whereas we have become more nationalistic in our approach.

The need for IJC reform is not restricted to the powers of the commission but bears also on the structure and staffing of the commission itself, particularly in the United States Section. This area of needed reform has been too long neglected by virtually all writers in this field. Specifically, we are referring to the need to improve the quality of the product in the Washington Section and staff. The successful effort of Senator Gaylord Nelson of Wisconsin to pass an amendment to a public works bill requiring Senate approval of the president's nominees to the IJC is a step in the right direction. Although the Senate Committee on Foreign Relations and the full Senate probably will regard this duty as one of very low priority, nevertheless it may have the effect of encouraging the president to exercise more care in selecting nominees in the future.

Other needed reforms include the following. (1) Separation of the IJC annual budget appropriation from the overall State Department budget, where it now appears as a line item, is a necessity if complete autonomy, as intended in the treaty, is to be maintained for the commission. (2) Equal funding of the IJC by both governments should be mandated; currently, the Canadian Section is clearly better funded and has greater manpower allocation. (3) All commissioners should be full-time, whereas currently only the chairmen are, and there appear to be problems attracting good talent in return for the relatively low half-time pay available. (4) All commissioners should have specific terms of office, with reappointments possible and with terms staggered to insure no more than a one-third turnover at any one time. Currently, only Canadian commissioners have terms; U.S. commissioners serve at the pleasure of the president. (5) Eligibility qualifications should be set for appointees to the IJC, including that any nominee should be required to have professional career experience in environmental affairs and should demonstrate interest in or sensitivity to Canada-U.S. relations. (6) An appointed citizens advisory committee needs to be established to provide input to the IJC. Such a committee would be composed of academic scholars and non-government representatives of citizens' groups. The prevailing membership should have environmental credentials, but should include a few experts on Canada-U.S. relations to achieve balance (perhaps in a 7:3 ratio). (7) A final reform pertains to the composition of the technical boards and various other IJC boards of inquiry which assist the commission in making its recommendations. These boards have been composed almost exclusively of federal, and less frequently, state and provincial bureaucrats. Most often, these bureaucrats come from an engineering background. The need to vary the composition of these boards is now beginning to be answered, as we begin to see the appointment of biologists, economists, geologists, soil scientists, and an occasional social scientist, but the pace of this reform is all too slow and proportionately insufficient. Additional non-engineering input is greatly needed to balance the approach taken and the recommendations submitted by these boards. In no case should more than half of a board's composition be engineering in background.

A second reform in the area of board composition relates to the almost total dominance by government officials. Public servants from federal, state, and provincial levels do have a place as long as they have the professional expertise, but they should not comprise over half of a board's membership. There is great need for the participation of academics (including social scientists), businessmen, citizen leaders, and others to balance both the approaches and the views of the boards. Of course, this would be more expensive than the present system, at least on paper, for the common IJC practice of "seconding" federal bureaucrats in both countries could no longer be as predominant as it has been. These public servants face the dilemma of dual allegiance. This is not to cast aspersions on those individuals who have worked tirelessly and devotedly on IJC boards in the past, but it is to say that, no matter how hard they try, they cannot be something other than what they are: veteran employees of government agencies who must, by definition, reflect the ways of doing business, if not the views themselves, of the agencies from which they are seconded. Hence, the approaches, methods, and views of Canada's Inland Waters Directorate and the Army Corps of Engineers, Bureau of Reclamation, and Geological Survey in the U.S. cannot help but dominate all IJC boards, as these agencies are essentially the source of current board membership. In proper proportion, there is nothing wrong with these approaches and this thinking, but it must be balanced by the intelligence and creativity that the non-government sector in each country is ably willing to contribute.

These "structural" rather than conceptual reforms are suggested in order to strengthen the capability and the prestige the IJC should be able to command in our society; such reforms have too long been ignored. As Maxwell Cohen, former Canadian co-chairman of the IJC, has explained:

The International Joint Commission will not be pressed into the service of resolving all the problems that bedevil both countries in their joint ecosystem dilemmas; but it is at the very least an instrument for approaching some of these difficulties and perhaps it is, also, a model for other means to deal with new problems now on the horizon of the common environmental future.[39]

The Current Situation

From the foregoing discussion, and indeed from the essays throughout this book, it is evident that environmental relations between Canada and the United States range from active cooperation to unilateral assertion of national positions. Political difficulties have arisen when some local problems grew into matters of national concern and the existing institutional framework was found inadequate to resolve such disputes. Until now, however, both countries have regarded such divergent views simply as minor irritants in their relationship. But a change has been noticed recently in the overall relationship between the two countries. As pointed out by Mitchell Sharp in his paper on "Canada-U.S. Relations: Options for the Future":

It is fair to assume that, in the 1970's and 1980's, Canadian-American relations may become more complex than they have been in the past. . . . It is also to be assumed that, if national interest were interpreted in a new and possibly narrower focus, the issues arising between us would, on occasion, be judged to bear more critically on it than when the relationship was more relaxed.[40]

The above statement seems all the more appropriate when one considers such controversies as those over the Skagit River and the tanker routes along both coasts. It appears that the period of "special relationship" or "personal diplomacy" is slowly being replaced by a period of readjustment and mutual appreciation of each other's national interests and aspirations.

At the same time one should realize that "perhaps no two countries in the world have the degree of economic and social intimacy that characterizes the day-to-day and long term relations between Canada and the United States."[41] It is within the context of this political reality that Canadian-American environmental relations should be examined. It would be equally pertinent to ask the vital question: has the time come to take joint stock of all existing mechanisms pertaining to transboundary pollution control? If so, are such mechanisms adequate? If not, what options are open to both countries to accommodate current environmental problems?

On the basis of the examination in this paper of five institutional mechanisms and three case studies, it becomes apparent that both federal governments are trying not to add any further jurisdiction to the International Joint Commission than is absolutely necessary and legally imperative under the Boundary Waters Treaty. The seeming reluctance on the part of the two nations to see the IJC becoming a "super international environmental protection agency" arises perhaps from the fact that both countries envisaged the major role of the Joint Commission, under the treaty, as an agency resolving disputes of water resources management. Consequently, the IJC was not given any enforcement power to deal with the co-ordination and administration of pollution abatement programs along the common borders. It has, of course, acquired over the years a reputation for being objective and not being drawn into national controversies. Its appropriateness is demonstrated in the following statement, that

> . . . the true measure of the Commission's usefulness to the people of the United States and Canada lies not so much in its positive as in its negative qualities, not so much in the cases it has actually settled as in the much larger number of cases that never come before it for consideration, simply because the Commission is there, as a sort of international safety-valve and therefore the sting is taken out of the situation.[42]

Although such a statement appears to be a weak testimonial to the effectiveness of the IJC, it should be realized that the commission, given its limited staff and restricted jurisdiction, has performed remarkably well the investigatory role pertaining to pollution references. However, abatement of pollution in transboundary areas requires a more wide-ranging international approach than the present structure and authority of the IJC permits. Pollution control is but one aspect of the total Canadian-American relationship that cannot be dissociated from a complex and interrelated web of physical, geographical, economic, and cultural factors, which together define and comprise that relationship.[43] The IJC, as currently constituted, is well-suited for its investigatory and mediative roles and related administrative tasks, although, as noted above, certain structural reforms are needed to improve the efficiency and objectivity of the IJC and to extend its intellectually informed base.

If we assume that the IJC is not likely to receive from the two countries a greater mandate than it presently has, and this seems to be a fair assumption, then some form of transnational organization should be established to take a holistic view of environmental questions concerning both Canada and the United States. One option that should be considered for broadened environmental cooperation is a joint "Canada-United States Transnational Environment Committee," composed of federal, provincial, and state representatives. Observer status could be extended to such entities as the IJC, the Great Lakes Basin Commission, and other agencies dealing with transboundary water resources questions. This committee would examine various aspects of environmental questions, including oil pollution, by appointing sub-committees to report on specific issues. At the same time, re-examination of all existing treaties (including the Boundary Waters and Columbia River treaties) and agreements (including the Great Lakes Water Quality Agreement) would be undertaken. While diplomatic negotiations continued, emerging environmental problems could be attended to either by the IJC or by creating an administrative framework similar to the Saint John River Committee. Such an option, it is hoped, would result in better appreciation and consideration of mutual problems. From this starting point, a better framework of understanding could be built to find agreeable solutions to transnational environmental problems. To achieve some success, however, Canadians will have to be more aggressive in this regard, if for no other reason than to maintain the constant attention of its "big brother," who has other equally pressing problems to tackle and who, consequently, is not always "watching" or overly concerned.

NOTES

1. For the historical development, see, for example, *Papers Relating to the Work of the International Joint Commission* (Ottawa, 1929), 103-4; and N. F. Dreisziger, "The Great Lakes in the United States-Canadian Relation: The First Stock-Taking," *Inland Seas*, 28 (Winter, 1972), 259-71.
2. Treaty between the United States and Great Britain relating to Boundary Waters, and Questions Arising Between the United States and Canada, January 11, 1909, *Canada Statutes 1911*, chapter 28.
3. Maxwell Cohen, "Canada and the United States – Possibilities for the Future," *Columbia Journal of Transnational Law*, 12, 2 (1973), 198.
4. The Alberta Ministry of Intergovernmental Affairs maintains an office in Ottawa which is facetiously known as the "Alberty Embassy."
5. Appearing before the Senate Standing Committee on Foreign Affairs, Hon.

Mitchell Sharp provided a List of Canada-United States Intergovernmental Bodies that consisted of seventeen such bodies, including the International Joint Commission. See Senate, *Proceedings Respecting Canadian Relations with the United States*, March 28, 1974, Appendix 13, pp. 1:34-1:39.

6. F. J. E. Jordan, "The International Joint Commission and Canada-United States Boundary Relations," in R. St. J. MacDonald *et al.* (eds.), *Canadian Perspectives on International Law and Organization* (Toronto, 1974), 525. The literature on the working of the IJC is extensive. There are three well-known book-length studies: C. J. Chacko, *The International Joint Commission* (New York, 1932); G. W. Kyte, *Organization and the Work of the International Joint Commission* (Ottawa, 1937); and L. M. Bloomfield and G. F. Fitzgerald, *Boundary Waters Problems of Canada and the United States* (Toronto, 1958).

Various IJC commissioners and officials also have written on it. See, for example, A. D. P. Heeney, "Diplomacy with a Difference: The International Joint Commission," *Inco Magazine*; J. L. MacCallum, "The International Joint Commission," *Canadian Geographical Journal*, 72 (March, 1966), 76-87; Matthew E. Welsh, "Role of the International Joint Commission," in *Proceedings of the Great Lakes Water Resources Conference* (Toronto, 1969), 871-5; M. E. Welsh and A. D. P. Heeney, "International Joint Commission – United States and Canada," 5th International Conference on Water for Peace, 1967 (paper p. 217), pp. 104-9; Eugene W. Weber, "The Role of the International Joint Commission," in *Water Management: Basic Issues*, OECD Report (Paris, 1972); Lawrence J. Burpee, *Good Neighbours* (Toronto, 1940); and Canada, *Papers Relating to the Work of the International Joint Commission* (Ottawa, 1929). Also see the various writings of Maxwell Cohen, some of which are referred to in notes 3 and 39.

Other articles on the IJC include: W. R. Willoughby, "The Appointment and Removal of Members of the International Joint Commission," *Canadian Public Administration*, 12 (Fall, 1969), 411-26; G. Graham Waite, "The International Joint Commission – Its Practice and Its Impact on Land Use," *Buffalo Law Review*, 13 (Fall, 1963), 93-118; Richard B. Bilder, "Controlling Great Lakes Pollution: A Study of United States-Canadian Environmental Cooperation," *Michigan Law Review*, 70 (January, 1972), 469-556; and O. P. Dwivedi, "The International Joint Commission: Its Role in United States-Canada Boundary Pollution Control," *International Review of Administrative Sciences*, 40 (1974), 369-76.

7. Boundary Waters Treaty, preamble, note 2.
8. *Ibid.*, articles III and IV.
9. *Ibid.*, article VIII, paragraph 4.
10. *Ibid.*, article VIII, paragraph 7.
11. *Ibid.*, article IX.
12. *Ibid.*, article X.
13. *Ibid.*, article IV, paragraph 2.
14. International Joint Commission, Pollution of Boundary Waters, Docket No. 4.
15. The Canadian Section has identified these three cases when the commission was divided along national lines. (1) Under the Boundary Waters Treaty, a provision was made, under article VI, for an equitable apportionment of the waters of the St. Mary and Milk Rivers for irrigation purposes (Docket No. 9). The IJC submitted its findings on October 4, 1921, to both governments

but the U.S. government was not satisfied. Further discussions among the commission members resulted in an equal division on national lines in February, 1932. (2) In the Belly-Waterton Rivers Investigation (Docket No. 57), where the interpretation of the intent of terms of reference was disputed, the two sections could not agree upon the recommendations to be sent to the two federal governments. (3) The third instance is related to the Skagit River Controversy (Docket No. 46), when in 1942 an order for raising the existing height of Ross Dam was approved by the IJC on the condition that an agreement was to be entered into between the City of Seattle Light and Power Company and the Province of British Columbia. But the W. A. C. Bennett government, which came into power in 1952, did not want to proceed with the required agreement. Consequently, Seattle appealed to the commission in 1958 to enforce its 1942 order. The commission could not reach a joint decision and was divided along national lines.

16. Lawrence J. Burpee, "An International Experiment," address before the School of International Law, University of Michigan, in *Papers Relating to the Work of the IJC*, 33, note 6.
17. Jordan, "International Joint Commission," 539, note 6.
18. Great Lakes Water Quality Agreement, 1972, article VI (4).
19. For further information, see James R. Huntley, *Man's Environment and the Atlantic Alliance* (Brussels: NATO Information Service, 1971); and Patrick Kyba, "CCMS: The Environmental Connection," *International Journal*, 29 (Spring, 1974), 256-67.
20. Canada, Department of External Affairs, Note to the Ambassador of the United States of America, Ottawa, No. GWU-310, dated Ottawa, September 21, 1972, Annex, p. 1.
21. See, for further elaboration, Kim Richard Nossal, in *International Perspectives* (November-December, 1978), 22-5.
22. Premier of Ontario and Governor of Michigan, Great Lakes Water Quality Agreement, *Communique*, April 10, 1974, p. 2.
23. Toronto *Globe and Mail*, June 29, 1973.
24. United States Senate, Committee on Foreign Relations, *Canada-United States Interparliamentary Group, Report on the Eighteenth Meeting, Held at Victoria, British Columbia, May 27-31, 1977* (Washington, 1977), 1.
25. Senate of Canada, Standing Senate Committee on Foreign Affairs, *Canada-United States Relations, Volume 1—The Institutional Framework for the Relationship* (Ottawa, 1975), 80.
26. Canada-United States Environmental Council Memorandum to Canadian Members of CUSEC from Theodore Mosquin, Canadian Co-chairman, September 21, 1976.
27. John E. Carroll, "The Boundary and the Environment: A Conservationist's Perspective," paper presented to 4th Biennial Meeting of the Association for Canadian Studies in the United States, Burlington, Vermont, October 8, 1977.
28. Many articles have been written on the *Torrey Canyon* disaster: see, for example, D. J. Bellamy, "Effects of Pollution from the *Torrey Canyon* on Littoral and Sub-Littoral Ecosystems," *Nature*, 216 (December 23, 1967), 1170-3.
29. Royal Commission on Pollution of Canadian Waters by Oil and Formal Investigation into Grounding of Steam Tanker "Arrow," *Report* (Ottawa: Information Canada, 1971).
30. *Ibid.*, 122.

31. Canada Shipping Act, 1970-71, chapter 27, section 762(1). In this direction, an important step to control sea pollution by oil has been taken by the member states by signing the *International Convention for the Prevention of Pollution of the Sea by Oil* (London, 1954), and subsequent amendments in 1962 and 1967.
32. International Joint Commission, Skagit River Dam and Reservoir, Docket No. 46, pp. 3-4.
33. Boundary Waters Treaty, chapter 28, article VIII, paragraph 7 (italics added).
34. Among the various critics, Mr. John A. Fraser, MP, has consistently taken this line of argument to advance his views that Canada should stress this aspect of legality in dealing with the Americans. See his statement in House Commons, *Debates*, February 14, 1973, p. 1296.
35. International Joint Commission, *Environmental and Ecological Consequences in Canada of raising Ross Lake in the Skagit Valley to elevation 1725* (Ottawa, 1971), 2.
36. *Ibid.*, 157.
37. *Ibid.*, 158.
38. House of Commons, *Debates*, November 2, 1973, p. 7473.
39. Maxwell Cohen, "The International Joint Commission – Yesterday, Today and Tomorrow," in *Proceedings of the Canada-United States Natural Resources and Environmental Symposium* (Durham, N.H.: University of New Hampshire, 1978), 33.
40. Hon. Mitchell Sharp, "Canada-U.S. Relations: Options for the Future," *International Perspectives* (Autumn, 1972), 23.
41. Cohen, "Possibilities for the Future," 198, note 3.
42. Burpee, "An International Experiment," 61.
43. Richard B. Bilder has used a similar argument while examining the question of Great Lakes pollution; see Bilder, "Controlling Great Lakes Pollution," 548, note 6.

Index

335